Tiki and Temple

Tiki and Temple

The Mormon Mission in New Zealand, 1854–1958

Marjorie Newton

Greg Kofford Books
Salt Lake City, 2012

Copyright © 2012 Marjorie Newton
Cover design copyright © 2012 Greg Kofford Books, Inc.

Cover information: Hamilton New Zealand Temple, 1965, photographer not identified.

Cover design by Loyd Ericson.

Published in the USA.

All rights reserved. No part of this volume may be reproduced in any form without written permission from the publisher, Greg Kofford Books. The views expressed herein are the responsibility of the author and do not necessarily represent the position of Greg Kofford Books.

Greg Kofford Books
P.O. Box 1362
Draper, UT 84020
www.koffordbooks.com

2015 14 13 12 11 5 4 3 2 1

Library of Congress Cataloging-in-Publication Data

Newton, Marjorie, author.
  Tiki and temple : the Mormon mission in New Zealand, 1854-1958 / Marjorie Newton.
     pages cm
  Includes bibliographical references and index.
  Summary: Details many events that happened from the very beginning of the Church of Jesus Christ of Latter-day Saints in New Zealand in the 1850s. Behind each is a story of faith, devotion, and many hardships.
  ISBN 978-1-58958-121-0
  1. Church of Jesus Christ of Latter-day Saints—New Zealand. 2. Mormon Church—New Zealand. 3. Mormons—New Zealand. I. Title.
  BX8617.N45N49 2012
  266'.9393—dc23
                                   2011045482

For Jenny
1959–2005

Contents

Foreword *by Elder Glen L. Rudd*   xi

Preface   xiii

Chapter 1   "... the Lord will not forget them"   1

Chapter 2   "... ripe for the gospel ..."   41

Chapter 3   "... the noblest of all aboriginal races"   81

Chapter 4   "... you are some of Hagoth's people and there is no pea about it"   121

Chapter 5   "... you will get a Temple"   155

Chapter 6   "... we need buildings, buildings and more buildings ..."   193

Chapter 7   "... two great strains of the house of Israel ..."   231

Glossary of Maori Words   267

Appendix A: New Zealand Mission Presidents, 1851–1958   269

Appendix B: LDS European Branches in New Zealand, 1855–1900   273

Appendix C: First Maori District Presidents   275

Bibliography   277

Photograph References   303

Index   305

About the Author   328

List of Maps

Cartography by John C. Hamer

1   Map of New Zealand North Island   8
2   Map of New Zealand South Island   9

List of Illustrations

1.1   Advertisement for Carl Asmussen's Christchurch business   11
1.2   William Michael Bromley (1839–1911)   28
1.3   Thomas and Hannah Cox   33
2.1   Georgiana G. and Moroni S. Marriott   55
2.2   Te Whatahoro (John A. Jury)   59
2.3   Missionary group in New Zealand in 1887   66
3.1   Hirini Whaanga   82
3.2   Headstone of Hirini and Mere Whaanga   114
3.3   The first LDS meetinghouse in Auckland, 1909   116
4.1   The Maori Agricultural College on dedication day, 6 April 1913   127
4.2   Visiting Maori Saints at the Salt Lake Temple, 1913   130
4.3   The MAC Band in a patriotic parade, August 1914   135
4.4   James N. Lambert teaches his wife, Edith, to ride a bicycle   138
4.5   Relief Society Conference, Kiri Kiri, 1918   148
5.1   MAC students at Thanksgiving picnic   156
5.2   MAC faculty and students, 1919   161
5.3   Apostle David O. McKay and other leaders, hui tau, 1921   167

5.4 A group of leading Maori brethren, c. 1927   178

5.5 Hastings, seven miles from the MAC, after the 1931 earthquake   190

6.1 John Ephraim Magleby, Elder Harold T. Christensen, and Sister Jennie Magleby   195

6.2 Tent city at Tamaki hui tau near Dannevirke, 1936   199

6.3 Percy Stanley Connorton Going   206

6.4 Gertrude Cutforth Going   206

6.5 Maromaku Chapel, constructed by the members from a single giant kauri tree, contributed by the Going family, 1940   206

6.6 President Matthew Cowley and his driver, Elder Glen L. Rudd, c. 1940.   209

6.7 Polly (Pare) Duncan, mission Relief Society president (1932–53)   211

7.1 At the New Zealand Temple, 1958, E. Albert Rosenvall, George R. Biesinger, Wendell B. Mendenhall, and Edward O. Anderson   254

7.2 The David O. McKay Auditorium, Church College of New Zealand, Hastings   258

7.3 More than 113,000 visitors came to the New Zealand Temple openhouse in 1958   262

Foreword

This lovely book, *Tiki and Temple*, has been written with more than one purpose. First, it details many events that happened from the very beginning of the Church in New Zealand in the 1850s. Behind each is a story of faith, devotion, and many hardships. As I read these stories, I was made more aware of the great sacrifice that many early missionaries made for the gospel.

Another purpose that I discerned was to highlight the spirit of the marvelous people of New Zealand, both the Pakeha and the Maori. Much has been said over the years about the goodness of these people, but in this book are many wonderful events and moments when it is easy to be touched spiritually by the goodness and devotion of the people.

This book gives the reader a picture of the Lord's purposes in sending the gospel to New Zealand, a country of great natural beauty and a country blessed with spiritual giants, Maori prophets, priesthood leaders, and dedicated missionaries who diligently and constantly battled against the many problems they encountered as they fulfilled the missions assigned to them by the Lord.

It has been a great privilege to read this book. My heart has been touched, my mind and intellect increased, and my spirit made tender by the lives and missions of great and wonderful people. May all who read find in these pages a testimony that the purposes of the Lord can and will be fulfilled.

— Glen L. Rudd
April 8, 2010

Preface

This book seeks to tell the simple yet inspiring story of the growth of Mormonism in New Zealand from a small and tentative beginning in 1854 to a large mission ready for the responsibilities of stakehood and a temple a century later. This story will, I hope, convey a sense of the faith, courage, and dedication of the North American missionaries, and the corresponding faith, courage, and dedication of their converts, whether Maori or Pakeha. It features the stories of pioneers of the Church in New Zealand, some of whom are otherwise uncelebrated.

Other writers have preceded me, and I acknowledge their fine work. One is Brian W. Hunt, whose *Zion in New Zealand: A History of the Church of Jesus Christ of Latter-day Saints in New Zealand, 1854-1977* (Temple View, New Zealand: Church College of New Zealand, 1977) is now out of print. Another is Professor R. Lanier Britsch, who included an excellent short history of the LDS Church in New Zealand in his *Unto the Islands of the Sea: A History of the Latter-day Saints in the Pacific* (Salt Lake City: Deseret Book, 1986). While *Unto the Islands of the Sea* is breathtaking in its scope and combines scholarly integrity and faithful history in a truly inspiring way, there is still a need for more comprehensive individual mission histories.

Because the major sources available are LDS Church records and missionary journals, the story is mostly, and unavoidably, told from this perspective; but wherever possible, I have included material from other sources.

This book ends in 1958 with the dedication of the New Zealand Temple, the organisation of the first stake in New Zealand, and the division of the New Zealand Mission. From that point the story, like a family tree, divides into many branches with simultaneous histories, as more stakes were organised and LDS Church membership in New Zealand soared to more than 100,000. It would need more than one volume to even begin to bring the story to the present day. But it was the New Zealand Mission that was the cradle of today's strong, stable Church, respected in the community and now sixth in size among the Christian churches of New Zealand.

This is the second of my studies of the Latter-day Saints in New Zealand. My doctoral thesis, "Mormonism in New Zealand: A Historical Appraisal," written for the Religious Studies Department of the University of Sydney (1998; forthcoming from Greg Kofford Books), was primarily an in-depth examination of several issues in New Zealand Mormon history, including the cultural conflict that developed between Mormonism and Maoritanga. Readers seeking scholarly treatment of those topics may find the thesis helpful.

This present volume is primarily intended for a Latter-day Saint audience. A chronological narrative of Mormonism in New Zealand between 1854 and 1958, it does not attempt to address recent scientific debate over Maori origins or current LDS teachings on the subject, but rather explains what the Mormon missionaries believed and taught in their own day and how those teachings resonated with their Maori converts.

I realise that as an Australian, I am vulnerable to errors of fact and interpretation in both New Zealand and American history, and especially in Maori culture. I hope that one day a Maori historian will produce a scholarly history of Mormonism in New Zealand that will remedy any omissions and defects in both my works. I also hope to see additional work done with the hundreds of stories of New Zealand Saints, both Maori and Pakeha, that are still waiting to be told. Much of this gap is being filled by Rangi Parker, whose dedicated work over many years collecting and preserving stories and photographic records of the Maori Saints and Mormon missionaries is unique and is now receiving the recognition it deserves.

British spelling and American punctuation have been used throughout except, of course, in quotations. Since New Zealand is now officially bilingual, I have generally used the roman typeface for Maori words, including those in quotations. I have not, however, adopted the convention of diacritical markings, since this largely postdates the historical sources that form the basic research documents for this study.

Distances are given in miles because imperial measurements were standard in New Zealand for the entire period covered in this book, but five miles equal eight kilometres. Likewise, until 1967, New Zealand currency was pounds, shillings, and pence; and monetary values in this book are expressed in the terms of the period. The value of the American dollar in New Zealand fluctuated over the hundred years of this volume but, for much of the twentieth century, ranged from five American dollars to one New Zealand pound in 1928 to three American dollars to one New Zealand pound in 1958. Monetary sums are expressed in either American dollars (US$) or New Zealand pounds (£) according to the context.

I am deeply grateful to the Institute for Polynesian Studies (now the Pacific Institute) at Brigham Young University—Hawaii for a small grant towards the initial research for my dissertation, and to the Mormon History Association for travel grants that facilitated both my participation in MHA conferences and my research. The Joseph Fielding Smith Institute for Latter-day Saint History at Brigham Young University—Provo provided a research award that assisted me in preparing this manuscript for publication. The staffs of the LDS Church History Library, the L. Tom Perry Special Collections and Manuscripts at BYU's Harold B. Lee Library, the New Zealand Government Archives, and the Wellington City Libraries were unfailingly courteous and helpful during my research, and I am grateful for permission to publish extracts from documents they hold.

Many people have helped me over the years, and I am grateful to each of them and wish I could name each one individually. This is not possible, but I must sincerely thank Elder Bruce C. Hafen for suggesting to Ronald K. Esplin and Richard L. Jensen of the Joseph Fielding Smith Institute for Latter-day Saint History at Brigham Young University that I should write this book, and to Elder Glen L. Rudd (formerly of the Seventy, a "Cowley" missionary, former mission president in New Zealand, New Zealand Temple president, and Pacific Area president) for his Foreword and his encouragement. I would also like to acknowledge Lavina Fielding Anderson and Richard L. Jensen without whose significant help, encouragement, and mentoring this book would not have been published. I owe a great debt of gratitude to Patricia Lyn Scott for her meticulous checking of Utah archival references as the manuscript was prepared for publication and for obtaining most of the photographic illustrations. As always, I am grateful for the never-failing support given by my husband, Don, and daughters Cecily and Jennifer as I wrote this book in the most difficult of family circumstances.

Chapter 1

"... the Lord will not forget them"

In November 1832 the Church of Jesus Christ of Latter-day Saints (at that time known as "the Church of Christ") had been organised for just two-and-one-half years. Church members were largely located in two centres: at Kirtland, Ohio, and in Independence, Missouri. Among those in Missouri was William W. Phelps, who edited a Mormon newspaper there.

One day, Phelps read a short sketch that described the physical beauty and superior intellect of the Maori people. Impressed by what he read, Phelps reprinted the passage in his Mormon paper, *The Evening and the Morning Star*. Then he added some comments about the Maori people that reflect how early and how clearly the early Saints and their leaders understood the mission of the infant Church: "It really affords consolation to think that such a people exists upon the Islands of the sea," he wrote, "for the Lord will not forget them. The Isles are to wait for his law, and the gospel of the kingdom, is to be preached to every nation on the globe so that some may be gathered out of every kindred, tongue and people, and be brought to Zion."[1] This was several years before the beginning of either organised British settlement in New Zealand or LDS foreign missionary work.

Years passed, and persecution forced the Latter-day Saints to flee from Missouri to Illinois. Under Joseph Smith's direction they began to build the city of Nauvoo and to further the missionary work of the Church, which by 1837 extended to Canada and England. Thousands joined the Church (officially named the Church of Jesus Christ of Latter-day Saints in 1838) in England; and in 1840, the first company of gathering Brit-

---

1. W. W. Phelps, "We accidentily [sic] came across ...," *The Evening and the Morning Star* 1, no. 6 (November 1832): 44. Phelps is best known today for his hymn "The Spirit of God like a Fire Is Burning."

ish converts arrived in Nauvoo. In New Zealand, the Treaty of Waitangi between Great Britain and Maori chiefs was signed in February that year. In the same year the first British colonists sent from England by the New Zealand Company arrived in Port Nicholson (Wellington). Just three years later, in 1843, the first LDS missionaries left Nauvoo to labour in the islands of the Pacific.

These missionaries sailed from the east coast of America on the *Timoleon*. The vessel crossed the Atlantic and Indian Oceans, passed south of Australia and, in March 1844, turned north-east into the Tasman Sea. If the weather was favourable, its captain intended to call at the flourishing port of Auckland on the North Island of New Zealand.

After hearing from shipmates and crew members of the *Timoleon* about the large British population now living in Auckland, Elders Addison Pratt, Noah Rogers, and Benjamin Grouard made up their minds to disembark there, instead of continuing on to the Sandwich Islands (Hawaii) as they originally intended. However, bad weather forced the captain to bypass New Zealand and turn eastward across the South Pacific Ocean. Pratt finally disembarked at Tubuai, the others in Tahiti. But Pratt wrote home to Nauvoo, suggesting that New Zealand would be "a great and delightful field for our elders to occupy."[2] By the time his letter arrived in Nauvoo, however, Joseph Smith, founder of the Church, and his brother Hyrum were dead, victims of assassination by an armed mob that stormed the jail where they were being held. Even in the turmoil and trials of the post-martyrdom years, Addison Pratt's suggestion that New Zealand would be a fruitful field for missionary endeavour was not forgotten by the Church's presiding body, the Quorum of the Twelve, though it could not immediately be acted upon.

Driven from their homes, farms, and temple in Illinois in 1846, the Saints began their epic trek westward; the first pioneers arrived in the Salt Lake Valley in July 1847. Soon after being formally sustained as Church president in December of that year, Brigham Young turned his mind to expanding missionary work in the Pacific. Addison Pratt, who arrived in the Salt Lake Valley via California in 1848 after several years in French Polynesia, soon left to serve another mission there, followed by his family and other missionaries.[3] While they were still serving, President Young in 1851 com-

---

2. Addison Pratt, letter to Elder W. W. Phelps, dated Ship *Timoleon*, Pacific Ocean, 25 April 1844, *Times and Seasons* 5, no. 21 (15 November 1844): 710.

3. The story of Addison Pratt and his companions can be read in R. Lanier Britsch, *Unto the Islands of the Sea: A History of the Latter-day Saints in the Pacific*. See also S. George Ellsworth, *The Journals of Addison Pratt: Being a Narrative of Yankee Whaling in the Eighteen Twenties, a Mormon Mission to the Society Islands, and of*

missioned Apostle Parley P. Pratt[4] to preside over all Mormon missionary endeavours in a pan-Pacific region stretching from California in the east to Australia in the west, from Hawaii in the north to Chile in the south.

Elder Pratt was given a task force of nine missionaries (including himself but not counting those already serving with Addison Pratt in French Polynesia) to cover this vast area. Their numbers were increased to ten when Pratt recruited former missionary Charles Wesley Wandell in San Francisco. From this group, Elder Pratt assigned veteran missionary John Murdock to preside over the work in the English colonies in Australia and New Zealand.[5] Charles Wandell was appointed to accompany Murdock, while Elder Pratt himself sailed for Valparaiso.

Elders Murdock and Wandell arrived in Sydney on 31 October 1851 to open the Australasian Mission.[6] They baptized their first converts before Christmas, and organised the Sydney Branch on 4 January 1852. Elder Murdock soon learned that there was a potential missionary field not only among the British immigrants in New Zealand, but among the Maori, "many of whom," he wrote, "can read and write, and all of them industrious and intelligent."[7]

The two elders begged for more missionaries, specifically mentioning the need for some to go to New Zealand. John Murdock was elderly and ill; he sailed for home in June 1852 after only seven months in Australia; and a year later, Elder Wandell prepared to follow. Neither missionary had been able to visit New Zealand.

Because an exchange of letters between Salt Lake City and Sydney could take more than a year, Elder Wandell did not know that President

---

Early California and Utah in the Eighteen Forties and Fifties.

4. No relation to Addison Pratt.

5. Parley P. Pratt Jr., ed., *Autobiography of Parley Parker Pratt*, 384.

6. "Australasia" was an inclusive term describing both countries, Australia and New Zealand but is now seldom used. Murdock's arrival date is usually given as 30 October 1851, from his journal, but he did not allow for the time difference as he sailed west. The vessel is recorded in the Sydney Harbour Master's records and in Sydney newspapers as arriving on Friday, 31 October. The Australasian Mission Minutes begun by Elder Wandell show that he recorded the date correctly as 31 October, and that the name "Australasian Mission" was used from that date, not from 1854 as is frequently stated. However, these mission minutes are catalogued in the Library and Archives of the Church of Jesus Christ of Latter-day Saints, Salt Lake City, Utah (hereafter LDS Church History Library), as "Australian Mission Minutes."

7. "Elders' Correspondence: Extracts of a Letter from Elder John Murdock, 5 February 1852," *Deseret News*, 24 March 1852, [74]. Some issues of the *Deseret News* in the 1850s and 1860s were unpaginated, and the pages have been counted in order to calculate the bracketed page numbers given in this and subsequent citations.

Brigham Young had responded to their pleas. Ten new missionaries—as many as Parley P. Pratt eighteen months earlier had had at his disposal for the entire Pacific Rim—arrived in Sydney on 31 March 1853, just as Elder Wandell and a party of gathering Saints were about to sail for California.

Charles Wandell had urged that the reinforcements for whom they begged should take passage directly to the various British colonies in Australia and New Zealand. If the missionaries assigned to the other colonies travelled to Sydney first, he warned, "they will find that it will cost nearly as much to get from here to their fields of labor as it would from San Francisco."[8] Unfortunately, this sound advice was not followed, and all ten arrived in Sydney. One of the party was mortally ill, and the other nine could not even cover all six Australian colonies. The new mission president, Augustus A. Farnham, had to postpone opening the work in New Zealand but was anxious to do so as soon as possible.

President Farnham, like John Murdock before him and William W. Phelps twenty years earlier, knew that the message must go to the Maori. "I have received some little information from that Island, New Zealand," Farnham wrote to Brigham Young. "I am informed the chiefs of the tribes say the [sectarian] missionaries do not preach them the right gospel, that they are keeping back the part they need. And they do not feel to receive their teaching. From what I can learn, the field is ready to harvest; and as soon as possible, we shall send some laborers there to weed the crop and try to gather the wheat."[9] Meanwhile, the work flourished in Australia, and some of the new converts were called to augment the missionary force. Among these was William Cooke.

William and Sarah Ann Cooke, both English-born, had reached Salt Lake City on their way to California in July 1852. Here they heard the Mormon gospel and were struck by its "simplicity and beauty." Cooke left his family in Utah, where Sarah was baptized in September, while he himself pushed on with the journey to California. Once there, he decided to move on to the Australian gold mines and sailed to Sydney where he found the Mormon missionaries and was baptized on 7 June 1853.[10] Ordained an

---

8. Chas. Wesley Wandell, Letter to Prests. B. Young, H. C. Kimball, and W. Richards, dated Sydney, 11 February 1852, *Deseret News*, 27 November 1852.

9. "Extracts of a Letter from Elder Augustus A. Farnham to Brigham Young, 14 August 1853," *Deseret News*, 8 December 1853, [96].

10. "General Intelligence," *Zion's Watchman* 1, nos. 4–5 (12 November 1853), 40; "The Half-Yearly Conference of the Church of Jesus Christ, of Latter-day Saints [sic], Held in the Old Assembly Rooms, King Street, Sydney, Sunday, October 1st, 1854," *Zion's Watchman* 1, nos. 20–21 (14 October 1854), 156; "General Intelligence," *Zion's Watchman* 1, nos. 30–31 (15 March 1855), 247; *Western Standard*, 6

elder immediately, he sailed down the coast to Melbourne two weeks later, assigned to proselytise with American Elder Burr Frost on the Victorian goldfields.[11]

The newly baptized and ordained Elder Cooke proved a valuable ally to Elder Frost, and several branches were soon organised on the diggings. Before long Frost and Cooke met Francis and Emma Evans and their children, a young family from New Zealand. Francis and Emma were baptized in September 1853, thus becoming the first-known New Zealanders to join the Mormon Church. Evans introduced the Mormon elders to four young friends from New Zealand—Thomas Holder and three brothers, Alfred, Frederick, and Charles Clement Hurst. The Hurst and Holder families had both arrived in New Zealand in the 1840s as British immigrants, and both families had settled in Karori, near Wellington, an offshoot of the New Zealand Company settlement there.[12] Holder was just eighteen, Fred Hurst twenty, and Charles sixteen when they travelled together to the Victorian goldfields. Frederick and Charles Clement Hurst were baptized by William Cooke on 12 January 1854, while Thomas Holder was baptized by Elder Burr Frost a week later.[13]

In April 1855, Fred and Charles[14] Hurst sailed from Melbourne on the *Tarquinia* with a large company of converts gathering to Utah. Meanwhile, William Cooke and Thomas Holder sailed up the coast to Sydney to represent the Victorian Conference (District) at the semi-annual mission conference in October 1854. During this conference President Farnham announced that, with William Cooke as his companion, he intended to visit New Zealand himself to open the work there.[15] The assembled Sydney Saints dug deep in their pockets to finance the venture.[16] As a result, the two missionaries were able to leave almost immediately and were accompanied by Thomas Holder, returning to live with his family near Wellington and personally introduce them to the missionaries of the restored gos-

---

September 1856; Patricia Lyn Scott, "Sarah Ann Sutton Cooke: 'The Respected Mrs. Cooke,'" in *Worth Their Salt, Too: More Notable But Often Unnoted Women of Utah*, edited by Colleen Whitley, 1–27.

11. "Half-Yearly Conference," *Zion's Watchman* 1, nos. 20–21 (14 October 1854): 155.

12. Peter J. Lineham, "The Mormons and Karori," *Stockade* 24 (1991): 4–13.

13. Samuel H. and Ida Hurst, comps., *Diary of Frederick William Hurst*, 13.

14. In his diary, Fred Hurst sometimes referred to his younger brother as Clement, but usually more familiarly as "Charley" or "Charlie."

15. "Half-Yearly Conference," *Zion's Watchman* 1, nos. 20–21 (14 October 1854): 159.

16. John Perkins, Diary, 20 October 1854.

pel. John Jones, a Welsh convert who was president of the Sydney Branch, wrote an acrostic that he printed in the mission paper:

> **F**ear not, for the Lord will you bless,
> **A**nd crown your labours with success;
> **R**ighteousness shall win its way,
> **N**o power can withstand its sway.
> **H**ell may rage and the Hirelings howl,
> **A**nd cry, alas! our crafts will fail,
> **M**aori's son will the truth obey.[17]

During President Farnham's absence in New Zealand, Jones also composed and printed a poem called "Address to the Aboriginals of New Zealand," which began

> Awake ye sons of Mauri—
> Your day is drawing nigh,
> For there is now amongst you
> Servants of the Most High . . .

and concluded nineteen verses later with a ringing exhortation to the "sons of Mauri" to listen to the message brought by the Mormon missionaries.[18] It is clear that the missionaries and Church members alike were eager for the restored gospel to be preached to the Maori.

The steamship *William Denny* docked in Auckland, already New Zealand's largest city, on 27 October 1854. The missionaries preached several times without success.[19] Although John Murdock had heard that there were some British Mormon immigrants in Auckland, none of them attended Farnham's meetings or made themselves known to the missionaries. Accordingly, the missionaries took ship for Wellington.

Arriving in Wellington on 18 November 1854, Elders Farnham and Cooke hired public rooms in Barrett's Hotel on Lambton Quay and advertised a series of meetings.[20] Attendance was very disappointing, but greater interest was shown in nearby Karori, the small settlement that was the home of the Holder and Hurst families.[21] Leaving Cooke there to con-

---

17. "Editorial and General Intelligence," *Zion's Watchman* 2, no. 1 (15 May 1855): 12. The "hirelings" referred to the salaried ministers of other churches.

18. "An Address to the Aboriginals of New Zealand," *Zion's Watchman* 1, nos. 24–25 (15 December 1855): 200.

19. A. Farnham, Letter to Brother F. D. Richards, Sydney, 26 January 1855, *Millennial Star* 17, no. 18 (5 May 1855): 283.

20. "The Latter Day Saints," *The New Zealand Spectator and Cook Strait Guardian*, Wellington, 13 December 1854, 1.

21. "Quarterly Conference of the Australasian Mission of the Church of Jesus

tinue the work, President Farnham returned to Australia on the *Mountain Maid*, reaching Sydney just after Christmas.

Although he and Elder Cooke did not find an opportunity of preaching to the Maori at this time, President Farnham was optimistic. "The natives are a fine race of people, tho' none of them speak the English language to any perfection," he wrote as he reported his journey to Brigham Young. "We made some effort to get a portion of our works translated, which I am in hopes will soon be done. As soon as we can get the latter-day faith before the Maori's [sic]," he prophesied, "it will spread quite rapidly."[22]

William Cooke baptized his first convert in New Zealand (Thomas Holder's mother, Martha) on the last day of 1854. By April 1855, he had organised a branch of the Church at Karori with ten or eleven members including Martha Holder, her son Thomas, and her eleven-year-old daughter Louisa.[23] Elder Cooke stayed in New Zealand another year, travelling almost constantly. He spent the autumn of 1855 in Nelson, on the South Island, where he was given lodging by a Mr. Jones, who remembered him by name twenty-five years later.[24] He wrote to Sydney for help, but no missionaries were available.[25]

Elder Cooke returned to Sydney in March 1856, and then worked his passage back to California on the *Jenny Ford*. After the *Jenny Ford* sailed from Sydney in May 1856 with a company of 120 converts and missionaries, only two American elders remained in the Australasian Mission, one in Sydney and one in Melbourne. The work in the other Australian colonies and in New Zealand was virtually at a standstill until another fifteen missionaries arrived some months later.

Once again the whole party shipped to Australia, arriving in three groups between 28 October and 18 December 1856. Three were assigned to New Zealand, but as they had no money, were forced to remain in Australia. Despite being left without a shepherd, several of the little flock at

---

Christ of Latter-day Saints, Held at the Old Assembly Rooms, King Street, Sydney, 7 January 1855," *Zion's Watchman* 1, nos. 26–27 (15 January 1855): 204.

22. "Elders' Correspondence: Extracts of a letter from Augustus A. Farnham to Brigham Young," dated Newcastle, New South Wales, 12 January 1855, *Deseret News*, 6 June 1855, 100.

23. "Annual Conference of the Church of Jesus Christ of Latter-day Saints, in Australasia, Held in the Old Assembly Rooms, King Street, Sydney, on April 1st, 1855," *Zion's Watchman* 1, nos. 32–33 (12 April 1855): 257.

24. "Correspondence: Interesting from New Zealand – [Letter from] 'Miles' Boy' to Editor, Auckland, December 6, 1880," *Deseret News*, 26 January 1881, 831.

25. Augustus Farnham, Letter to President F. D. Richards, dated Sidney [sic], 31 May 1855, *Millennial Star* 17, no. 37 (15 September 1855): 591.

8 Tiki and Temple

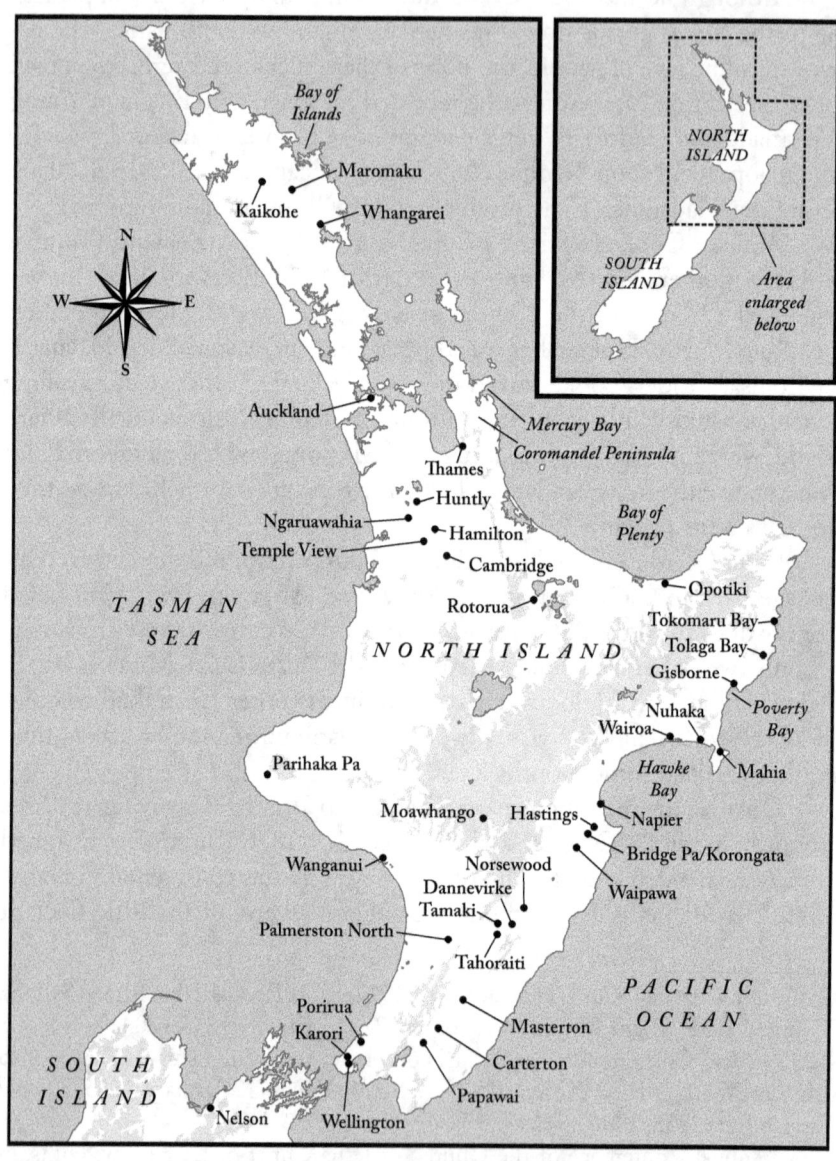

North Island of New Zealand, showing places significant in the history of the Mormon mission, 1854–1958. Cartography by John C. Hamer.

"... the Lord will not forget them" 9

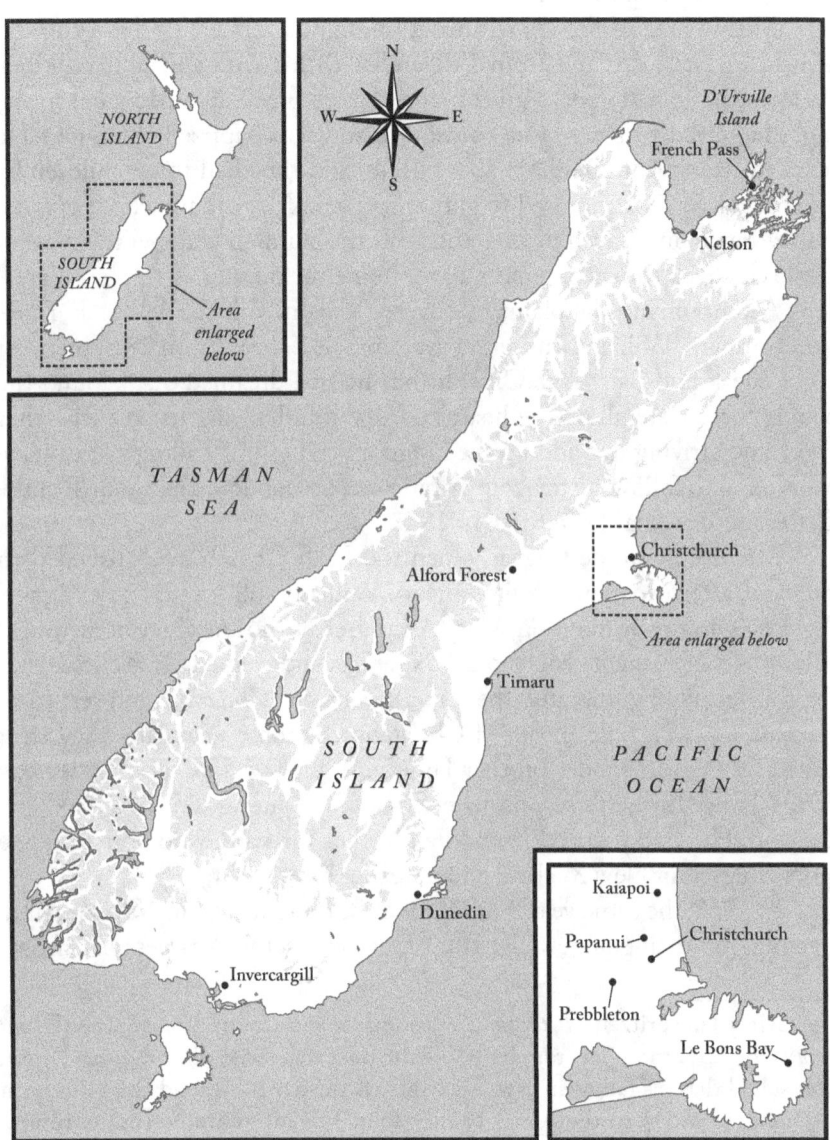

South Island of New Zealand, showing places significant in the history of the Mormon mission, 1854–1958. Cartography by John C. Hamer.

Karori remained faithful to the gospel, among them the Holder family. More than fifteen years were to pass before they again had personal contact with Mormon missionaries.

Meanwhile, in 1858, a Mormon immigrant named William Burnett arrived in New Zealand from England with his wife and four children. As a youth, he had gone with some friends to break up a Mormon meeting. He stayed to listen, was converted, and was baptized in 1844.[26] He married Mary Ann Denham about 1848, and they had three children by 1854 when William wanted to gather to Utah. Mary Ann, who was not a Latter-day Saint, stayed in England with the children while William went ahead to check things out and make a home for them.

After crossing the plains by covered wagon with the Moses F. Thurston company, William Burnett arrived in Salt Lake City on 28 September 1855. He found Salt Lake City all that he had dreamed of: "I found the people there were all of one heart and one mind, trying to do each other good, and striving to build up the kingdom of God."[27] Failing to persuade Mary Ann to follow, he reluctantly returned to London. Their fourth child, Catherine Jane, was born there in 1857.

Mary Ann Burnett never joined the LDS Church. Dissatisfied with England after experiencing life abroad, William still wanted to emigrate. According to family tradition, Mary Ann agreed to go anywhere in the world as long as there were no Mormons.[28] New Zealand seemed a safe choice, and the Burnett family migrated there in 1858 on the *Zealandia* and settled in Kaiapoi, fourteen miles north of Christchurch. Some years later they were joined by William's elder brother James and his two sons, also Latter-day Saints. James Burnett's second wife, Susan, died during the voyage to New Zealand. He soon married Fanny Fairbrother Orchard, who bore him five more children in New Zealand and a further three in Utah.[29]

In 1858, the same year that William Burnett arrived in New Zealand, a young, multi-lingual jeweller from Denmark set up business in Christ-

---

26. Mary Jane Fritzen, *History of George Brunt and Elizabeth Susan Burnett Brunt Family*, 6. A footnote records that William Burnett's son-in-law, George Brunt, later stated that his father-in-law was baptized the day his second child was born (28 October 1851), at the age of twenty-four. This may have been a rebaptism, frequently performed when original records were not available, or in preparation for health blessings, or simply for renewal of covenants.

27. William Burnett, Letter to President F. D. Richards, 1 January 1868, *Millennial Star* 30, no. 14 (4 April 1868): 220–21.

28. Fritzen, *History of George Brunt and Elizabeth Susan Burnett Brunt Family*, 7.

29. Ibid., 7–9; Genealogical Society of Utah, Ancestral File, http://www.familysearch.org (accessed 1 May 2004).

"... the Lord will not forget them"   11

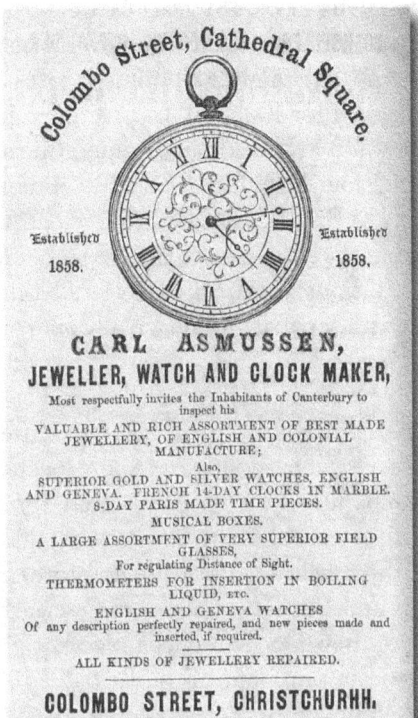

Advertisement for Carl Asmussen's Christchurch business. *The Southern Provinces Almanac, Directory, and Year Book for 1861*, [202]. Courtesy Wellington City Libraries.

church.[30] Carl Christian Asmussen, born in 1825 in Copenhagen, had already packed a lifetime of travel and adventure into his thirty-two years. After first travelling on the Continent, he sailed for the Australian gold diggings. Following a short stint of gold-mining at Sofala, near Bathurst, New South Wales, he moved on to Melbourne where he opened a jewellery store at 50 Queen Street.[31] This venture prospered; and Asmussen sold the business and returned to Denmark via England. After three years in Europe, Asmussen sailed for New Zealand in 1857, arriving in 1858, the same year as William and Mary Ann Burnett, though they did not travel on the same ship or know each other at this time, despite the common assumption that Asmussen converted Burnett. For several years Asmussen conducted a flourishing jewellery business in Christchurch until, one day in 1864, he found a Mormon tract on the street.[32]

---

30. *Chapman's New Zealand Almanac for the Year 1862*, 210; *The Southern Provinces Almanac, Directory, and Year Book for 1861, 1862, 1863*.

31. P. W. Pierce, comp., *The Melbourne Commercial Directory, including Collingwood and Richmond, and Almanac for the Year 1853*, 67.

32. Thomas Arthur Gladman Shreeve, "The Story of the New Zealand Mission from the Journal of Elder Thomas A. Shreeve," [1880].

Asmussen was intrigued with what he read. The tract he so fortuitously found was probably dropped by an immigrant Mormon from Great Britain. Unable to find any Mormons in Christchurch, Asmussen left his business in the care of a manager and sailed for England. In Liverpool, he sought out the office of the British Mission at the address printed on the tract he had found and was baptized by Elder E. A. Groves on 29 September 1864. A few months later, he went to Salt Lake City and decided to make his home there. But first he needed to return briefly to New Zealand to sell his business in Christchurch. Although not called as a full-time missionary, he was ordained a Seventy and set apart to preach as opportunity offered during his travels.[33]

Asmussen did not go straight to New Zealand, but travelled via England, and did not arrive back in Christchurch until early in 1867. After baptizing a German immigrant he met on board ship, he soon located the Burnett brothers at Kaiapoi and rebaptized them on 6 March 1867, as was commonly done at that time, for renewal of covenants previously made. Asmussen is often credited with converting the Burnett brothers, but LDS Church membership records and Burnett family records clearly show that they were already members of the LDS Church, baptized originally in England. As well, in a letter to the president of the British Mission, Asmussen explicitly stated that William Burnett was rebaptised.[34] On 17 March he reordained William Burnett an elder and James a priest. Together the three began the work of converting a city.[35]

As Mary Ann Burnett remained intractably opposed to her husband's religion, James and Fanny Burnett opened their home for meetings.[36] Asmussen baptized six—four males (including the rebaptism of the Burnett brothers) and two females[37]—before leaving Christchurch for Europe on 6 June 1867 via Panama.[38] From Copenhagen he wrote to Apostle Franklin

---

33. Julia Amussen Dalley, "Carl Christian Asmussen (Amussen)" in Daughters of Utah Pioneers Lesson Committee, *An Enduring Legacy*, 4:217–33. Asmussen was fluent in English, German, Spanish, and Italian as well as his native Danish.

34. Carl C. Asmussen, Letter to President F. D. Richards, dated Copenhagen, 31 August 1867, *Millennial Star* 29, no. 41 (12 October 1867): 653.

35. William Burnett, Letter to President F. D. Richards, dated New Zealand, 4 September 1867, *Millennial Star* 29, no. 48 (30 November 1867): 764–65.

36. Carl C. Asmussen, Letter to President F. D. Richards, dated Copenhagen, 31 August 1867.

37. William Burnett, Letter to President F. D. Richards, dated Kaiapoi, Canterbury, [New Zealand], 3 December 1867, *Millennial Star* 30, no. 8 (22 February 1868): 125.

38. This was, of course, long before the Panama Canal was built. Travellers sailed

D. Richards, presiding over the Church in England, and reported on the Church in New Zealand, unaware of the little group of Saints in Wellington.[39] Asmussen (who changed his name to "Amussen" in Utah) reached Utah for the second time in the summer of 1868, still single at the age of forty-two. He married in 1869 and later took second and third wives. Flora, his youngest daughter, married Ezra Taft Benson, who later became an apostle and then the thirteenth president of the Church of Jesus Christ of Latter-day Saints.

Although the Saints in Christchurch were few, they were choice souls, and the value of Asmussen's work can scarcely be overestimated. However, the branch grew very slowly for a few years after his departure. William Burnett baptized two (one of whom was his future son-in-law George Brunt) and ordained his own fifteen-year-old son a deacon.[40] The two Burnett families planned to remove to Utah as soon as they could. "I know it is as much a duty for us to gather to Zion out of Babylon, as it was a duty to be baptized," wrote William Burnett.[41]

In March 1870, William and James Burnett were still assiduously distributing tracts around Christchurch and lending copies of the *Millennial Star* (the British Mission paper) to anyone who would take them. In the meantime they looked forward to a visit from the newly appointed president of the Australasian Mission, Robert Beauchamp. Across Cook Strait in Wellington, the little group at Karori also waited eagerly for Beauchamp's visit.[42]

Nearly fifteen years had passed since William Cooke left the little branch in Karori, four miles from Wellington. During that time, Thomas Holder married a young woman named Caroline Allington. Thomas Holder got on well with his brother-in-law, Henry Allington, who was a serious-minded, studious man. Allington, two years younger than Holder, was born in Warwickshire, England, and, like the Hursts and Thomas Holder,

---

across the Pacific Ocean, disembarked at Panama, and travelled across the isthmus by rail to Colon, where they embarked on another vessel bound for North American or European ports.

39. Carl C. Asmussen, Letter to President F. D. Richards, dated Copenhagen, 31 August 1867.

40. William Burnett, Letter to President F. D. Richards, dated New Zealand, 4 September 1867.

41. William Burnett, Letter to President F. D. Richards, dated Canterbury, 1 January 1868.

42. William Burnett, Letter to President A. Carrington, dated Kaiapoi Island, Canterbury, 20 March 1870, and H. Allington, Letter to Albert Carrington, Esq., dated Karori, 27 March 1870, *Millennial Star* 32, no. 22 (31 May 1870): 346–47.

had come to Wellington with his emigrating family. After an adventurous youth that included gold digging in Australia and surviving shipwreck as a crew member of a whaler which sank in New Caledonia, Allington settled down to teaching school in Karori. He and Thomas Holder had many conversations about religion, and Holder loaned Allington copies of Orson Pratt's works and a Book of Mormon.[43]

After reading these works, Allington was converted, and began teaching his family and friends about Mormonism. He wrote to Robert Beauchamp, the new mission president in Sydney, and begged him to come to New Zealand to baptize him and a dozen others whom he and Holder had taught.[44]

Robert Beauchamp, the new mission president, is the first person known to have been baptized in Australia.[45] However, after his baptism in Adelaide in 1842, he had no further contact with Mormonism until 1854, when he met Elders Burr Frost and Robert Owen in Tasmania. Frost rebaptized Beauchamp, who then moved his family back to Geelong on the mainland. In 1868, Beauchamp took his wife and children to Utah, where he was almost immediately called to return as president of the Australasian Mission. He sailed from San Francisco on 24 August 1869 on the *Sarah and Mariah*, bound for New Zealand, where he trans-shipped to a Melbourne-bound vessel.[46] Within a few months, he had reorganised the Australian branches and then travelled back to New Zealand in April 1870.

---

43. Robert Beauchamp, Letter to President A. Carrington, dated Karori, near Wellington, 30 April 1870, *Millennial Star* 32, no. 27 (5 July 1870): 425–26.

44. Henry Allington, Letter to Albert Carrington, 27 March 1870; Robert Beauchamp, Letter to President A. Carrington, 30 April 1870.

45. Robert Beauchamp, Letter to President B. Young, jun., dated Melbourne, 26 August 1866, *Millennial Star* 28, no. 44 (3 November 1866): 701–3; Victoria District Record of Members, 1868–1906, Genealogical Society of Utah microfilm 105322, Item 3, p. 247. The latter record states that Beauchamp was baptized by William Barrett [sic] in Adelaide in 1842 and rebaptized in Melbourne by John L. Blythe on 24 October 1885. Beauchamp presumably gave the information himself at this time.

46. Robert Beauchamp, Letter to President Carrington, dated Maiden Town, 4 December 1869, *Millennial Star* 32, no. 8 (22 February 1870): 123. Beauchamp, described on arrival in South Australia in 1840 as a painter and glazier, had theatrical aspirations and adopted "Beauchamp" (pronounced "Bee-cham") as a stage name. His wife and children were known by his real name, Dolling. They remained in America when he returned to Australasia as mission president in 1869. Beauchamp never returned to America or his family. After his second rebaptism in 1885, he continued some association with the LDS Church in Victoria until he died in Geelong in 1890.

On Sunday morning, 17 April 1870, Robert Beauchamp rebaptized Thomas Holder and baptized Henry Allington and four others. He then reorganised the Karori Branch, with Henry Allington as president and Thomas Holder and William Fawcett as counselors.[47] The following weekend, Beauchamp baptized Allington's wife Ellen, his mother Elizabeth and Holder's wife Caroline, among others. Holder's mother and his married sister Louisa Clark were received on their original baptisms. The Karori Branch prospered, with fifty-five people on the records by 1871. Branch meetings were held in an empty barn.[48]

Both Mormon missionaries, William Cooke in 1854–55 and Robert Beauchamp in 1870–71, found success in Karori but virtually none elsewhere on the North Island. It was the network of personal introductions to friends and relations that paved their way in Karori. That the Church of England and Methodists had somewhat neglected Karori for some years undoubtedly helped, as did Allington's respected position as schoolmaster.[49] But of the fifty-five people whose names appear on Karori LDS membership records between April 1870 and December 1871, only five males do not appear to have been related to other branch members. The remainder all belonged to just three extended families—the Allington/Holder family, the Drydens, and the Fawcetts. This pattern was repeated time after time in LDS branches in both Australia and New Zealand. To this day, personal introductions are the most prolific source of new converts, and LDS Church members are encouraged to provide such introductions for the full-time missionaries. Detailed analysis of the historical membership records of both countries testifies to the efficacy of this procedure.[50]

After holding a few public meetings and attracting some unfavourable press comment,[51] President Beauchamp moved on to Christchurch, on the South Island, to visit the Kaiapoi Branch. Here he appointed William Burnett president of the New Zealand Conference (District) of the Australasian Mission, with his brother James as first counselor and Henry

---

47. Karori Branch Membership Record, front page certified by Beauchamp and Allington, Genealogical Society of Utah microfilm 128889, Item 21.

48. "Amongst the Passengers by the '*Colima*,'" *The Daily Southern Cross*, Auckland, 15 December 1875.

49. Lineham, "The Mormons and Karori," 8–9.

50. Marjorie Newton, *Southern Cross Saints: The Mormons in Australia*, chap. 5; "Mormonism in New Zealand: A Historical Appraisal," chap. 3; and "Nineteenth-Century Pakeha Mormons in New Zealand," in *Proclamation to the People: Nineteenth-Century Mormonism and the Pacific Basin Frontier*, edited by Laurie F. Maffly-Kipp and Reid L. Neilson, 238.

51. "New Zealand," *Millennial Star* 32, no. 35 (30 August 1870): 552.

Allington in Wellington as second counselor.[52] By the end of May, the Kaiapoi Branch had eighteen members.[53]

Robert Beauchamp found life stressful, alone in a mission that covered all Australia and New Zealand. "When I am in the colony of New South Wales, the Saints in the colonies of Victoria and New Zealand send letters begging me to come to them, and as soon as I pay a visit to either of those colonies, then the other colony wants me very badly," he wrote to the mission president in England.[54]

In October 1871, President Beauchamp again visited New Zealand. On this occasion, newspaper comment stirred up opposition, with the Mormon association with polygamy providing the focus. Rotten eggs and rocks were thrown into the house where the Saints met.[55] These events prompted the first discussion of Mormonism in the New Zealand Parliament. In the House of Representatives on 18 October 1871, the Premier, the Honourable William Fox, was asked whether the government intended to take steps to halt the spread of Mormonism in the colony. Fox replied that "unless circumstances were brought under their notice to show that any individual or number of persons were acting in a manner contrary to the public welfare, they could not interfere in the matter."[56]

The Kaiapoi Branch near Christchurch grew slowly but steadily under the care of the Burnett brothers, while the Karori Branch near Wellington was decimated by the emigration to Utah of its strongest members. In the nineteenth century, all Mormon converts were encouraged to "gather" in one place to build up the Church and prepare for the Second Coming of the Saviour. Branches were organised as a temporary expedient to look after new converts until they could gather to America. Unfortunately, this procedure worked well only when there were sufficient missionaries or strong local priesthood left to preside over the converts remaining in the little branches. With no missionaries at all, the Karori Branch did not survive the emigration of its strongest converts.

---

52. William Burnett, Letter to President Albert Carrington, dated Kaiapoi, 25 May 1870, *Millennial Star* 32, no. 32 (2 August 1870): 486–87.

53. Henry Allington, Letter to *Deseret News*, 31 May 1870, quoted in Manuscript History of the New Zealand Mission, LDS Church History Library, hereafter cited as New Zealand Mission, Manuscript History.

54. Robert Beauchamp, Letter to President Albert Carrington, dated Melbourne, 12 August 1871, *Millennial Star* 33, no. 41 (10 October 1871): 653.

55. "The Church in New Zealand," *Millennial Star* 34, no. 2 (9 January 1872): 24–26.

56. Ibid. See also *New Zealand Parliamentary Debates*, 11:390–91, as cited by Lineham, "The Mormons and Karori," p. 13.

It is a moot point whether the Hurst brothers and the Evans family should be regarded as the first New Zealand converts to gather to Utah. All were immigrants to New Zealand from England who were converted to Mormonism on the Australian gold diggings; all emigrated to Utah from Melbourne, starting their journey on the *Tarquinia* in April 1855. Charles Logie, another New Zealand resident who was baptized in Australia, sailed from Sydney on 7 September 1855 on the ill-fated *Julia Ann*, which was wrecked 200 miles west of Tahiti four weeks later. Logie, his English-born wife, and their baby daughter were among the survivors of the shipwreck, finally settling happily in Utah after their dramatic voyage.[57]

Carl C. Asmussen was the next New Zealand resident to gather to Utah (1867). Three years later, in 1870, Henry Allington reported the first departure from New Zealand of a Latter-day Saint actually converted and baptized in New Zealand. "The Saints . . . all desire to gather to Zion and are laboring to accomplish that object," he wrote to President Albert Carrington in England. "One of our number left here for Utah by the last San Francisco mail-boat, the first fruits of the New Zealand Mission."[58] Tantalisingly, Allington did not identify the member, but it was probably George ("Gus") Clark, Thomas Holder's brother-in-law.

Clark's wife, Louisa, had been baptized by William Cooke in 1855 as an eleven-year-old girl. Louisa, her four children, and her mother, Martha Young Holder, were the first converts to sail from New Zealand whose names are definitely known. They left on 6 August 1871; and while it is clear from contemporary references that George did not travel with them, he also emigrated. It seems likely that he was the unnamed convert who left in 1870, going to prepare a home in Utah for his wife, children, and mother-in-law. The family settled in Mayfield, Sanpete County, where Clark became a justice of the peace.[59] In December 1871, another eleven converts sailed on the *Nevada*, to be followed a few months later by a group that included Henry and Ellen Allington and their children.

Meanwhile, the Maori people were not forgotten. Despite the entire absence of American missionaries, James Burnett "opened a mission to the natives" early in 1872. On one occasion, he preached to a gathering of between 100 and 150 "Maories," some of whom "seemed pleased with his testimony, while others disliked it."[60] As far as presently available records

---

57. Newton, *Southern Cross Saints*, chap. 6.
58. Henry Allington, Letter to President Albert Carrington, dated Karori, 30 July 1870, *Millennial Star* 32, no. 41 (11 October 1870): 649.
59. "Correspondence: New Zealand Mission: 'Frater,' Letter, Mayfield, Utah, 17 January 1881, *Deseret News*, 2 February 1881, 843.
60. "New Zealand," *Millennial Star* 34, no. 25 (18 June 1872): 394.

show, James Burnett was the first Mormon to preach to the Maori people and should be recognised for this, even though no baptisms resulted from his efforts.

Robert Beauchamp was released in 1873 after Saints in the Australasian Mission complained of his behaviour to the British Mission president, alleging intemperance and immorality.[61] Another lone missionary, William Geddes, was sent from the British Mission to take over. The shortage of missionaries virtually halted all Mormon proselytising in both Australia and New Zealand until Thomas Steed arrived (via England and Australia) in November 1875.[62] Elder Steed found his way to Kaiapoi where he was warmly welcomed by the Burnett families. A month later he was joined by reinforcements. Eleven missionaries were on board the schooner *Colima* when she called at Auckland in mid-December 1875. Four of them (Elders William McLachlan, John T. Rich, and Frederick and Charles Clement Hurst) disembarked there, while the remaining seven, including the new mission president, Isaac Groo, continued their voyage to Sydney.

Fred and Charles Hurst had not had an easy passage to Utah in April 1855. Sailing on the *Tarquinia* from Melbourne with some seventy other converts, they found themselves stranded in the Sandwich Islands (Hawaii) when their vessel was condemned as unseaworthy. Many of the company experienced considerable hardship, as they had paid their passage all the way to California and had no money to pay a second time for the Honolulu-San Francisco leg of the journey. Fred and Charles gave their savings—more than $1,000 in cash and gold—from their years on the goldfields to help the destitute *Tarquinia* families in Hawaii, and then looked for work to earn their own passages to San Francisco.[63] But first they were called to serve as missionaries in the islands. The brothers finally worked their way to California in November 1856, arriving with just seventy-five cents between them.[64] They reached Utah in December 1857, where Frederick Hurst married in 1858, and Charles in 1869.[65]

In October 1875, the brothers were called to return to New Zealand "on a special mission to the Maoris,"[66] though what Church authorities intended by this is not recorded. It was not easy for Fred to leave; he and his wife Aurelia had just lost a small daughter, and he had to leave his grieving wife to care for their six living children, including six-month-old twins,

---

61. Joseph Royal Miller and Elna Miller, eds., *Journal of Jacob Miller*, 127, 158.
62. Thomas Steed, Diaries, 1875–77.
63. Hurst and Hurst, *Diary of Frederick William Hurst*, Appendix.
64. Ibid., 67.
65. Ibid., 108; Floyd Harris Hurst, "Australian Converts and Missionaries," 12.
66. Hurst and Hurst, *Diary of Frederick William Hurst*, 112.

with little means of support. Mindful of the charge to preach to the Maori, Elder Hurst managed to pick up a Maori New Testament and dictionary in California and used his time during the voyage to study the language.[67] Having learned some Hawaiian during his earlier Sandwich Islands mission, he made fair progress with Maori, as the languages are related.[68]

William McLachlan was appointed presiding elder for New Zealand and travelled with his three companions by coastal steamer from Auckland to Wellington. Here the Hurst brothers remained to visit their mother, while Elders McLachlan and Rich continued on to the South Island to meet up with Thomas Steed. The three elders stayed in Kaiapoi for a few weeks; then, wanting to be in a more central area, they rented a room in Christchurch and started housekeeping. By February 1876, they had had 1,000 copies of Lorenzo Snow's tract, *The Only Way to Be Saved*, printed and began distributing them throughout the city.[69] This pamphlet was the first recorded Mormon imprint in New Zealand. They hired the Temperance Hall and about seventy people came to their first advertised meeting.

Back in Wellington, feeble and in ill health, the widowed Mary Ann Hurst, now seventy-five years old, was overjoyed to see her younger sons again. Fred set out to visit the remaining Latter-day Saints in the Wellington area. Having a parcel from Ellen Reading Allington in Utah to deliver to her parents, he visited them and was cordially entertained, although Mrs. Reading was now very opposed to Mormonism. The feelings of other members of the extended Allington/Holder clan towards the Mormon Church also varied from lukewarm to hostile, influenced by the Dryden family. The Drydens, early converts who went to Utah in 1871, were bitterly disappointed with their reception in Utah and returned to New Zealand in an apostate condition. Elder Hurst tried to encourage the wavering Saints: "I told them it put me in mind of when I went to the mines in Australia; every day we would meet people coming back discouraged and said the mines were all a failure and humbug, but that did not prove true, far from it."[70]

---

67. Ibid., 116.

68. Tahiti, New Zealand, Hawaii and the Cook Islands are classed as Eastern Polynesian cultures, and native speakers from one of these island groups could usually communicate with those from the other groups.

69. Steed, Diaries, 31 December 1875; William McLachlan, Letter to the Editor, dated Christchurch, 8 February 1876, *Juvenile Instructor* 11, no. 5 (1 March 1876): 59.

70. Hurst and Hurst, *Diary of Frederick William Hurst*, 126. Mary Ann Dryden's mother, Hannah Eagle, returned with them. Her husband, Robert, remained faithful to the Church but also returned to New Zealand, hoping in vain to

Just before Christmas, the Hurst brothers in Wellington talked over their situation. They felt impressed to join the other missionaries in Christchurch on the South Island but, not having enough money for two passages, decided that Charles should sail on the *Taranaki* on 23 December. After spending Christmas with his mother, Fred walked to the Ohariu Valley and found William Fawcett (baptized by Robert Beauchamp in 1870) living with his married daughter.

With Fawcett's help, Elder Hurst was able to locate other Latter-day Saints. While prepared to do all they could for him, they were not optimistic about the success of his mission. "They think it is hopeless to undertake to preach here or hold meetings," he wrote in his diary on 6 January 1876. "There is so much prejudice." For some years, apostate Mormons who had emigrated to New Zealand from England and a few New Zealand converts who had returned from Utah disillusioned had combined with the press to turn the minds of the general public against the Mormons, usually with sensational stories about polygamy. With a little help, Hurst was able to rent a hall and advertise some public meetings. The first two were reasonably well attended, but no one at all—not even his LDS friends—came to the third.[71]

He found it difficult to find openings among the Maori, who were also being prejudiced against Mormonism, in their case by their ministers. He realised that, although he could read and write Maori "tolerably well," preaching in Maori would be much more difficult but decided to persevere with his studies.[72]

Things were not easy in Christchurch either. The resources of the few Saints were stretched to the limit, and the missionaries had to work to support themselves. "It was either work or starve and go naked with them," wrote Hurst.[73] McLachlan, Rich, and Steed found most of the Europeans in Christchurch uninterested in their message.[74]

Elder McLachlan thought that the prosperity of the people hindered their conversion, as their chief preoccupation was amusement. Polygamy was at once a big stumbling block to serious investigation and the chief drawcard to their meetings. The principle of polygamy (more correctly polygyny) or plural marriage had been acknowledged as part of LDS Church teachings since 1852. Although the practice was limited and entered into under strict conditions, it deeply offended the religious mores of the day,

---

persuade his wife to return to Utah.

71. Ibid., 17, 23 January 1876, 134, 135.

72. Ibid., 146, 148.

73. William McLachlan, Letter to the Editor, *Juvenile Instructor* 11, no. 17 (1 September 1876): 202; Hurst and Hurst *Diary of Frederick William Hurst*, 155.

74. Steed, Diaries, 6 April 1876.

and all Mormons were frequently regarded as dissolute and immoral. At the same time, there was avid interest in the details of life in polygamous families in Utah. Besides, Mormonism was not new to a great many. "There are thousands of people here who have heard our missionaries in their own countries," McLachlan reported, "and then there is a considerable number of old country apostates, and who wish to remain so."[75]

Steed and McLachlan found themselves in trouble when the husband of a newly baptized convert, Mrs. East, threatened to cut the throats of the "Salt Lake Mormon buggers." He was arrested for disturbing the peace. In court next day, East alleged that his wife had been "tumbled three times head over heels in the Waimakariri River" by the Mormons. The missionaries explained that Mrs. East, having told them she had her husband's permission, had been immersed once only. The magistrate fined East ten shillings, and the case was closed.[76]

The little group of Saints gave the missionaries as much moral and financial support as they could muster. "Brother James Burnett and wife have done all we could ask of them and more," Elder McLachlan wrote. Others of the Saints gave weekly cash donations to help the missionaries.[77]

In June 1876, Charles Hurst returned to Wellington and the brothers set up housekeeping together for a few months, supplied with various items of furniture and food by the few Latter-day Saint women in Wellington. A postal order from Elder McLachlan was received with gratitude, as they were literally reduced to their last halfpenny. Only one of the brothers could go to the Post Office to cash the money order, as they had only one pair of boots between them, which they wore in turns.[78] Both were studying Maori in preparation for a trip to Napier, from whence they planned to visit inland Maori tribes. Before they could leave, Elder McLachlan wrote, summoning both to the South Island.

The brothers travelled to Christchurch at the end of October 1876. Fred was overwhelmed to the point of tears by the kindness of their reception by the Saints. A few days later, he walked several miles to Sunday meeting at Papanui. During the meeting, he was overjoyed to receive the sacrament for the first time since leaving Utah more than a year earlier.[79]

---

75. William McLachlan, Letter to the Editor, dated Christchurch, 28 June 1876, *Juvenile Instructor* 11, no. 15 (1 August 1876): 172–73.

76. William McLachlan, Reminiscences and Journals, 1863–86, 11, 12 April 1876; Steed, Diaries, 12 April 1876.

77. McLachlan, Journal, 30 January 1876.

78. Hurst and Hurst, *Diary of Frederick William Hurst*, 159.

79. Ibid., 170–71.

Soon after arriving in New Zealand, Elder McLachlan wrote home about the Maori people. "[They] resemble our Indians very much, and are undoubtedly of the same race," he wrote, "but are much more civilized, and dress like white men. They own large tracts of land, secured to them by the Government. This they rent or lease to the whites, having no privileges to sell or dispose of it in any other way. Thus it becomes a source of permanent income and benefit to them, and in this way they live, many of them being well off."[80] He also reported King Tawhiao's new "reformatory religion," currently being promulgated at Hikurangi, which led the editor of the *Deseret News* to prophesy that the Maori people would listen if the true gospel were to be preached to them as "their hearts are being prepared beforehand."[81]

A few months later, McLachlan summarised the traditional history of the Maori, telling of the arrival of the Great Fleet from the legendary place Hawaiki. "Strong evidence that there is truth in their tradition of this exodus is supplied by the facts that all the tribes agree in their accounts of the doings of the principal 'canoes' or of those who came in them, after their arrival in New Zealand, and that there is also agreement in tracing from each 'canoe' the descent of the numerous tribes which have spread over the islands," he wrote.[82]

In January 1877, the missionaries in New Zealand received news of their release from Mission President Isaac Groo in Sydney.[83] By May all had sailed for home, and it was not until August the following year that the first replacement arrived.

As has been seen, between 1854 and 1878 Mormon missionary work in New Zealand was spasmodic. Even if missionaries had been available, little missionary work could have been done on the North Island before the 1870s, owing to the Maori Wars (or Land Wars, the name many historians prefer). While the wars began with localised conflicts between the settlers and Maori inhabitants, British regiments were soon called in to aid the settlers and quell the Maori uprisings.

By 1860, British settlers outnumbered the indigenous Maori population, and there was growing Maori resistance to selling land to the encroaching colonists. The issue was complicated by traditional tribal ownership, making it difficult to decide who had title to, and thus could legally sell, any particular plot. Originally meant to protect the Maori from un-

---

80. "A Religious Phenomenon[:] New Zealand Missionaries," William McLachlan, Letter to George Goddard, 10 January 1876, *Deseret Evening News*, 5 March 1876, [5].
81. Ibid.
82. McLachlan, Letter to the Editor, 28 June 1876.
83. Hurst and Hurst, *Diary of Frederick William Hurst*, 28 January 1877, 182.

scrupulous buyers, one provision of the 1840 Treaty of Waitangi stipulated that Maori owners could sell land only to the government. But, of course, the government sold it on to white settlers at a handsome profit. This procedure severely disadvantaged the Maori. At the same time, the growth of the King movement, a pan-tribal quest for Maori unity (particularly with regard to opposition to further land sales), led to increasing difficulty for the government and administrators.

While some Maori tribes such as Ngati Porou and Ngati Kahungunu supported the British, much of the central North Island, especially Taranaki and the Waikato, was in turmoil as British regiments fought rebel Maori tribes. Even though they vastly outnumbered their Maori opponents, the British did not have it all their own way; but eventually, and inevitably, their superior numbers and weapons prevailed. The Maori king and his followers retreated into near inaccessible lands in the central Waikato, still known today as the "King Country." Peace gradually returned as the British regiments sailed away and the Maori prisoners were repatriated, though skirmishes continued into the early 1870s.

In a punitive measure of the mid-1860s, more than three million acres of Maori land in Taranaki, the Waikato, and the Bay of Plenty were confiscated, though eventually about half was either paid for or returned. The government hand fell with little regard to justice; some opposing tribes, such as those in the fertile central Waikato, found their land taken almost wholesale, while other rebel tribes such as the Ngati Maniapoto, whose land was less desirable, lost none. Even some tribes in the lower Waikato who had supported the British found their land confiscated, while loyal Ngati Kahungunu chiefs had to sell or mortgage lands to pay for their participation in the war on the British side.[84] The consequent resentment strained relations with the British for many years in some areas and was a factor in the Mormon success among the Ngati Kahungunu and Ngapuhi, and in Porirua. It was also a factor in Mormon difficulty in making headway in Taranaki, the King Country, the Waikato, and the East Coast, where the Maori tribes now looked on all white people with deep suspicion.[85]

In a more pervasive cultural rebellion, indigenous prophets such as Te Ua Haumene and Te Kooti instituted new religions—Pai Marire (also known as the "Hau Haus" from an element of their ritual), and Ringatu (an amalgam of Old and New Testament teachings with traditional Maori

---

84. M. P. K. Sorrenson, "Maori and Pakeha," in Geoffrey W. Rice, ed., *The Oxford History of New Zealand*, 2d ed., 158–59.

85. Ian R. Barker, "The Connexion: The Mormon Church and the Maori People," 47–49.

culture) respectively. Their hold on the Arawa and East Coast Maori hindered Mormon progress in these areas. In the Taranaki area, local leaders and Maori prophets Eruiti Te Whiti-o-Rongomai III and Tohu Kakahi founded a religious and pacifist enclave at Parihaka, though their influence came to spread far beyond Taranaki. Thousands of disillusioned Maori left the Christian churches, many of whose ministers had served as chaplains to British regiments during the wars, and followed one or other of these prophet-chiefs. The smouldering animosity that many Maori felt towards the English missionaries was another factor that made many of them, some years later, willing to listen to the American Mormon missionaries.

So while the dearth of Mormon missionaries in New Zealand in the 1860s was not caused by the Land Wars, they would have made little headway during that turbulent decade. By the late 1870s, the time was right and Mormon interest and success in New Zealand gradually increased. The arrival of Elder Thomas Shreeve in August 1878 marked the beginning of a continuous Mormon mission there. Although Shreeve and his companion, Elder Fred J. May, are usually included in lists of New Zealand mission presidents, to date no evidence has been found that they were officially appointed as such. In reality May was presiding elder in Australia and Shreeve presiding elder in New Zealand, and they were sustained as such at a conference at Prebbleton, on the South Island of New Zealand, on 15 September 1878. As soon as the new mission president, Elijah F. Pearce, arrived in New Zealand, they were released as presiding elders at a conference in Papanui on 18 January 1879.[86]

In the meantime, Elder Shreeve at first worked in the Christchurch district, where twenty-five European converts were baptized during the next three months. During this time, he reorganised the Papanui Branch and organised a new branch at Prebbleton, while the original Kaiapoi Branch continued.[87] Just over a year later, on 26 December 1879, Shreeve organised New Zealand's first Relief Society in Christchurch, with Ann James as president and Johanna Larsen and Agnes Doak as counselors.[88] Other branches of the Church were organised in the South Island, at Alford Forest, Sydenham, and Timaru. During these years, a number of Latter-day Saints from the Canterbury District left New Zealand for Utah, including, at various times, members of the extended Burnett families.[89]

---

86. Shreeve, "Story of the New Zealand Mission," 4–5.
87. Ibid., 6.
88. "Mormons in Canterbury," *Millennial Star* 42, no. 9 (1 March 1880): 133.
89. Hurst and Hurst, *Diary of Frederick William Hurst*, 202; "Correspondence: Mormonism in New Zealand," George Batt, Letter, dated Christchurch, 27 March 1880, *Deseret Evening News*, 3 May 1880, [4]; U.S. Census 1880, Utah. Mary Ann

By the late 1870s, about 4,500 Scandinavian immigrants had settled in New Zealand; and in 1879 two missionaries who were natives of Scandinavia, Elders John P. Sorensen and Neils J. Gronlund, were sent to New Zealand. Although they were meant to work primarily in the Scandinavian settlements further south, there was so much work to do in Auckland that Elder Sorensen initially stayed there.[90] Elder Gronlund moved on to Christchurch but soon became ill and sailed for home. Elder George Batt (a New Zealand convert who had gone to Utah in 1876 and returned as a missionary in 1879) took over as mission president *pro tem* from Elder Elijah Pearce on 3 March 1880.[91] Elder Batt sent Thomas Shreeve to the North Island, where he held the first Mormon meeting in Napier in April before going to Auckland to join Elder John P. Sorensen.

Elder Sorensen had already baptized several extended family groups in Auckland, and on 6 June 1880, Elders Sorensen and Shreeve met with their converts in the Orange Hall in the inner suburb of Newton and organised the first LDS branch in Auckland. Local convert William John McDonnel, superintendent of the Auckland dry dock at the bottom of Hobson Street, was appointed branch president.

Thomas Shreeve sailed for home on the *Zealandia* on 28 June 1880, leaving only Elders Batt and Sorensen in the field, Sorensen in the North Island and Batt in the South Island. The work in the South Island was still growing, and Elder Batt especially praised the work of the Christchurch Relief Society.[92] Among Batt's converts was a young Danish immigrant named Jens Jensen. Jensen was ordained to the priesthood and then devoted himself to full-time proselytising until he too sailed for America in April 1881. It was Jensen who actually began the first Mormon preaching in the Scandinavian settlements on the North Island.

Elder John P. Sorensen was born in Aalborg, Denmark, on 17 October 1837, and had become a ship's carpenter. After spending ten years in New Zealand, in 1869 he set out to return to Europe via America. While passing through Utah in 1872, he married an LDS woman, settled there, and joined the LDS Church.[93] A Danish-speaking convert who was well ac-

---

Burnett remained in New Zealand with her married daughter and son-in-law.

90. New Zealand Mission, Manuscript History, January–May 1880.

91. New Zealand Mission, Manuscript History, 3 March 1880.

92. Journal History of the Church of Jesus Christ of Latter-day Saints (chronological scrapbook of typed entries and newspaper clippings, 1830–present), 13 July 1880, hereafter cited as Journal History.

93. International Genealogical Index, http://www.familysearch.org, accessed 6 September 2003; "Within These Hallowed Walls," Auckland Chapel Dedication Program, 1953.

quainted with New Zealand was exactly what the First Presidency needed in 1879, and Sorensen was promptly called on a mission to New Zealand. He was a zealous worker and a preacher of power; while in New Zealand, he performed some sixty baptisms and blessed thirty-eight children under eight.[94] However, Elder Sorensen, though very ardent, had an abrasive personality and some personal weaknesses.[95] He seems to have been the catalyst for some serious problems in the Auckland Branch, so Mission President George Batt travelled north from Christchurch and reorganised the branch. He then sent Elder Sorensen south to work with Jens Jensen in the Scandinavian settlements of Norsewood and Dannevirke.[96]

Like every New Zealand missionary before him, George Batt's concern was not limited to the Pakeha (as all non-Maori were termed). "I would like to call your attention to the Maoris, the natives of this country," he wrote to Church leaders in Utah. "It strikes me very forcibly that they are about ripe for the gospel. They are firm believers in present revelation from God . . . and it is well-known that they practice plural marriage. . . . They have no inclination for fighting now, and they are looking for something important to take place. Who knows? It might be the 'Mormon' Elders taking them the word of the Lord as revealed through the Prophet Joseph Smith, even the Book of Mormon."[97]

Elder Batt's information was coming from Charles Hardy, "a friend to the Maories." Hardy, an Englishman, was baptized on the Australian gold diggings in 1853. He helped pay for Elder William Cooke's 1854 mission to New Zealand[98] before he himself sailed for California with the *Tarquinia* company in 1855.[99] In California, Hardy learned from Apostle Francis M. Lyman that work was very scarce in Utah, so he worked his passage back to Sydney, then went back to England where he married and eventually emigrated to New Zealand. By 1880, Charles Hardy was living at Dairy Flat just north of Auckland, well-to-do, well-educated, and

---

94. John Peter Sorensen, New Zealand Mission Diaries, 1879–81.

95. Fred Bromley Hodson, *None Shall Excel Thee: The Life and Journals of William Michael Bromley*, 157.

96. "The Work in New Zealand," George Batt, Letter, dated Auckland, September 10, 1880, *Deseret Evening News*, 27 October 1880, 821.

97. "Correspondence: Interesting from New Zealand," George Batt, Letter to the Editor, 7 October 1880, *Deseret Evening News*, 6 November 1880, [2].

98. "Correspondence: Interesting from New Zealand," George Batt, Letter, 6 December 1880, *Deseret News*, 11 January 1881, 831, copy in New Zealand Mission, Manuscript History.

99. Hardy was reportedly excommunicated during the voyage. No reason was given. Hurst and Hurst, *Diary of Frederick William Hurst*, 18.

something of a self-taught expert in the infant science of Maori ethnology. Soon after his first contact with Elder Batt and the Auckland Branch of the Church, he was rebaptized. He was reordained to the Melchizedek Priesthood in 1881 and would have liked to gather to Zion, but his wife would not agree.[100] He stayed in New Zealand and remained a pillar of the mission till his death in 1907.

Meanwhile, Elders Sorensen and Jensen rebaptized Hans Henrik Mortensen and his wife Mette, LDS immigrants from Denmark. On 17 October 1880, Sorensen organised the first Latter-day Saint branch in Napier before he and Jensen moved inland to the Scandinavian settlements of Dannevirke and Norsewood. Here they made some converts and organised the Norsewood Branch on 12 December 1880 with Johannes C. Widerup as president. The following Sunday they preached the first Mormon sermon in Dannevirke.[101]

A new mission president, William M. Bromley, arrived in Auckland on 14 January 1881. President Joseph F. Smith, second counselor in the First Presidency, told President Bromley before he left for New Zealand that "the time had arrived when the natives of New Zealand . . . would receive the gospel. He believed them to be of the house of Israel."[102] President Smith had a particular interest in the Polynesians and their origins, as he had spent some years as a missionary in Hawaii from the age of fifteen. He was still in the Hawaiian Islands when the *Tarquinia* company from Australia was stranded there and probably learned much about the Maori people from the Hurst brothers who, after abandoning the *Tarquinia*, also served as missionaries in Hawaii.

Two new missionaries arrived with President Bromley. He sent one, Elder N. Harmon Groesbeck, to join George Batt in Christchurch, and the other, Elder John S. Ferris, to work in Napier. At the request of Auckland Branch members, on 20 January 1881 Bromley officially changed the mission headquarters from Sydney to Auckland.[103]

---

100. Hodson, *None Shall Excel Thee*, 99, 121.
101. New Zealand Mission, Manuscript History, 12 December 1880.
102. William M. Bromley, "Introduction of the Gospel to the Maories," *Juvenile Instructor* 22, no. 1 (1 January 1887): 6. While President Bromley is often thought to have been the first to be given specific instructions to open the work among the Maori people, it should be remembered that Brigham Young on several occasions had given the same instructions to previous missionaries.
103. Hodson, *None Shall Excel Thee*, 97. In reality, mission headquarters had been at Christchurch for some time.

William Michael Bromley (1839–1911), the LDS mission president who in 1881 organized the first systematic preaching to the Maori. Courtesy LDS Church History Library.

Large crowds attended Elder Batt's open-air meetings in Christchurch, but they were disrupted by a rowdy element.[104] Nevertheless, Batt and Groesbeck persevered with some success. On the North Island, despite being mobbed and pelted with rubbish in Palmerston North and having to sleep two nights at Woodville in the shelter of a fallen tree and some old sheets of iron, Elders Sorensen and Ferris began to find success among the Scandinavian settlers. Sorensen had 200 copies of a small Danish hymnal printed and sent two of his converts from Norsewood to proselytise in Carterton, where they organised a branch on 20 February 1881.[105] Sorensen himself organised another small branch, this time at Wanganui, on

---

104. "Correspondence," George Batt, Letter, dated Timaru, 25 February 1881, *Deseret Evening News*, 8 April 1881, [4].

105. New Zealand Mission, Manuscript History, 20 February 1881. A copy of Sorensen's forty-eight-page Danish hymnal survives in the LDS Church History Library. It was printed at Napier in 1881 by R. C. Harding.

3 April 1881.[106] Although neither Carterton nor Wanganui were Scandinavian settlements, both branches soon had several Scandinavian families among their members.

Just as Elders McLachlan and Batt found that lectures on Utah's "social conditions"—a pleasant euphemism for polygamy—drew bigger crowds in the South Island than did preaching on faith and repentance, President Bromley in Auckland found a similar lack of interest in first principles and great curiosity about polygamy.[107] Nevertheless, the Auckland Branch grew and a Relief Society was organised there, the second in New Zealand.

In March 1881, President Bromley, accompanied by three Auckland church members, visited the Maori village at Orakei. Despite language problems, they asked the chief if he would forward an epistle-cum-tract, which Bromley had written, to the Maori prophet Te Whiti.[108] Bromley experienced some difficulty finding a translator, but the letter was finally translated by a half-caste Maori, William Thompson Warbeck;[109] and on a second visit to Orakei, the chief was persuaded to send Bromley's translated letter to both the Maori king, Tawhiao, and the prophet Te Whiti.[110]

These visits are popularly regarded as the beginning of Mormon work among the Maori, and President Bromley is often honoured as the founding father of this work because of these visits, and, indeed, claimed that honour for himself.[111] An element of caution is necessary in any claim to a historical "first;" but certainly, the record is clear that James Burnett had preached to a large gathering of Maori as early as 1872. President Bromley's efforts at Orakei were no more intensive and had no better results than those of James Burnett or Fred Hurst, or those of any other missionary who preceded Bromley. But it was President Bromley who organized the first serious and sustained missionary work among the Maori, and it was he who was the first to achieve the translation into Maori of the principles of the restored gospel. These efforts, rather than his personal preaching, laid the foundation for Mormon success and justify Bromley's reputation as the founding father of Mormonism among the Maori people.

By the end of April, the Maori tract had been printed (the cost paid by Charles Hardy), and President Bromley immediately despatched 250

---

106. Sorensen, Diary, 3 April 1881.
107. Hodson, *None Shall Excel Thee*, 105.
108. Ibid., 106, 108, 109, 113.
109. Ibid., 114–16.
110. Ibid., 118.
111. Ibid., 506.

copies to Elder Ferris in Napier.[112] Bromley also set apart local convert William John McDonnel as a missionary to the Maori.[113] McDonnel filled a satchel with the Maori tracts and began work.

Elder George Batt was released at the end of April 1881 and escorted a company of twenty-seven Saints bound for Utah aboard the steamer *City of Sydney*. At the same time, two young converts, Joseph Wallace and Ben Hansen, decided to travel to Utah via Europe. They sailed for Melbourne on the *Tararua*, intending to trans-ship there for London. The vessel ran onto rocks off the South Island and over 100 passengers, including the two young Mormon converts, were drowned.[114] Both young men had relatives in the *City of Sydney* company. Both have been omitted from previous accounts and lists of casualties of the Mormon gathering. Another group of twenty-four, this time from the Auckland Branch, sailed on the *Australia* for San Francisco on 24 May 1881.[115]

In June 1881, William McDonnel met a Maori chief named Ngataki (reputed to be one of King Tawhiao's advisers) during the course of his work; he took the opportunity to preach some Mormon doctrine to him. That evening, Bromley and McDonnel spent three hours with Ngataki, pointing out significant passages in the Bible which Ngataki followed in a Maori Bible. "He took some tracts with him and promised to lay the matter before the king," wrote President Bromley. "Thus the way is being opened in a miraculous manner for the natives to hear the Gospel." Ngataki promised to return in a few days but did not keep the appointment; he was eventually baptized four months later, on 18 October 1881.[116] He was not, however, the first Maori to be baptized into the Mormon Church, though he was the first baptized in New Zealand. According to Assistant Church Historian Andrew Jenson, an Elder Richard G. Lambert baptized a Maori seaman in Hawaii about 1874.

In the meantime, Elder Sorensen visited Parihaka, home of Maori prophets Te Whiti-o-Rongomai and Tohu Kakahi and their followers, on

---

112. Ibid., 129.
113. Ibid., 123.
114. "Sad Occurrence," George Batt, Letter, *Deseret Evening News*, 29 June 1881, [2].
115. Hodson, *None Shall Excel Thee*, 140.
116. Ibid., 147, 186; New Zealand Mission, Manuscript History, 18 October 1881; William John McDonnel, "The Start of the Mission among the Maoris." McDonnel intimates here that Ngataki's baptism took place a day or two after his initial contact but has obviously telescoped the events of a few months into a few days. In another account, he places it in October 1881, which date is confirmed by other sources.

Wednesday, 15 June 1881. He gave away sixty-eight copies of Bromley's Maori tract during this first visit, including one to Tohu. Sorensen's timing was bad: Parihaka was preoccupied with the return of prisoners being repatriated by the British, 112 arriving at the time of this visit, with 300 more expected daily. Two days later Sorensen returned to Parihaka from his base at a Maori camp two miles away, and approached the prophet Te Whiti with the offer of a tract, which was refused. Sorensen reacted with characteristic volatility, rebuking the "unclean spirit" in Te Whiti and symbolically shaking the dust of Parihaka from his feet.[117]

Elder John S. Ferris preached at Opotiki several times during June 1881. Speaking through an interpreter, he introduced his Maori listeners to the Book of Mormon and the restoration of the gospel in the last days by the angel of God.[118] Ferris told them that both the American Indians and the Maori were descendants of Ephraim and therefore of Israel, and reported that the Maori were very pleased with and interested in these teachings. "He . . . states that the Maories tell him that more than a year ago the king said a White man would come across the sea and preach to them the true gospel and they affirm that they believe he [Ferris] is the man . . . This is strange news," wrote President Bromley, "and I am led to exclaim God moves in a mysterious way his wonders to perform. It seems as though the time has arrived for the Maories to have the Gospel presented to them."[119]

In July 1881, Elder Ferris reported an invitation from King Tawhiao to visit him the following December. Ferris was elated at the invitation; he noted in his journal that whichever church the king and Te Kooti joined, all his people would also join.[120] This is the first of many recorded instances which show that Mormon missionaries became well aware of the influence of the chiefs or rangatira in a community-based society like that which prevailed in Maori villages. The classic "top-down" conversion pattern is found in Christian mission history from medieval times, and it had been experienced by other religious denominations in New Zealand before the Mormons began proselytising among the Maori.[121]

---

117. "Latest from Parihaka," *Auckland Evening Star*, 18 June 1881; New Zealand Mission, Manuscript History, 15, 17 June 1881; Hodson, *None Shall Excel Thee*, 148, 150.

118. John Solomon Ferris, Journal, 3 June 1881.

119. Hodson, *None Shall Excel Thee*, 148.

120. Ferris, Journal, 4 June 1881; see also "Correspondence: Opotiki," John S. Ferris, Letter, *Deseret Evening News*, 10 November 1881, [4].

121. For a fuller discussion of the "top-down" conversion pattern in Mormon missionary work in New Zealand, see Newton, "Mormonism in New Zealand,"

President Bromley noted with satisfaction that "the king wishes the book of Mormon translated in to the Maori language." He urged Elder Ferris to learn the Maori language and continue his work among them.[122] However, the lonely life began to tell on Ferris; and over the next few months, his mental stability was questioned at different times by his mission president, his Maori friends at Opotiki, and the Saints in the Auckland Branch where he laboured for some time after an ignominious return from Opotiki.[123]

Six new missionaries arrived from America on 14 December. All six were assigned to work in New Zealand, rather than Australia, four of them on the South Island, and the other two in the Wellington, Napier, and Wanganui districts. With eight full-time missionaries, plus the help of local elders, conversions began to escalate. By 21 May 1882, when President Bromley presided over a mission conference in Christchurch, Mormonism had been preached in all settlements from Christchurch south to Invercargill and in most centres of population in the southern part of the North Island.

President Bromley arranged to have 10,000 English tracts printed on the South Island. By October, eight branches (Christchurch, Auckland, Timaru, Carterton, Alford Forest, Dunedin, Le Bons Bay, and Invercargill) were reporting, and Elders Alma Greenwood and John Ferris had made the first missionary journey north of Auckland, travelling as far as Warkworth, though without success.[124]

In August 1882, Thomas and Hannah Cox, English immigrants who joined the Mormon Church in Auckland in 1880, moved to Cambridge in the Waikato, where Thomas set up business as a boot and shoemaker. Here they became friendly with a local Maori tribe, who had been miraculously prepared for the gospel.[125] On Christmas Eve, a Sunday, Cox, President Bromley, and William McDonnel spent the evening preaching to some of their number. Later that evening, after discussing Mormon doctrine in the chief's home, they laid hands on and blessed his sick daughter, who quickly recovered.

On Christmas Day 1882, the Maori chief Hare Teimana, his wife, Pare, and another Maori, possibly Hare Katere (Harry Carter) were baptized in the nearby river.[126] After the confirmations, the Maori chief testi-

---

chap. 8.

122. Hodson, *None Shall Excel Thee*, 155.
123. Ibid., 185, 208.
124. New Zealand Mission, Manuscript History, 26 September 1882.
125. Ibid., 25 December 1882.
126. Bromley's journal gives the name as "Hane Takare" (sometimes spelled "Takara" or "Tahere"). Other sources name him as Hare Te Katere (Harry Carter).

Thomas and Hannah Cox, influential in the conversion of the first Maori in the Waikato. Courtesy LDS Church History Library.

fied with great earnestness that he had been visited several months before by the Apostle Peter, who showed him in vision the men who would bring the gospel to him, and that Bromley, Cox, and McDonnel were these men.[127] Another six Maori were baptized the following week, and Thomas Cox was appointed president of the Waikato District before Bromley and McDonnel returned to Auckland.

Samuel Cox, the eldest son of Thomas and Hannah Cox and a witness of these events, later testified of the part played by his mother in winning the confidence of the Maori. Her many kindnesses, he wrote, "made a lasting impression upon the minds of the Maoris.... She truly has proven herself a ministering Angel of mercy, and her name will ever be remembered in connection with those, who under the providence of God, first presented the Gospel to the Natives on the Waikato."[128] President Bromley

---

Both McDonnel and Samuel Cox state clearly that the third person was a woman; Cox says she was Teimana's sister-in-law. However, in his report on his return home, Bromley stated that the third person was Teimana's *brother*-in-law, presumably Hare Te Katere. See "The Church in New Zealand," *Deseret News*, 15 August 1883, 476–77.

127. McDonnel, "The Start of the Mission among the Maoris"; Hodson, *None Shall Excel Thee*, 294–95.

128. Samuel Cox, Letter dated Pocatello, Idaho, 13 March 1957, to *Relief*

confirmed this, writing in his journal that "Sister Cox was very energetic in administering to the sick among the natives, teaching them cleanliness and explaining many of the principles of the Gospel to them."[129]

Later in January, Elders Alma Greenwood and Ira Noble Hinckley travelled about 100 miles from Auckland to Huntly, walking most of the way. At each settler's home they would stop to leave a tract and beg a drink of water. Most of the settlers were very hospitable, and usually offered milk or tea, and bread and butter. "[O]ne individual filled us up with beer," recorded Elder Greenwood, "which caused us to walk and talk very lively for some time."[130]

Elder Greenwood described his feelings as he and his companion baptized a Maori convert on Thursday, 1 February 1883: "We led another Maori into the waters of baptism. He was as humble as a babe. All day long he lingered near, eagerly asking questions about the gospel. Some invisible power was preying upon him causing a longing for the salvation of his soul. It was the spirit of God. After being immersed contentment, joy and peace apparently characterized his general appearance. His once eager countenance wore an aspect of smiles and gratitude. While standing . . . on the brink of this beautiful river. . . my eyes fell on the dark image undressed sitting at my feet and I thought that the light of heaven has dawned upon the minds of these aborigines who have wandered in gross darkness."[131] Greenwood and Hinckley assisted Thomas Cox with the baptisms of several other Maori converts, and then returned to Auckland, pledging Elder Greenwood's watch to the station master at Huntly as security for their train tickets.

By mid-February 1883, there were sixty-five Maori members of the Mormon Church in the Cambridge-Huntly area. The first LDS Maori branch was organised at Waotu on 25 February 1883, with twenty-six adult members. Hare Katere (Harry Carter) was ordained a priest and set apart as branch president.[132] Unfortunately, Thomas Cox's business failed;

Society Magazine, typescript copy in New Zealand Mission, Manuscript History, following entry for 22 June 1880. Punctuation modernised.

129. Bromley, "Presenting the Gospel to the Maories," in Hodson, *None Shall Excel Thee*, 311.

130. Alma Greenwood, Diary and Scrapbook, 28 January 1883. Although the Mormon dietary code (known as the Word of Wisdom, now canonised as LDS Doctrine and Covenants 89), was dated 1833, rigid adherence to it was not required until the early decades of the twentieth century.

131. Greenwood, Diary, 1 February 1883.

132. Hodson, *None Shall Excel Thee*, 307; transcription of Louis G. Hoagland's interview with William John McDonnel, December 1919, inserted in New Zealand Mission, Manuscript History, at end of 1882. Note that on this occasion,

he filed for bankruptcy and took his family back to Auckland. Without help and leadership, the initial enthusiasm of the Waikato Maori waned, and the mission to the Maori in the Waikato was temporarily abandoned by the end of July 1883, though success began to occur elsewhere and soon resumed in the Waikato.[133]

President Bromley was released in July 1883. During his two-and-a-half-year term as mission president, 210 baptisms had taken place, 120 children and infants had been blessed, and 130 European Saints had emigrated to Utah. Two Maori tracts had been printed, and five American elders were spending most of their time proselytising among the Maori and learning their language. There were ten branches, three Sunday Schools, two Relief Societies, and 370 members still in the mission, of whom eighty-five were Maori.[134] "There is much enquiry amongst the native race, but very little amongst the Caucasian," President Bromley reported to the First Presidency when he reached home. "There is no doubt in my mind but the natives will receive the truth in large numbers in a short time."[135]

Elders Greenwood and Hinckley frequently visited Maori villages at Papawai and Te Ore Ore. There was a European branch at nearby Carterton, where the Ridgway, Christensen, and Wiley homes provided a convenient base for missionary visits among the local tribes. The extended Wiley family was connected to the Fawcetts, who had been early Wellington converts, and Elder Fred Hurst had several times recorded preaching to members of the family in the 1870s.[136]

Greenwood and Hinckley baptized fifteen Maori converts (nine men and six women) on 21 July 1883, including two influential Wairarapa chiefs, Manihera Te Whenuanui Rangitakaiwaho and Ihaia Hopu Te Whakamairu.[137] Elder Greenwood described Manihera as an imposing figure, "about sixty years of age, stands about 6 feet 4 inches high, well-built, weight 210 lbs. His hair is tinged with grey and whiskers white. Has a large noble forehead and large keen black eyes, very intelligent and

---

McDonnel specified that the first Maori baptized at Cambridge were Harry Carter, his wife, and another woman.

133. New Zealand Mission, Manuscript History, 27 July 1883.
134. Ibid., 17 July 1883; Hodson, *None Shall Excel Thee*, 348.
135. Ibid., 348–49.
136. Hurst and Hurst, *Diary of Frederick William Hurst*, e.g., 165. Priscilla Fawcett Wiley was originally a member of the Fawcett family of the Karori Branch reorganised by Robert Beauchamp in 1870.
137. New Zealand Mission, Manuscript History, 21 July 1883; Greenwood, Diary, 21 July 1883.

witty, understands the scriptures . . ."[138] Ihaia, a prominent Ngati Kahungunu chief, was a Justice of the Peace and had been appointed a native assessor by Governor Sir George Grey. He was a wealthy and cultivated man, who had served as a lay minister in the Church of England for forty years before accepting Mormonism. He became the first Maori to receive the Melchizedek Priesthood and served as president of the Te Ore Ore Branch from its organisation to his death on 27 April 1886.[139] His home was beautifully furnished and decorated with wallpaper, carpets, and a piano that his well-educated daughter played for the missionaries.[140] The baptism of these men set an example that encouraged many others to listen to and learn from the missionaries. These conversions also sparked some opposition to Mormon efforts, including a spate of complaining letters in the *Wairarapa Standard*. Alma Greenwood wrote many replies, which were published, as was a letter from Mormon converts Ihaia Whakamairu and K. N. Piharau who aired some specific grievances. They pointed out that when the Anglican Church Missionary Society (CMS) missionaries first came to the Wairarapa, local Maori tribes acceded to their request for land for schools, giving 400 acres at Papawai. "Now, where is the missionary schools for the Maori children? We have not seen these schools. The only Maori schools are those supported by the Government," they wrote.[141] This school land was a major grievance among the local Maori tribes and eventually resulted in court action. It was also another major reason for the open-minded reception of the Mormon missionaries by members of the Ngati Kahungunu and Ngapuhi tribes.

Elders Greenwood and Hinckley organised three Maori branches in 1883, at Papawai (26 August), Manaia (2 December) and Te Ore Ore (16 December). At the end of December, the first Maori priesthood meeting was held in the Wairarapa district, with eighty-eight Maori Saints attending.[142] This figure probably included several Maori women, who enthusiastically attended priesthood meetings until the missionaries began to organise concurrent testimony meetings for them. Early the following year, Elders Greenwood and Hinckley received an urgent request from an influential Hawkes Bay chief, Otene Meihana, to visit Taonoke in the Hawkes

---

138. Ibid., 3 April 1883.

139. "Death of a Distinguished Maori," *Deseret Evening News*, 17 June 1886, [1].

140. Greenwood, Diary, 7 July 1883.

141. Clippings of letters to the editor, *Wairarapa Standard*, in Journal History, under date of 2 January 1884, but not specifically identified by date of publication.

142. Greenwood, Diary, 30 December 1883.

Bay district.¹⁴³ Within two weeks they had baptized Meihana and another thirteen Maori converts—six males and seven women. On 18 May, the two elders baptized another twenty-three Maori at Korongata.

Not yet fluent in the Maori language, the Mormon missionaries relied on interpreters, usually finding someone in attendance at their meetings who could translate. Six more missionaries arrived in June 1884, specially called to preach to the Maori. Within six months, a few of them were able to speak and understand Maori reasonably well, but the constant turnover as missionaries arrived and departed meant that Maori converts were in demand as interpreters for several years. They were more than willing. "Our native brother, Otene Meihana, is very ambitious in the work, having an ardent desire to bring all his race into the truth," wrote Elder Greenwood to his wife in Fillmore, Utah. "He brings many to us to preach to. By this means the word of truth is being carried to many of them. Nearly all are very anxious to hear the Gospel."¹⁴⁴ Stalwart Maori converts such as Meihana and Takarei Ihaia not only travelled with the missionaries and interpreted for them, but were soon ordained priests and began preaching and teaching themselves, with considerable success.¹⁴⁵

It was an exciting time to be a missionary in New Zealand. During the last months of 1884, Elders William T. Stewart, Ira N. Hinckley, and Alma Greenwood travelled extensively in the Wairoa, Hawkes Bay, Poverty Bay, and Bay of Plenty areas, baptizing groups of Maori in Nuhaka, Mahia, Kopuawhara, and Muriwai, all of which, plus Taonoke and Korongata, became Mormon strongholds. Truly in these areas, the Maori people, especially the Ngati Kahungunu, were "ripe for the gospel" and were ready and waiting for the Mormon elders, whose coming was prophesied to them. Members of these branches became, as their descendants are to this day, pillars of strength of the LDS Church in New Zealand. When a conference was held at Taonoke, Hawkes Bay, on 18 January 1885, in a meeting house specially built by Otene Meihana, it was reported that there were 811 Maori and 265 Europeans on the records of the Mormon Church in New Zealand.¹⁴⁶

As success with the Maori increased, the emphasis of Mormon missionary work in New Zealand changed. European work was never termi-

---

143. Greenwood, "My New Zealand Mission," *Juvenile Instructor* 20, no. 16 (15 August 1885): 251.

144. "Cause of Truth in New Zealand: Alma Greenwood to Mrs. F. M. Greenwood, Taonoke, Hawkes Bay, 14 May 1884," *Deseret Evening News*, 2 July 1884, [2].

145. Greenwood, Diary, 29 July 1883.

146. New Zealand Mission, Manuscript History, 18 January 1885.

nated but was certainly overshadowed by the excitement of success among the Maori. It was felt necessary for American missionaries to preside as district presidents, to be "shepherds" over the Maori branches, living with the Maori Saints and giving pastoral care to their converts. Because of the sheer scale of success, almost all available missionaries were channelled into this work.

Although this emphasis changed the missionary thrust, there was far more success among the European population of New Zealand than is generally recognised. There were at least twenty-eight "European" branches organised in New Zealand between 1855 and the end of the nineteenth century. (See Appendix B.) They were spread from the Bay of Islands to Invercargill. Many of the branches were very small indeed, comprising sometimes just two or three families and their children. Sometimes a branch continued for many years; at other times, as families gathered to Zion or moved to another part of New Zealand, a branch would lapse, sometimes to be reorganised a few years later. This pattern was regarded as normal; as stated earlier, branches were not intended to be permanent before the beginning of the twentieth century because converts were taught that it was their duty to gather to Zion in America as soon as possible.

Altogether, the names of 1,170 European converts who were baptized between 1855 and 1900 are known, and the records refer to numerous others whose names are not known, so even a figure of 1,400 or 1,500 is likely to be conservative. Of the 1,170 whose names are known, 708 were in the North Island and 451 were in the South Island. Contrary to contemporary stereotypes, which saw the Mormon missionaries looking for single women to take home to their "harems" in Utah, the gender ratio was almost even, with a small preponderance of males. This latter factor could be expected, however, in the context of the prevailing scarcity of European women in colonial New Zealand. Most of the European converts belonged to nuclear or extended family groups whose members also joined the Church.

Mormonism, as stated earlier, spread mainly by personal and family networks, and family groups predominated in all branches. Most of the adult converts were British-born emigrants, and about 20 percent were Scandinavian. Nearly 45 percent of the European converts gathered to Utah, a more than favourable percentage compared with other missions.[147] A few were well-to-do, but most struggled to find the money to migrate

---

147. For a fuller discussion of the nineteenth-century European converts to Mormonism in New Zealand, see Newton, "Mormonism in New Zealand," chap. 3, and Newton, "Nineteenth-century Pakeha Mormons in New Zealand."

to Utah. The Saints on the South Island seemed rather better off than those in Auckland, where the branch members were mostly working-class families. In the Bay of Islands, Wairarapa, and South Island districts, many of the European Saints owned their own farms and were in a somewhat better financial position than those in the cities.

However, there was certainly much less interest among the Pakeha than among the Maori, and the missionaries had to work much harder for fewer converts. It took fifty years from the organisation of the Church for the work to reach the Maori people; but as William W. Phelps had foretold in 1832, the Lord had not forgotten them. When the time was right, the missionaries became available; and after 1882, the mission presidents were overwhelmed with the response of the Maori people to Mormonism. They simply did not have enough missionaries to work with both the Pakeha and the Maori. Missionary efforts among the Europeans never totally ceased, but for the next three-quarters of a century, the Mormon Church in New Zealand owed most of its growth and stability to its faithful Maori converts.

Chapter 2

"... ripe for the gospel ..."

By the 1880s, the Maori people were, as George Batt phrased it, "ripe for the gospel."[1] For at least half a century, since Christianity was first preached among them, their own prophets and holy men (tohunga) had foretold the coming of a new religion for the Maori.[2] The significance of these prophecies was not lost on the Mormon missionaries. As has been shown, Augustus Farnham, presiding over the Australasian Mission from his Sydney headquarters, heard that the Maori chiefs wanted something more than they were hearing from the Christian missionaries. Twenty years later, William McLachlan's reports made it clear that he believed the hearts of the Maori were "being prepared beforehand" for the restored gospel. George Batt, presiding over the mission in 1880, reported that the Maori people believed in revelation and were "looking for something important to take place."[3]

The earliest contemporary reference to a specific prophecy that many believe foretold the advent of Mormonism is found in the journal of mission president William Bromley. In June 1881, President Bromley received a letter from Elder John S. Ferris who was preaching at Opotiki in the Bay of Plenty. Ferris reported that he had been told by the local Maori tribe

---

1. George Batt, "Correspondence: Interesting from New Zealand," Letter to the Editor, 7 October 1880, *Deseret Evening News*, 6 November 1880, [2].

2. *He Poropititanga Enei: Na nga Poropiti Maori o nga wa o mua*; Matthew Cowley, "Maori Chief Predicts Coming of L.D.S. Missionaries," 696–98, 754–56; Brian W. Hunt, *Zion in New Zealand: A History of the Church of Jesus Christ of Latter-day Saints in New Zealand, 1854–1977*, 9–11; R. Lanier Britsch, "Maori Traditions and the Mormon Church," 37–46.

3. Augustus A. Farnham, Letter to Brigham Young, 14 August 1853, *Deseret News*, 8 December 1853, [96]; William McLachlan, Letter, *Deseret Evening News*, 25 March 1876, 5; Batt, "Correspondence: Interesting from New Zealand," [2].

that "more than a year ago the king [Tawhiao] said a White man would come across the sea and preach to them the true gospel and they affirm that they believe he [Ferris] is the man."[4] Mormon historians Brian Hunt and R. Lanier Britsch have identified several prophets who foretold the arrival of a religion that many Maori identified with Mormonism. They specifically list Arama Toiroa, Toaroa Pakahia, and Apiata Kuikainga[5] but agree that the most important prophecy was that made by Paora Potangaroa in 1881.

Potangaroa had been revered as a prophet, holy man, and leader since the 1860s.[6] At a large Ngati Kahungunu gathering at Te Ore Ore, near Masterton in the upper Wairarapa Valley in 1881, he was asked which church the Maori race should join. After prayer and meditation, he told his questioners that the church for the Maori people had not yet come; but that when it did, they would recognise it because it would come from the east, brought by emissaries who would travel among them in twos, live in their homes, and learn their language. They would raise their right arms when they prayed. A scribe wrote the prophecy, plus a covenant which, Paora stated, came from Jehovah. The written prophecy and covenant were sealed in a stone monument, but not before a local man photographed it. In 1928 or 1929, followers of a later Maori prophet, Ratana, opened the monument, but nothing had survived.[7]

More than sixty years after the document was sealed in the monument, Mission President Matthew Cowley attended a conference in the area in 1944 where Eriata Nopera, a faithful Mormon leader who had been ordained a high priest in 1928, spoke about Paora's prophecy and covenant. Nopera, baptized into the Church on 15 August 1886, had attended the 1881 gathering at Te Ore Ore as a very young man, and had witnessed the events he now related at the 1944 conference. When the meeting ended, a Maori sister asked her husband to go home and bring back a certain document wrapped in brown paper. He did so, and she handed it to Brother Nopera, who found it contained a print of the 1881 photograph of the covenant. The photograph was given to President Cowley, who had it framed and eventually hung it in his Salt Lake City home.

The prophecies of all these men contained one or more similar elements: the true church for the Maoris had not yet come. When it did, it would come from the east, its preachers would travel two by two, raise their arms to the

---

4. Fred Bromley Hodson, *None Shall Excel Thee: The Life and Journals of William Michael Bromley*, 148.

5. Hunt, *Zion in New Zealand*, 9–11; Britsch, "Maori Traditions and the Mormon Church."

6. Angela Ballara and Keith Cairns, "Te Potangaroa, Paora, ?–1881," *Dictionary of New Zealand Biography*.

7. Cowley, "Maori Chief Predicts Coming of L.D.S. Missionaries."

square when praying,[8] and would eat and sleep with the Maori people. They would teach that the Maori were of Israel and would teach baptism by immersion and salvation for the dead.[9] Other religions have been seen by their adherents as fulfilling some of these prophecies. In particular, the followers of the Maori prophet Ratana believe that Te Potangaroa's prophecy foretold the coming of the Ratana church in the 1920s.[10] But to Mormons, Te Potangaroa's prophecy and covenant explicitly identify Mormonism.[11]

From the reports made by early Mormon missionaries, there can be little doubt that still other such prophecies were made, even if contemporary documentation and dating are not always available. Many Mormon families have told of visions received by their ancestors, guiding them to accept Mormonism.[12] The significant point is that the Maori people were accustomed to revelation from living prophets. Disenchanted with mainstream Christianity, many were looking for a new religion. The story of Joseph Smith was not something incredible to them; to believe that God had spoken to Joseph was not such a leap of faith to Maori Christians as it was to many Pakeha Christians but instead was confirmation of a vital part of Maori indigenous religion. "In the eyes of Polynesians, the Mormon Church possessed God's favour for He continued to reveal His will to it," wrote one scholar, contrasting the teachings of the orthodox Protestant churches that revelation and miracles had ceased.[13]

Sixty-six Mormon missionaries arrived in New Zealand from America between 1885 and 1889. Almost all learned the Maori language, and most lived and worked exclusively among the Maori people. While in some areas most Maori understood English, there were many places where

---

8. It was often the custom into the early twentieth century for officiators "offering public prayers" in LDS meetings to raise either one or both hands "in a worshipful attitude," a gesture now confined to baptisms and other ritual occasions. James B. Allen and Glen M. Leonard, *The Story of the Latter-day Saints*, 379. I remember seeing elderly priesthood holders raise their right arm to the square as they blessed the sacrament when I was a child in Sydney in the 1930s and 1940s.

9. Britsch, "Maori Traditions and the Mormon Church"; Hunt, *Zion in New Zealand*, 9–11.

10. Peter J. Lineham, "The Mormon Message in the Context of Maori Culture," *Journal of Mormon History* 17 (1991): 87; Ballara and Cairns, "Te Potangaroa."

11. Cowley, "Maori Chief Predicts Coming of L.D.S. Missionaries"; Stuart Meha, "A Prophetic Utterance of Paora Potangaroa," *Te Karere* 43, no. 10 (October 1948): 298–99.

12. For example, see the Hamon family story in George Shepard Taylor, Private Journal, 14 March 1921.

13. Ian R. Barker, "The Connexion: The Mormon Church and the Maori People," 32.

the opposite was true at this time. So it was very important that the missionaries learned to speak Maori, which was most easily accomplished by living among them.[14] They kept journals and wrote many letters home, some of which were published in the *Deseret News*. Many of these letters and journals have survived and provide a rich and heretofore largely untapped source of observations about life in Maori villages in the late nineteenth century. All of them convey a feeling that the Lord was guiding their work among a people who were of Israel and who had been prepared by the Lord for their coming.

As with the European Saints, economic conditions among the Maori Saints varied widely in different parts of New Zealand as well as within each district. A few of the Maori Saints in the Wairarapa Valley and Hawkes Bay were quite wealthy and lived in European-style houses furnished with elegance. "Staying at Kohonui with one of the biggest rangatiras [chiefs, or highly respected local leaders] in this valley," Elder Nelson S. Bishop wrote to his half-sister Susan at the end of February 1889. He described the two-storey house with its beautiful furnishings, then added, "He dresses like a gentleman and attends to his own business affairs. He runs a large farm with horses, sheep and cattle and has a good income besides rent from the land." Bishop was intrigued to note that while the chief's family were all good workers, they needed additional help and kept a couple of European "hired men."

This situation was the exception rather than the rule, and Bishop explained that not all Maori homes matched this standard. "There is some that is to the reverse," he added. "They want nothing and know nothing besides being dirty and anything but inticeing [sic]."[15] In Korongata, for instance, there was only one European-style house when the Mormon missionaries first visited.[16] On the other hand, Elder Bishop reported his surprise on first visiting Waipawa, some miles farther south, to discover that part of it was a Maori town "whith [sic] fine houses as the Europeans have. No Maori huts as I had been accustomed to seeing."[17] Elder William Douglass described the homes found in a typical Maori pa (village). "The poorer class of Maori reside in small huts 10' x 20' ft, made of rushes, wood and willows

---

14. William Gardner, Diaries, 29 June 1884, 17 May 1885; Charles Anderson, "The New Zealand Mission, 3 December 1884, Waotu," *Deseret Evening News*, 9 February 1885, [4].

15. Nelson Spicer Bishop, Letter to Susan Meeks, 28 February 1889, New Zealand Mission Diaries, 445.

16. Alma Greenwood, "Gospel Work among the Maoris," *Deseret Evening News*, 15 October 1884, in Journal History, 22 August 1884, 4.

17. Bishop, Diaries, 11 April 1887, 79.

and tied and fastened by flax, which grows in abundance and is shipped to England and America for making ropes, etc."[18] In the Waikato, most of the Maori Saints were very poor. Here and in many other parts of New Zealand, the Maori mainly relied on subsistence farming and seasonal labour such as fencing, shearing, timber felling, and digging kauri gum, for which New Zealand had a big export market.[19] However, rich or poor, the missionaries were sure that "this people ... are evidently a branch [of the house] of Israel, ... an intelligent race indeed among whom a great work is sure to be done."[20]

Elder Charles Anderson viewed the various Maori prophets and religions as a reaction to the "folly and uselessness" of the different Christian sects. "They see that they have been grossly imposed upon by the Ministers who have through strategy stolen their lands from them," he wrote. "Especially are they down on the Church of England... [T]hey think by having creeds of their own it will cost them less money and less land for they have paid the Christian ministers dearly for their false religion."[21]

Anderson's territory covered nearly half of the North Island, and he and his companions were constantly travelling. "This country is extremely difficult to traverse," he wrote. "The inclemency of the weather, much rain, muddy state of the roads and numerous unbridged rivers and creeks render walking both laborious and disagreeable."[22] As well as travelling between the Maori branches, Elder Anderson supervised the Auckland Branch, which had seventy-one European members on its records in August 1885. In Wellington, where Henry Allington, now returned from Utah, was trying to revive the Karori Branch, LDS numbers remained small, and Allington could report only six members in March 1885.[23]

Missionary work among the Maori was quite different from work in the European towns and cities. In New Zealand cities, the Mormon missionaries followed a similar regimen to those in the Australian and British missions—house-by-house visits along suburban streets, offering tracts, holding cottage meetings and, by the end of the century, street meetings. They travelled between the European towns and cities, staying with LDS

---

18. William Douglass Jr., Journal Notes, New Zealand Mission, after record of ordinances following entry for 17 March 1892.

19. Michael King, "Between Two Worlds," in Geoffrey W. Rice, ed., *The Oxford History of New Zealand*, 290.

20. Charles Anderson, "New Zealand Mission," [4].

21. Ibid.

22. Chas. (Charles) Anderson, "Correspondence: New Zealand Letter to Editor, 5 August 1885, Auckland." *Deseret Evening News*, 11 September 1885, [1].

23. Henry Allington, Letter to the Editor, *Millennial Star* 47, no. 20 (18 May 1885): 319.

families whenever possible. Few Maori lived in urban areas. For several decades from the 1880s, therefore, elders assigned to Maori work made their headquarters in the various Maori pa, often living in an "Elders' house" constructed Maori-style for their especial use.[24] Many became very attached to their "Maori mothers" who cooked for them and did their laundry. They spent many hours each day studying the Maori language and took part in village life, attending karakia (community prayer meetings) morning and night, tangihanga (funerals), and weddings, finding many opportunities to preach as they did so. Public transport was nonexistent except on main routes; to travel between the various villages in their districts, the elders walked or, more commonly, were supplied with horses by the ever-generous Maori Saints. They frequently rode many miles for the opportunity to preach when the peripatetic land courts were held in their vicinity.

Maori baptisms, conferences, and the dedication of Maori meetinghouses were all accompanied by feasts. Describing the April 1885 mission conference in Taonoke, Elder Anderson wrote that "a Maori gathering of any kind is always accompanied by a great feast. The first day [of the conference] the 'whare' [house] was dedicated and after the dedication services, a great feast was served to all present. . . . The next day a number of natives were baptized, among whom was an influential chief, the father of 'Otene Meihana,' and another feast, with great rejoicing, was held over that."[25] When President William T. Stewart spoke at the first district conference at Uawa, Tolaga Bay, in August 1885, he explained the concept of a conference, "it being a new thing to the Maori people," in terms of feasting, "not [just] of food for the body, but of food for the spirit."[26]

Missionaries from the Church Missionary Society sponsored by the Church of England had maintained a social distance, living in European houses and eating European food at European-style dining tables. Most were "career" missionaries, with wives and families accompanying them to New Zealand; their aim was to set an example of civilisation for the Maori. The Mormon missionaries, in New Zealand for comparatively short, three-year missions, mostly left their wives and families at home. Their cultural immersion was near total; and while many suffered from initial culture shock, most developed a genuine love for, and appreciation of, their Maori converts and their culture as they slept on flax mats in smoky, unventilated

---

24. See, for example, Bishop, Diaries, 1 October 1886, 8.

25. "Correspondence: Interesting Letter from New Zealand, [Charles Anderson to YMMIA (Young Men's Mutual Improvement Association) of Elsinore]," *Deseret Evening News*, 28 April 1885, [4].

26. "Conference in New Zealand [Letter from Sondra Sanders Jr., 19 August 1885, Uawa]," *Deseret Evening News*, 8 October 1885, [4].

whare, sat on the ground and ate shellfish, eels, and potatoes with their fingers from a communal dish, taught school, and supervised the work of the Maori branch presidencies.

In return, the Maori Saints loved the "Zion elders" who believed their prophecies, found striking similarities between Maori culture and Israelite customs as recorded in the Old Testament, and validated their firm conviction that the Maori people were of Israelite blood, something they had been taught by the Christian missionaries for sixty years from the days of Samuel Marsden.[27] But no other church offered a coherent, exact explanation of Polynesian origins to match the story of the Book of Mormon, nor could any other church offer anything as relevant as the story of Hagoth that so aptly fitted the pan-tribal canoe stories. To Maori converts, the Mormon Church was "their church" in a very personal and particular way. Enthusiastically adopting their Mormon identity as "Lamanites," they felt a real sense of ownership of the LDS Church, a feeling that continued for several generations.

There were still many Maori villages without government schools in the 1880s; so, like the CMS missionaries several decades earlier, the Mormon missionaries began to establish schools for Maori children in some of these villages. The first LDS primary school in New Zealand was established in the village of Nuhaka in the Mahia District on 11 January 1886.[28] Schoolwork was conducted in English. Additional Mormon schools were opened in Waiapu in November the same year, in the Waikato during 1887, and at Te Aroha in the Hauraki District in August 1888. "Although we have none of the books and other appliances that we have at home," wrote Elder Thomas C. Young, appointed teacher of the Te Aroha school, "the children are learning very fast. . . . The Maori children have excellent memories, and they are also very anxious to learn the English language." About half the children enrolled at this school were not Latter-day Saints, but the missionaries welcomed them all and felt they were having a good influence on the whole community. When a government school was opened in the area some months later, the missionaries closed the "Mormon" school and encouraged their former pupils to attend the state school.[29]

On 8 November 1886, Elder John E. Magleby helped start the Waiapu school. The children were so excited that they came running to

---

27. Samuel Marsden, "Journal of Proceedings at New Zealand 29 July 1819–19 October 1919," holograph copy made in New South Wales, signed by Samuel Marsden (II New Zealand Journal), Hocken Library, University of Otago; quoted in Judith Binney, *The Legacy of Guilt: A Life of Thomas Kendall*, 31.

28. History of Mahia Conference, 1886, New Zealand Mission, Manuscript History.

29. New Zealand Mission, Manuscript History, October 1888, 10 March 1889.

school two hours early at seven o'clock in the morning. With only a blackboard and twelve slates for forty-seven children, and no desks or tables, the missionaries found the school a major undertaking. "The children are quite noisy and poorly dressed, a great many of them only having a shirt on & quite ragged," Elder Magleby wrote. "Those who have pants don't know how to keep their shirt tail in nor their pance [sic] up, but judge not for it is the best they have," he concluded philosophically, but could not resist adding, "It looks rather a funny school outfit."[30]

Maori branches of the Mormon Church began to proliferate across the North Island. There were sixteen in August 1885, and more than twenty-five six months later, with a total of nearly 1,800 members.[31] Opposition began to mount in some districts, especially among the Ngati Porou in the Urewera. Here the defection of Maori converts from the Church of England was opposed by both a local chief and a Maori lay preacher, who unsuccessfully petitioned the New Zealand government to deport the Mormon elders. Their opposition was sparked partly by a genuine belief that the converts were being misled, and partly by resentment at the loss of monetary support, as the Church of England ministers charged for officiating at weddings and funerals while the Mormon elders gave their services free.[32] In October 1885, at Taumata o Tapuhi, a committee led by a well-known Maori preacher, Mohu Turei, summoned the Mormon elders to debate their beliefs. Committee members read aloud the names of sixty-three Mormon converts, who were called on in turn to state his or her choice between renouncing Mormonism or facing either death or the whareherehere ("jale," as Elder Magleby, a dedicated missionary but an indifferent speller, parenthetically explained).[33] The missionaries were proud of their little flock, whose testimonies were strong. Only two succumbed to the opposition pressure.[34] Of course such threats were illegal, and no immediate penalties were imposed on the Mormon converts, but Elders Richards and Magleby were kept busy reassuring their flock.

Over the next few weeks, the Waiapu area simmered. In February 1886, a local chief, Te Hatiwira, and his followers attacked the homes of Latter-day Saints in the village of Te Rimu. After throwing the belongings

---

30. John Ephraim Magleby, Journal, 8, 9 November 1886, 106–7.
31. Statistical report of the Australasian Mission, 1 August 1885; Report of Second Annual Conference of the Australasian Mission, 6 March 1886; both in New Zealand Mission, Manuscript History.
32. Magleby, Journal, 24 September 1885, 64.
33. Ibid., 1 October 1885, 75.
34. Ezra Foss Richards, Journal, 1 October 1885.

of one family into the street, they proceeded to tear down the house.³⁵ Attempting to return to the village a few days later, Elder Magleby and his companion, Elder Elias Johnson, were ambushed a mile out of Kawakawa by Te Hati and several of his men. "He caught the horses by the bits determined we should not pass," wrote Magleby. "We then backed the horses, one one way and one the other, thinking if we strove a little we might get by but he hung to the bits like a lion calling for his men to come and tie us.... When they had arrived he yanked us from our horses, likewise our ropes with which he tied us hands and feet, placing us up against the fence where he made fast the rope tying it real tight and then left us while he counselled what to do with us."

After a short time, Te Hati demanded that the missionaries sign an agreement to leave the area and never return. When they refused, they were left tied up for over an hour before being released and taken into the pa where they were fed and allowed to participate in karakia (communal prayers). Finally they were given a place to sleep with "a flax mat for a bed spread on the floor, with a little blanket to spread over us," reported Magleby. "Though being under persecution, and abuse, we were under the influence of a cheerful spirit and felt as the Apostle of old, glad to be counted worthy of suffering persecution for the name of Christ and his gospel."

The missionaries held out for two days; then Te Hati accepted the following note written on a page of Magleby's notebook: "Kawakawa. 13 February 1886. We hereby testify or witness that we will not come and endeavor to preach the doctrine which we proclaim to be the word of God to Te Hati or any of his people who reject us or don't want to hear us." They were released and left immediately, travelling about twenty-five miles that night. They arrived at Waiapu about 2 a.m. on the morning of Sunday, 14 February. The Saints there were overjoyed to see them safely back. "After forenoon meeting our noses were almost rubbed of[f] honging [sic] with the Saints, they were so glad to see us as they had heard that we were tied and might be killed; I must say we appreciated their love," Magleby wrote. The Mormon elders charged Te Hati with assault; but although the matter went to court, the charges were later dismissed on the grounds that the missionaries had suffered no actual bodily injury.³⁶

Hearing that the Hon. John Ballance, Minister for Maori Affairs, was expected at Waiomatatini, in the northern part of the Ngati Porou territory, the Mormon elders decided to approach him through John A. Jury (Te Whatahoro), an influential Maori convert who had come north

---

35. Magleby, Journal, 8 February 1886, 124.
36. Ibid., 11, 13, 14 February, 9 March 1886, 126–32, 142–47.

to help the missionaries. In the meantime, other chiefs in the area invited the Mormons, "one and all, to come and partake of their hospitality" at Whakato. Eleven missionaries and 219 Maori Mormons formed a procession headed by twelve buggies and followed by most of the remainder on horseback, with a few walking. They were kindly and ceremoniously welcomed at Whakato, the chiefs explaining that they wanted the Mormons to know they did not agree with the actions of the Ngati Porou, and "they did not sanction the instruction Archdeacon Williams [of the Church of England] had given that the natives should not feed us but oblige us to go to hotels." Despite their kindly gesture and the plentiful food offered, the hosts showed no desire to learn more about Mormon doctrine; they did, however, issue a standing invitation to the Mormon missionaries to visit whenever they passed that way.[37]

About 100 men, women, and children accompanied the elders to Waiomatatini on 7 April to meet John Ballance. Ballance and his party were received by the local Maori people with customary ceremony, and everyone adjourned for lunch before an afternoon meeting held in the courthouse. While they were eating dinner, Ballance was given a printed copy of the LDS Articles of Faith. When the meeting began, Ballance was requested by some of the Ngati Porou chiefs to expel the Mormon elders from New Zealand. After listening to speeches from both sides, he "complimented the Saints very much on their belief, stated that the 12th article was a splendid one, and that if they lived up to it they would be sustained and protected by the government but said he, 'The Thirteenth Article is the best of all, and if they lived up to it they could not go wrong.'" Ballance made it clear to the assembled Maori that the government "would sustain all churches under the Law; that the Mormons had as much right as the English church."[38] Ballance was adamant that the Mormons must not be harmed. "You must not persecute them," he told the assembled crowd. "If you do, the government will punish you."[39]

Although he could speak little Maori in September 1885 when he and Elder Richards first confronted opposition in Waiapu, Elder John E. Magleby quickly became fluent in the language and was later acknowledged to be the best Maori speaker of any Mormon missionary ever in New Zealand. He became very much beloved of the Maori people and

---

37. Richards, Journal, 9 March 1886.
38. Sondra Sanders Jr., Journal, 11 April 1886; Richards, Journal, 9 March 1886.
39. "Correspondence: Elders Arrested by Maories [sic], Progress of the Work, Curious Customs [Edward Cliff, Letter to the Editor, 15 July 1886, Hastings, Hawkes Bay]," *Deseret Evening News*, 12 August 1886, [2].

returned twice more to New Zealand after his initial mission which lasted from July 1885 to February 1889. From 1900 to 1902 and again from 1928 to 1932, he presided over the New Zealand Mission (formally separated from the Australian Mission from 1898). The story of his 1886 kidnapping became the stuff of legend and was exaggerated so much that Magleby, in later years, was embarrassed when the story was referred to.[40]

A few months later, the missionaries, along with the entire population of New Zealand, were shocked when Mount Tarawera erupted during the night and early morning of 9–10 June 1886. Ninety-five Maori were killed at Te Ariki, as well as some forty Europeans. Elder Ezra F. Richards recorded in his journal on Thursday, 10 June, "[A] dreadful night of storms.... We also distinctly felt the earth reel five times from earthquakes." Charles Hardy heard the explosions, which sounded to him like cannon fire, at his home in Dairy Flat, north of Auckland and about 110 miles from the scene, and thought that either the French or the Russians were bombarding Auckland.[41] A week later, Elder Sanders reported that the damage was much more disastrous than at first thought. "Several pas [sic] . . . are destroyed, and many people have perished. Lakes have risen fifty and sixty feet. The beautiful terraces are gone.... The Maories are tanging [crying] over their dead." Elder Sanders wrote also that ash had fallen four inches thick on a ship ten miles out to sea.[42]

Elders Ezra F. Richards, James A. Slater, and the new mission president, William Paxman, visited the scene six months after the disaster. Roads were still washed away, and a heavy coating of mud, ash, and debris had destroyed most vegetation. Trees were uprooted or shattered and the once beautiful lake was still what Richards described as a "nasty, clayey color." The three men wandered down the main street of Te Ariki, noting carts almost buried and the ruins of tourist hotels near the once-famous terraces. The elders collected a few small bottles as souvenirs, and Slater pointed out the whare where he and Elder Francis H. Wright had preached and borne testimony just two weeks before the disaster. "Started on our return trip about 12 noon having felt a thousand times paid for our time and trouble," Elder Richards wrote, "as it was an additional testimony to the Almighty power of God to save or to destroy . . . instantaneously; 'twas indeed a solemn and solitary sight to behold; one that caused me much reflection concerning the dealings of the Lord with his people an-

---

40. For a discussion of the subsequent mythologisation of this incident, see Newton, "Mormonism in New Zealand: A Historical Appraisal," chap. 6.
41. Richards, Journal, 10 June 1886; Charles Hardy, "Interesting in New Zealand," *Deseret Evening News*, 23 June 1886, in Journal History, 18 June 1886, 6.
42. Sanders, Journal, 16 June 1886, 236.

ciently, as recorded in the Book of Mormon; where whole towns had been destroyed, swallowed up or buried up."[43]

Elder William Gardner visited the ruins in February 1887 and collected several souvenirs including a large shell from a whare in which he had preached the previous summer. "I viewed the scene and and [sic] wondered at the situation. I had warned the people one year ago to repent and be baptized but they failed to hear me and Te Ariki was covered up to 50 feet in mud," he wrote.[44] Despite popular belief, the infamous Te Hati was nowhere near Mount Taranaki at the time of the earthquake, and no contemporary Mormon account attributes the earthquake to divine retribution on him.

It was just a month after the eruption of Mount Tarawera that Elder William Gardner set out on a country trip. After visiting European convert Thomas Locke at Te Puru, north of Thames, he walked further north to Tapu and then set out to cross the Coromandel Peninsula to Mercury Bay, taking a trail over the mountains which, although very rough, was much shorter than the road. On reaching the top of the mountain, he became lost. After wandering many miles in heavy rain, he spent a miserable night in the dense bush with no food, blanket, or fire. The ground was so wet he could not sit down. He prayed for protection and comfort, and then sang hymns and practised his Maori till dawn. But great good was to come from his apparent misadventure.

After a long, miserable night, he worked his way back down the mountain until he found a trail, where he knelt and thanked God for his deliverance. About a mile further on, he came to the Maori village of Kiri Kiri where he was soon fed and warmed and his clothes dried. He was invited to return, which he did some weeks later, arriving after dark and finding his way to a home with a lamp burning in the front window. Here he was entertained by the Watene family, most of whom were soon baptized, as were others in the village.[45] The Watene home became a refuge for the missionaries from that time, and a branch was organised there in 1888, with Taramana Hei Watene as branch president. He was still serving as branch president when he died in 1895. "His fine dying testimony was read in public throughout all Maoridom long afterwards," wrote Andrew Jenson, Assistant Church Historian, who visited New Zealand in 1895. "[He was] one of the most faithful Maori Elders who ever joined the Church."[46] Watene descendants still provide leadership and strength in numerous Mormon congregations today.

---

43. Richards, Journal, 3 December 1886.

44. William Gardner, Diary, 24 February 1887.

45. Matthew Cowley, "Tribute to Prest. Gardner," *Deseret Evening News*, 7 October 1916, Section 3, 8.

46. History of Kiri Kiri Branch, New Zealand Mission, Manuscript History, vol. 1.

With the numbers of both missionaries and converts increasing, there was great demand for Mormon literature in Maori. While there had been interest in translating the Book of Mormon and other works from the time of Augustus Farnham (1854), only two tracts and the Articles of Faith had been translated and published by 1886. Early that year, Mission President William T. Stewart began translating the Book of Mormon with the assistance of Elder Ezra Foss Richards (son of Apostle Franklin D. Richards) and Maori convert John A. Jury, but the work did not progress very fast.[47]

President Stewart and his nephew, Clarence Stewart, who was also serving in New Zealand, sailed for home on 25 May 1886, taking with them nine-year-old Pirika Whaanga, in anticipation of his family's following shortly. Pirika was thus the first Maori to gather to Utah. Stewart's successor was Elder William Paxman, the first mission president to take his wife with him to New Zealand. The following year, President Paxman assigned Elder Ezra F. Richards and Elder Sondra Sanders Jr. to recommence translation of the Book of Mormon immediately after the forthcoming mission conference.

The third annual conference (hui tau) of the Australasian Mission was held at Muriwai, near Gisborne, in March 1887. The annual mission conferences were numbered from 1885, although there had been several Australasian Mission conferences held in Sydney in the 1850s and at least one in Christchurch in the 1870s. The 1885 conference, from which subsequent conferences were numbered, was the first in which the majority of those attending were Maori and at which most of the proceedings of the conference were in the Maori language. Each conference lasted several days, usually from Friday to Monday or Tuesday of the following week. Providing food and shelter for those attending from long distances provided a major logistical challenge.

Preparing to go to the 1887 hui tau, Elder Ezra F. Richards was overwhelmed by the generosity of local Maori Saints, who were far from wealthy, when the Maori sister who had his old calico shirt to launder gave him instead a new shirt, and the local Maori brethren bought him a new suit to wear to the conference. A pall of sadness was cast over the conference when the Paxmans' baby daughter died on the eve of the conference. Small Sarah had been ill with teething troubles, diarrhoea, and whooping cough for three months before she finally succumbed to "canker" (probably diphtheria). Her illness and death must have been a severe test for her mother. For many years, her little grave in the Whakato cemetery, with

---

47. W. T. Stewart, Letter to Elder Franklin D. Richards, in Journal History, 12 March 1886.

its picket fence and white marble headstone, was a place of pilgrimage for LDS missionaries.[48]

There were three husband-and-wife teams in the mission, Moroni S. and Georgiana Marriott, who arrived in December 1885, followed in the next few months by Heber and Belle Sears, and William and Kate Paxman. Kate Paxman and Georgiana Marriott in particular displayed intrepid spirits and undaunted faith during their husbands' missions, but they have never been officially recognised as missionaries. Kate Paxman was the fourth (plural) wife of William Paxman, and little Sarah was seven months old when they arrived in Auckland. Moroni Stewart Marriott had married Georgiana Geertsen, his second (and plural) wife, in January 1883. She was just twenty and pregnant when his mission call to New Zealand came. Leaving his first wife to care for their farm in Ogden, Moroni and Georgiana arrived in New Zealand just before Christmas 1885. Georgiana's first baby, Winifred, was delivered with the help of Harriet Herd, a Presbyterian midwife whom the Marriotts always remembered with affection and gratitude, at Wairoa on 20 June 1886. By the time she was two, the child was fluent in Maori and was something of a mascot and a curiosity to the American missionaries.[49] The third woman missionary of this period, Belle Sears, was not a plural wife. She had lost her first baby a few months before their mission call. Her second child was born after her return home.

All three women did far more than keep house for their husbands. All performed actual missionary labour, working with the Maori women, teaching school, keeping books, learning Maori and acting as interpreters for new male missionaries. As well, Kate Paxman and Georgiana Marriott actively assisted with the Book of Mormon translation; Kate kept house for the assigned missionaries, checked references, and occasionally suggested a better translation or pointed out errors, while Georgiana transcribed more than 400 pages of the manuscript, making a fair copy for the printer. All three women suffered incredible hardship along with their husbands as they lived in primitive villages through the New Zealand winters, with inadequate heating and often inadequate supplies of food. Elder Nelson S. Bishop, riding to Nuhaka, described his journey. "The road was a trail over the mountains. There was fifteen miles of the way over the mountains that was either ascent or descent and in places the trail was washed out from 2 to 5 feet and just wide enough to admit of a horseman. Over roots[,] rocks

---

48. Francis Washington Kirkham, Journal, Book 8, 14 March 1898; Rufus K. Hardy, "With Church Leaders in New Zealand," *Deseret News*, 25 June 1938, Journal History, 25 June 1938, 2.

49. Bishop, Diaries, 3 April 1888, 278.

Georgiana G. and Moroni S. Marriott, who served as missionaries in New Zealand from 1885 to 1888. Courtesy LDS Church History Library.

and through the mud and so steep that it seemed as though we were either going over the horse's head or tail and the horse would flounce and jump and the banks would hold him from falling broadside and so on we went. ... Two of our sisters from Utah, Katie Paxman and Georgiana Marriott, rode over this road on horseback and had babyes [sic] along," he marvelled.[50] In December 1887, Kate Paxman suffered severe concussion when she and Georgiana Marriott both fell from a shying horse at Rakaututu. Georgiana luckily suffered nothing worse than some bad bruises.[51]

Although these women were regarded in the field as missionaries, and obviously saw themselves as missionaries, they were apparently never certified as proselytising missionaries.[52] Instead, Harriet Nye, set apart as a proselytising missionary in 1898 when her husband was called to preside over the LDS Mission in California, is honoured as the first official female Mormon missionary; a dormitory complex for sister missionaries at the Missionary Training Centre at Provo, Utah, has been named in her honour.[53] The 200 women who preceded Harriet Nye, including four (Geor-

---

50. Ibid., 25 October 1886, 15.
51. Richards, Journal, 15 December 1887.
52. Jessie L. Embry, "LDS Sister Missionaries: An Oral History Response, 1910–1970," 104–7.
53. Diane L. Mangum, "The First Sister Missionaries," *Ensign*, July 1980, 62;

giana Marriott, Belle Sears, Kate Paxman, and Ida Dunford) who served in New Zealand, have been largely forgotten in LDS Church history. It is a pity that the work and sacrifice of these women are not more widely known.

Between 400 and 500 Maori Saints attended fourteen conference meetings held at Muriwai over three days from 11 March 1887. The main business of the 1887 hui tau was the proposal to complete the translation of the Book of Mormon into Maori and then publish it. Mindful of Maori resentment of the mainstream churches' requests for money and land, the missionaries were somewhat nervous about putting the idea to the Maori members. However, the work could not be done without their financial help, as virtually no financial support was received by the mission from Church headquarters at this time or for some years to come. The mission president's only funds were small tithing donations from the Pakeha Saints, donations totally inadequate to meet mission expenses. Individual missionaries were supported by their savings, or by their families or wards at home, and were fed and housed in the Maori villages.

While the Pakeha Saints in city branches such as Auckland and Wellington were taught the law of tithing and were observing it as early as 1880,[54] this principle was introduced gradually to the Maori Saints. As early as 1887 the First Presidency counselled the missionaries in New Zealand to teach the principle of tithing to the Maori.[55] However, no systematic teaching of tithing was done for at least another ten years. While a report on the Mahia District Conference held at Nuhaka on 3 August 1890 indicates that the Maori Saints there had some understanding of tithing, contributions were quite spontaneous, paid in either cash or kind. As this record states, this practice was unique to the Mahia District at this time.[56] Individual missionaries at times taught the principle of tithing; Elder Benjamin Goddard in Porirua in 1892 is one example.[57] But it was not until 1897 that, following renewed instructions from the First Presidency, a consistent effort commenced. The mission president advised the elders to present the principles of tithing and fast offering "with all kindness before [the Maori Saints] with explanations of the blessings to be gained with the keeping of these laws."[58] Mission President Ezra T. Stevenson, sending the

---

"Dedication of Church Facilities in Provo and Argentina," *Ensign*, June 1994, 74.

54. John Peter Sorensen, "Tithing" and "Tithing and Donation," Diary 1, 1880–81.

55. Richards, Journal, 12 March 1887.

56. New Zealand Mission, Manuscript History, 3 August 1890.

57. Phoenix (pseud. of Benjamin Goddard), "Letter from New Zealand, 11 July 1892, Palmerston North," *Deseret Evening News*, 9 August 1892, 7.

58. New Zealand Auckland Mission, General Minutes, 14 February 1898, 133.

1898 annual report to the Presiding Bishopric, specifically explained that the "principle or law, of tithing has not been taught directly to our Maoris. We have, however, begun thereon."[59]

Thus, in the 1880s, the major and vital contribution of the Maori Saints was providing food, shelter, and horses for the missionaries; and the missionaries were reluctant to ask the Maori Saints for donations to support the translation team and pay for eventual publication of the Book of Mormon. But their nervousness was unnecessary.

As President Paxman could not speak Maori, he assigned Elder Ezra F. Richards to present to the conference the proposal to publish a Maori edition of the Book of Mormon. A vote was then taken on whether the Church members were willing to raise the money. The response was enthusiastic. "Three or four would get the floor at once and they were so full of the good spirit it seemed almost impossible for each to wait his turn," Elder Richards recorded.[60] The motion was carried unanimously, and the project became the most significant work of the New Zealand mission during the next two years.

A few weeks after hui tau, Elders Richards and Sanders, together with Sister Paxman (who was to act as cook and housekeeper), moved into a small weatherboard house in Rakaututu, near Gisborne. On Tuesday, 26 April, President Paxman set them apart for the work. He spoke solemnly to the two elders about the sacred nature of the work they were beginning. One room of the house was dedicated for the translation and was not to be used for any other purpose so that the Spirit would be unrestrained.[61]

The two elders started by revising the chapters that had already been translated, but this was slow work. By Thursday, 5 May 1887, they had finished only five chapters—Richards writing, Sanders researching words and grammar, and Sister Paxman making clean copies of the completed pages. By mid-May, they were so deeply immersed in the work that Richards found himself constructing Maori sentences in his sleep. Words like "insomuch" gave them great trouble, and Kate Paxman was drawn into the translation process, searching between the English and Maori Bibles for examples of usage and translation of such phrases. Elder Richards was nearing the end of his three-year mission, and President Paxman anxiously asked if he would stay longer in order to finish the translation. Elder Richards replied that he came to New Zealand to serve until he was released and that his release date was up to his mission president.

---

59. New Zealand Mission, Presidents' Correspondence, 17 February 1899.
60. Richards, Journal, 12 March 1887.
61. Ibid., 26 April 1887.

By July, Richards and Sanders had decided it would be quicker to work separately, as it took them so long to agree on the translation of individual verses. By September they were more than half-way through the text, and President Paxman visited printers to get quotes for 3,000 copies of a book in the Maori language, from 650–700 pages, seven by five inches, with type and paper quality similar to those of the Maori New Testament. Paxman wanted the translation finished by Christmas, so that the volume could be printed in time to be distributed at hui tau at Easter 1888. This goal was too ambitious, for the book was barely ready for the 1889 mission conference.

While Elders Richards and Sanders remained isolated and absorbed in their task, regular missionary work proceeded throughout the mission. Most missionaries were working among the Maori, but the Carterton (European) Branch was reorganised on 12 June 1887 with David Thomas Wiley as president and Charles Petersen and Robert Wiley as counselors. Wherever President Paxman went, he held conferences and accepted donations ranging from a few shillings to many pounds for printing the Maori Book of Mormon, from both Maori and Pakeha Saints.

On Thursday, 24 November 1887 (Thanksgiving Day in America), Elder Richards finished the translation of the Book of Mormon. Sister Paxman cooked a pudding to celebrate. After supper, they completed the index and the front matter, "and at 8.43 p.m. we finished them which was all the Book of Mormon and we rejoiced immensely in having been thus far so wonderfully blessed and prospered of the Lord in the important work."[62] A carefully drawn up chart survives, detailing exactly which chapters and pages each of the two translators produced, Richards being credited with translating 116 chapters and Sanders seventy-seven; the remaining forty-six chapters were a joint effort.[63] Richards and Sanders spent the next few months revising the manuscript with the help of Henare Potae,[64] one of the great Ngati Porou rangatira of the Poverty Bay area. Rewarded by the British for his services in the 1860s, Potae was both wealthy and influential. He was baptized into the LDS Church in 1884 by William T. Stewart.[65]

Elder Ezra F. Richards sailed for home on 23 April 1888. Two faithful Maori brethren, John A. Jury and Piripi Te Maari, spent the next four months

---

62. Ibid., 24 November 1887.
63. Magleby, Journal, chart by Francis H. Wright between entries for 14 and 15 December 1887, 85.
64. Richards, Journal, 28 December 1887.
65. "Missionary Work in New Zealand," *Deseret Evening News*, 11 December 1884, [2]; Steven Oliver, "Potae, Henare, ?–1895," *Dictionary of New Zealand Biography*.

Te Whatahoro (John A. Jury), a prominent and influential early Maori convert. Courtesy LDS Church History Library.

helping Elder Sanders revise the manuscript yet again.[66] Both were among the best-educated and most prominent Latter-day Saint Maori converts. John Alfred Jury (Hoani Te Whatahoro) was the son of a British father and Maori mother, and incidentally a son-in-law of Henare Potae. Jury was born in 1841 near Gisborne but grew up in the Wairarapa where the land court awarded him 400 acres of his deceased mother's land. He travelled around the North Island as an advocate in the native land courts. He was baptized in November 1884, and combined his activities helping the Mormon elders with his work for Te Kotahitangi (Maori parliament) movement. Piripi Te Maari, born about 1836–37, was another prominent leader in the Wairarapa area. A successful businessman, he passionately defended Maori rights to Wairarapa land in the land courts and elsewhere. He was baptized in 1887 and a few months later became the first president of the Kohunui Branch, a calling he held faithfully till his death in 1895. He was a fine orator and was frequently invited to speak at hui tau meetings.[67]

Fund-raising for the printing now began in earnest. The sums raised to date had simply covered the expenses of the translation team.[68] The 1888

---

66. New Zealand Mission, Manuscript History, vol. 2, 31 August 1888.

67. M. J. Parsons, "Jury, Hoani Te Whatahoro, 1841–1921"; Angela Ballara and Mita Carter, "Te Maari-o-te-rangi, Piripi, 1837?–1895." Both in *Dictionary of New Zealand Biography*.

68. Richards, Journal, 24 December 1887, 135.

annual conference was held at Te Hauke in April. The missionaries met in council with some of the leading Maori Saints on Saturday evening, 7 April, and decided to have 2,000 copies of the Maori Book of Mormon printed and bound in leather at a cost of five shillings each. They then considered ways and means of raising the necessary £500 (US$2,500). The meeting lasted four hours, as a small minority of the Maori Saints now thought the Church should pay for the printing. "We took great pains to show them that this sacred and holy Book concerned them especially, as it was a history of God's dealings with their forefathers," wrote Mission President William Paxman.[69] However, most donated as much as they could, and enough cash was raised during the conference to get the printing started. The missionaries understood why some of the Maori Saints had reservations. "The amount of it is the Maories [sic] have been robbed and cheated by the whites until they have learned to look upon them with suspicion," wrote one.[70]

This conference was also a landmark because seventeen Maori elders were called to serve as home missionaries. The annual report showed eleven organised districts, 1,917 members, and 657 children under eight, making a total of 2,574 Latter-day Saints on the records of the Australasian Mission. Of these, 2,243 or 87 percent were Maori.[71] Of the 331 European Saints, only forty-two were in Australia.[72] For several decades, the European Saints in New Zealand were found mainly, but not exclusively, in cities. The Maori Saints, on the other hand, were overwhelmingly in rural areas—rural pockets in the North Island, as scholar Ian Barker has noted, pointing out two focal areas among the Ngati Kahungunu in Hawkes Bay and Nga Puhi in North Auckland.[73] In the Mahia district, for example, of 537 Latter-day Saints on the Church records as late as 1895, only two were European.[74]

Elder John E. Magleby was still working in the Uawa-Tolaga Bay area. His new companion, Elder Ezra T. Stevenson, described a trip they made around the East Cape and Bay of Plenty area, where the trail crossed a sandy beach for a short distance and then climbed a steep mountain. "In . . . places the narrow path leads round the steep mountain sides, the ocean waves beating up at the base; where a single mis-step would be likely to

---

69. William Paxman, Excerpt from Journal, in New Zealand Mission, Manuscript History, 7 April 1888.
70. Bishop, Diaries, 13 October 1888, 380.
71. New Zealand Mission, Manuscript History, 7 April 1888.
72. Angus Taylor Wright, Journal, Statistical Report, 31 January 1888.
73. Barker, "The Connexion," 8.
74. History of Mahia Conference.

cause an ocean bath, or at least a wet suit of clothes. When the rocks are too steep, steps are cut, and we realise what it is to ride up stairs horseback." One morning they rode fifteen miles up the bed of a river, tacking across the stream ninety-five times.[75]

Elder Nelson S. Bishop divided his time between the European branch at Carterton and the Maori branches in the Wairarapa. He and his companion, Elder Alonzo Stewart, enjoyed Christmas dinner with Sister Manihera, who spread two long tablecloths on the floor for her extended family, and a round table at one end for the missionaries. "Bread, butter, potatoes, five kinds of cakes, two kinds of pies, beef, pork, mutton, eels, and goose," Bishop wrote. "A full set of dishes of the finest kind, with flower pots and flowers to deck the table."[76]

The Mormon missionaries frequently recorded their observations of Maori life and customs. They were particularly fascinated with tangihanga (funeral customs). The actual funeral service and burial were only part of the tangihanga, which often lasted a week. Although protocol varied in different tribal areas, between villages within tribal areas, and even between marae in the same village,[77] the basic procedure was similar. The main elements of a tangihanga included the body lying in state on the marae, in an open coffin, with (after the introduction of photography) pictures of the deceased and other deceased relatives displayed.[78] The chief mourners (women with green wreaths in their hair) sat beside the casket, and the arrival of successive parties of manuhiri (visitors) was marked with formal wailing, hongi, and speeches to the deceased and to the living. The visitors were next fed (to remove tapu)[79] and then watched the welcome of later arrivals.

The actual burial usually took place on the third or fourth day, with personal possessions accompanying the corpse to the cemetery. After the funeral, the deceased's home was visited by women who carried out specific rites to remove tapu. Finally, there was an elaborate haakari (funerary feast). Specific rituals regarding tapu were followed at every stage. One year later,

---

75. E[zra] T. S[tevenson], "Among the Maories [sic]: Conference in New Zealand—Labors among the Natives," *Deseret Evening News*, 24 October 1888, [4].

76. Bishop, Diaries, 25 December 1888, 412.

77. Cleve Barlow, *Tikanga Whakaaro: Key Concepts in Maori Culture*, 122.

78. The actual position of the body on the marae (whether in a meetinghouse and if so, where positioned, on the porch of a meetinghouse, in a tent or in the open air), varied according to regional and tribal traditions. Joan Metge, *The Maoris of New Zealand: Rautahi*, 261.

79. Food is noa (ordinary, commonplace), and contact with food nullifies the tapu of death as well as any tapu inadvertently brought on to the marae by te manuhiri (the visitors).

further ceremonies were held when a memorial gravestone was unveiled, the modern equivalent of the pre-European-contact custom of exhumation and reburial.[80] Face-laceration as a sign of mourning, an early practice, was seldom seen by the time the Mormons began working with the Maori.

Elder Bishop came from thrifty, pioneering Mormon stock, and some aspects of the tangi shocked his Puritan soul, especially the Maori belief that the belongings of a dead person were tapu. "Bro. Taylor, Sandres [sic], Sister Marriott and myself took a walk up the river," he wrote on one occasion, "and on the way back we stopped at a grave of a Maori. There was a house built over the grave and fence around it with geraniums planted all around which made it look quite nice but on looking in we saw a second-hand store. They had everything that he owned in the clothes line there, even to his bed."[81] Two years later, Elder Bishop was asked to dedicate a grave. "They lowered the body and then according to custom they buried all his clothes with him. I would have been pleased to have changed shoes with him," he commented somewhat enviously. "The Maoris said they would rather go naked before they would wear anything belonging to one who was dead." While in the early years of Mormon contact, the tangihanga was more a matter of curiosity than concern to the missionaries, by the 1950s it was becoming a focus of cultural misunderstanding and conflict between the Maori Saints and American presiding officers, not fully resolved to this day.[82]

Another aspect of Maori life that shocked the missionaries was what they perceived as moral laxity. In reality, pre-European Maori society had strict standards of modesty and sexual morality and meted out effective punishments for violating these standards. Despite some fifty years of Christianity, many of these cultural mores persisted into the twentieth century. The problem the Mormon missionaries faced was that Maori standards of morality differed from those of the LDS Church.

For example, young people were allowed considerable sexual freedom and only the daughters of chiefs were expected to be virgins at marriage. However, adultery involving a married woman was a serious crime.[83] There

---

80. For a fuller discussion of both pre- and post-European Maori death customs, see Cleve Barlow, *Tikanga Whakaaro: Key Concepts in Maori Concepts*, 14, 16, 120; Metge, *The Maoris of New Zealand: Rautahi*, 27–28, 261–264; James Irwin, *An Introduction to Maori Religion: Its Character before European Contact and Its Survival in Contemporary Maori and New Zealand Culture*, 49–59.

81. New Zealand Mission Journals, 21 November 1886, 27.

82. Ibid., 18 February 1889, 439. For an extended discussion of Maori funeral customs and Mormonism, see Newton, "Mormonism in New Zealand," chap. 7.

83. Metge, *The Maoris of New Zealand: Rautahi*, 20; Bruce Biggs, *Maori*

was no marriage ceremony as the missionaries understood it; a union was arranged by conferences between the two families, and the young couple simply set up house together. The families often celebrated with a feast. Because there were no legal documents or even ritual to be cancelled, dissolution of a marriage could occur by mutual agreement, usually for reasons such as barrenness, adultery, or desertion. In these cases, utu (satisfaction, or payment) was exacted from the family to which the erring party belonged, and both parties were then free to establish another union. Many Maori chiefs practised polygamy (or more precisely, polygyny), taking up to four wives each.

During the latter half of the nineteenth century, many Maori couples had their marriages solemnised by Christian ministers, but such marriages did not have to be registered until early in the twentieth century and were not legally required until the 1950s. So the Maori people were free to marry either by tribal law or Christian marriage rites, or to "mix and match" elements of both.

Very early, the Mormon missionaries recorded concern about moral standards; but as long as the LDS Church officially espoused the practice of polygamy (until 1890), they showed no concern about this aspect of Maori culture. But while they were quite willing to baptize a Maori chief and his plural wives, they began to excommunicate converts who married "Maori fashion."[84] Once the LDS Church retreated from the practice of polygamy, Maori marriage customs caused the missionaries a great deal of worry. More than half a century passed before LDS standards of morality and marriage were fully accepted by the Maori Saints, and at times there was considerable tension in the intervening period as different mission presidents required more or less strict obedience to LDS standards.[85]

The 1889 mission conference was again held in Te Hauke. Some of the Saints rode several hundred miles from the Bay of Islands district, where Elder Magleby had opened the work with great success. Each district president had to report. "Wairarapa District was reported by district president N[elson] S. Bishop," Bishop wrote, tongue-in-cheek, in his journal. "The report was somewhat flattering, telling the good and leaving out the bad as is the custom."[86] But the great event of the conference was the distribution of the first 500 copies of the Book of Mormon.

Marriage: An Essay in Reconstruction, 15.

84. R. H. Manihera, "Account of Missionary Work in N.Z. in 1880s"; Bishop, Diaries, 8 July 1888, 337.

85. For a fuller discussion of Mormon/Maori cultural conflict, including marriage customs, see Newton, "Mormonism in New Zealand," chaps. 7–9.

86. Bishop, Diaries, 4 April 1889, 473.

Elder Angus T. Wright had spent the previous few months proofreading each sheet as it came from the printer, four times. "Have taken much pleasure in my labor on that sacred work," he wrote on 28 February 1889. "Will finish printing one week from now." With the printing completed, the next step was binding, and Wright worried about getting any copies in time for the conference. "I saw the bookbinder and tried to hurry him up but he don't seem to hurry much," he wrote on 1 March. On 28 March he finally took delivery of the first 500 copies, had them hastily packed, and dispatched them by a vessel bound for Hawkes Bay.

On arrival at Napier, he was unable to get the boxes unloaded, so he went to Te Hauke for the weekend conference sessions. On Monday, he returned to Napier, only to be told that the boxes could not be found. After considerable worry and some judicious tipping, they were located and transhipped to the railway office just in time to catch the afternoon train to Te Hauke. Amid great excitement, about 340 copies were distributed next morning, Tuesday, 9 April 1889, the final day of the conference.[87]

"Never were children more anxious to receive their Christmas presents, than were this people to receive that holy book," wrote President Paxman. He was particularly impressed that, even though most of those present had already donated from five shillings to five pounds and thus were entitled to receive their copies free, about eighty of the Saints insisted on paying the five shillings again to help raise the final payment to the printer and to begin a fund towards publishing other Church works in Maori.[88]

President Paxman was released in July 1889 and was instructed by the First Presidency to appoint Elder Angus T. Wright his successor as mission president. Paxman, Nelson S. Bishop, and three other elders, plus three emigrating Saints, sailed on the *Zealandia* on 12 August 1889. Before leaving, Elder Bishop, with Elder Joseph S. Groesbeck and a Maori companion, Edward Manihera, made a three-month visit to the South Island. Here there were no Maori Saints to provide horses, and the three walked great distances, sleeping in shearing sheds where they were sometimes fed and sometimes not. Their feet blistered and bled. Back in Wellington, they were hospitably received by the Allington family. "My sleep was sweet for Bro[ther] and Sister Allington gave us their bed," wrote Elder Bishop.[89]

Bishop was a meticulous record keeper, and it is not difficult to read between the lines and gauge the devotion and dedication of such men to

---

87. Wright, Journal, 28 March, and 8, 9 April 1889.

88. "Correspondence: Wm. Paxman, Letter to President Geo. Teasdale, dated Hastings, New Zealand, 29 April 1889," *Millennial Star* 51, no. 28 (15 July 1889): 436–38.

89. Bishop, Diaries, 6 August 1889, 528.

the work of the Lord. Between his departure from Salt Lake City in August 1886 and his arrival home on 9 September 1889, he travelled 12,631 miles by steamer, 2,429 miles by train, rode on horseback 6,017 miles and walked 1,032 miles, a total of 22,309 miles travelled. He attended 257 meetings at which he did not speak, and 400 at which he did, making a total of 657 meetings attended. He received 194 letters and wrote 242, performed thirty-one baptisms, and assisted in a further twenty-one. His expenses for his mission totalled US$546.80 cents (approximately £125). A final note in his missionary journal catalogued some of the food consumed at hui tau in April 1889: 23,550 lbs. potatoes; 1,050 lbs. kumara (sweet potato); 2,000 lbs. eels; 2,080 lbs. sugar; 1,600 lbs. shellfish; 5,500 lbs. flour; 19 hogs, 58 sheep, and 4 "beeves."

Like Elder Bishop, Elder Heber S. Cutler, who arrived at the end of March 1889, was fascinated by Maori culture. He, too, described the protocol of greeting visitors to any pa, and the tangi or weeping that preceded the welcome speeches if any member of either tribe had died since their last meeting. "The same operation is gone through as often as any new person arrives who has not previously wept," he wrote home.[90] Cutler lived with Maori in the Taupo region, where the people were very poor. He deplored the unhygienic conditions in which food was prepared, but praised the needlework of the women and the fondness they showed for babies and children. Childless Maori, he reported, would borrow a child from relatives for months at a time and very often babies were given away altogether. This Maori custom, too, perturbed the missionaries. "I searched the scriptures and found a few passages to assist me in breaking down the old Maori tradition of giving their children away," wrote Elder Ezra F. Richards one day in 1886. "I was very desirous of getting them to realise the necessity of raising their children up in the Church."[91] When a Maori Saint and his wife gave their newborn twin girls to non-LDS relatives as late as 1918, Mission President James N. Lambert talked seriously to the parents of the possible consequences of the children being raised out of the LDS Church. "They ... seemed to feel very badly about it," he commented. "I believe they wish now they had kept them."[92]

Elder Cutler was assigned to teach at the Mormon primary school in Taupo. Late in 1889, he reported that the local Maori tribe planned to build a bigger schoolhouse for the missionaries; and when it was built, he

---

90. "In Maori Land" (Heber S. Cutler, Letter to his parents, 27 November 1889), *Deseret News Weekly*, 4 January 1890, 52–54.
91. Richards, Journal, 23 May 1886.
92. James Needham Lambert, Journal, 3 September 1918, 596.

Missionary group in New Zealand in 1887, including William Gardner, centre (seated), Ezra T. Stevenson, seated (front) and Nelson S. Bishop, far right. Courtesy Harold B. Lee Library, Brigham Young University, Provo, Utah.

expected children to come from surrounding villages. "All the natives have made extra preparations to have large crops of potatoes this coming season, so there will be plenty of food for the children and I expect there will be a great many outside [non-LDS] children come. I trust the school will be the means of doing much good," he wrote.[93] Elder Cutler implied that the plans were for a residential school; and although such a school did not eventuate at this time, the scheme was discussed for some years and was the genesis of the Maori Agricultural College.

The Maori Saints enthusiastically adopted Mormonism as a way of life, attending Sunday School, sacrament services, priesthood meetings, and Relief Society meetings as well as their regular daily karakia. Local men served as presidencies of all Maori branches, several of the branch presidents being ordained elders and others priests, while American missionaries served as conference (district) presidents. Branch presidents were chosen by consensus, rather than "called" as Latter-day Saints today understand the procedure.[94]

---

93. Cutler, "In Maori Land," 53.
94. New Zealand Mission Minutes, 17 August 1902; Magleby, Journal, 31 January 1901.

All Maori branch presidents spoke at district conference, and each year a few were invited to speak at the annual hui tau. Public speaking held no fears for the Maori, for oratory was a highly developed art among them. "The fixed etiquette of welcoming visitors with oratorical speeches, replying, open discussions of affairs of tribal or family interest, and orations connected with birth, marriage, and death, all led to the development of high standards of speech and oratory," wrote Sir Peter Buck (Te Rangi Hiroa).[95] For example, at hui tau in 1889, Henare Potae, "who has devoted much time and means in connection with the publication of the Book of Mormon," spoke in the Sunday morning session. "This conference was not called by man, but by God," Potae told the assembled Saints. "I know that God takes the weak things of the earth to establish His purposes." Another frequent speaker at conferences was Piripi Te Maare, "an eloquent expounder of the gospel, . . . an intelligent and exemplary man."[96]

Talks and testimonies of these and other Maori branch presidents were often commended by the missionaries for their eloquence and superior oratory. At hui tau in 1895, Ngawaea Poipoi "was listened to with breathless interest, as he fluently reviewed the history of Lehi and his sons, showing how the Maoris inherited the dark skin through the disobedience of their ancestors," wrote Elder Benjamin Goddard. "This native Demosthenes most eloquently portrayed the Gospel plan of salvation, and with appropriate gestures, he forcibly emphasised these saving principles and urged all his people to render obedience to the laws of God."[97] Demosthenes, of course, was the greatest orator of ancient Athens.

Sunday Schools were organised in most branches, divided according to numbers into two, three, or four classes, for both children and adults. Many Maori could read their own language and an ever-increasing number were able to read English.[98] In Porirua, Elder Goddard organised two adult classes, one in English and one in Maori. "English" denoted the language of the text studied, not the ethnicity of the class members, and indicates that a substantial number of the Maori Saints in that branch could

---

95. Te Rangi Hiroa (Sir Peter Buck), *The Coming of the Maori*, 360.

96. John F. Smellie, "Australasian Mission," *Deseret News Weekly*, 25 September 1889, 678; Phoenix (pseud. of Benjamin Goddard), "Distant Maoridom," *Deseret News Weekly*, 27 January 1894, 172–73; "New Zealand Conference," *Deseret News Weekly*, 28 May 1892, 746–47.

97. Phoenix (pseud. of Benjamin Goddard), "In the Antipodes: An Annual Conference of the Australasian Mission," *Deseret Evening News*, 19 May 1894, 11.

98. Maori was an oral language; but the early Christian missionaries devised a written form, and large numbers of Maori learned to read in the mission schools in the years before the Land Wars.

both speak and read English.[99] Sunday School classes studied a variety of materials. These included the scriptures (especially the Book of Mormon after the Maori edition appeared), volumes such as Wilford Woodruff's *Leaves from My Journal* (in English), and Sunday School cards. A generous supply of these cards, translated into Maori, was sent to the mission from the Deseret Sunday School Union in Salt Lake City. However, by 1889, many of the Saints, both adults and children, had committed all the cards to memory and were anxiously hoping for more.[100] The Maori gift for memorisation was well known to the missionaries; many were what Elder Benjamin Goddard called "living compendiums" of the scriptures, which were recited daily at karakia.[101]

The Maori Saints delighted in testimony meetings. "The floor was continuously occupied," Elder Heber S. Cutler reported of one such meeting, held on 12 January 1890. "No sooner did one speaker close his remarks than another was found eagerly waiting to improve the fleeting time. In fact several would remain standing to claim the next opportunity to speak. This was kept up for four hours and thirty-five minutes, during which time forty-two persons had borne their testimony."[102] Four-hour testimony meetings were common. The participants were of all ages, and the missionaries occasionally drew unflattering comparisons with the youth in their home wards in Zion. We "started for Kikokino [Tiko Kino] where we will hold the monthly priesthood meeting. It is as good as a conference with them as they all come out both men and women and children. It makes one feel good to see them so merry with a smile on their face and a sparkle to their eye," wrote Elder Bishop in 1887. "After the business was over it was [time] for testimony and there was no time lost[,] two and sometimes three jumped up at a time. All wishing to say something I often think did our young at home have a little of their spirit of jumping up in a testimony meeting they would be better prepared for [becoming] missionaries than a great many are."

The youth added much to the spirit of branch meetings. "Their minds are free from malice and they are freerer [sic] from sin, and they trully [sic] do speak well," Elder Bishop wrote of those in the Papawai Branch, noting that youth speakers ranging from ten to fifteen years spoke from five

---

99. Bishop, Diaries, 1 July 1888, 334–35; Phoenix (pseud. of Benjamin Goddard), "Letter from New Zealand, 11 July 1892."

100. Smellie, "Australasian Mission," 678–79.

101. Phoenix (pseud. of Benjamin Goddard), "Letter from New Zealand, 6 September 1892, Palmerston North," *Deseret News Weekly*, 8 October 1892, 494–95.

102. Cutler, "The Australasian Mission," 325–26, in New Zealand Mission, Manuscript History, 12 January 1890.

"... ripe for the gospel..." 69

to fifteen minutes each. Assistant Church Historian Andrew Jenson, who visited Nuhaka in 1895, also commented on the willingness with which all participated, noting that the members felt slighted if not called on in turn. "That peculiar timidity with which every young American or European Elder is so well acquainted, seems to be almost unknown among the Maoris, who generally arise with an air which would indicate that they consider themselves perfectly able to do anything in the line of singing, preaching or praying that is required of them."[103]

Almost every branch had a choir, and music was an important part of every meeting, whether local, district, or mission. For several decades, branch choirs competed for a trophy or monetary prizes at hui tau. Elder Orson D. Romney told of a testimony meeting held as part of a district conference in the Bay of Islands. "Both male and female, old and young, bore faithful testimonies to the work of God," he wrote, "and the sweetness and solemnity of their songs and praises unto the Lord are beyond my power to describe."[104] At first the Church of England hymnal was used, but soon the missionaries introduced LDS tunes to some of these hymns and began translating LDS hymns into Maori. A small Maori hymnal was compiled by the New Zealand Missionary Society (formerly Zion's Maori Association) in Salt Lake City in 1910, containing a dozen hymns with a mixture of English and Maori words. An LDS Maori hymnal was printed in New Zealand in 1917.[105]

On the whole, then, the missionaries were pleased with the devotion and dedication of their Maori converts. "The [Maori] members are generally quite intelligent and perform their religious duties with zeal and ability," reported Elder Alma Greenwood on his return to Salt Lake City. "They are as a rule exceedingly hospitable and quite exemplary in their conduct or at least soon become so when they embrace the gospel. In fact the change that takes place for the better in them is almost marvellous in its suddenness. The reformatory work among them introduced by the Elders was so striking that it was even observed and commented upon

---

103. Bishop, Diaries, 4 June 1887, 1 July 1888, 103–4, 335; Andrew Jenson, "Jenson's Travels: Letter No. 34," *Deseret News Weekly*, 4 April 1896, 498–99.

104. Orson D. Romney, Letter, 30 September 1889, printed in unidentified newspaper, clipping pasted into New Zealand Mission, Manuscript History, 1 November 1889.

105. Bishop, Diaries, 12–30 July 1888, 338–44; Phoenix (pseud. of Benjamin Goddard), "Letter from New Zealand, 19 April 1893," *Deseret News Weekly*, 27 May 1893, 706–7; Jenson, "Jenson's Travels: Letter No. 34"; New Zealand Missionary Society, 1910, Maori Hymnal; Lambert, Journal, 29 March 1917.

by some of the public journals, usually unfriendly to Mormons."[106] "Very satisfactory reports were made by the [district] presidents," wrote Elder Cutler, reporting a conference in January 1890, "showing that the natives are desirous of remaining firm to the principles of truth which have been taught them; and though there are some who give way to temptation and folly, yet there is a marked change for good in the Saints."[107]

The Maori Saints themselves commented on the improved state of those who joined the Church and remained faithful. For example, Hoera Te Ruruku, president of the Rangitoto Branch on D'Urville Island, "stated that the members were leading exemplary lives, and many outsiders were favorably impressed." Maori convert John A. Jury (Te Whatahoro) told Elder Nelson S. Bishop that, although he was previously a member of the Church of England, he used never to pray, and regularly drank liquor and smoked; but from the day of his baptism, he had given up drink, tobacco, tea, and coffee; he also prayed regularly, and "such a change he dident [sic] think could have been made." At hui tau at Tamaki in 1895, Piripi Te Maari and Arapata Meha "both testified to the benefits derived by the Maori people through the indefatigable labors of the Elders of Israel."[108] As early as 1884, Chief Otene Meihana wrote to the family of Elder George S. Taylor in Utah, expressing the gratitude of one who was "small in the gospel" to God and the Church authorities "for sending the Gospel to us in New Zealand."[109]

While the missionaries may have been biased in reporting the "marked change for good" in their converts, similar reports also came from "outsiders" (as non-Latter-day Saints were termed by the missionaries). President Angus T. Wright told the editor of the *Millennial Star* in England that the work of the Mormon missionaries among the Maori had received many "flattering notices" in the local press, that the Minister for Native Affairs had reported to Parliament that Mormonism was the only church which had made any advance in the King Country, and that their converts were "the most sober and industrious Maories in New Zealand."[110]

---

106. Alma Greenwood, quoted in "Return from New Zealand: The Australasian Mission Prospers," *Deseret Evening News*, 6 December 1884, [3].

107. Heber S. Cutler, "The Australasian Mission," 12 January 1890, *Deseret News Weekly*, 1 March 1890, 325–26.

108. R. G. Meikle, "New Zealand Conference," *Deseret News Weekly*, 25 March 1893, 429; Bishop, Diaries, 9 October 1885, 10; B[enjamin] Goddard, "Australasian Conference," *Deseret News Weekly*, 14 June 1895, 818–21.

109. "Brother Otene's Letter, 4 December 1884," *Deseret News*, 14 January 1885, 820.

110. Angus T. Wright, Letter from Auckland, New Zealand, 3 October 1890, *Millennial Star* 52, no. 46 (17 November 1890): 731.

Articles which appeared in provincial newspapers were sometimes picked up by the metropolitan journals. An article from the Napier *Telegraph* was reprinted in the *Auckland Weekly News* in 1890. The *News* reported:

> According to the Napier *[Daily] Telegraph*, Mormonism is making great way among the Maories in that province.... The Mormons can be easily picked out at any place by their temperance, as well as superior cleanliness and tidiness of dress, both among the men and women ... and we are informed that similar effects are being observed among the natives who adopt Mormonism in several other parts of the country.... The missionaries, we are also told, devote themselves very earnestly to their work, live and move among the natives, and devote their attention as much to moral as religious teaching.[111]

The Word of Wisdom was preached to the Maori much earlier than the law of tithing. The Mormon missionaries were dismayed at the intemperance of the Maori population and also that women and children smoked as well as the men. "Liquor is easily obtainable from the whites, who have framed their laws so they can sell to the natives without stint or hindrance, finding it much easier to accomplish with their accursed grog what they failed to do with powder and ball—viz., robbing them of their lands," wrote Mission President W. T. Stewart in 1884, adding, "The Maories [sic] are the most confirmed smokers and tea drinkers I have ever seen, these practices being limited neither to sex nor age. From the time they are able to run about till they go into the grave, they suck away at the pipe as if their life depended upon it. However, some who have joined the Church have put away their pipes, and we think it is only a matter of time before many more will do the same."[112]

Observance of the Word of Wisdom did not come easily to many of the Maori Saints, although when Elder Henry F. McCune preached the first sermon on the subject at Uawa in 1885, fifty pipes were thrown into the fire then and there. Nelson S. Bishop had somewhat less spectacular success at Papawai when, after preaching on the Word of Wisdom, he called on those willing to stop smoking to stand. Only three arose—the branch president, a deacon, and one young woman. However, as time passed, more and more of the Saints faithfully abstained from liquor, tobacco, tea, and coffee.[113]

---

111. *Auckland Weekly Star*. Article, no date. Reprinted in *Millennial Star* 52, no. 26 (30 June 1890): 414.

112. W. T. Stewart, Letter dated Papawai, 22 April 1884, *Millennial Star* 46, no. 24 (16 June 1884): 378–79.

113. H[enry] F[rederick] McCune, Autobiography and Diary, 30 October 1885,

While the first Latter-day Saint meetinghouse in Australia was not built until 1904, many Maori LDS branches built meetinghouses from the mid-1880s. Branches were encouraged to build their own specifically LDS meetinghouse, as whare karakia on the marae were traditionally open to all denominations.[114] Occasionally, a whare karakia built for the Church of England was simply turned over to the Mormons when the village converted.[115] Sometimes the Maori ministers would be converted also; some leading chiefs who embraced Mormonism, such as Ihaka and Te Whatahoro (John A. Jury), were reputed to have been Church of England lay preachers for many years.[116]

Most branch meetinghouses were not permanent structures, nor did the LDS Church own the land on which they were built; some were built on land owned by an individual rangatira and others on communally owned land. They were usually slightly larger versions of the traditional whare karakia, sometimes containing windows as a concession to the missionaries' inexplicable desire for fresh air. Great efforts were made to have new buildings ready for district and mission conferences, and often the missionaries helped the host branch with the construction.

For example, two large buildings, one timber-framed, were erected for the 1892 hui tau at the small village of Te Rahui on the Awanui River near the East Cape, a village which normally consisted of a few Maori huts. All the Mormons in the district co-operated in preparing for the conference. The whare karakia, with a traditional carved front, seated 500 on flax mats, which the Maori preferred to benches or chairs. The dining room was 150 feet by 20 feet, and here an improvised table seating 200 ran the full length of the building.

Elder Benjamin Goddard described the journey as missionaries from the southernmost and northernmost parts of the island left their assigned areas up to a month before the scheduled date of this conference, collecting other "pilgrims" as they passed through various towns and villages. Two groups converged at Gisborne, and more than 200 Latter-day Saints set out from there on the morning of 2 April.

"The scene reminded the observer of a regiment of cavalry, minus the uniforms," wrote Goddard, "except that the company was improved by being composed of both sexes (many mothers carrying their babes) and instead of the clanking of the weapons of war, they rode forth singing the

---

1:74; Bishop, Diaries, 27 September 1887, 158; History of the Mahia Conference.

114. Barker, "The Connexion," 16–17.

115. Elwin W. Jensen, Papers, item 2.

116. L[ouis] G. Hoagland, "In Distant New Zealand," *Deseret News Weekly*, 8 October 1893, 494–95.

songs of Zion or merrily conversing together." The large party spent the Sabbath at Uawa, and set out again on Monday, their numbers almost doubled. "The road from Uawa to Tokomaru Bay, our next stopping place, was over mountain trails, where we rode in single file, often along narrow ledges, passing deep chasms and descending into the bush where the vegetation was so dense that even one horseman could scarcely pass through," Goddard continued. A day or two later, they were welcomed to the little town of Jerusalem, where most of the inhabitants belonged to the "Missionary Church" (Church of England), with hoisted flags and ceremonial dances, as well as being given food and shelter for the night. Whereas in the cities, and in some rural areas, the ministers often led the opposition to Mormonism, in many districts there was a remarkable spirit of ecumenical hospitality and cooperation.

Next day they set out on the last leg of the journey to Te Rahui, one horseman riding ahead with the Union Jack and the rest of the company marshalled into lines, four abreast. At Te Rahui, the local Maori formed two companies, one of LDS members and the other of members of the "Missionary Church," each group divided into male and female participants. The ceremonial dances and haka continued for over an hour.[117]

The custom of holding karakia morning and evening had been begun by the earliest Christian missionaries in Polynesia and was still observed faithfully throughout the islands.[118] Mormon missionaries in New Zealand encouraged the practice, which in New Zealand was conducted for an entire pa rather than in individual households as in other parts of Polynesia. Elder Benjamin Goddard, who helped finance his mission by writing for the Utah papers, described karakia in Porirua, about fourteen miles north of Wellington:

> It is customary with our Maori members to assemble at the meeting house, morning and evening, for prayers. In this branch we are roused by the bell ringing at half-past six in the morning, and at this winter season it is scarcely daylight at that hour.
>
> Half an hour is allowed for dressing and washing, and at seven o'clock the second bell rings. The Saints may then be seen wending their way to the meeting house; mothers carrying their babies on their backs in true Maori style. The services usually last about half an hour. A hymn is sung and a chapter read from the Bible or Book

---

117. Phoenix (pseud. of Benjamin Goddard), "New Zealand Conference," *Deseret News Weekly*, 2 May 1892, 710–12.

118. T. Lindsay Buick, *The Treaty of Waitangi: How New Zealand Became a British Colony*, 8–9.

of Mormon, after which the members chant or recite what they term the "Rongo Pai" or Gospel.

This consists of passages of scripture on the various principles of the Gospel, and most of the members have memorized all the scriptural references to the first principles of the Gospel, the scattering and gathering of Israel, restoration of the Gospel, tithing, etc. All present take part in the exercise, from the aged and feeble to the children who can only lisp the words. Some of the little ones, yet unable to read, will repeat correctly many of the scriptural passages. After prayer, the members disperse to attend to their daily duties, but at five we are summoned together again by the ringing of the bell. This routine is continued summer and winter, and the inclement weather does not affect the attendance.[119]

Elder Goddard warmly appreciated the hospitality of the Maori, whether they offered much or little. On a journey from Porirua to the Manawatu District Conference in 1892, Goddard wrote of the affectionate greeting he and his companion received from an elderly Maori widow. "A good fire was built in the middle of the whare, or house.... Our good sister spread our supper on the floor, consisting of potatoes and salt seasoned with love an[d] esteem." The following day they arrived at Awapuni, where elaborate preparations had been made for the conference. "All comers were made happy and comfortable," he wrote, "and the Maori sisters had evidently been busy cooking several days, judging from the abundance of puddings, sponge cakes, etc. Our dining table was loaded with meats, vegetables, jellies, jam and cakes, all prepared by the native sisters of the branch, who are excellent cooks, and it would be difficult to excel them. As we had been traveling in the rain all day we appreciated our comfortable quarters and the warm fire, and when called to supper we proved our appreciation by doing justice to the luxuries spread before us."[120]

In fact, the missionaries were unanimous in praising the generosity and hospitality of the Maori people. "It makes no difference to our reception whether the Saints are at home [when we arrive] or not," wrote Heber S. Cutler. Cutler was reporting a trip that he and the new mission president, John S. Bingham (who succeeded President Wright in October 1890), made through the Bay of Islands district, "as the outsiders here treat us just as kindly." He described a meal of potatoes and eels. "Feeling rather hungry after our ride, we dived into the dish and ate our frugal meal with

---

119. Phoenix (pseud. of Benjamin Goddard), "Letter from New Zealand, 11 July 1892," 7.
120. Ibid.

as much relish as though we had been born and reared Maoris," Cutler wrote. After supper, the elders participated in evening prayer and then prepared for sleep. "All down one side of the house are spread mats upon rushes, and the natives showed us a spot about the centre of the room where a few extra rushes have been thrown to render it a little softer. Here we made our bed while the natives slept close by on either side."[121]

In 1893, President William T. Stewart and Elder John M. Hendry travelled south along the east coast, calling at every pa till they reached Uawa. Hendry reported that they were more kindly received by the Hauhau, followers of Te Kooti, than by orthodox Christian congregations. "[In] some places entertainment was not given, which is a very unusual thing among the Maories as they will generally divide their last potato with the stranger. Yes, frequently starve themselves to provide for a person or company thrown upon their hospitality. In fact, hospitality may be said to be their national trait, and a native is strongly prejudiced indeed when he will not feed and house the traveler."[122]

Despite the enormous expenditure of money and labour involved in staging the annual hui tau, the mission districts competed keenly for the privilege of hosting it. In 1894, it was held at Waiwhara in the Mahia District. A "spacious building," sixty feet by twenty feet, was specially built of native reeds for the conference, and all meetings were dimly lighted as the only light entered from the doorway and a small opening for ventilation. There was a small table with a rough bench and a pulpit for the speakers, and the usual flax mats spread down each side of the hall. The congregation sat, squatted, or reclined on these mats, which were also the evening's bedding. There were plenty of blankets and pillows, so it was possible to lie at ease listening to the proceedings. "The deacons pace to and fro through the centre aisle armed with long rods and occasionally poking drowsy members of the congregation to prevent them falling into the arms of Morpheus [the Greek god of sleep]," wrote Goddard. "The Argus eyes of these vigilant officials were often fixed upon the Elders who were also compelled to lie upon the mats as there were only two chairs in the village. The brethren would often chat till late in the evening and were aroused early in the morning hence it was no wonder if, in a four-hour testimony meeting, some were found nodding and a watchful deacon, enjoying the opportunity, would give the Kaumatua [elders] a gentle reminder."[123]

---

121. Heber S. Cutler, "Letter from New Zealand, 11 November 1890, Whangaroa, Bay of Islands," *Deseret News Weekly*, 3 January 1891, 153–55.
122. New Zealand Mission, Manuscript History, 20 January 1893.
123. Phoenix (pseud. of Benjamin Goddard), "In the Antipodes."

Serious gospel inquiries from Europeans were now more frequent than for several years past, and the missionaries decided that they should make a renewed effort with the Pakeha.[124] President William T. Stewart and Elder Goddard held a series of European meetings at Fielding, Colyton, Ashurst, and Palmerston North in 1893, all of which were well attended. Indeed, the elders were so surprised at their friendly reception that they found it hard to realise they were addressing "outsiders."[125] Goddard made another visit to the South Island in November, and over 300 Europeans attended one of the Wairau District conference meetings. Even after the Maoris present graciously vacated the hall and sat on the ground under the windows to listen, there was not room for all the Europeans who wished to attend.[126] When Archdeacon T. S. Grace of the Church of England denounced Mormonism from his own pulpit, the elders felt he accomplished little more than "scattering the seed" for them.[127]

Within a few years of hearing the gospel, many of the Maori Saints became anxious to emigrate to Zion. From John Ferris in 1881 on, the missionaries had linked the Maori people with the Lamanites of the Book of Mormon. Just one example of many was Mission President William Paxman. President Paxman, as quoted earlier, appealed to the Maori Saints for donations to pay for printing the Book of Mormon in 1888 and "took great pains to show them that this sacred and holy Book concerned them especially, as it was a history of God's dealings with their forefathers."[128] A later example is Assistant Church Historian Andrew Jenson, who, during a record-gathering tour of the Church missions, spoke at a northern district conference in 1896, tracing "the history of the ancestry of the Maoris since 600 B.C., when Lehi and family left Jerusalem."[129]

---

124. "The Work Is Spreading," Thomas L. Cox, Letter dated Milton, Otago, 12 April 1894, *Deseret News Weekly*, 9 June 1894, 770–71.

125. Phoenix (pseud. of Benjamin Goddard), "In Far Off New Zealand," *Deseret News Weekly*, 15 July 1893, 107–8.

126. Phoenix (pseud. of Benjamin Goddard), "Distant Maoridom," *Deseret News Weekly*, 27 January 1894, 172.

127. *Millennial Star* 56, no. 13 (26 March 1894): 205. Archdeacon Grace was the son of the Rev. Thomas Samuel Grace, a well-known CMS missionary in the North Island in earlier decades.

128. Paxman, Journal excerpt, in New Zealand Mission, Manuscript History, 7 April 1887.

129. "Over in Maoriland," John Johnson, Letter, 23 January 1896, *Deseret News Weekly*, 9 May 1896, 644; Andrew Jenson, "Jenson's Travels: Letter No. 61," *Deseret News Weekly*, 18 April 1896, 562–64.

Most of the missionaries were very circumspect about a Maori "gathering." As early as 1884, Elder Edward Newby wrote home that "the spirit of gathering is making itself manifest in H[awkes] B[ay] but as yet I do not say anything about it."[130] "The principle of gathering has never been preached to the Maories by the Elders but they seem to have imbibed it and many of them are very anxious to emigrate," reported Elder Henry F. McCune on his arrival home in January 1886.[131] "The Saints here [in the Mahia District] has got the spirit of gathering and all they can think of and talk of is that and they want to go right away," wrote Elder Nelson S. Bishop in November 1886, "and I told them that the time was not yet but was near in the future and when the time came God would let it be known through the Prophet."[132] "The spirit of gathering is working considerably upon some of the natives," wrote Elder Ezra F. Richards to his father, Apostle Franklin D. Richards. "A good many of them are also making inquiry as to what can be done for their ancestors that have never heard the true Gospel; and the feeling that seems to be fast growing on them will, I think, cause a company of them to emigrate soon."[133] As Latter-day Saints believe that saving ordinances for the dead can only be performed in temples and the only temples at this date were in Utah, the Maori Saints began to plan to gather to Utah.

Apostle Richards was somewhat perturbed at this news from his son. He foresaw difficulties in a large-scale Maori emigration and urged "great caution and prudence; for the condition of things here, during the present [anti-polygamy] crusade, being so different from their surroundings in their native lands, it would be a severe test of their faith." He suggested that "a few of the leading men" might visit for a few months, then return and testify of what they had seen and done; but that a general gathering would not be permitted by the Church leaders, at least during the unsettled conditions incident to the anti-polygamy campaign in Utah.[134]

It seems likely that Apostle Richards mentioned the matter in Quorum of the Twelve meetings, for at the 1887 hui tau, President Paxman read a letter from the First Presidency, counselling that "the principle of tithing be presented or taught to the Maoris" but "discouraging the idea of

---

130. "Missionary Work in New Zealand," *Deseret Evening News*, 11 December 1884, [2].

131. "A Mission to the Antipodes: Elder McCune Returns," *Deseret News*, 10 February 1886, 62.

132. Bishop, Diaries, 28 November 1886, 28.

133. "The New Zealand Mission," *Deseret Evening News*, 23 March 1886, [2].

134. Franklin D. Richards, Letter to Ezra F. Richards, 8 April 1886, in Ezra F. Richards, Journal, 28 May 1886.

the Maori gathering in a body immediately as it would not be advisable."[135] Despite having received this counsel, the missionaries believed that their Maori converts should, and eventually would, gather to Utah, and that the First Presidency embargo was a temporary one. During a round of farewell visits before his release in July 1889, President Paxman told the Maori Saints that he looked forward to the time when "you shall be gathered to the land of your forefathers, the land blessed above all others, where you can help to build up Zion and labor in the temples for your dead friends."[136]

In view of such statements, it can scarcely be said that the missionaries were not preaching the doctrine of gathering. Benjamin Goddard, describing scripture recitation at karakia in Porirua in 1892, reported that "most of the members have memorized all the scriptural references to the first principles of the Gospel, *the scattering and gathering of Israel*, restoration of the Gospel, tithing, etc."[137] Goddard also reported that the Saints in Porirua were "diligent in performing their duties, and many are earnestly praying for the time when they can gather to Zion."[138] The Maori translation of the Book of Mormon was circulating through the mission. Maori Saints soon began to regard its numerous prophecies that Israel would be gathered from the four quarters of the earth, including "the isles of the sea," to the "lands of their inheritance" as a divinely ordained solution of their land grievances.[139]

Goddard's mission president, William T. Stewart, who was serving his second term (1891–93), referred the matter of Maori gathering to the First Presidency, then consisting of Wilford Woodruff, George Q. Cannon, and Joseph F. Smith. They answered on 14 October 1893, their reply tempered by the experiences of other Polynesian Saints. By this time, a Hawaiian settlement at Iosepa in Skull Valley, Utah, was some four years old, and beset with problems caused by the economic depression, severe weather conditions, and a high mortality rate.[140] "As you are aware, we have hitherto felt reluctant to encourage the emigration of any of this people

---

135. Ibid., 12 March 1887.

136. Heber S. Cutler, "The Australasian Conference," *Deseret News Weekly*, 17 August 1889, 254.

137. Phoenix (pseud. of Benjamin Goddard, "Letter from New Zealand," 7; emphasis mine.

138. Ibid.

139. Ian G. Barber, "Between Biculturalism and Assimilation: The Changing Place of Maori Culture in the Twentieth Century New Zealand Mormon Church," 151. Barber notes some two dozen explicit Book of Mormon promises to this effect.

140. Tracey E. Panek, "Life at Iosepa, Utah's Polynesian Colony," 64–77.

from their native islands to Zion," the First Presidency wrote to Stewart, "our experience with our Kanaka [Hawaiian] brethren and sisters not having been altogether encouraging; but after perusing your letter and learning therefrom their characteristics, their industry and their capability, for such work as is incidental to the opening of a new country, we have felt that a limited number of the best and most capable brethren and their families might, at the present time, be permitted to gather."

They were to be escorted to Utah by returning missionaries. "Neither do we think it would be well to treat them as our immigrants of the white races are treated," continued the Presidency. They would not be permitted to make their own way and choose where they would live but were to settle at Kanab in southern Utah. Stewart, who was due to return to his home in Kanab, was to continue to have responsibility for them after their arrival, "that they still may have a father to look to for the instruction, guidance and support that they will undoubtedly need."[141]

While Church authorities were initially apprehensive of the difficulties that would face the Maori Saints in such a vastly different climate and with such different social conditions as they would find in Utah, by the 1890s there were additional concerns. Utah was suffering from a major depression, part of a worldwide recession that also affected Australia and New Zealand.[142] Utah's economy was particularly hard hit. It has been estimated that about 48 percent of the labor force of Salt Lake City was out of work by the spring of 1894, symptomatic of conditions throughout the territory. Church revenue from tithing funds was correspondingly affected.[143] For some years, jobs had been scarce; and even before the international depression of the 1890s, it was becoming apparent that Utah had already reached its optimum population.[144] With the added worry of the depression, by June 1894 the First Presidency and Council of the Twelve were not singling out Polynesian Saints but were counselling mission presidents

---

141. First Presidency (Wilford Woodruff, George Q. Cannon, Joseph F. Smith), to Prest. W. T. Stewart, New Zealand, 14 October 1893, in William Thomas Stewart, Papers.

142. New Zealand had, in fact, been suffering from what became known as "the Long Depression" since 1878. The Baring Bank failure, which triggered the 1893 depression in England, America, and Australia, exacerbated but did not cause the New Zealand depression. However, later historians argue that, as real income did not fall, it was a period of economic stagnation rather than a real depression. W. J. Gardner, " A Colonial Economy," 75.

143. Thomas G. Alexander, *Utah: The Right Place*, 210–11.

144. Leonard J. Arrington, *Great Basin Kingdom: An Economic History of the Latter-day Saints, 1830–1890*, 354.

throughout the world to discourage converts from gathering, especially if they were earning good wages in their homelands, as they would almost inevitably face severe economic hardship on arrival in Utah.[145]

President William T. Stewart was released from his second term as mission president, and William Gardner, also back in New Zealand for a second mission, was appointed to take over as mission president.[146] President Stewart and three other missionaries sailed from Auckland on 30 December 1893, but without any Maori emigrants, as there had not been time between receipt of the First Presidency permission and the missionaries' departure for the Maori Saints to organise their affairs. It was left to President William Gardner to organise the departure of the chosen group six months later.

---

145. Richard L. Jensen, "The British Gathering to Zion," in *Truth Will Prevail: The Rise of The Church of Jesus Christ of Latter-day Saints in the British Isles 1837–1987*, edited by V. Ben Bloxham, James R. Moss, and Larry C. Porter, 189.

146. First Presidency to Prest. W. T. Stewart, 14 October 1893.

Chapter 3

"... the noblest of all aboriginal races..."

On Saturday, 16 June 1894, the *Monowai* sailed from Auckland with the first group of emigrating Maori—"the first Maori Saints permitted to return to the ancient inheritance of their ancestors"[1]—in the care of three returning missionaries. The party consisted of Hirini Whaanga; his wife, Mere; his sister-in-law Apikara Whaanga and her two sons, Ihaia (age twelve) and Ihaka Kanapa (age four); one of Hirini's grandsons, Hirini Whaanga Hirihiti (Sidney Christy, ten); an adopted daughter, Edna Pomare (twelve); and Watene Mete (Walter Smith, ten), Mere Whaanga's nephew. Another of Apikara's sons, Pirika, had been living in Utah since 1886 when Elder John Clarence Stewart took him home; Pirika was thus actually the first Mormon Maori to gather to Utah. He travelled north from Kanab to Salt Lake City to be reunited with his mother and brothers.

Hirini Te Rito Whaanga was an influential chief of the Ngati Kahungunu. Born in the East Coast Mahia district in 1828, Hirini, like many of the Ngati Kahungunu people, worked in the whaling trade for many years and then became a successful farmer. Mere Mete (Mary Smith) was his third (monogamous) wife, and it was she who was first converted to Mormonism and influenced Hirini towards the new religion.[2] The Whaanga family were Anglicans and were loyal to the British government during the Maori wars of the 1860s, resisting the appeal of the Pai Marire religion. However, when the first Mormon missionaries came to the Mahia peninsula in 1884, Mere and Hirini were baptized, along with some two hundred others of his Ngati Kahungunu tribe.

---

1. Phoenix (pseud. of Benjamin Goddard), "In the Antipodes: An Annual Conference of the Australasian Mission," *Deseret Evening News*, 19 May 1894, 11.
2. Louis G. Hoagland, Letter to M. Charles Woods, 11 May 1937, in Louis Gerald Hoagland Papers, 1915–41.

Hirini Whaanga, patriarch of the first Maori family to emigrate to the United States. Courtesy LDS Church History Library.

There were nearly 450 members and eight branches in the LDS Mahia Conference (District) at the time of the Whaanga departure. Hirini had been president of the Nuhaka Branch of the Church for some years and was sixty-six years old when he left for Utah.[3] He had proved to be an excellent speaker at conferences and Church services.[4] He had helped with home missionary work and was a wise and faithful branch president while Mere cared for the missionaries. For many years, the missionaries supervising the Mahia District spent a week in each branch, always staying with the Whaanga family while in Nuhaka. Forty years later, one missionary recalled that Mere "was one of the very first to turn to the Elders. . . . [For] years and years when it was the Elders' week to be in Nuhaka, she would leave an important gathering, Maori tangihanga and the like, and ride back to her home so as to have the home ready and clean for the Elders."[5] When the couple emigrated, they specified that their New Zealand home was to be available as missionary headquarters for the Mahia District.

---

3. Peter J. Lineham, "Whaanga, Hirini Te Rito, 1828–1905," *Dictionary of New Zealand Biography*, updated 7 April 2006, http://www.dnzb.govt.nz/ (accessed 10 March 2007); *San Francisco Examiner*, 15 July 1894, reprinted as "Hirini Whaanga, the Maori Chief," *Deseret Weekly News*, 19 February 1898, 313, accessed digitally 20 June 2009.

4. William Douglass Jr., "Journal Notes of William Douglas [sic] Jr., while on a Mission to New Zealand," 28 February 1891–July 1893, 24 September 1893.

5. Hoagland to Woods, 11 May 1937.

In later years, Walter Smith wrote an account of their journey. "The first stage ... by horseback from Nuhaka to Gisborne through the mountain bush and mud, is still fresh in my mind," he wrote. "Gisborne to Auckland was made in a small coastal steamer." Smith recalled their amazement at the "horseless cars" (cable trams) in San Francisco which "went up hill and down without any apparent reason, or so it seemed to the young untutored savage mind."[6] The Whaanga family marvelled at other sights of San Francisco but had no desire to stay there. "The people are very great here, but there is one thing I don't understand," Hirini told a reporter from the *Examiner*. "They don't observe the Sabbath. In Auckland, Brisbane or Wellington you can look all around on the Sabbath and not see anything sold, but here it is very different."[7]

At last the three Maori adults and five children arrived in Salt Lake City, where the children had their first taste of ice cream, which ten-year-old Walter Smith thought was butter and tried to spread on his bread. A reception in their honour was well attended by former New Zealand missionaries. After a week in Salt Lake City, they travelled by covered wagon to Kanab, in southern Utah, where the First Presidency apparently hoped the warmer winters would make them feel at home, even though the harsh desert environment was so different from the lush green countryside and high rainfall of the Mahia Peninsula.

Unfortunately, within a year, two returned missionaries, who took over management of Hirini Whaanga's affairs from William T. Stewart, had mismanaged his funds and were even accused of defrauding the venerable Maori Saint. When news of Hirini Whaanga's financial problems reached the First Presidency, they appointed William Paxman, a former mission president, to "a short mission" to Kanab to investigate the rumours and take whatever action was necessary.[8] The Whaanga family was relocated in Salt Lake City, where the adults spent most of their time in the Salt Lake Temple and were very happy.

---

6. Walter Smith, "The First Maoris to Emigrate to Zion," n.d., [2]. Photocopy of typescript in Church College of New Zealand Library. A condensed version appeared in *Te Karere* 35, no. 5 (May 1941): 658–60.

7. "Hirini Whaanga, the Maori Chief," *Deseret Weekly News*, 19 February 1898, 313. The date was the eve of Whaanga's departure for his full-time mission to New Zealand.

8. First Presidency (Wilford Woodruff, George Q. Cannon, and Joseph F. Smith), Letter to President William Paxman, Nephi, February 1895, copied into William Gardner, Diary, 2 April 1895; John Ephraim Magleby, Letter to George Reynolds, 25 April 1902, in New Zealand Mission, Minutes.

Hirini Whaanga had confidently expected that many other Maori Saints would follow him to Utah. "I think many of my people will come and live with me," he told reporters in San Francisco.[9] In fact, however, exactly sixteen years were to pass before another Maori family emigrated to Utah. The effects of the disastrous Iosepa experiment and the near-disaster of the Whaanga immigration led the First Presidency to continue its embargo on Maori gathering, especially as they were encouraging all Saints to stay in their homelands and build up the Church worldwide. Instead of emigrating to Utah, the Maori Saints were asked to record their genealogies and send them to Hirini and Mere Whaanga who then performed the necessary temple work.[10]

Elder Benjamin Goddard, who served as clerk of the Australasian Mission, was released to return home in May 1895. Soon after his arrival in Salt Lake City, he and his fellow former New Zealand missionaries organised "Zion's Maori Association," with William Paxman as the first president, Goddard as vice-president, and John M. Hendry as assistant secretary and treasurer. Membership in the association was open to all returned missionaries from the New Zealand Mission. One of the aims of the society was to provide literature for the mission, Goddard having several times reported the shortage of tracts and books. Zion's Maori Association became an extremely important influence in the future of the New Zealand Mission. The First Presidency assigned the Whaanga family to the association's care, and one of its first projects was relocating the family from Kanab to suburban Forest Dale in Salt Lake City.[11]

More than 115 European converts whose names and sailing dates are known departed from New Zealand for Utah in the ten years between 1884 and 1894, and there were many others whose names were not recorded. The sudden success with the Maori in this decade meant that the European branches were often left to fend for themselves, and many stalwart converts staffed these branches. Even with First Presidency discouragement, European Saints desirous of attending the temple continued to trickle to Utah, but no Church assistance was available and there were no more organised companies. It was an individual decision taken by each person or family.

William Gardner reinstituted work among the European residents of New Zealand during 1894 and 1895. The Auckland Branch had fallen

---

9. "Hirini Whaanga, the Maori Chief," 313.

10. Ezra F. Richards, Letter to First Presidency, 18 January 1897, in Journal, Reel 2, Ezra Foss Richards Papers, 1885–1927.

11. New Zealand Missionary Society, "Book prepared for David O. McKay and Hugh J. Cannon, 26 November 1920."

into disarray for some years after the emigration of some of its strongest members. Towards the end of 1894, Elders John Johnson and Jedediah Goff were appointed to labour in Auckland, the first missionaries so assigned for several years. After much diligent searching, they located between twenty and thirty former members, and by October they were holding two "hall" meetings every Sunday and a cottage meeting during the week. They reorganised the Auckland Branch, which functioned continuously from that time, with Charles Hardy serving as branch president till his death in 1907.

The Christchurch Branch lapsed when the Larsen, Porter, Clark, and Nordstrand families left, the first two going direct to Utah. The Clarks and Nordstrands moved first to Auckland, though only the Clarks completed the journey to Utah. The missionaries who went home from Christchurch were not replaced as new arrivals were channelled into Maori work on the North Island. At the April 1895 conference, President Gardner, responsible for all Australia and New Zealand, appointed Elders W. O. Best and Charles Petersen to reopen the European work in the South Island. Missionaries were again finding success in Brisbane, Sydney, and Melbourne; with the work reinvigorated in the Australian part of the mission, President Gardner eyed the Chatham, Fijian, and Cook islands and pondered how to get enough manpower to send missionaries to these islands.[12]

Like all the mission presidents before him, President Gardner's greatest difficulties were a shortage of literature, a shortage of missionaries, and a shortage of money. He had no funds other than the small amounts that came in as voluntary tithing donations, and these were totally inadequate to meet the expenses of the mission. While most missionaries lived with the Maori Saints and their additional needs were supplied either from their savings or by their families, the Church undertook to pay their fares home to America and to provide each departing elder with a new suit of clothes.[13] Every few months, President Gardner was called upon to pay the steamship fares of two or more returning missionaries. Time and again he borrowed large sums from local Church members such as Charles Hardy and Thomas Finlayson, repaying the loans when the money was refunded from Salt Lake City months later. Mission presidents were frequently embarrassed at the time it took to receive funds from Salt Lake City to reimburse these Saints.[14]

---

12. William Gardner, Diary, 1 August 1894.
13. New Zealand Mission, Minutes, 20 July 1895, 20.
14. Ibid., 14 October 1895 and 23 January 1896; Richards, Journal, 11 February 1897, 10 April 1897; George Reynolds for the First Presidency, Letter to William Gardner, 28 May 1898, and Ezra T. Stevenson, Letter to Presiding Bishopric, 10 June 1899, both in New Zealand Mission, Presidents' Correspondence.

The 1896 hui tau was held at Tamaki, near Dannevirke, 3–6 April. More than 700 Maori Saints travelled from various parts of New Zealand to attend the conference. Twelve Maori meetings and four "European" meetings were held at the pa, with another three European meetings at nearby Dannevirke. New assignments were given to the fifty-two missionaries in the mission. Six were assigned to European work in Auckland, Christchurch, and Dunedin. Twelve missionaries—the most since the 1850s—were in Australia. Letters of greeting from the First Presidency and from Zion's Maori Association were read to the conference.

In June 1896, Ezra F. Richards, principal translator of the Book of Mormon, arrived in Auckland to succeed William Gardner as president of the mission. The old and new presidents made an extended tour of the mission, visiting the major centres of both New Zealand and Australia. On 10 September, President Gardner and six other missionaries sailed from Sydney for Vancouver on their way home, leaving President Richards to return to New Zealand alone.[15]

Richards reached New Zealand on 18 September 1896 and found that he needed more missionaries to take advantage of the openings that presented themselves. He appealed to the First Presidency to double the missionary force, which had already grown to sixty-one. With the intention of increasing missionary work in the European cities of both Australia and New Zealand, President Richards attempted to introduce systematic methods for tracting (as the missionary effort of calling at houses and leaving tracts was called) and also insisted on receiving detailed monthly reports.[16]

A letter from the First Presidency soon brought momentous changes to the Australasian Mission. "For some time past, the First Presidency, in considering the growth and development of the Australasian Mission, and the vast extent of territory it covers, have thought that the time was now at hand when it would be for the best interests of the church and of the saints to separate it into two missions; one comprising Australia and Tasmania, the other New Zealand and contiguous groups," wrote the First Presidency through their secretary, George Reynolds. "It is felt that it is placing too much upon one man's shoulders to expect him to care for so large a field and accomplish as much for the advancement of the Kingdom of God as could be done if there were two presidents, one in New Zealand and one in Australia."[17] This was indeed welcome news.

---

15. Gardner, Diary, 10 September 1896.

16. Richards, Auckland, Letter dated Porirua, New Zealand, 20 April 1897 and copied into Richards, Journal, between entries for 28 and 29 April 1897; also in New Zealand Mission, Presidents' Correspondence.

17. George Reynolds, Letter to Ezra F. Richards, typescript, on First Presidency

Every mission president since John Murdock had lamented the size of the mission and the impossibility of successfully proselytising in such an enormous territory, given the shortage of missionaries and literature and the difficulties of transportation between and within the various colonies.

President Richards was warmly in favour of the proposed division. "I have felt for some time that a move of that kind would contribute largely to causing the work to progress more rapidly in Australia and Tasmania," he replied. Virtually admitting that Australia had been neglected over the previous fifteen years, he pointed out that "the Maori people and work are of so peculiar a nature as to wholly absorb one president's time."[18] Richards, and those before him, were essentially presiding over three separate missions—one in Australia, and two (Maori and Pakeha) in New Zealand. Supervising the work in New Zealand and attending branch and district conferences there kept the mission presidents busy. Roads to many areas where Maori branches were located were often almost impassable, and much time was spent simply travelling from one district conference to another—usually on horseback. Available funds were inadequate to pay steamship fares for regular supervisory visits to Sydney, let alone the other five Australian colonies. Only three mission presidents—Augustus Farnham, Robert Beauchamp, and William Gardner—visited both countries.[19] The division, though announced earlier, took effect on 1 January 1898;[20] and from that time, the New Zealand Mission flourished as never before.

There was great excitement among the Maori people of New Zealand, Mormon and non-Mormon alike, when Hirini Whaanga returned to New Zealand as a missionary. He travelled from Utah with the new mission president, Ezra T. Stevenson, and his expenses were paid by Zion's Maori Association. President Stevenson and Elder Whaanga arrived in Auckland just as the 1898 hui tau got under way, and reached the conference site at Papawai on the second day of the conference, Monday, 4 April. The scheduled conference sessions were postponed while a full ceremonial welcome was given to Hirini.

---

letterhead, 19 March 1897, pasted in Richards, Journal, between entries for 5 and 6 May 1897.

18. Richards, Letter to Wilford Woodruff, 26 May 1897, copied into Richards, Journal, 26 May 1897.

19. Richards had toured Australia with Gardner, but his journal makes it clear that he had not yet assumed the role of mission president, even though the books had been transferred to his name in Auckland before their departure. New Zealand Mission, Manuscript History, 9, 13 July 1896.

20. First Presidency, Letter to Andrew Smith Jr., 28 October 1897, postscript to letter, in Journal History, 10–11.

Next day, Elder Whaanga addressed the conference, telling the Maori Saints of a small book titled *The Latter-day Saints*, specially written for them by James H. Anderson, which had been translated into Maori and published by Zion's Maori Association. He and President Stevenson had brought with them the first 1,800 of 5,000 copies.

After the conference, Elder Whaanga accompanied President Stevenson on a tour of the North Island districts. He was welcomed wherever he went, as were his companions, and the way was opened for the elders to work in many areas where they had previously had little success. Many false stories had circulated during Hirini's absence, even reports that he had been killed by the Mormons,[21] and Maori chiefs in many districts were happy to see for themselves that these reports were untrue. They listened intently to Elder Whaanga's testimony.[22]

In November, President Stevenson and Elder Whaanga travelled north into the Bay of Islands district, and were entertained at a village from which the elders had been driven a few years previously with orders never to return.[23] Before they left, two baptisms were performed, and others were requested. "We feel that the testimonies of Bro[ther] Hirini's have been and will be a source of much good," President Stevenson reported to the First Presidency. "His ... fine appearance and happy countenance with the spirit he manifests is of itself a testimony and they cannot say nay."[24]

At the Te Horo District Conference, Elder Whaanga spoke to the assembled Saints on the redemption of the dead and offered to take the names of their dead ancestors with him when he returned to Utah so that he and his family could perform the temple ordinances for them. One of his listeners objected on the grounds that whakapapa (genealogies) were tapu (sacred). Whaanga pointed out that the objector and many others present had already given their genealogy to the land courts in order to obtain legal title to their land, so that it was inconsistent to object to Maori Saints giving it for the purpose of temple work. This counter-argument effectively silenced his opponent.[25]

---

21. "Maori Chief Returns Home," *Deseret Evening News*, 13 May 1899, 17.

22. Ezra T. Stevenson, Auckland, Letter to Wilford Woodruff, 9 June 1898, New Zealand Mission, Presidents' Correspondence.

23. New Zealand Mission, Manuscript History, 10 November 1898.

24. Ezra T. Stevenson, Auckland, Letter to George Reynolds, Secretary to the First Presidency, 11 January 1899, in New Zealand Mission, Presidents' Correspondence.

25. "Mission Fields: Letters from Hirini Whaanga," *Deseret Evening News*, 7 January 1899, 15.

Before Christmas, Elder Whaanga visited the LDS Maori district on the South Island, then returned to the North Island for another round of district conferences. His health was not good, and President Stevenson worried about his riding horseback to conferences through another New Zealand winter. Accordingly, Elder Whaanga was released at the April 1899 mission conference. He sailed with Elder Francis W. Kirkham and three other missionaries on the *Moana* on 17 April 1899, having served just over one year and having done much good for the work of the mission.

For some years, the mission presidents had lived with Auckland Branch members, whose homes were often an inconvenient distance from the centre of the city. The mission had no office space, and no suitable accommodation for arriving and departing missionaries. In October 1898, President Stevenson rented office space and living quarters for the mission staff on the fourth floor of the Mutual Life Assurance building on Queen Street, Auckland. This was an improvement, but Stevenson believed that the mission needed a permanent headquarters. At the April 1899 hui tau at Uawa, Tolaga Bay, President Stevenson proposed the idea to the assembled missionaries and raised £57 in donations within a few minutes from the missionaries and Charles Hardy. Stevenson soon began a search for a suitable site and reported his "pet scheme" to the Presiding Bishopric, estimating the cost at £400.[26]

The Presiding Bishopric handed the matter over to Benjamin Goddard, who was gradually becoming a *de facto* counselor to the General Authorities of the Church on all matters to do with New Zealand. Goddard talked the matter over with the First Presidency and reported their cautious approval to Stevenson on condition that the mission did not get into debt over the project. There was no suggestion that local tithing funds could be used or that other Church funds would be made available. In any case, the tithing collected in the New Zealand Mission still barely covered postage and similar expenses for the mission office. In Salt Lake City, Zion's Maori Association immediately began to ask for donations from returned missionaries and New Zealand expatriates in Utah. In the meantime, President Stevenson and Elder John E. Magleby (who, like President Stevenson, was back in New Zealand serving a second mission) were dismayed to find that land in Auckland was selling at the equivalent of US$50 per foot of street frontage.[27]

---

26. New Zealand Mission, Manuscript History, 10 April 1899; John Ephraim Magleby, Journal, 10 April 1899.

27. Magleby, Journal, 18 April 1899.

Elder Magleby had brought a "magic lantern" and assorted views of Utah with him. For the next year or two, the projector was passed from one missionary to another and travelled far and wide through New Zealand. Local halls were rented for slide shows, and donations were collected as admission fees; any excess after the hall rent was paid was given to charities such as local cottage hospitals. If the hall was free, no collection was taken. Sometimes the halls were crowded; at other times, the audience consisted of a few small boys.[28] On the whole, the missionaries were happy with this "high tech" boost to their proselytising techniques.

President Stevenson was released in February 1900 and was succeeded by Elder Magleby. Magleby was enjoying his second mission. He loved the Maori people; and while he recorded their habits and customs with interest, he was remarkably nonjudgmental about what he saw. "Nearly everybody both men and women smoke, cough, and spit there being no spittoons," he wrote in his journal one day in January 1899, while travelling among non-LDS Maori. "I noticed that some of them spit in their dress or waist one lady used her hat as a spittoon into which she then threw match sticks &c. as well as spit in it."[29]

He enjoyed his occasional visits with LDS Pakeha families. "Came to a place where there is a fine family of European Saints with whom we intend spending Sunday. We were royally received," he wrote, "given a good dinner, & afterwards treated to a large dish of blackberries, sugar and cream. We were given a fine apple pudding or apple pie according to the english stile [sic] for supper. It seems that the saints can't do to[o] much for the Elders when they come around. We ate until we were nearly bloated."[30]

President Magleby toured the mission, asking permission of local government officials to hold street meetings in the European cities. At the turn of the century, fewer than 10 percent of Maori lived in urban areas, so that missionary work in the cities always targeted the largely Pakeha population.[31] As the Latter-day Saints had no chapels to which the public in the cities could be invited, open-air meetings were one way to reach the populace. President Magleby was disappointed that few passers-by stopped to listen to his outdoor sermon in Invercargill, and among those who did were some hecklers. "Though

---

28. Ibid., 8 August and 4 October 1900, Reel 2.
29. Ibid., 26 January 1899, Reel 1.
30. Ibid., 4 February 1899, Reel 1.
31. Until World War II, three-quarters of the Maori population of New Zealand lived in rural areas; the next thirty years saw the Maori drift to the cities. Three-quarters of the Maori population were living in urban areas by the mid-1970s. Michael King, "Between Two Worlds," 289–90; Graeme Dunstall, "The Social Pattern," 457.

we said nothing about who we were, yet they soon knew and threw out insults, asking how many wives we had &c. We did our part as best we could, to warn the people thronging the streets," he wrote.[32]

It seemed to the Mormon elders that, as soon as they started to find success with the Europeans, opposition arose. In Auckland on 31 March 1901, a man named Rimmer delivered what the missionaries reported as "a very slanderous lecture" on "Mormon Idolatry" at the Fire Bell on Queen Street, a favourite spot for "stump" speakers. The mission clerk, Elder Ernest P. Brown, was so upset that he prophesied dire consequences to Rimmer if the latter did not repent and was laughed at for his pains. About 300 people gathered to listen to the missionaries' rebuttal and seemed satisfied with what they heard. Two weeks later during another Mormon street meeting, Rimmer managed to get into the Mormon "ring" or circle, "saying vile things" against the missionaries in particular and Mormons in general. Help came from an unexpected quarter, and Rimmer withdrew when a stranger spoke up, claiming to be a man of the world who knew the Mormons to be a "God-fearing, honest and virtuous people."[33]

President Magleby visited the Maori prophets Te Whiti and Tohu at Parihaka, the "new Jerusalem," in May, and was received coolly by Te Whiti. The elderly and ailing Tohu was altogether milder. Magleby had several conversations with both Maori prophets, telling them that the New Jerusalem was to be established in America and "showing them that Parihaka or New Zealand was not the place. Leaving them my testimony against theirs." The following month, Elders John E. Taylor and George T. Hislop accepted an invitation from the Maori of Parihaka to be present on 18 June 1901 and "see the Savior come" as prophesied by Te Whiti. Arriving a few days early, they warned the people that the looked-for advent would not take place. "But they made great preparations for the event and danced hakas and poi dances and sang powhiris (welcomes) to the Lord to come to their New Jerusalem," the elders reported. When the Saviour did not appear, Te Whiti blamed the Duke of York, who was visiting New Zealand and was at that time being entertained by more than 7,000 Maori at Rotorua. The Duke of York was a grandson of Queen Victoria who, according to Te Whiti, was "the mother of harlots spoken of in Revelation."[34]

President Magleby was still anxious to see European work pursued and wanted street meetings held regularly in each city.[35] Following Elder

---

32. Magleby, Journal, 11 August 1900.
33. New Zealand Mission, Manuscript History, 31 March and 14 April 1901.
34. Ibid., 1, 2, 3 May and 7 September 1901.
35. New Zealand Mission, Minutes, 8 April 1901, 231.

Ernest Brown's successful rout of the opposition in Auckland, he was sent to the South Island for a few months to help the missionaries establish regular outdoor meetings. After getting permission from the mayor of Christchurch in April 1901, the elders held seventeen street meetings over the next few months. Several times they were "hustled" and driven through the streets by mobs. The trouble continued after Brown moved on to Dunedin, and the Christchurch elders were warned on 19 May that police protection would no longer be available to them if they persisted in speaking on the streets.

With three other missionaries, Brown began to hold street meetings in Dunedin on 3 May. They were undisturbed for a week; but on 11 May, two missionaries were knocked down, stoned, and spat on. As the police could not guarantee their safety, the missionaries gave up street meetings for the time being and returned to tracting and holding cottage meetings. Similar meetings were held in Australia without exciting any opposition greater than heckling, but incidents similar to those at Mormon street meetings in New Zealand occurred in England from time to time when anti-Mormon agitation in the press was high.[36]

Elder Brown returned to Auckland, calling on Police Commissioner John Bennett Tunbridge at Wellington on his way and on Frank Dillingham, the American consul-general, when he arrived in Auckland. Both assured Brown that the Mormons were entitled to every privilege allowed other denominations and that the Mormon elders had every right to expect the government to protect them.[37] The missionaries were delighted that Dillingham was friendly but found ironic the fact that his father, as governor of Vermont, had been responsible for appointing George F. Edmunds to the U.S. Senate.[38] The Edmunds Act (1882) and the Edmunds-Tucker Act (1887), both introduced by the senator, were the principal legislative means that had forced the LDS Church to abandon polygamy in 1890.

On hearing these assurances of their rights, President Magleby sent Elder Brown back to preside over the work in the South Island and to try street meetings again. After some minor skirmishes, Elder R. A. Jones was

---

36. Richard O. Cowan, "Church Growth in England, 1841–1914," 224; Louis B. Cardon, "The First World War and the Great Depression 1914–39," 343–45, both in *Truth Will Prevail: The Rise of the Church of Jesus Christ of Latter-day Saints in the British Isles 1837–1987*, edited by V. Ben Bloxham, James R. Moss, and Larry C. Porter.

37. "News from New Zealand," *Deseret Evening News*, Journal History, 8 October 1901, 4.

38. New Zealand Mission, Manuscript History, 25 July 1904.

kicked and dragged along a Christchurch street on 22 September; Elder Leslie C. Atwood was struck on the head, a torch (flashlight) belonging to the missionaries was lost, and their hats were kicked around the square like footballs. As historian Peter Lineham has written of opposition to Robert Beauchamp in Wellington three decades earlier, "Issues of morality were more important than theology in producing opposition [to Mormonism]. . . . The stigma of polygamy legitimised folk violence."[39]

Elder Brown reported the damage to the mayor and police inspector who promised assistance. The following week, a police guard attempted to keep the crowd away from the missionaries but without success. Stones and rubbish were thrown at both missionaries and police, and only valiant work by the police saved the elders from a forced ducking in the Avon River.[40] The local press reported in indignant headlines: "Another Mormon Hunt—Disgraceful Scenes in the City—Pursued by a Howling Mob of Larrikins," and estimated the crowd at about 2,000, most of whom were attracted by the disturbance and did not really know what it was about.[41] By and large, the New Zealand newspapers came out in support of the Mormons, lamenting the lack of tolerance in the community.[42]

The memory of this period of persecution in Christchurch has lingered in the minds of Church members and leaders in New Zealand, becoming somewhat exaggerated over the years. Many New Zealand and American Mormons (including two General Authorities) believe that a missionary was killed by the Christchurch mob at this time.[43] It seems likely that the death of twenty-four-year-old Elder Leslie C. Atwood in Auckland on 21 July 1902 has become associated with his part in the Christchurch riots. Elder Atwood sent his own account of the incident to his friend and fellow-missionary, John W. Gardner:

> We started street work again. . . . The crowd made a rush for us. I got hit once in the short ribs and my coat and vest just about taken off from me. Bro. Jones got knocked down and dragged a little way, but fortunately we all got out safely, though they made a football of Bro. Jones's hat and a bond fire [sic] of our torch. It was humming times

---

39. Peter Lineham, "The Mormons and Karori," 12.

40. "News from New Zealand," *Deseret Evening News*, Journal History, 8 October 1901, 4.

41. "Another Mormon Hunt," *The Star* (Christchurch), 30 September 1901.

42. "Anti-'Mormon' Mobocracy" (editorial), *Deseret News*, 2 December 1901, Journal History, 2.

43. Robert L. Simpson, Oral History, 10; Glen Larkin Rudd, Oral History, 23. In Elder Simpson's version, the missionary was stoned to death; in Elder Rudd's, he was pushed into the Avon River and held under with sticks until he drowned.

for a while.... We went out again last Sunday night. We had not much more than got started till they made a rush.... The police had all they could do to keep them off of us. As we went over the bridge of a river that runs through the town, cries went up for a rush to be made and us thrown over but they were unsuccessful. When they saw that they could not get at us they began throwing mud and rocks. I was struck twice and Bro. Duncan once but no damage done.... None of us were hurt. I can see that the helping hand of our Heavenly Father was there or those few police could never have kept such a mob from us.[44]

Elder Atwood continued his missionary work in Christchurch from the date of this incident, 22 September 1901, until shortly before his death in July 1902. He began to suffer violent headaches and mental disturbance about three weeks before his death, and the Christchurch doctors recommended that he go to Auckland for specialist treatment, which was unavailing. His death was ascribed to tuberculous meningitis.[45] There was no contemporary suggestion whatsoever that it may have resulted from the Christchurch attack nine or ten months earlier. After a memorial service in Auckland on 26 July 1902, his remains were shipped to his home town of Spanish Fork, Utah, for burial.

There were still many Maori Latter-day Saints who wanted to gather to Utah. However, Church authorities continued to discourage gathering to Utah from all the missions of the Church, not just from New Zealand, urging the Saints to stay and build up the Church in their homelands. President Magleby wrote to Church President Lorenzo Snow suggesting that if the Maori Saints were not permitted to gather to Utah, a Mormon "colony" should be established somewhere in New Zealand. He urged the advantages that would come from having the Maori Saints together in a central place where Church programs could function better and more fully. He particularly urged the First Presidency to consider the benefit such a colony would be to the youth of the Church in New Zealand.

President Magleby also begged President Snow to send an apostle to the next hui tau in April 1901. "For some time, ever since I was here before in the year 1888, there has been and is a great desire on the part of the Maori Saints to be visited by one of the Twelve," he wrote. "We think

---

44. Letter from L. C. Atwood, in Eldon J. Gardner and Alice Gardner, eds., "Day Journal of John W. Gardner in New Zealand LDS Mission, 17 July 1901 to 23 January 1904," 43–44; initial capitals and terminal punctuation added.

45. "A Sad and Sorrowful Homecoming," *Deseret Evening News*, 29 August 1902, 8; Leslie Atwood, Death Certificate, 21 July 1902, Registrar of Births, Deaths, and Marriages, Wellington, New Zealand.

the magnitude and nature of the Gospel work in these islands is scarcely realized in the fullest sense."[46] Samoa and Australia could be included in such a trip for very little extra expense and receive comparable benefits, President Magleby explained. "'Ask and ye shall receive,'" he quoted hopefully, but fruitlessly. Another twenty years passed before the first General Authority visited the South Pacific.

President Magleby and the mission presidents who both preceded and succeeded him were very concerned about the future of the Maori race. Up till the turn of the century, the Maori were thought by many to be dwindling into oblivion and were expected to either die out or become "amalgamated" into the larger European population. Maori numbers were shrinking not only as a result of the inter-tribal "musket wars" of the 1820s and the Maori/Pakeha struggles of the 1860s, but also as European diseases took their toll. By the 1891 census, the Maori population had decreased from Captain Cook's estimated 100,000 to about 42,000. Some Maori felt that their best option was separatism, and two Mormon converts were among the founders of the Te Kotahitanga (Maori Parliament) movement in the 1890s. A different outlook was promoted by the Young Maori Party, a group of young professional Maori leaders, most of them educated at the prestigious Anglican Te Aute College. The Young Maori Party believed that the Maori should take advantage of all that was good in the dominant European civilisation and particularly promoted measures to improve their health, sanitation, and education.[47]

While Relief Societies were organised in Christchurch (1879) and Auckland (1880) for European sisters, it was not until 1901 that the first Relief Societies were organised in Maori branches. President Magleby felt that the Relief Society would mobilise the energies of the Maori women to do much good in their own communities as well as improve their standards of health, hygiene, and housekeeping. The first Maori Relief Society was organised at Te Horo, in the Bay of Islands District, on 23 March 1901, with Mangu Rewiti as president, Ere Hari first counselor and Kewa Waa, second counselor. The next was organised at Kiri Kiri, in the Hauraki District, on 8 June 1901, followed by three in branches of the Hawkes Bay District and three in the Mahia District in August.[48]

At a district conference on 10–11 August 1901, President Magleby met with the nine Maori sisters who had been called to preside over the

---

46. New Zealand Mission, Minutes, 24 September 1900, 203.
47. King, "Between Two Worlds," 293–96.
48. New Zealand Mission, Manuscript History, 23 March, 8 June, 9, 25 August 1901.

Relief Societies of Te Hauke, Korongata, and Tamaki in the Hawkes Bay District. He spoke on the purpose of Relief Society, asked each woman if she smoked, and queried whether she was willing to act in her appointed office. He told them that they should teach the young people to be virtuous, clothe the poor, visit the sick, and do many other good works.[49] Up till this time, there had been no opportunity for Maori women to give service in the Church beyond caring for the needs of the missionaries, so these sisters were truly pioneers and needed much counsel and advice from the mission president as they learned their duties and the standards of conduct expected of them in these callings.

The inexperienced Relief Society officers often turned to the young male missionaries for guidance. Elder John W. Gardner found himself writing up Relief Society minutes and ruling up an account book so that the very new secretary in Papawai had a guide to refer to.[50] A few years later, Elder James King sent an urgent plea for a female missionary to be sent to the Te Hauke district to help with Relief Society work. "I am doing all I can to help them out but I am sure a woman could do more," he wrote to the mission president. "I am sort of up a stump as to what to give them to do and make it interesting at the same time."[51]

Meanwhile, Elder Alexander Wright and his wife, Emma, arrived in the mission in July 1902. Sister Wright was immediately called to be mission Relief Society president, and "Te Hui Atawhai a Nga Wahine" (a very free translation would be "the Women's Benevolent Society") was adopted as the organisation's name.[52] Relief Society sessions soon became a feature of each mission and district conference, welcomed and enjoyed by most of the women. President Magleby toured the mission urging the Relief Society officers to teach cleanliness and child care, in line with traditional Church practice that linked temporal well-being with spiritual health.

This initiative was timely and reinforced government action, which in turn was prompted by the Young Maori Party. Maori doctor Maui Pomare, returned from training in the United States, was appointed the first Maori Health Officer in 1900 and toured New Zealand promoting better sanitation and hygiene in Maori villages. Pomare's visits occasionally coincided with a Mormon conference; and when they did, he was invited to speak to

---

49. Magleby Journal, 10, 11 August 1901.

50. Gardner and Gardner, "Day Journal of John W. Gardner," 3 October 1902, 180.

51. James King, Letter to Louis G. Hoagland, 6 November 1906, in Hoagland Papers, Reel 3.

52. Charles B. Bartlett, Journal, 23 August 1902, 42; New Zealand Mission, Minutes, 23 August 1902, 314.

the assembled Saints. President Magleby felt that Pomare's teachings were wonderful corroboration of the Word of Wisdom. "The gentleman did us much good as the people could not help see on the face of it that we are working for their good and now the government is following up as this man is hired by the government."[53]

The following year, Dr. Pomare, this time accompanied by Member of Parliament James Carroll, again spoke at some district conferences. "In the evening the time was given to the Hon. James Carroll (the Maori Minister), Dr Pomare and others who were here in the interests of the Government," wrote Elder Richard H. Solomon, reporting from Muriwai in March 1902. "[They] came to explain the duties of the Maori Council which, if enforced, will be a great benefit to the Maori people, as it will have a tendency to elevate them to a higher standard; all intoxicating liquors will be prohibited and children under sixteen will also be prohibited from smoking... Many things were advanced which were highly endorsed by the Elders, as it will be the means of putting down many of the growing evils among the young."[54]

The missionaries saw Pomare's work as a direct answer to prayer. "The Government is now taking steps, in answer to our semi-annual fasts and prayers, to enforce laws which would bring about conditions among the Maoris that the Elders have been striving for since they commenced to labor, namely, to get the natives to live in clean houses and clothes, abstain from all narcotics, and live on a higher standard of civilization."[55] President Magleby was not backward in telling Pomare and Carroll that the Church had been in advance of the government initiatives. Carroll, in reply to the welcome speeches, spoke approvingly of the work of the Mormon missionaries in New Zealand. "He also said the Government wanted them to keep their genealogical records and also their mythology. He encouraged the Saints in their faith," recorded the mission clerk. Magleby voiced approbation of Carroll's words, telling Pomare and Carroll that the Spirit of God was working upon the government to bring about these reforms.[56]

Many branch Relief Societies were very successful. While there was never a suggestion that any Relief Society in Australia should have its own building, as was common in American wards, by March 1902 the Tamaki Branch Relief Society women had raised £17 and were erecting a Relief

---

53. Magleby, Journal, 2 April 1901, Reel 2; see also New Zealand Mission, Manuscript History, 15 March 1902.

54. R. H. Solomon, "New Zealand: Traveling in the Mission," letter 30 March 1902, *Deseret Evening News*, 10 May 1902, 22.

55. New Zealand Mission, Manuscript History, 15 March 1902.

56. Ibid.

Society hall for meetings and storage of supplies.[57] At the Hawkes Bay district conference, the minutes recorded that the sick and distressed were being looked after, and that the sisters had made many quilts and "kites" (ketes or baskets) to sell.[58]

President Magleby was determined to start a mission paper. He began canvassing the idea among the missionaries and in letters from February 1902; and at the April hui tau in Tokomaru Bay, a committee was appointed to research and report on the viability of the project.[59] By mid-April, Magleby and the mission secretary had obtained quotes for printing a sixteen-page octavo-size journal modelled on the British Mission's *Millennial Star*. Magleby wrote to Salt Lake City regarding his plans. "We hope ... to make it self-sustaining which we think we can do by having an elder given a mission to edit the paper.... We propose to hire the printing done. There are young Maoris who we think would be able to handle the whole affair after two or three years' experience."[60]

President Magleby also applied to the New Zealand government to have missionaries licensed as marriage celebrants.[61] However, he was released soon afterward, and it was his successor, President Charles B. Bartlett, who successfully negotiated official recognition of the Church of Jesus Christ of Latter-day Saints so that this could be done. The first Mormon marriage celebrant in New Zealand, Elder David Elmer Davis, was officially gazetted on 8 July 1903,[62] and the first marriage in New Zealand solemnized by a Latter-day Saint occurred between an LDS man, Alfred Parsons, and his non-LDS fiancée, Amelia McCormack, on 5 December 1903 in Auckland.[63] The names of both Charles B. Bartlett and David E. Davis were gazetted the following year, and President Bartlett performed his first marriage ceremony on 9 February 1904.[64]

Once again the mission was looking for new headquarters, having been asked in February 1903 to vacate the offices rented from an insurance company. A few days later, President Bartlett leased a seven-roomed

---

57. Ibid.
58. Ibid., 23 March 1902.
59. Ibid., 17 February, 10 and 23 March, 6 April 1902.
60. John E. Magleby, Letter to George Reynolds, 25 April 1902, in New Zealand Mission, Minutes.
61. New Zealand Mission, Manuscript History, 6 April 1902.
62. "Officiating Ministers for 1903," *The New Zealand Gazette* no. 56 (9 July 1903): 1571.
63. New Zealand Mission, Manuscript History, 5 December 1903. Parsons, age thirty-one, died of blood poisoning eighteen months later. Ibid., 9 May 1905.
64. Ibid., 3 and 9 February 1904.

cottage on the corner of Upper Queen Street and Edwin Street. In July, he purchased a building lot on Paice Avenue, Mount Roskill, for £85, intending to build mission headquarters and a chapel on it.[65] The First Presidency belatedly approved this purchase in October.

The new reporting system inaugurated by President Richards and refined by President Bartlett made possible the collection of various data for the annual report. The year 1903 closed with 4,823 members on the books, of whom 275 were European and the remaining 4,548 Maori. The missionaries, who numbered forty-three at the end of the year, had called at 30,851 homes during 1903 and distributed 23,278 tracts. They had held 275 outdoor (street) meetings and 1,557 indoors. While the records do not define the terms, the 1,557 "indoor" meetings were presumably missionary meetings in homes or halls, not the regular branch meetings, which would have come to a far larger total.[66] "We have active missions in the larger cities, and a great portion of the country has been canvassed," wrote President Bartlett. "The principle [sic] methods available to use are tract distributing, street meetings, and private conversations. Halls and school houses are so expensive as to render their use almost impossible to us."[67]

President Bartlett thoughtfully evaluated the situation of the Maori. He deplored the introduction of European vices and their effect on the Maori, who, he said, were "the noblest of all aboriginal races.... They were long lived, strong, vigorous and athletic, but now they are fast fading away. The average life of the native is constantly shortening." It was not enough to preach to the Maori, he explained. The New Zealand Mission needed additional measures. "The problem of how to regenerate the race is one of a serious nature, and, so far as our Maori Saints are concerned, demands a solution at our hands. The day has gone by when we can treat this simply as a mission among outsiders. We will be compelled to take direction of their temporal as well as of their spiritual affairs. We will have to give them technical instruction in every department of life."[68] In view of the vigorous measures being taken by the New Zealand government and the Young Maori Party, plus the upward turn already occurring in Maori population figures, Bartlett's concern seems well meaning but perhaps unduly paternalistic.

While this feeling of responsibility by LDS Church leaders soon led to the foundation of the Maori Agricultural College, President Bartlett did not agree with President Magleby's proposal for a Mormon colony

---

65. Ibid., 10 July 1903; Charles B. Bartlett, "The New Zealand Mission," *Millennial Star* 66 no. 32 (11 August 1904): 499.

66. New Zealand Mission, Manuscript History, 31 December 1903.

67. Bartlett, "The New Zealand Mission," 499.

68. Ibid., 501.

somewhere in New Zealand.[69] He felt that there were still too many intertribal jealousies to allow such a proposal to succeed. The complicated Maori land laws were a further hindrance.

The 1904 hui tau was held at Moawhango. In the priesthood meeting on Sunday, 3 April, President Bartlett discussed establishing a boarding school for Maori boys in the village, where they could be taught gospel principles as well as academic subjects. There was no government secondary school system for Maori children at this time. "In doing this it will give us a better hold on the rising generation and will make them stronger in the faith," he explained, pointing out that at present the only option for Maori youth seeking secondary education was to attend schools conducted by other religious denominations. "Through this we have lost many of our young people," he told the assembled Maori Saints.

Most of those present supported the idea, and even a non-member, Eruiti Arani, promised to make a substantial donation. As he had just paid £45 for an organ for the Mormon conference, it did not appear to be an empty promise. Only a small school was visualised, with one American elder as the teacher. In addition to local children, it was decided that at least one student should be accepted from each Church district in New Zealand.

A subscription list was opened, headed by President Bartlett's personal contribution of £5. It was decided to set a yearly assessment of five shillings minimum for each Church member in New Zealand. President Bartlett and two missionaries (Elders David E. Davis and M. Charles Woods) were appointed as a school committee, and Elder Woods was designated mission architect. Two other missionaries, John W. Gardner and Asa L. Curtis, were assigned to design a curriculum.[70]

Elder Woods was kept busy in his new calling as architect for the New Zealand Mission. Sometimes an existing hall was turned over to the Latter-day Saints, as at Mangakahei in the Bay of Islands;[71] at other places, such as Korongata and Te Horo, meetinghouses were designed by Woods or later missionaries and built by the missionaries with local help, at least one (that at Te Horo) having a European-style spire.[72]

Land titles sometimes proved a problem. In Korongata, the Church bought one acre of land from local landowner J. P. Donnelly, who promised to deed an additional acre to the Church. The missionaries began building a chapel, only to be advised by the Church's solicitors that Donnelly did

---

69. Ibid.
70. New Zealand Mission, Manuscript History, 3, 4, and 11 April 1904.
71. Ibid., 30 October 1904.
72. Ibid., 24 February 1906.

not have a clear title to the land. President Bartlett counselled the missionaries to obtain permission from the Maori Saints to move the building onto their land, but it was completed on Donnelly's property. Eventually Donnelly solved his title problems and agreed to deed the land on which the meetinghouse stood to the LDS Church.[73] An LDS primary school had been started in the Korongata chapel the previous May.[74]

Another feature of Bartlett's presidency was a monthly newsletter of current mission events, circulated to all missionaries in the field as well as to some who had returned home to Utah.[75] The first was prepared at the end of July 1904 and was the first step towards the mission paper that President Magleby had proposed.

Meanwhile, President Bartlett promoted the boarding school at every district conference, and donations continued to trickle in. Eruiti Arani, the non-LDS chief at Moawhango, engaged Elder Woods to design a large modern home for him and to supervise a group of American elders who were to build it. In return, the elders would receive £60 for the school building fund, plus their board.[76] Eruiti was baptized on 1 October 1904 and was accordingly welcomed among the "prominent Saints" attending the 1905 hui tau, rather than being listed as previously with the "prominent outsiders."[77]

By February 1905, President Bartlett, Elder Woods, and Elder William M. Paxman, son of the former mission president, constituted a formal board of education for the mission's schools. One New Zealander, Wiremu Takana (William Duncan Sr.), was added to the board at the April hui tau. Eleven missionaries were assigned as "temporal workers" to raise funds for the new school by building Eruiti Arani's new nine-roomed home.[78] "The move is in the interest of our College which I believe to be the most important move in our mission," wrote President Bartlett to Elder Frank Atkin, instructing him to leave the Chatham Islands and report to Arani's building project at Moawhango.[79]

President Bartlett did not get to see what he now called the "LDS Maori College." On 5 June 1905, another former missionary, Louis G. Hoagland, bishop of Salt Lake City's Twenty-sixth Ward, arrived to take over presidency of the mission. Bartlett sailed from Auckland on 5 Au-

---

73. Ibid., 13 September 1905.
74. Ibid., 1 May 1905.
75. Ibid., 31 July 1904.
76. Ibid., 12 December 1904.
77. Ibid., 6 April 1905.
78. Ibid., 18 May 1904, 22 May 1905.
79. Charles B. Bartlett, Letter to W. Frank Atkin, 24 November 1904, in William Frank Atkin Papers.

gust 1905; but before he left, the old and new presidents made a mission tour, including a visit to Korongata where President Hoagland delivered young David (Rawiri) Kamau's belongings to his sorrowing parents. David, whom President Magleby took to Utah in 1902 as a ten-year-old, had died there of pleurisy three years later on 30 April 1905.[80]

Two other deaths—one in New Zealand, one in Utah—saddened the LDS community in New Zealand and the members of Zion's Maori Association in Utah. Arapata Meha, an influential chief and stalwart of the Mormon Church since the 1880s, died at Waipawa, where he was the branch president, on 7 July 1905. A few months later, on 17 October 1905, Hirini Whaanga died of complications following an appendectomy in Salt Lake City. "The news of the death of our venerable Maori Father, Hirini Whaanga... came as a great surprise and shock to all in New Zealand," recorded the mission clerk. "Many were the hearts that were saddened and eyes that were stained with tears in behalf of one whom all had learned to love."[81]

Meanwhile, the missionaries pursued their work with vigour. American elders served as district presidents, and their work and routine varied little from the mid-1880s to the late 1920s. Elder John E. Magleby described a typical Sunday for "Maori missionaries" in 1885. He and his companion walked three miles in the early morning to attend sacrament meeting, at which his companion spoke. After a dinner of bread and milk, they conducted a baptismal service, confirmed six adults, and blessed four children. They held afternoon meeting, then stayed for some time answering questions from non-Latter-day Saints in the village. "When all was over, we went back to our place of staying, rejoicing over the day's labor we had performed," he wrote. But their day was not yet over, for after supper they were called out to visit and administer to one of the Saints.[82]

The missionaries regularly visited from twelve to twenty villages in each district. Most districts had several branches, so not all could be visited every Sunday, or even one Sunday a month. In the Hawkes Bay District in 1906, for example, Elder James King reported that visiting the three strong branches of Korongata, Tamaki, and Te Hauke took three Sundays out of four, leaving only one Sunday (or occasionally two) on which to visit the other six. "Therefore three are visited well and six visited poorly," he wrote.[83] While on the whole the Saints were faithful and committed, there were of course "backsliders," both European and Maori. The Maori branches in

---

80. New Zealand Mission, Manuscript History, 27 June 1905.
81. Ibid., 21 November 1905.
82. Magleby, Journal, 13 September 1885.
83. James King, Letter to Louis G. Hoagland, 6 November 1906, in Hoagland Papers, Reel 3, fd. 6.

particular were subject to quick collapse if neglected. Elder W. D. Walton, labouring in the King Country in 1906, reported that the Saints "have all joined another church because they say the Elders do not come up often enough."[84] "The Maoris are a weak people, easily led; hence, it requires an elder among them continually," wrote Elder F. W. Halls in 1911, "because, when the shepherd is gone, wolves break in and scatter the flock."[85] Ironically, some years earlier William Cowie, Anglican archbishop of Auckland, reported the same problem in reverse, but with the identical metaphor: "At the Huntly station, when we arrived, we saw a large gathering of Maories [sic], taking leave of a Mormon preacher, who had been making converts in the district. . . . The Rev. Heta Tarawhiti, our Maori clergyman of this district, has been in delicate health lately, and not able to travel much; consequently his flock . . . have been left without a shepherd, and the wolf has been tearing the sheep."[86] As late as 1938, a returning mission president, addressing general conference in the Salt Lake Tabernacle, told the Saints that "your sons among the Maoris are not doing regular preaching, but are acting like bishops and helping with the taking care of the sick, building and gardening and other things to further the mission work."[87]

The missionaries frequently attended the land courts where large numbers of Maori assembled. The native land courts converted Maori communal and customary land ownership into titles derived from the crown. Paper title deeds were easily negotiable, making it easier for British settlers to obtain, by purchase or lease, such land as the Maori retained after the widespread confiscations following the wars of the 1860s. Seduced by the easy money obtained by selling land to Pakeha, many Maori sought to have their claims to land validated; unless their claim had been cleared by the land court, they could neither sell nor lease. The periodic land court hearings became occasions for large tribal gatherings, often accompanied by feasting and drunkenness. Usually ministers of at least two or three churches were present, all holding karakia (communal prayer meetings) and vying for the largest congregations. Sometimes the Mormon missionaries were invited to speak in the karakia of another religion, and sometimes they were able to conduct their own services.[88]

---

84. W. D. Walton, Letter to Louis G. Hoagland, 8 January 1906, in Hoagland Papers, Reel 1.

85. F. W. Halls, "New Zealand Conference," *Deseret Evening News,* in Journal History, 28 October 1911, 4.

86. William Garden Cowie, *Our Last Year in New Zealand: 1887,* 211.

87. M. Charles Woods, 6 April 1938, *Conference Report,* 90.

88. New Zealand Mission, Manuscript History, 24 May 1905.

Maori Saints, especially rangatira, had for some years now been called on short-term missions at each hui tau. They were extremely successful, often gaining entrance to villages from which American missionaries were excluded. The first Maori husband-and-wife couple called to one of these short-term, full-time missions were Eru and Erena Rewiti of Te Horo, who in 1905 were called to work among Eru's people in the Manawatu District.[89] While a Maori woman, Takare Takana, wife of Wiremu Takana (William Duncan Sr.), had been called to serve as a counselor to Emma Wright, an American missionary wife whom President Magleby had called as mission Relief Society president in 1902, Erena's calling appears to be the first instance of a Maori woman being called as a missionary.

The American district presidents were instructed to place all these "home missionaries" in areas where they already had mana (prestige).[90] The mission presidents were still well aware of the "top-down" conversion patterns and also aware, after some painful experiences, that it could work both ways: If a chief would not accept the gospel, few of his tribe would either.[91] For example, in 1885, Otene Meihana quarrelled with the missionaries because, they alleged, he wanted to run the missionary work in his area because of his rangatira status; eventually, after several years, problems came to a head when the missionaries disagreed with some of his doctrinal teachings. The missionaries laboured with him, but he was excommunicated in 1891 and others apparently left with him.[92] As late as 1951, a rangatira branch president who resented his release from his Church calling threatened to leave the Church and to take all his hapu (extended family) with him.[93] Because of experiences like these, missionaries were counselled never to excommunicate a chief or rangatira without the mission president's consent.[94]

The missionaries frequently participated in formal debates with other ministers, even though, under instructions from the First Presidency, the elders seldom initiated such encounters. On one occasion, two Plymouth Brethren ministers refused to debate with anyone but Mission President Charles B. Bartlett. Bartlett agreed, but Wiremu Takana (William Dun-

---

89. Ibid., 21 July 1905.
90. Ibid., 6 April 1906.
91. John E. Magleby, "Among the Maoris, Funeral of a Chief—Queer Native Customs" (letter to the editor), *Deseret News*, 30 November 1887, [2].
92. Henry Frederick McCune, Autobiography and Diaries, July 1885, 69; Douglass, Journal, 23 May, 18 June 1891, January 1892.
93. Gordon C. Young, Journal, 26 April 1951, in Gordon Claridge Young Papers, 1948–72.
94. Richards, Journal, 31 March 1897.

can) made a comment before the debate began. One of the opposing ministers replied, and the debate proceeded forthwith with Duncan representing the Mormons so eloquently that President Bartlett merely watched and listened till the Plymouth Brethren preachers confessed themselves relieved when supper was announced. Two missionaries at Kiri Kiri, John S. Evans and Thomas W. Henderson, were invited to debate with a Catholic priest. After two days' discussion, members of the priest's congregation were so impressed with the Mormon elders that they promptly invited them to take over as their regular preachers—as long as they would conduct Catholic services. The missionaries declined.[95]

The Maori Saints actively helped promote Mormon standards. When the "outsiders" at Moawhango tried to sabotage a Mormon Christmas hui in 1905 by scheduling a free dance with free whisky and beer, Hakopa Te Ahunga and Eruiti Arani told visiting Maori to choose between the opposing functions. They warned the visitors that not only would they get no liquor at the Mormon gathering, but they would also be charged two shillings each to attend the Mormon dance. The proceeds would go to the relief of a group of impoverished Maori whose potato crop had failed. "Not one of the visitors left and a nice little purse was sent to the suffering natives," reported the mission clerk.[96]

By the early 1900s, the missionaries were beginning to take a strong line with Maori cultural customs which they no longer perceived as mere curiosities, but as pagan relics which their converts should abandon. Some customs, such as moko (face tattooing for women), were gradually falling into disuse in any case in the larger Maori population. While women who had been tattooed before conversion were accepted into the Church without question, quite early the elders began to counsel female converts against the practice and to regard new tattoos as grounds for Church discipline. Usually the missionaries treated the erring women leniently, and punishment simply involved asking their local congregation for forgiveness. But in at least one instance, in 1887 the Maori branch president was determined to excommunicate a member woman who had her face tattooed. He was quite disappointed when the missionaries settled for a public confession of disobedience and a request for forgiveness.[97]

The facial markings, which were thought to have deep hereditary meaning, were applied by the tohunga or priests. "Tohunga" basically meant "expert" and designated not only priests, but also skilled crafts-

---

95. New Zealand Mission, Manuscript History, 10 April, 24 November 1905.
96. New Zealand Mission, Manuscript History, 25 December 1905.
97. Nelson Spicer Bishop, New Zealand Mission Diaries, 23 October 1887, 173.

men—in most cases qualified by the name of the appropriate craft, as tohunga ta moko or tohunga whakaira (expert carver). Because sickness and disease were thought to be of supernatural origin, or the result of a breach of tapu, the roles of priest and doctor became fused in the person of the tohunga. Elaborate and unorthodox rituals and healing rites were prescribed for those who were ill, treatments that undoubtedly resulted in the deaths of many patients. By the 1890s, the Mormon missionaries were trying by every means possible to discourage their sick converts from consulting tohunga Maori but had only partial success. Even with the concurrent teaching of the Young Maori Party and the new government health officers, the traditional and deeply ingrained influence of the tohunga could not be negated in one generation.

The American missionaries translated the term tohunga as "sorcerer" or "witch doctor," showing something less than complete cultural understanding as they did so. They encouraged sick members of their flock to visit a qualified medical practitioner and, in addition, to ask for the LDS ordinance of administration (anointing with oil while a blessing was pronounced by priesthood holders who laid hands on the sufferer's head). Those who persisted in consulting tohunga were frowned upon; those who practised as tohunga were excommunicated.

Until at least World War I, relatively few Maori had access to European doctors, and even fewer were able to pay them. The choice for most Maori Mormons, therefore, was usually between tohunga Maori methods and the blessings offered by the missionaries to all who had faith to be healed. The Maori had and have a deep and simple faith; countless healings credited to administrations have been recorded. Matthew Cowley, New Zealand missionary, mission president, and later apostle, credited these healings to the profound faith and trust of the Polynesian Saints. "They accept miracles as a matter of course," he said. "They never doubt anything."[98]

But before the majority of the Maori converts accepted these teachings, there was some unavoidable strain in the Mormon-Maori relationship in various parts of the mission. Even after the New Zealand government passed the Tohunga Suppression Act in 1907, in an effort to curb the worst excesses of the tohunga (many of whom, by this time, were regarded as charlatans rather than being traditionally trained), Maori Latter-day Saints continued to consult them. Some mission presidents reacted sharply, while others were more tolerant. Elder Robert L. Simpson, later a mission president, General Authority, and Area President, recalled that, during his first mission in the late 1930s, the Maori Saints "felt comfortable about being

---

98. Matthew Cowley, "Miracles," 44.

Mormons while holding onto most of their Maori traditions. . . . When there were sick among them, they'd not only call in the Elders but think to themselves, 'Why not make sure that we've touched all the bases?' and they'd call on the old Maori tohunga to give them a blessing at the same time."[99]

While it was inevitable that there should be some conflict between Maori culture and Mormon doctrine and practice, the situation was complicated because of lack of firm guidance from Church headquarters. The General Authorities had no first-hand knowledge of Maori culture and customs and left policy-making on such matters to the judgement of the mission presidents. The result was a fairly fluid situation, as, in many instances, those mission presidents who had been most thoroughly immersed in Maori culture during their first missions, such as John Ephraim Magleby, responded with more sympathy and tolerance to Maori customs than those who had served in European areas and did not speak Maori. Even this pattern was not always predictable, and the swings between presidents who were willing to accommodate Maori customs and those who enforced prohibition of them when they conflicted with LDS standards caused confusion. It was probably not until the 1970s and 1980s—almost a century after Mormonism was introduced to the Maori people—that clear guidelines were established in every area of cultural dissonance.

President Bartlett left the mission in good condition, with more than 5,000 Latter-day Saints on the Church records.[100] Making a stopover in Samoa on his way home, he was intrigued to find the Mormon missionaries there working hard to establish boarding schools. "They are acquiring land wherever possible and the temporal labors of the Elders is one of the strongest features of their Mission," he wrote back to President Hoagland in New Zealand. "Their achievements under desperately discouraging circumstances (particularly in German Samoa) have been marvelous." Bartlett repeated his conviction that both Mormon schools and American families to lead by example were needed in New Zealand. "I am thouroughly [sic] convinced that the school system, [and] the establishing of permanent homes for elders and sisters and the developement [sic] of the ability of the saints in temporal matters is the key to permanent success in the New Zealand Mission."[101]

---

99. Simpson, Oral History, 5.
100. New Zealand Mission, Manuscript History, 31 December 1904.
101. Charles B. Bartlett, Letter to Louis G. Hoagland, dated At Sea, 13 August 1905, in Hoagland Papers, Reel 1.

President Hoagland spent the rest of 1905 and all of 1906 working towards the boys' secondary boarding school and establishing a mission paper. To his disappointment, an offer of free land at Wanganui was withdrawn in February 1906. But Hoagland soon decided that, because of possible land court complications, it would in any case be wiser for the Church to buy land for the school from Pakeha owners, and then lease additional farming land from local Maori members.[102] A general priesthood meeting endorsed this view, and Kopuawhara and Nuhaka were considered as alternative sites for the proposed college.[103]

In September, a letter signed by leading missionaries and Maori Saints was sent to Church president Joseph F. Smith, outlining the need for an "academy" and stressing that it would do as much good as seventy-five elders in the field. President Hoagland estimated that the mission would need $15,000 to acquire land, erect suitable buildings, and establish farming, which would see the project become self-sustaining. Seven hundred dollars had been donated so far, mainly from American missionaries, and Hoagland was confident that the Maori Latter-day Saints could raise $5,000. "This amount we consider all they could be asked for under distressing circumstances," wrote the committee. "Owing to the failure of crops for the past two years the government has been compelled to partly provide for some of them. In view of the above we are compelled to appeal to you for assistance to the extent of ten thousand dollars."[104]

While he waited for the First Presidency's answer, President Hoagland continued Bartlett's chapel-building program. He urged the missionaries to consider local membership numbers and to keep meeting-house projects within the means of the local members.[105] Both Bartlett and Hoagland wanted the missionaries to make chapel-building an opportunity to teach building skills, a concept that reemerged as a basic feature of the labor missionary program half a century later. While Maori-style raupo-walled whare were frequently built in many villages in the 1880s and 1890s for conferences and were afterwards used by the local branches, during the first part of the twentieth century many branch buildings incorporated both European-style construction and traditional Maori carved fronts—"half-caste house[s]," as one Maori Saint termed them.[106]

---

102. New Zealand Mission, Manuscript History, 6 April 1906.

103. Re [Ray Gudmansen], Letter to L[ouis] G. Hoagland, dated Nuhaka, 23 May 1906, in Hoagland Papers, Reel 2.

104. New Zealand Mission, Manuscript History, quoted in annual report, 31 December 1906.

105. Ibid., 7 April 1906.

106. Tiaki Haeata, Oral History, interviewed by Kenneth W. Baldridge, at

It took great and consistent effort for Maori communities to build the European-style meetinghouses preferred by Church leaders. The Te Horo meetinghouse, dedicated in February 1907, required two years to build. It was sixty-five feet long, thirty feet wide, and eighteen feet high. The steeple (complete with belfry) rose sixty feet. It needed 22,000 feet of lumber, most of which was cut and sawn by the Maori members and the missionaries in a saw-pit dug for the purpose on Maori land. Other Maori Saints, in addition to working on their own farms, worked for local European farmers or dug kauri gum (an important New Zealand export) to earn money to feed the builders. The community raised funds for the hardware, paint, and other items they could not produce themselves by leasing grazing lands to Percy Going, a prominent Pakeha LDS dairy farmer.

The question of a Maori "gathering" still occupied much of the mission president's time. President Bartlett had discouraged schemes to establish a communal Mormon gathering place in New Zealand, but President Hoagland began to consider establishing a Maori colony away from New Zealand, following the plan of Iosepa, the Hawaiian colony in Skull Valley, Utah. "This he thinks would be a great incentive for those here to live better lives," wrote the mission clerk.[107] According to one of his missionaries, W. Frank Atkin, President Hoagland thought that Mexico, where there was a Mormon colony at Colonia Juarez, would be suitable.[108] However, nothing came of the Mexico idea. In view of the expense and problems incurred at Iosepa, the First Presidency would scarcely have been willing to finance a second such venture.[109]

President Hoagland next turned his attention to the long-looked-for mission paper. With £5 donations from Charles Hardy and Eruiti Arani, and a number of smaller contributions, he arranged for the purchase of a second-hand press at Wanganui for £35. It was shipped to Auckland, sustaining considerable damage en route. The missionaries managed some repairs. "We put most of it together [but] there are a few pieces we can't find a place for," admitted the mission secretary, David P. Howells, in a letter to President Hoagland, who was in Dunedin when the press arrived in Auckland. Howells suggested that the paper should be a joint venture with the Australian Mission, an idea which he hoped would double the circulation and halve the cost. President Hoagland liked the idea, but nothing came of

---

Masterton, New Zealand, 19 December 1971, 6.

107. New Zealand Mission, Manuscript History, 6 April 1906.

108. W. Frank Atkin, "Mission Notes 1906," Atkin Papers, fd. 15.

109. Tracey E. Panek, "Life at Iosepa, Utah's Polynesian Colony," 64–77; Thomas G. Alexander, *Mormonism in Transition: A History of the Latter-day Saints, 1890–1930*, 202.

it though, from time to time, some issues carried Australian Mission news and articles from Australian members in the years before the Australian Mission began its own paper, the *Austral Star*, in 1929.

The first issue of the *Elders' Messenger* was published at the end of January 1907. Consisting of eight octavo (A5) pages, the first five pages were in English under the *Elders' Messenger* banner; pages 6–8 were in Maori, with the title of *Te Karere* ("The Messenger"). The pages in English were not just for the Pakeha Saints but were a deliberate attempt to provide "an incentive [for] our young Maori friends to learn the English language and to learn the Gospel in English. It is hoped they will work diligently to acquire the use of the English language since it will be such an aid to their intellectual and business welfare."[110] The size of the paper was increased to twelve pages by the third number. The journal was published fortnightly, with subscriptions costing 5/- per year, and became a much-loved institution of the New Zealand Mission, enduring for more than half a century.

A new mission president, Rufus K. Hardy, arrived on 28 March 1907. Travelling with him were his wife Adelaide, Benjamin and Emma Goddard, and Mere Whaanga, widow of Hirini Whaanga. Mere had come home to serve a mission among her own people as her husband had done nearly a decade earlier. Goddard had served as mission secretary in the 1890s and was now in charge of the Bureau of Information on Temple Square. He had maintained an active interest in the New Zealand Mission through Zion's Maori Association and seemed to have unlimited access to the First Presidency and a considerable degree of influence with them regarding the affairs of the New Zealand Mission. The First Presidency had sent him to help President Hardy choose a site for the Maori college and also a site in Auckland for mission headquarters.[111]

Plans to establish the school in Moawhango or Kopuawhara were shelved, and instead land was sought in the Hawkes Bay district. J. P. Donnelly, from whom the Church had bought land for the Korongata Branch meetinghouse, offered to donate £100 and also promised to support any land purchase application that the Church made for the college. He advised Elder David P. Howells, then the district president, to enlist the help of Members of Parliament such as Sir Robert Stout, Apirana Ngata, or James Carroll. Stout was a former Premier, still very powerful; Ngata and Carroll were both Maori, and the latter was Minister of Native Affairs from 1899 to 1912. "If we have their recommendation to anything that we

---

110. *Elders' Messenger* 1, no. 1 (January 1907): 1.

111. New Zealand Mission, *Catalogue and Announcement of the Latter-day Saints Agricultural College, First Year 1913–1914*, 11.

might put before Parliament our success is assured," Elder Howells wrote to his mission president. Howells visited Te Aute College near Hastings, founded in 1871 by Archdeacon Samuel Williams (son of CMS missionary Henry Williams) for the sons of Maori chiefs. Howells was not impressed with anything about Te Aute except the number of acres owned by the school. "I feel more encouraged than ever," he reported to President Hoagland, "for surely we will have no difficulty in surpassing them. Their buildings are all old, cheaply constructed affairs." He even contemplated asking the government for a section of Te Aute College land.[112]

Stout was polite but declined to help. He was a firm opponent of denominational schools and had previously urged the government to take over Te Aute College, which was the leading Church of England secondary school in the southern part of the North Island; he could not now consistently come out in favour of another denominational school. Ngata agreed that an agricultural college would be beneficial for Maori boys but did not show great initial enthusiasm.[113]

President Hardy soon changed the name of the mission paper from the *Elders' Messenger* to *The Messenger*, then separated the English and Maori sections on 5 February 1908, publishing each on alternate fortnights.[114] Editorial matter was different in each; Pakeha subscribers received only the English edition, while Maori subscribers who could read English received both at no extra cost. Both papers were increased in size to sixteen pages. Purchase of a petrol motor for the printing press made it possible to print 5,000 tracts as well as the mission paper. When the U.S. fleet visited New Zealand in 1908, nearly every missionary within a reasonable distance of the city came to Auckland for the occasion. Hardy capitalised on their presence by having them fold and staple the freshly printed tracts.[115]

The "European" missionaries worked very hard for small advances in the number of their converts. During 1906, for example, they visited 31,159 homes, leaving 21,255 pamphlets as they went. When it is taken into consideration that, as President Hoagland had justly pointed out, fewer than one third of the mission's fifty-seven missionaries were engaged in tracting (the remainder worked with the Maori people, where no tracting

---

112. David P. Howells, Letter to President L[ouis] G. Hoagland, dated Wednesday [27 March 1907], in Hoagland Papers, Reel 3.

113. David P. Howells, Wanganui, Letter to Louis Hoagland, [29 March] 1907, in Hoagland Papers, Reel 3.

114. *The Messenger* 1, no. 12 (January 1908): 139; New Zealand Mission, Manuscript History, 5 February 1908.

115. New Zealand Mission, Manuscript History, 10 and 18 June, 9 August 1908.

was done), it must be seen as a prodigious effort. Despite official discouragement, European families continued to emigrate to Utah during this period, though usually only one or two families left each year.

The American missionaries experienced many health problems in the decades around the turn of the century. The mission office was shocked on 12 March 1908 when Elder John A. Southwick died of typhoid fever. This was the fourth death of a Mormon missionary in New Zealand (the fifth, counting that of Sarah Paxman, the baby daughter of William and Kate Paxman in 1887).[116] Southwick's body was embalmed and shipped home. Records from the 1880s onward show that the missionaries were often ill. Frequent bouts of typhoid fever, rheumatic fever, diphtheria, bronchitis, asthma, measles, boils, sores, and "the itch" were recorded. Those with typhoid were hospitalised; those with other illnesses recovered as best they could, usually with little aid other than an administration (laying on of hands) from fellow missionaries. "Having been troubled with sores on my head for about three weeks & they were getting worse, Elder J. W. Ash & myself repaired to the bush about ¼ mile from the house, consecrated a bottle of oil & he anointed my head and administered to me," Elder Ezra F. Richards had written at Uawa, Tolaga Bay, on 1 January 1885. Even the comfort of a companion to administer was not always available, so when Alma Greenwood experienced bad chest pains one evening when he was alone in the Wairarapa, he anointed himself with oil. "This relieved me very much," he wrote.[117]

Another unorthodox administration took place when Elder Nelson S. Bishop and his companion were travelling by horseback in hilly countryside near Petone, in the Wellington district. They were dismayed when one of their horses went lame and they had to lead him. "Horse gets worse all the time, and we make it a matter of pray[e]r," recorded Bishop. "Also administer to him, when he travells easyer [sic]."[118]

For two or three decades around the turn of the century, it is hard to tell from their journals whether fleas or boils caused the missionaries more distress as they walked and rode through rural New Zealand. One elder wrote to Elder Frank Atkin from Kamo, mentioning that he had had boils

---

116. Previous deaths were those of Elders Brigham W. Young (1887), Leslie C. Atwood (1902), and G. W. Stevens (1906).

117. Richards, Journal, 1 January 1885; Alma Greenwood, Diary, 21 May 1883, 100.

118. Bishop, Diaries, 6 September 1887, 148. It was frequently the case that the missionaries had one horse between them. In that case, they would travel by the time-honoured method of "ride and tie"—taking it in turns to ride a mile, tie the horse to a tree, and walk a mile.

for about two months. "About the time one gets well another comes," he wrote. "I have two now.... I tell you they are anything but pleasant, as they are right where the saddle goes, and we have to ride all the time, so I just have to grin and bare it [sic]."[119]

"New Zealand is the champion island south of the Equator for fleas," wrote Elder Alma Greenwood in 1883. "Why, they are as numerous as Abraham's seed."[120] Nelson S. Bishop used a battlefield analogy when he and his companion waged war on their tiny but numerous enemy, reporting that "although we were in the manority [sic] we came out victorious as the deaths was greatest with our opponents. My partner was not alarmed as he said he had been in battle before and was always the winner."[121] Several others described their encounters with fleas in a similar mock-heroic vein. "The fleas are my best companions," wrote seventeen-year-old Elder Matthew Cowley in 1914. "I call them my best companions because they stick to me so close." Next evening Cowley rubbed himself all over with flea powder and spread a thick layer of the powder on his bed, waking next day to find "a multitude" of dead fleas. "It made me feel like Napoleon to be the victor of such a battle," he wrote.[122] Fleas were not Cowley's only problem. A note in the mission paper records: "We have a modern Job in the mission. Elder Matt Cowelly [sic] is suffering intensely from an attack of boils."[123] The problems with boils and fleas abated somewhat as time went by, but one elder was invalided home to Utah as late as 1972 because of his allergic reaction to fleabites.[124]

In April 1908, the New Zealand Mission bade farewell to Sister Mere Whaanga as she sailed for her home in Salt Lake City. "Since her arrival in New Zealand, March 28, 1907, she had been a most humble, obedient and faithful missionary among her people, and her influence for good would never be forgotten. Too much praise cannot be accorded her," wrote the mission clerk.[125] Just before Mere's return to Utah, Zion's Maori

---

119. L. J. Bowen, Letter to W. Frank Atkin, dated Kamo, 19 December 1903, in Atkin Papers, fd. 4.

120. Greenwood, Diary, 26 February 1883, 52.

121. Ibid., 20 October 1886.

122. Matthew Cowley, Journal, 1, 2, 3 February 1915, 37–38, in Cowley Collection, Box 1, fd. 1.

123. "College Notes," *The Messenger* 9, no. 21 (20 October 1915): 246–47.

124. Leo W. Russon, Letter to Mr. and Mrs. M. F. Huffaker, dated Auckland, 27 October 1972, in New Zealand Auckland Mission, Presidents' Correspondence, 1967–75, fd. 21.

125. New Zealand Mission, Manuscript History, 4 April 1908.

Headstone of Hirini and Mere Whaanga in the Salt Lake City Cemetery. Courtesy Patricia Lyn Scott.

Association had erected a striking marble monument over the grave of her husband, Hirini, in the Salt Lake City cemetery.[126]

As the first mission president since William Paxman to bring his wife to New Zealand, President Rufus K. Hardy had looked at the rented mission home on Queen Street, Auckland, with different eyes. He immediately purchased new linoleum, carpets, and furniture to make the house more comfortable, then began to look for a site on which to build a permanent mission home.[127] Whether the Church still owned the lot at Mount

---

126. Mere Whaanga died in Salt Lake City in 1944. In 1995, fifty years after her death and burial in Hirini's grave, her name had not been added to the memorial. This omission was brought to the attention of officers of the New Zealand Missionary Society (successor of Zion's Maori Association), who undertook to rectify it.

127. New Zealand Mission, Minutes, 13 August 1907, 3:74.

Roskill which Bartlett had bought for this purpose is not clear, but Hardy and Goddard eventually bought land on the corner of Upper Queen Street and Esk Street (later renamed Scotia Place).[128] Plans were drawn up for a home for the mission president and an all-purpose meeting hall. Tenders were called on 1 October 1908, the successful bidder being W. E. Trevarthen. Work proceeded quickly, and President and Sister Hardy moved into the mission home in mid-January 1909.

President Hardy wrote enthusiastically about the site to his predecessor, Louis G. Hoagland. "Since you left there have been large shops built from the [Baptist] [T]abernacle to Karangahape Road, three stories high; on the opposite side from our property eight brick shops, seven of which are two stories high and one is a one-story place; these are all between Grey's Monument and Karangahape Road. The corner of Grey Street will soon be torn up for the city hall. . . . It is a location that must advance rapidly in value, and in fact double itself so that the Church will make a splendid investment, besides giving us the location that we have all so much desired."[129]

Seventy-five people were present when Charles Hardy,[130] president of the Auckland Branch, dedicated the mission home on Saturday, 30 January 1909. The following morning, after Charles Hardy had recounted the history of the LDS New Zealand Mission, President Rufus K. Hardy dedicated the "Assembly Hall," the first building for European worship built by the LDS Church in New Zealand. For many years, the hall doubled as a chapel on Sundays and a recreation hall for the Mutual Improvement Association on week nights. The basement provided storage space for missionary literature, a baptismal font, and a room for the printing press.[131]

Meanwhile, President Hardy had negotiated with William and Thomas Thompson, butchers in Hastings, for land near Korongata, some seven miles from Hastings, for the proposed boarding school. The Thompson brothers originally offered the land at £22/10/- per acre but, when the Church showed serious interest, raised their price to £26 per acre. After receiving cabled instructions to proceed with the purchase, President Hardy finally secured an option for just under 130 acres at £22 per acre, and the contract was signed on 1 April 1908.[132] He also took an option to purchase

---

128. New Zealand Mission, Manuscript History, 6 July 1908.
129. Rufus K. Hardy, Letter to L[ouis] G. Hoagland, dated Kamo, 1 July 1908, in Hoagland Papers, Reel 3.
130. No relation to Rufus K. Hardy.
131. New Zealand Mission, Manuscript History, 30 January 1909.
132. Ibid., 20 January 1908; New Zealand Mission, Minutes, 9–11 March 1908.

The first LDS meetinghouse in Auckland, dedicated 1909 by Rufus K. Hardy. Courtesy LDS Church History Library.

a further 130 acres. Controversy over the suitability of this site for the purpose continued for several decades, long after the Maori Agricultural College was defunct.[133]

Initially, most of the college land was leased back to the Thompson brothers for pasture. President Hardy hired Maori Latter-day Saints from Korongata to fence the Church property and plough fifty-five acres that were sown with grain. By the end of August, the grain crop was ready to harvest. Eleven American missionaries cut and stacked the crop, using borrowed drays and horses. This done, Hardy had concentrated his attention on the erection of the mission home in Auckland.

The purchase of the school land and the building of the mission home and chapel in Auckland were the crowning achievements of Rufus K. Hardy's term as mission president. On 29 March 1909, George Bowles arrived as President Hardy's replacement. Thanks to the new home, President Bowles was able to bring his wife, Christine, and their small son, George. Following now-established custom, the old and new presidents conferred over the mission records and accounts and then toured the mission before Rufus K. and Adelaide Hardy departed from New Zealand on 12 May 1909.

---

133. See Marjorie Newton, "Mormonism in New Zealand," chap. 4.

President Bowles spent most of his time in routine missionary work. He and his fellow missionaries were amused when Bowles was verbally attacked by the Reverend T. Hopper, a Wesleyan Methodist minister, after a public meeting in Tauranga in February 1910. About 200 Europeans had come to hear Bowles preach on "Mormonism." Hopper was indignant, feeling that the crowd had been enticed to attend under false pretences; he accused Bowles of preaching Christianity instead of the advertised "Mormonism." He was "somewhat chagrined," the mission clerk recorded, when he finally understood that what he had heard was the doctrine that the world called "Mormonism."[134]

In June 1910, another Maori family, consisting of Tamihana Te Awe Awe, his wife, Waitokorau (Victoria), and their daughters Adelaide and Nora sailed for Utah. Tamihana was a chief of the Rangitane tribe and his wife was of equal rank in her own right.[135] Since joining the LDS Church, Tamihana had served as a travelling missionary and a branch president, while Waitokorau had been a respected Relief Society leader, riding many miles on horseback in the interests of her calling. They sold their extensive property, and Bowles testified to the Maori land court that their presence in Salt Lake City had been requested by Church authorities. It was virtually a mission call, to continue the Maori temple work begun by Hirini and Mere Whaanga years earlier.

In Salt Lake City, Tamihana and Waitokorau (known there as Brother and Sister Thompson) made their home in the Forest Dale Ward where Mere Whaanga also lived.[136] Tamihana was employed as a custodian in the Salt Lake Tabernacle at a salary of $60 a month.[137] Within a year, Adelaide had won a scholarship at the LDS University in Salt Lake City. Former missionary M. Wallace Woolley, reporting this achievement to the New Zealand Saints and missionaries, remarked that this "was surprising to the [American] Pakehas who did not realize that some of the New Zealanders

---

134. New Zealand Mission, Manuscript History, 15 February 1910.

135. Maori genealogical pedigrees are ambilineal, that is, can be traced through either male or female lines according to choice, usually following the nobler line. Tribal leadership was settled by primogeniture in the male line. However, the firstborn daughter of a chief was honoured as an *ariki* or chief. Te Rangi Hiroa (Sir Peter Buck), *The Coming of the Maori*, 337–45.

136. "Tamihana Te Awe Awe Dies in New Zealand," *Deseret Evening News*, Journal History, 28 November 1918, 4.

137. "Amongst the Mormons," reprinted from *Manawatu Evening Standard*, date not given, in *The Messenger* 8 no. 3 (11 February 1914): 28.

know the English language better than many of us."[138] Adelaide graduated three years later with high honours.[139]

After two years, President Bowles was succeeded in March 1911, as was now customary, by another ex-New Zealand missionary, Orson D. Romney. President Romney was accompanied by his wife, Emma, and four teenage children (Vilate, Orson Jr., Melbourne, and William.) Orson Jr. and later Melbourne were set apart as missionaries.

Presidents Bowles and Romney travelled to Papawai for the annual hui tau, which this year was scheduled to follow the unveiling of a monument to Chief Tamahau, a wealthy and influential Maori leader who had developed the Maori centre at Papawai and who had died in 1904. Thousands of Maori gathered—so many that government officials hastily sent for a further thirty large tents to add to the many already erected. On 30 March 1911, Rev. A. O. Williams of the Church of England conducted the ceremonies, the Mormon choir provided the music, and the Hon. James Carroll, Minister for Native Affairs, unveiled the monument. President Bowles read greetings to the assembled crowd from the First Presidency of the LDS Church.

The following day, the hui tau commenced. President Romney addressed the conference in Maori, pleased to find that his fluency in the language had not been lost in the twenty years since he had served in New Zealand as a young missionary. The record of business shows seventeen districts and seven primary schools (at Awarua, Tauranganui, Kopuawhara, Korongata, Kohunui, Porirua, and Wairau).

Sister Romney was sustained as the mission Relief Society president, with her daughter Vilate and another American missionary wife, Laura S. Johnson, as counselors. The mission was divided in two for Relief Society work, and a presidency of Maori women was sustained for both the northern and southern portions of the missions, to work under the direction of the mission Relief Society officers. The conference also passed a motion that each member of the Church over eight years old should contribute one pound for the proposed secondary school.[140]

The New Zealand Mission had gone from strength to strength, far outstripping its parent Australian Mission. By the end of the first decade of the twentieth century, there were nearly 6,000 Latter-day Saints in New Zealand, and barely 1,000 in Australia. While the Brisbane Chapel pre-

---

138. W. Wallace Woolley, "A Letter from Zion," *The Messenger* 7, no. 1 (1 January 1913): 2.
139. "Mission Notes," *The Messenger* 7, no. 24 (19 November 1913): 283.
140. New Zealand Mission, Manuscript History, 3 April 1911.

ceded the Auckland Chapel by four years, another twenty years were to pass before the LDS Church owned a mission headquarters in Sydney. *Te Karere*, the New Zealand mission paper, was established more than twenty years before the *Austral Star*. The undeniable difference was the conversion of a significant portion of the Maori population and their faithful adherence to the restored Church. Most New Zealand Latter-day Saints were Maori, about 12 percent of the estimated Maori population of approximately 40,000. However, it should be clearly understood that while most New Zealand Mormons were Maori, most Maori were not Mormon. As the number of Maori converts grew, new branches were organised. "A battalion of active young Elders could be utilised in this beautiful evergreen land," wrote Elder M. N. Johnson, "and there is nowhere to be found where an Elder can gain a better experience."[141] The situation in Australia caused an unhappy circular effect; fewer missionaries were called to the mission, and consequently convert numbers stagnated to the point where the First Presidency seriously considered closing the Australian Mission. At the same time, the New Zealand Mission was poised for its most exciting period yet as the Maori Agricultural College became not just a dream, but a reality.

---

141. M. N. Johnson, "New Zealand," *Deseret Evening News*, 10 June 1911, in Journal History, 29 March 1911, 4.

Chapter 4

"... you are some of Hagoth's people and there is no pea about it"

In August 1911, President Orson D. Romney received a cable from Church headquarters in Salt Lake City instructing him to proceed immediately with the erection of the college buildings.[1] Auckland architect John M. Walker was appointed to oversee the construction by Hastings builders W. M. Hay and Son, who submitted the winning tender. The foundations were staked out on 31 October. By late January 1912, the brickwork on the dormitory building was up to the second storey, and foundations had been laid for a second building.[2] Seeing the quick progress, President Romney planned to open the school in February 1913, the beginning of the academic year in the southern hemisphere. He wrote asking the First Presidency to send one of the Quorum of the Twelve to dedicate the school at its opening.

President Romney's routine work in the mission office in Auckland was now punctuated by hurried visits to Korongata every few weeks to inspect progress of the college buildings. In between, he conducted district conferences. On 10 March, he dedicated a new meetinghouse at Nuhaka, the largest in the mission, and was pleased to report that it had been built and completely paid for within a nine-month period. The 1912 hui tau was held at Awapuni, near Palmerston North, 5–7 April. Progress on the college buildings was a topic of eager discussion at this conference, and President Romney returned to Auckland with nearly £300 paid as tithing and donations for the college. He was especially touched when the mis-

---

1. New Zealand Mission, Minutes, 18 August 1911, 3:194.
2. New Zealand Mission, Manuscript History, 31 October and 22 November 1911; New Zealand Mission, Minutes, 23 January 1912, 210.

sion Relief Societies turned over their entire treasury of £200 to the college building fund.³

Meanwhile, in Salt Lake City, Horace Hall Cummings, who served as Superintendent of Church Schools from 1906 to 1919, was assigned to nominate a principal for the new agricultural high school in New Zealand. Advising him were members of Zion's Maori Association, including Ezra T. Stevenson, Rufus K. Hardy, and Benjamin Goddard. Their choice fell on another former New Zealand missionary, John Johnson, who was then president of the Oneida Stake Academy in Preston, Idaho. "You are the man we want for the position," Church President Joseph F. Smith told Johnson. During July, Johnson and Rufus K. Hardy solicited gifts of agricultural equipment from various implement companies. International Harvester Company donated a wagon worth $450, Deering donated a harrow, drill, and cultivator, and other contributors offered gifts ranging from a cream separator to a corn sheller. John and Eva Johnson were set apart for their mission—so designated despite the fact that they were to receive a generous salary—by the First Presidency on 26 September 1912. After the business of the meeting was concluded, President Smith admonished the Johnson children (John Jr., Vivian, Edith, and baby Eva) to be obedient to their parents and to set a good example to the Maori children.⁴

The Johnsons sailed from Vancouver, Canada, and arrived in Auckland on 23 October 1912. Leaving their families in Auckland, Mission President Romney and Elder Johnson took the overnight express to Hastings a few days later to inspect the college chapel (which would double as a classroom) and the dormitory, both nearly completed. Johnson was very enthusiastic about the dormitories but realised at once that there were not enough classrooms to make the projected curriculum feasible.⁵

During the next three months, Principal Johnson accompanied President Romney on a mission tour, visiting both islands. Everywhere they travelled, Johnson spoke to the Saints about the college and extolled the benefits to be obtained from an education in an LDS Church school.⁶ Romney and Johnson also appointed a small school board that held its first meeting on 22 December. The board's first major decision was to build a faculty home, and Hay and Son were awarded that contract as well.

---

3. New Zealand Mission, Manuscript History, 7 April 1912.

4. John Johnson, "Journal of Second Mission to New Zealand," in John Johnson, Journals, 1893–1925, 16, 18, 19 June, 2, 29 July, 26 September 1912, Reel 3.

5. Ibid., 29 October 1912, 128–29.

6. New Zealand Mission, Manuscript History, November–December 1912, January 1913.

Within weeks the board was formally constituted as the College Board of Education and enlarged to fifteen members. Romney (president of the board), John Johnson (college principal), and Elder Hugh S. Geddes (Hawkes Bay district president) became members *ex officio*; with Stuart Meha as secretary, they formed an Executive Board. As far as possible, every district in the mission was represented.[7] Meha was the only New Zealander on the executive board and was the only person, as Kenneth Baldridge points out, who was officially connected with the college from its opening to its closing.[8]

With the help of Meha, a prominent, well-educated Maori Latter-day Saint, Johnson wrote the "catalogue" or prospectus of the college. Stuart (Tuati) Meha was the son of Arapata Meha, one of the earliest Maori rangatira to embrace Mormonism; his mother was a sister of Apikara Whaanga in Utah. Born in 1878, Meha was baptized as a child of eight by Elder Sondra Sanders Jr. and was educated at the prestigious Te Aute College. Now an adult, tragically widowed,[9] he was an automatic choice for the College Board, and played an influential part in college life during the eighteen years of its existence.[10]

The opening of the new school was postponed from February, the beginning of New Zealand's academic year, until the 1913 hui tau, scheduled for April at Korongata. January, February, and March were busy months for both Romney and Johnson. They continued their visits to as many

---

7. New Zealand Mission, *Catalogue and Announcement, 1913–1914*, 12; Johnson, Journal, 23 January 1913.

8. Kenneth W. Baldridge, "The Maori Agricultural College: An Experience in Rural Education," 24.

9. Stuart Meha married Meri Hineiturama Tapihana at Dannevirke about 1897, and his biographer states that the couple had at least three sons and one daughter before his wife died in 1912. Two years later, in 1914, Meha married Rosina Jane Edith Morris, and another four children were born to this union before Rosina died in 1920. On the advice of mission president George S. Taylor, Meha was married for the third time to a sister of his second wife, Ivory Tepora Morris. After giving birth to seven children, Ivory also died in 1937. Meha himself lived until 1963. Peter J. Lineham, "Meha, Stuart, 1878–1963," *Dictionary of New Zealand Biography*, updated 7 April 2006, http://www.dnzb.govt.nz/ (accessed 10 March 2007).

10. Meha's name is variously spelled "Stuart" and "Stewart" in Mormon documents; however, he signed his name "Stuart," and his second marriage in 1914 is registered under the name "Stuart." It is likely that he was named for Edward Craig Stuart, who was consecrated Anglican Bishop of Waiapu, succeeding William Williams, consecrated in December 1877, twelve months before Stuart Meha's birth. Maori children were frequently named for beloved CMS missionaries.

branches and districts as they could reach, publicising the college and soliciting both prospective students and financial donations. They also gratefully received donations of bed linen from the mission Relief Societies.[11] Between conference visits, they shopped for furniture and furnishings—linoleum, blinds, beds, sixty mattresses at fifteen shillings and sixpence each, ten dozen chairs—and took tenders for building benches and school desks.

Another American teacher, Rodney C. Allred, arrived on the *Mulawa* on 16 February 1913. Also on board were the agricultural implements that had been donated to the school, all of which were admitted duty free. In early March when the faculty home was finished, President Romney engaged Mr. Hay to build a manual training room, containing two classrooms each thirty by twenty feet, for an additional £260.[12] Six hundred catalogues had been printed, and Johnson mailed copies to prominent European and Maori leaders and to the parents of prospective students throughout the mission.

A substantial, octavo-sized booklet of forty-eight pages, the "catalogue" or prospectus was printed in both English and Maori. The catalogue stated that the specific aims of the Maori Agricultural College were "to teach the Maoris the principles of agriculture that they may better utilize their valuable land holdings; to instruct them in the manual arts that they may build their own houses, barns, bridges, etc.; to train them in the secular branches of education that they may cope successfully with their associates in the commercial and social world, and to furnish them an opportunity to possess themselves of that education that will imbue them with a better understanding of the obligations of life and a higher appreciation of its opportunities and blessings." Fees were a moderate £12 per year—less for each student, the prospectus pointed out, than the cost of his food—plus uniform (£3/10/-) and books (£3).

While the prospectus stated that both LDS and non-LDS pupils would be admitted, it specified that there would be no girls (except for music lessons) and no Pakeha boys (presumably because it was felt there were sufficient government secondary schools for them). However, exceptions were made from the beginning: Johnson's elder son and daughter, plus Cyril Going, one of a large pioneer Mormon Pakeha family from a remote township in the Bay of Islands, were enrolled.[13] Liquor, tobacco,

---

11. Johnson, Journal, 27 January 1913.

12. New Zealand Mission, Manuscript History, 3 March 1913; "Doings at the College," *The Messenger* 7, no. 7 (26 March 1913): 79.

13. Cyril Going, Oral History, interviewed by Kenneth W. Baldridge, 1 April 1973, in Laie, Hawaii. There was no local high school within reach of the Going family property.

and profanity were prohibited. Students were to share housework, laundry, and kitchen duties as well as work on the farm.

The prospectus outlined an ambitious program, but the faculty was too small for the program offered. Johnson was to teach theology and English; Allred, a graduate of the Utah State Agricultural College at Logan, was responsible for agriculture and manual training classes, while Eva Johnson was to be school librarian and teach vocal and instrumental music, as well as caring for her four children. A young missionary currently teaching at the LDS primary school in Korongata, Elder Sidney J. Ottley, was seconded as an assistant master for the agricultural college; and a local Maori woman, Ka Karaitiana, was employed as cook and dormitory overseer (matron).

The last few weeks before the opening were hectic. On Monday, 10 March, for example, Johnson recorded hanging blinds and oiling floors in the dormitories while the paperhanger worked around him. At the end of that week, the Johnson and Allred families moved into the newly completed four-bedroom faculty home. Goddard cabled that a piano had been shipped from San Francisco, and a few days later the agricultural implements arrived after being transhipped from Auckland. Johnson sent off a letter to all former presidents of the New Zealand Mission, asking each for the gift of a photograph of himself plus £1 to pay for framing. "This had a double purpose," explained Johnson, "first, to perpetuate the memory of the men who had done so much for the New Zealand Mission and for the Maori people and secondly to furnish wall decorations for the College."[14]

In the last week of March, Elder Ottley and two other missionaries, one of whom was the mission president's son, Melbourne Romney, were drafted to oil floors and erect beds. Parties of visitors from Hastings and Napier, including many influential Maori, visited the college and were shown through. There was a last-minute hitch when the toilets failed to flush satisfactorily but the plumber hastily returned to the building site and rectified the problem.

When the mail steamer from San Francisco arrived in Wellington on 27 March 1913, President Romney was at the wharf to meet it, hoping that it had brought both an apostle to dedicate the new school and the expected piano. "The President found neither apostle nor piano and was naturally somewhat disappointed," wrote Johnson.[15] However, nothing could dampen the excitement that mounted steadily as the time approached for the hui tau and college opening.

---

14. Johnson, Journal, 20 March 1913.
15. Ibid., 27 March 1913.

Although the conference was not scheduled to begin until Friday, 4 April 1913, parties of visitors began arriving in Korongata as early as Monday, 31 March. "[The] scene was indeed a lively one, automobiles and drays arriving every few minutes from the Hasting's [sic] station loaded with visitors for the hui," wrote the mission clerk.[16] More than two thousand Saints, friends and elders assembled, and everyone wanted to view the college buildings. Johnson conducted nonstop tours while traditional Maori welcome ceremonies went on outside. Each evening, dances were held in the assembly hall to raise money for the school, and conference sessions convened, beginning on Friday.

On Sunday, 6 April 1913, hundreds of European visitors came from Hastings and nearby towns to join the conference crowd at the dedication of the LDS Maori Agricultural College. Despite cold and bleak weather, the ceremony was held outdoors to accommodate the numbers present. An improvised speakers' rostrum was set up on the American farm wagon donated by the International Harvester Company. Johnson was amused to see the amount of interest aroused by the wagon, a novelty in New Zealand. A missionary quartet and the Korongata Branch choir sang, John Johnson spoke on "The Educational Spirit of the Latter-day Saints," and President Orson D. Romney offered the dedicatory prayer.

Throughout the afternoon, the buildings were crowded as long lines of visitors passed through, inspecting the new facilities. Johnson personally escorted Lady Carroll, wife of the former Minister of Native Affairs, Sir James Carroll, on a tour of the college. "She was delighted by what she saw and heard," he wrote, "and was full of praise for our people and what they are doing for her native race." At the end of her inspection, Lady Carroll made a generous donation to the college funds.[17]

The occasion brought the Church favourable notice in New Zealand as the press reported the dedication of the new college. "They [the Mormons] make the Maori a cleaner, more sober, more self-respecting man, and they are setting out to make him a more industrious man," wrote a reporter from the Christchurch *Evening News*. "... The Mormons at Salt Lake made a garden out of a wilderness. In New Zealand they find the garden, and see its Maori possessor letting it become a wilderness. So, having made him steady and sober, they proceed to make him industrious and skillful in the utilization of those portions of his heritage that remain to him.... It is rather a reflection that the first Maori agricultural college

---

16. New Zealand Mission, Manuscript History, 31 March 1913.
17. John Johnson, "Dedication of the Maori Agricultural College," *Millennial Star* 75, no. 24 (12 June 1913): 369–73.

"... you are some of Hagoth's people and there is no pea about it"   127

The Maori Agricultural College on dedication day, 6 April 1913. The dormitory building is to the right, the assembly hall (chapel cum classrooms) on the left. Courtesy Harold B. Lee Library, Brigham Young University, Provo, Utah.

should be established by a people alien to New Zealand in faith and in nationality, and with money brought from without the Dominion."[18]

On the following day, the non-LDS Maori chiefs present called a meeting to raise funds for the new school, and £523 ($2,500) was donated, with more promised. These donations were greatly appreciated, as the extras, such as the faculty home and classroom block and taking up the option on the additional land, eventually brought the total cost to about £18,000 ($90,000). Hay and Son had originally submitted a tender of £9,351, revised to £10,150 to include several extras (hot water service, gas plant, well, pump, and mill). Thanks to their diligence and President Romney's careful supervision, the buildings were constructed within this estimate.[19] It was the additional buildings that exceeded the budget; however, they were all constructed with First Presidency permission.

---

18. Reprinted as "The Mormon and the Maori," *The Messenger* 7, no. 10 (7 May 1913): 109–11.

19. "A Tribute to President Romney," *The Messenger* 8, no. 6 (25 March 1914), 69; New Zealand Mission, Minutes, 20 October 1911, 198–99. Although President Hoagland had originally suggested the sum of $15,000 to the First Presidency in 1906, President Romney had estimated £8,500 (about $40,000) in mid-1910, but felt Hay's tender was reasonable in view of at least 10 percent inflation in the intervening time.

It had always been understood that the school must be self-sustaining once the Church paid the initial construction costs. For the last few years, most of the land had been leased to the Thompson Brothers for £141 per year, money that went into the college building fund. Now the farm was to be worked as the practical component of the agronomy course and was expected to produce sufficient revenue to cover additional expenses. But already drought was causing Johnson to be cautious. "Of course it will be some time before the Institution can hope to be self-supporting," he wrote in April 1913, the very month the college opened.[20]

Thirty-five students and four teachers (John Johnson, Eva Johnson, Allred, and Ottley) were present on Monday, 14 April, when school formally commenced. During the week, farm machinery, the piano, and a typewriter arrived, and the first school assembly was held. A college Sunday School was organised, with faculty members presiding and teaching, but with students installed as "assistants" to receive training in church leadership. The student body and faculty attended sacrament meeting at the pa. One week later, there were forty pupils with more expected. From the beginning, all classes as well as Sunday School and other meetings were conducted in English.

In May, Allred prepared to sow seventy-five acres with oats. The American walking ploughs that had been donated by American firms proved quite inadequate to cope with the pumice subsoil, and local teams were hired to do the work, making the farm unprofitable from the beginning. The classrooms were bitterly cold by May, and it was becoming more and more apparent that the school could not function with such a small staff. Johnson had to make frequent business visits to Hastings to purchase food, stationery, and other supplies, leaving Allred to cover his classes as well as his own, an impossible situation. Another full-time missionary, Elder Samuel Morgan, was transferred from the LDS primary school in Porirua in June, and history and geography classes were added to the timetable. Although the Mission Board of Education had decided that New Zealand textbooks should be used in the college, a meeting of the all-American faculty decided to adopt American texts for the following year, which they persisted in calling the "1914–15" school year, despite the fact that the New Zealand academic year was (and is) fully contained in one calendar year.

---

20. Prof. Jno. Johnson, "Annual Conference of the New Zealand Mission; Dedication of Maori Agricultural College," *The Messenger* 7, no. 9 (23 April 1913): 107.

Soon after the college opened, six wealthy and influential Maori Latter-day Saints left New Zealand to visit Utah. Like converts worldwide, they longed to see "Zion" and receive their temple blessings. They also wanted to see for themselves whether conditions in Utah would be suitable for Maori emigration. Stuart Meha, Luxford Peeti, Wiremu and Takare Duncan, and Takarei and Ema Ihaia sailed on the *Niagara* in May 1913. After disembarking in Vancouver, Stuart Meha telegraphed news of their arrival to Benjamin Goddard before they began the overland leg of their journey to Utah. In his telegram, Meha said, "Who knows but that some of Hagoth's people have arrived, pea [perhaps]."[21] Zion's Maori Association organised a royal reception for them in Salt Lake City, where the First Presidency hosted a banquet in their honour on 3 June 1913. Other guests were members of the Quorum of the Twelve, Utah's governor William Spry, most of the former presidents, and many former missionaries of the New Zealand Mission. Benjamin Goddard was master of ceremonies. Both Governor Spry and President Joseph F. Smith gave welcoming addresses.

In his speech, President Smith related his experience as a very young missionary in Hawaii almost sixty years earlier. At that time, he said, when landing on the island of Hawaii, he had been impressed with the idea that the passage in the Book of Mormon that referred to the "sailing away" of Hagoth's ship was an evidence that the Polynesian people originated on the American continent. "He found on the beach at Hawaii, great saw[n] timbers which had been driven from the mouth of the Columbia River or other points along the west coast of America, by sea currents and winds, directly to the shores of Hawaii, and it is very probable, he said, that Hagoth's ship, which never returned, may have followed the currents likewise to the Pacific Islands."[22] Smith then quoted Meha's telegram and commented: "[You] brethren and sisters from New Zealand, I want you to know that you are some of Hagoth's people, and there is no pea about it."[23]

From the time the first European ships sailed into the Pacific Ocean, scholars have debated the origins of the Polynesian people. One prevalent theory was that they were descended from the Israelites, a belief supported by explorers and early Church of England missionaries such as Samuel Marsden. Their Maori converts to Christianity widely accepted this view. Later, scientists propounded three different theories—that the Polynesian

---

21. Stuart Meha, "A Request Talk for Sunday Evening the 15th April, 1962," 5.
22. "Reception for Visiting Maoris," *Deseret Evening News*, 4 June 1913, in Journal History, 3 June 1913, 2.
23. Meha, " Request Talk"; Tetuati [Stuart] Meha, Waiapa, Letter to Francis W. Kirkham, 14 March 1961.

The six visiting Maori Saints at the Salt Lake Temple, 1913, pictured with the three resident Maori (the widowed Mere Whaanga, and Tamihana and Waitokorau Te Awe Awe). Courtesy LDS Church History Library.

people had originated in the Pacific; that they had come from Asia, migrating from west to east; or that they came from the west coast of the American continent (east to west migration).

Brigham Young taught as early as 1858 that the Polynesians were of Israelitish origin; and in 1865, in a letter to King Kamehameha V of Hawaii, he specifically linked them with the Book of Mormon.[24] As has been shown, from 1881 the Mormon missionaries to New Zealand taught that the Maori were descendants of Lehi. (See chaps. 1–2.) It is not known how early others, including Church leaders, adopted the young Joseph F. Smith's idea that the Polynesians were specifically descendants of Hagoth and his people, who according to the Book of Mormon sailed away about 55 B.C. and did not return (Alma 63:5–8). But this belief was certainly current among the American missionaries in New Zealand by 1894.[25] Now, in 1913, when a

---

24. Brigham Young, quoted in Norman Douglas, "The Sons of Lehi and the Seed of Cain: Racial Myths in Mormon Scripture and Their Relevance to the Pacific Islands," 96.

25. For example, see Phoenix (pseud. of Benjamin Goddard), "In Maoridom,"

"... you are some of Hagoth's people and there is no pea about it"   131

Maori Saint again suggested the idea, Joseph F. Smith, sustained as prophet, seer, and revelator and president of the Church twelve years earlier, confirmed it. Although it has never been acknowledged as official doctrine of the LDS Church, several other Church presidents and General Authorities have since made similar semi-official statements, and the Maori Latter-day Saints widely accept Hagoth's people as their ancestors.[26]

The Maori party visited Brigham Young University at Provo and the Utah Agricultural College at Logan. BYU president George Brimhall invited them to send some Maori students to BYU to train as teachers for the Maori Agricultural College. Returned missionaries wrote to President Romney in New Zealand, reporting increased interest in the New Zealand Mission generated by the visitors and the good accomplished by their presence in Utah.[27] The travellers arrived back in New Zealand in November and were soon in demand as speakers to report on their journey.

In December 1913, veteran New Zealand missionary William Gardner arrived for a second term as mission president. He and President Romney visited the MAC at Korongata together. Several improvements had been made during the school's first year. Teachers and students together had built a greenhouse, pig-sty, and fowl-house. A garden competition had been instituted, and four acres of previously uncultivated land behind the college were ploughed, divided into individual plots, and turned over to the boys, who planted vegetables and melons. The grain crop was flourishing, and the Hui Atawhai (Relief Society) of Korongata had presented the college with a beautiful bell.

Deseret News, 13 October 1894, 516–17.

26. For a fuller discussion of Mormon teachings on Maori origins, see Marjorie Newton, "Mormonism in New Zealand: A Historical Appraisal," chap. 8. More recent scholarship has seen extensive discussion about DNA and Native American origins, which, while not relevant to the search for Polynesian origins *per se*, must carry over by implication if the Polynesians are recognised by Mormons as descendants of Lehi. For the implications of DNA research on American Indian and Polynesian origins, see Simon Southerton, *Losing a Lost Tribe: Native Americans, DNA, and the Mormon Church*. More recently the work of Simon Ho at the Universities of Sydney and Oxford has cast significant doubt on the DNA dating methods cited by Southerton and others. See Chris Rodley, "Time Lord: The Work of 25-Year-Old Researcher Simon Ho Is Overturning Established Ideas about the Pace of Evolution and Human Development," *Sydney Alumni Magazine*, Winter 2006, 10–11, and "Revolutionary Thinking on Evolution Forces Rethink on Species," *Sydney Morning Herald*, 29–30 June 2006. See also Jeff Meldrum and Trent D. Stephens, *Who Are the Children of Lehi? DNA and the Book of Mormon*, carefully outlining questions that DNA can answer but also its limitations.

27. "Mission Notes," *The Messenger* 7, no. 17 (13 August 1913): 198–99.

Walter Smith, one of Hirini Whaanga's grandchildren who had gone to Utah in 1894, had exceptional musical talent and played several instruments. He married Ida Mae Haley in Salt Lake City in 1910. Both Walter and Ida were called as missionaries to teach at the MAC and arrived in New Zealand in November 1913. Ida was not a Latter-day Saint and thus was perhaps the only woman ever to be called on an LDS mission while not a member of the Church. President Romney also assigned Reuben and Della Murdock, a missionary couple who arrived in New Zealand in July 1913, to teach at the college for the 1914 school year. Johnson was instructed to add rooms to the faculty home to accommodate the Murdocks and Smiths.

After the 1913 school year finished in December, Principal Johnson accompanied the two mission presidents and Walter Smith to a Christmas hui at Nuhaka, Smith's former home. "Have attended many tangis in Maoriland but none just like this one held in honor of the return of Walter Smith to his people after an absence in America for twenty years," wrote Johnson. "The meeting with his mother, his father, brothers and sisters was the most pathetic scene I had ever witnessed.... It is the only tangi at which I have really cried."[28] There was further rejoicing next day when Ida Smith was baptized.

During subsequent conference sessions, the first Primary in New Zealand was organised for the children of the Nuhaka Branch, with Sister Bessie Greening as president.[29] Also present were the four Maori men—Stuart Meha, Wi Duncan, Luxford Peeti, and Takarei Ihaia—who had recently visited Utah and who had now been called to serve as home missionaries. Because of their first-hand knowledge, they were given the special responsibility of helping the American elders correct false impressions held by many "outsiders" about Mormonism in Utah.[30]

The idea of a Maori gathering to Utah was still talked of from time to time; and Meha, Duncan, Peeti, and Ihaia had done some serious investigation into social and economic conditions there. They came home convinced that the Maori Saints should remain in New Zealand. Meha in particular was conscious that the Maori people lacked sufficient education to compete successfully in America, where no special government department would look after their interests as in New Zealand. He also thought that the Utah climate would not suit the Maori and returned with a new appreciation of his native land's beauty. The Maori party had been amused to find that a flock of 3,000 sheep made a man a great sheep farmer in

---

28. Johnson, Journal, 24 December 1913.
29. New Zealand Mission, Manuscript History, 28 December 1913.
30. "Mission Notes," *The Messenger* 7, no. 24 (19 November 1913): 283.

Utah.³¹ The four, already leaders of the Mormon Maori community before their overseas trip, gained even more mana afterwards. They were soon dubbed "the Yankee Maoris" or "American Maoris" and their home missionary work spread their influence throughout the mission.³²

Charles Hardy, the longest-serving European branch president in the New Zealand Mission, died at his Mount Albert home in January 1914.³³ Hardy, age eighty-two, had been president of the Auckland Branch for twenty-four years, giving unfailing support to successive mission presidents throughout this period. He wrote voluminously on gospel subjects, and his competently crafted verses were often featured in the pages of *The Messenger*. He loved and studied the Maori people, convinced that they were descendants of Lehi's family in the Book of Mormon. He left his large and important collection of works on Maori ethnography to the library of the Maori Agricultural College.

The 1914 college year began on Monday, 16 February, with twice the initial enrolment of the first year. More beds and desks were ordered. By the end of the week, sixty-five young men were enrolled, and ten registered at the April hui tau. Johnson decided that the dormitory bedrooms would have to hold three and even four beds instead of two. Another shipment of agricultural implements arrived from the United States—ploughs, a harrow, two incubators, and a white-top buggy.³⁴ On 11 February, two eighteen-year-old youths from Samoa, Earl Francis and Albert ("Max") Schwenke, arrived to attend the MAC. Schwenke's elder brother had distinguished himself at Brigham Young University in Provo a few years earlier. They were the first of numerous Pacific Island students to attend the MAC. Johnson assigned them a room, and then found that they were penniless, believing they could easily earn the money for their college fees. They had only tropical clothing, another worry for Johnson, who realized how inadequate it would be in the coming winter. Both young men stayed and became prized pupils of the college.

At the end of April 1914, fifteen brass instruments were purchased for the college, and a band was organised on 10 May. Just three weeks later, Walter Smith led the brass band in its first performance—a spirited rendition of "God Save the King" on the King's Birthday holiday, 2 June. By

---

31. "Impressions of Utah," reprinted from the *Dannevirke Evening News*, 12 November 1913, in *The Messenger* 7, no. 26 (17 December 1913): 309–11.

32. "Mission Notes," *The Messenger* 8, no. 2 (28 January 1914): 19, and "The Past Three Months in and around the M.A.C.," ibid., 20; James Needham Lambert, Journals, 1916–19, 27 January 1918, 440.

33. "A Death," *The Messenger* 8, no. 2 (28 January 1914): 19–20.

34. "College Activities," *The Messenger* 8, no. 6 (25 March 1914): 68.

now there were eighty boys enrolled. Smith composed a school song, "Our Good Old MAC" (later used, with words adapted, by the Church College of New Zealand), while his wife, Ida, stitched a striking blue and white banner for the college.

President Gardner spent the King's Birthday holiday at the college and attended a Board of Education meeting the next day. The board decided to buy a circular saw and more sheep and to install an engine for the windmill that provided water for the college. The board also decided to write to the First Presidency and request the purchase of the additional 130 acres for which the Church held an option. Permission for the purchase was received on 21 August 1914, and negotiations were completed on 18 September.[35]

World War I began on 4 August 1914. Patriotic concerts and parades were held in most New Zealand towns and cities, and the MAC students marched in a parade through Hastings on the last Saturday of August, led by their own brass band.[36] As the months went by, the band also played at farewells to local servicemen and at other patriotic functions.

Although non-Mormon boys enrolled at the college were not required to attend "theology" classes, most did, and three were baptized in October 1914. On 15 November, Johnson baptized another, Niki Paewai, who would become a leader in both Maori and Mormon affairs. "He had taken my class in theology and had manifested much interest from the beginning," wrote Johnson. "I was very glad to see him become a member of the Church."[37] A few days later, on 22 November 1914, the school was rocked by a severe earthquake, though it was not damaged. However, only five days later, the faculty home (built of timber) was gutted by fire. After hearing of this disaster by cable, the First Presidency authorised immediate rebuilding.

Just two days before the fire, a new principal, A. Royal W. Hintze, arrived with his wife, Jessie, and three-year-old daughter, Mildred. They landed in New Zealand on 23 November with a party of new missionaries, one of whom was seventeen-year-old Matthew Cowley, son of Apostle Matthias Cowley.[38] The Hintzes, escorted by President Gardner, travelled straight to Korongata, while Elder Cowley was assigned to Tauranga, in

---

35. New Zealand Mission, Manuscript History, 3 June, 21 August, and 18 September 1914.

36. Johnson, Journal, 29 August 1914.

37. Ibid., 15 November 1914.

38. Apostles Matthias Cowley and John W. Taylor had resigned from the Quorum of the Twelve in 1905 over their continuing support of plural marriage.

"... you are some of Hagoth's people and there is no pea about it"   135

The MAC Band marches in a patriotic parade in Hastings, August 1914.

the Hauraki District. The fire had cast gloom over the college community, and the Hintzes must have had a disappointing introduction to the school.

End-of-year activities at the college included annual examinations, complicated by harvesting a crop depleted by drought. Farm profits were further eroded when an unseasonable frost killed most of the vegetable garden. "Commencement week" (an American term which puzzled New Zealanders, as it was held at the end of the school year, not the beginning) began on 7 December, and featured a concert, an exhibition of the boys' work, a sports day, and an end-of-year dance as well as what in other New Zealand schools would have been called Speech Day. Hastings draper Matt Johnson presented a gold medal to the best student, James Elkington of French Pass. The students prepared a farewell banquet in honour of the Johnsons; and on 11 December 1914, the school broke up for the Christmas summer vacation.

The college military band toured the North Island during the holidays, with the double aim of advertising the college and raising funds for Belgian relief work and for comforts for the Maori contingent at the front. After only six months, the band had apparently achieved considerable facility. Elder Sidney J. Ottley (later the father of Mormon Tabernacle Choir conductor Jerold Ottley), described it as "the pippingest little band in New Zealand."[39] Walter Smith was a born musician and teacher, proficient on

---

39. Sidney J. Ottley, Oral History, interviewed by Kenneth W. Baldridge, 10

many instruments and a virtuoso on the guitar and mandolin. Under his direction, the college music program blossomed; the students revelled in the military band, string band, choir and glee club, and the band's reputation spread. During his twenty years in the United States, Smith had not only developed his natural musical talents but had learned a good deal of American showmanship. Crippled with rheumatism (probably rheumatic fever) during his youth, he turned his disability to advantage when, dressed in a ceremonial uniform of white trousers and a blue satin tunic, Smith, on horseback, led the marching band.

Involving at least seventeen concerts in twelve North Island centres, the tour began at Dannevirke and circled through Palmerston North and Wanganui to Hamilton, thence to Rotorua, north to Thames and on to Auckland, finishing at Whangarei. Travel was by train, bus, and steamer. Concerts were advertised ahead in each town, and the band paraded down each main street, playing rousing marches that attracted spectators, many of whom followed them to the concert venue. However, to the disappointment of mission and school authorities, the band tour was a financial failure as local papers published identical letters, purportedly from ministers in each town, warning people to stay away because the profits from ticket sales would be used to propagate Mormonism. Johnson sent letters of correction to these papers, which refused to print them.[40]

School fees were increased from £12 to £16 for the 1915 school year. The new school principal, Royal Hintze, was determined that the college standard would be above that of the "common schools" (primary schools) and recommended that all prospective students who had access to government primary schools attend them before coming to the MAC. For those from isolated areas lacking primary schools, the MAC offered a course equivalent to the fifth standard in public schools, as well as the four-year high school course.[41] After a few disastrous experiences with students who, entrusted with their tuition money and travelling expenses, managed to spend most of it en route from home to college, Hintze asked parents to forward the school fees directly to the college by registered post.

A remarkable and much-loved Maori woman died on 17 September 1915. Harata Hall, wife of David Hall of Huria (Judea), Tauranga, had been baptized during President Gardner's first mission and had been a "Maori mother" to many missionaries during the ensuing years. She had served as branch Relief Society president since its organisation and was a

---

August 1972, 2.

40. Johnson, Journal, 15–20 December 1914.

41. "College Notice," *The Messenger* 9, no. 4 (24 February 1915): 45–46.

stout defender of the Mormon faith. "[She] had unusual ability as a leader; and her advice was not only sought after by women, but by the men folks also," wrote Elder W. J. Olpin. "The elders and all who met, or even had been associated with her, have all learned to love her on account of her desire to live a good life and help others to do the same."[42]

Preliminary notices for the 1916 college year stressed that both fifth and sixth standard primary classes would be offered in addition to first, second, and third year high school work. There had been plentiful rain, and at last college crops were doing well. The lawns and flower beds around the buildings were at their best. The livestock was also doing well: there were horses, cows, pigs, seven hundred lambs, and hens that laid fifty to eighty eggs a day. The college sent a box of ten dozen eggs to mission headquarters in Auckland, and the office staff there inserted a note of thanks in *The Messenger*, with a special word to the hens: "Kia kahi i roto te mahi pai" (keep up the good work).[43]

In February 1916, missionary numbers were augmented by the arrival of four families: W. Frank and Annie Atkin and three children; Horace and Leona Holbrook and their four children; Lashbrook L. and Florence Cook and baby daughter Mabel; and Tamihana and Waitokorau Te Awe Awe, accompanied by their daughter Nora and granddaughter Ada. The Atkins family were sent first to the Bay of Islands; Cook, a farmer with a degree in agriculture, left immediately for the MAC; Tamihana and Waitokorau were sent to Palmerston North, and Dr. Holbrook was appointed to tour the southern part of the North Island, including the college.

President Gardner's seventieth birthday was celebrated with a party at mission headquarters on 22 May 1916. A week later, a new mission president, James Needham Lambert, his new wife, Edith, and his teenage children from his first marriage, Phyllis and Claude, arrived in Auckland on the *Niagara*. Together, President Gardner and the Lamberts set out on a mission tour, and President Gardner sailed for home six weeks later. Elder Matthew Cowley paid tribute to him in the columns of the Utah *Deseret Evening News*. He had been one of the first six Mormon missionaries to live among the Maori race, Cowley wrote. "President Gardner had an infinite love for the Maori people which caused his mind to be ever alive to their welfare and he was never ashamed to greet them with the customary rubbing noses even if it was on Queen Street in Auckland," Cowley

---

42. W. J. Olpin, "Passed to the Great Beyond," *The Messenger* 9, no. 21 (20 October 1915): 245.

43. "An Appreciated Gift," *The Messenger* 9, no. 24 (1 December 1915): 282; "To Parents and Students of M.A.C.," no. 25 (15 December 1915): 297; "College Notes," no. 26 (29 December 1915): 306.

Mission President James N. Lambert teaching his wife, Edith, to ride a bicycle in front of the mission home in Auckland, c. 1916. Courtesy LDS Church History Library.

continued. Despite his age, President Gardner had travelled over 50,000 miles during his second term as mission president.[44]

The Maori Agricultural College was, of course, of prime importance to the new mission president. President Lambert walked over the whole farm—266 acres—noting the use to which the land was put: thirteen acres for the actual college campus and faculty home; seventy acres sown with rape, seventy under grass, forty acres of lucerne, barley forty-five acres, and oats twenty-eight acres. "It's a beautiful tract of ground but for the last two seasons has not produced much because of a severe drought," Lambert noted. The six-mile distance from Hastings was ideal, Lambert thought. "—just far enough away so as to make it a little unhandy for the boys to go too often."[45]

Back in Auckland, President Lambert instituted renovations, extensions, and redecoration at the mission home. After some thought, he decided to move the print shop, presently located in the basement of the

---

44. Matt Cowley, "Tribute to President Gardner," *Deseret Evening News*, 7 October 1916, in Journal History, 7 October 1916, 4.

45. Lambert, Journal, 8 June 1916, 42.

Auckland chapel, to the MAC in Korongata, where some of the students could gain experience in the production of *Te Karere* and the mission's various tracts. The move took place in August 1916, and the paper was edited from the college for the next fifteen years.

Construction of the LDS temple at Laie, Hawaii, was nearing completion, and plans were being made for its dedication. It was the first temple outside mainland North America and the first for the Polynesian people. New Zealand Mission members were keenly interested in its progress, and President Lambert wanted to escort a party of Maori Saints to its dedication and the subsequent celebrations. He wrote to President Joseph F. Smith and Presiding Bishop Charles W. Nibley suggesting this plan, and inviting either or both men to visit the New Zealand Mission after the temple dedication.[46]

The war in Europe was beginning to affect missionary work. President Lambert recorded a train journey from Hastings to Palmerston North in July 1916. "All along the line the soldiers (which amounted to about half the passengers on board) were greeted by the children and bands at nearly every station." The soldiers were due to sail in a few days, the nineteenth contingent since the outbreak of war in 1914. In September, Lambert visited the New Zealand Army training facilities at Featherston in the Wairarapa. "Was quite surprised at the greatness of things around the camp," he wrote in his journal. "Cavalry, infantry, artillery, all here going through their maneuvers (manoeuvres). Nine thousand men now being trained and up to date nearly 70,000 have gone from New Zealand. About fifteen hundred Maoris have gone and a few hundred are in training. . . . The whole of the country for miles around has been confiscated by the government. A regular city with stores or shops as they are called has now sprung up."[47]

The New Zealand Saints, of course, were much more deeply involved in the war effort and the fortunes of the Allies than were the American missionaries and mission president. In 1918, fifty-eight New Zealand servicemen serving overseas with the Expeditionary Forces identified themselves as Mormon.[48] Several families, Maori and Pakeha, lost sons at Gallipoli. When Percy and Gertrude Going's son Stanley was killed in action in France in September 1916, the whole mission grieved with them. The Goings, one of the earliest Pakeha families to join the LDS Church in the Bay of Islands district, were successful dairy farmers at Maromaku and

---

46. New Zealand Mission, Manuscript History, 16 July 1916.

47. Lambert, Journal, 24 July 1916, 63, and 1 September 1916, 80.

48. "Religion of Soldiers," *Auckland Star*, 18 September 1918. In comparison, 32,700 recorded their religion as Church of England.

much loved by everyone, Maori and Pakeha. President Lambert visited the Goings on 7 October. "They are heart-broken over their son's death," he reported. " ... He left New Zealand about the first of the year and has seen considerable fighting in the trenches. He was a fine Latter-day Saint and partook of the Going spirit."[49]

Parents of twelve children, Percy and Gertrude Going ran their dairy farm as a family operation. Every mission president and missionary spoke highly of them, and President Lambert was no exception. "This home is, I believe, the cleanest I was ever in and I don't think of any place where I saw love for each other like is shown here," he wrote during this visit to the Going home.[50] The Goings had planned to sell out and emigrate to the United States. One son had gone ahead, and was married and working on a farm in Idaho. Wartime restrictions and, after the war, new United States immigration laws prevented their dream becoming reality but providentially left a strong family in New Zealand to provide future leadership for the Mormon Church there.

Once again the question of a Maori gathering was discussed. Many of the Saints favoured a gathering site in New Zealand and wanted the Church to purchase land. After long discussion, Lambert and Wi Duncan agreed that the scheme was currently impracticable. Land prices were high and could be expected to increase. The government was "resuming" land (compulsorily repurchasing crown lands which had been sold) from large landowners, paying compensation below market price, sometimes as little as two-thirds what aggrieved owners claimed they paid for it, in preparation for soldier-settlement schemes after the war.[51]

Signs of war were everywhere, and even the Americans, whose nation was not yet involved, could no longer ignore them. "War, war, war is all that is discussed everywhere," wrote Lambert. "In some places little else is considered and Missionary work is almost at a standstill."[52] After Woodrow Wilson's "peace without victory" speech to the U.S. Senate, missionaries were frequently insulted and even threatened. "The whole of New Zealand are up in arms," Lambert recorded. He cautioned the missionaries to be discreet and to use wisdom in what they said and did in regard to the war and the international situation.[53]

President Lambert negotiated with John Hislop, Under Secretary of the Department of Internal Affairs, and Dr. Maui Pomare for permission

---

49. Lambert, Journal, 7 October 1916, 98.
50. Ibid. 7, 8 October 1916, 97–99.
51. Ibid., 2 September 1916, 81.
52. Ibid.
53. Ibid., 26 January 1917, 164.

for Maori Saints to attend the dedication of the Hawaii Temple. Pomare, as Minister for Native Affairs, gave verbal permission, and Hislop indicated that, if Pomare approved, there should be no problem. Benjamin Goddard cabled on 30 March 1917 to invite James and Edith Lambert and ten Maori Saints to the dedication. Lambert assigned missionary wife Annie Atkin to organise sewing bees with the Maori women who had been endowed in the Salt Lake Temple—Sisters Duncan, Ihaia, and Te Awe Awe. Together they made ten full sets of temple clothing and robes for the anticipated visit.[54]

Because of wartime conditions, household help was virtually impossible to find. Edith Lambert, whom the widowed mission president had married just before leaving America, gave birth to a son on 1 April 1917. Dozens of Saints travelling to and from the hui tau in Kaikohe called at the mission home in Auckland. As her stepmother was still recovering from her confinement, sixteen-year-old Phyllis Lambert had to do the housework and cook meals (with missionary help) for forty to fifty people each day. "It was quite an experience for Phyllis," her father commented blandly.[55]

Anti-American feeling in New Zealand subsided somewhat when the United States entered the war on 6 April 1917. President Lambert reported that conversation on board an inter-island ship was all on the war. "One cannot disguise the fact that he is an American especially if he talks," he wrote. Still, a new problem presented itself: Since "the first [American] contingent has arrived in Europe we are, as a Nation looked up to." But "as Elders . . . [are] look[ed] on as able-bodied men who ought to go to War, we are *persona non grata*."[56] Dominion newspapers reprinted anti-Mormon articles from the English press; and the venom in some, such as those by apostate Hans P. Freece, affected Mormon-government relations in New Zealand and Australia. Pomare warned Lambert of growing hostility to the Mormons among cabinet members, including some suspicion about the plan to take Maori Saints to Hawaii for the temple dedication.[57] However, as the temple's construction was running behind schedule, this particular problem was not urgent.

President Lambert cultivated relations with the American consul, Alfred A. Winslow. As the Mormon missionaries accounted for about two-fifths of the American citizens in New Zealand, Winslow was well aware of the mission and its work. When the consul presented Lambert with a

---

54. Annie M. Atkin, New Zealand Mission Journal, 14, 16, 22 May 1917, 41, in William Frank Atkin, Papers.
55. Lambert, Journal, 10, 11, 12 April 1917, 217–18.
56. Ibid., 24 May 1917, 243.
57. Ibid., 25 May 1917, 244.

picture of President Wilson, Lambert bought a picture of King George V and had both portraits framed to hang in the dining room at the college.[58]

All of President Lambert's previous troubles faded into insignificance when the *Niagara* docked on 25 June 1917. He waited on the wharf for some time before he learned that the eight new missionaries he had come to meet had been off-loaded in Honolulu. As none of the eight had a New Zealand visa, the Union Steamship Company had refused to carry them further. Lambert cabled President Joseph F. Smith to ask if the missionaries would arrive on the next boat. Unknown to Lambert, the First Presidency had been aware of the situation since early June, when the British consul in Portland, Oregon, refused to issue visas to the eight New Zealand-bound missionaries.

Apostle Reed Smoot of Utah, whose election to the Senate in 1903 had sparked a protracted Senate subcommittee hearing involving polygamy, was now chairman of the powerful Senate Finance Committee in Washington, and the First Presidency enlisted his help as early as 2 June. Smoot contacted Sir Cecil Spring-Rice, then serving as British ambassador in Washington, who explained that the visas were refused at the request of the New Zealand government. Smoot reported the situation to the U.S. Secretary of State, adding that the British government had received identical requests from the governments of Australia and South Africa.[59]

Unable to get information anywhere else, President Lambert in New Zealand called at the offices of the Union Steamship Company on 13 July where a clerk told him that, by government order, no more Mormons would be admitted to New Zealand. Thunderstruck, Lambert finally reached W. B. Montgomery, public service head of customs, who confirmed the information but could not or would not tell Lambert whether the ban was the result of a new law, a cabinet order, or simply a ruling by a civil service department head. President Lambert tried to reach John Hislop, Under Secretary for Internal Affairs, and Dr. Maui Pomare, Minister for Native Affairs, but both had left their offices for the weekend. Lambert was almost frantic. "Thoughts rushed through my mind as to the consequences and I could picture the Elders who were here staying indefinitely," he wrote, noting ruefully in his journal that it was Friday the 13th.[60]

Meanwhile, as a result of President Lambert's representations, Alfred A. Winslow, the American consul in Auckland, wrote twice to New

---

58. Ibid., 2, 29 June 1917, 248, 266.

59. Reed Smoot, Letter to Secretary of State, 9 October 1917, in U.S. Department of State, Diplomatic Correspondence on Mormons and Mormonism, 1910–40.

60. Lambert, Journal, 13 July 1917, 276.

"... you are some of Hagoth's people and there is no pea about it" 143

Zealand's Prime Minister William Massey asking if any Americans were being discriminated against by New Zealand immigration policies. Massey assured Winslow that no Americans were being discriminated against. If they held U.S. passports (duly visaed) they would be admitted to the Dominion; but, of course, the problem was that they could not obtain visas. Massey told Winslow that the Mormons were guilty of "inoculating" people with their beliefs; rumours had reached his department that they were also guilty of inducing women to go to Utah; accordingly, they were not wanted in New Zealand. "I told Mr. Winslow we certainly were guilty of the first charge, that of preaching the gospel," wrote Lambert, "but denied *in toto* the latter charge."[61]

At Winslow's request, President Lambert wrote a lengthy letter to the consul, outlining the history of the New Zealand Mission and the MAC, for Winslow to use on his behalf. He forwarded a copy to Senator Smoot and sent Winslow a copy of Massey's letter.[62] Lambert was heavy-hearted. "I realised this was the result of an agitation started some time ago by the Ministerial Association," he wrote, "under cover, of course, due to our activity in preaching the Gospel. The devil seems to have the upper hand now, but not for long[,] it is hoped."[63]

For several months, letters and telegrams went back and forth between Auckland, Wellington, Salt Lake City, Washington, and London. Spring-Rice told Smoot towards the end of July that he had been advised that the measure was a temporary one, a result of wartime conditions.[64] This claim was viewed with some skepticism in government circles in Washington, as indicated by a confidential memorandum addressed to "Mr. Secretary" (presumably the Secretary of State) in which, after discussing the situation, the unidentified correspondent speculated "that the war may have been taken merely as an excuse for the exclusion of Mormon missionaries from NZ."[65]

While Smoot fought the battle against Mormon exclusion on the Washington front, President Lambert pursued the matter in New Zealand. In mid-August 1917, he was told that the government, far from allowing

---

61. Ibid., 11 August 1917, 293.
62. Ibid.; James N. Lambert, Letter to Senator Reed Smoot, 13 August 1917, in Diplomatic Correspondence on Mormons and Mormonism.
63. Lambert, Journal, 11 August 1917, 293.
64. Cecil Spring-Rice, Letter to Senator Reed Smoot, 24 July 1917, in Diplomatic Correspondence on Mormons and Mormonism.
65. U.S. Department of State, Bureau of Citizenship, Confidential Memorandum addressed "Mr. Secretary" and signed R.W.F., 16 October 1917, in Diplomatic Correspondence on Mormons and Mormonism.

more missionaries entrance, was considering deporting even missionaries already in New Zealand.[66] He called on every Auckland businessman he knew—including his barber, chemist, stationer, and the "candy merchant"—soliciting references. Armed with these letters, Lambert travelled to Wellington where, with the help of the American consul, he obtained an appointment with Prime Minister Massey on 17 August 1917. He was given just twelve minutes to state his case. Massey, who had been acquainted with Charles Hardy years before, promised to read the references Lambert brought and take the matter up in cabinet.[67]

In a second interview two weeks later, the Prime Minister intimated that a mistake had been made somewhere. "I think you people have been misunderstood," he told Lambert.[68] On 26 September, Massey wrote to President Lambert saying that six of the eight previously prohibited missionaries would be admitted. Lambert was not satisfied; by this time, more missionaries were due for release and numbers would be seriously depleted if they left. He needed assurance that more than these six could come. He spoke to Winslow, and together he and the consul decided to make another appeal to Massey and, at the same time, place the matter in the hands of the State Department in America.[69]

In December 1917, the New Zealand government decided to deport Elder Leslie A. Peel on the grounds that he had been making a house-to-house canvass in Wellington, allegedly for the purpose of raising money. "This line of action is resented by Government," stated the Minister of Internal Affairs, the Hon. G. W. Russell, in a letter to Winslow. Winslow immediately reported the case to the Secretary of State in Washington, and by mid-January he had received a letter from Massey admitting that the government did not have power to deport anyone without exceptional cause.[70] President Lambert followed up by visiting Russell and Under-Secretary John Hislop in Wellington on 21 January 1918.

Russell insinuated that the missionaries had sinister motives for tracting in the mornings between nine and twelve, when most women were alone in their homes. President Lambert asked hotly how many men would be home if they tracted in the afternoons, or even at night, and

---

66. John Shaw Welch, Journals, 1917–20, 15 August 1917, 1:150.
67. Lambert, Journal, 17 August 1917, 302.
68. Ibid., 31 August 1917, 313.
69. Ibid., 3, 4 October 1917, 344–45; New Zealand Mission, Manuscript History, 3, 4 October 1917.
70. G. W. Russell, Letter to American Consul-General, 3 January 1918, copied into New Zealand Mission, Manuscript History; see also New Zealand Mission, Manuscript History, 17 December 1917, 19 January 1918.

pointed out that most New Zealand men belonged to lodges or found other reasons for being out in the evenings. "Would it not be said that under cover of darkness we were doing our tracting?" he asked Russell. Russell refused to increase the total number of missionaries but reluctantly agreed that some of the missionaries who were returning home could be replaced. "The Minister was very narrow in many of his views," commented the mission clerk.[71]

There were seventy-five missionaries in New Zealand on 1 May 1917, but only fifty-nine by January 1918. Of these, three, including President Lambert himself, were attached to the Auckland office; six were teaching at the MAC, two were working on its farm, and two more were producing the mission paper. Of the remainder, seventeen were engaged in European work and twenty-nine were working among the Maori people.[72]

President Lambert enlisted the help of a prominent businessman, J. R. Hetherington of Ngaruawahia. Although Hetherington was not a Mormon, his mother, who had died in 1917, had been a member of the Church for twenty years. Hetherington was quite willing to write to Massey and Russell, with both of whom he was well acquainted, on behalf of the Church. His intervention was successful; and Russell replied, stating that replacement elders would be allowed into New Zealand. Hetherington passed on the news and copies of the correspondence to the mission office. "This was indeed gratifying news and the very thing for which we had all been hoping and praying," wrote the mission clerk.[73] Hislop also wrote directly to Lambert, confirming that each time a Mormon missionary departed from New Zealand, the British ambassador at Washington would be authorised to visa the passport of another elder.[74] Although President Lambert rejoiced, the system was to prove unworkable owing to the time lag involved.

The movie *The Mormon Maid*, billed as a sensational exposé of Mormonism, was shown in Auckland cinemas in January 1918. President Lambert went to see it, concerned about its impact at such a sensitive stage of negotiations with the government. He concluded that its "bark was worse than its bite . . . not nearly as bad as some other anti-Mormon pictures

---

71. Lambert, Journal, 21 January 1918, 433; New Zealand Mission, Manuscript History, 21 January 1918.
72. New Zealand Mission, Manuscript History, 31 January 1918.
73. Ibid., 13 February 1918.
74. John Hislop, Under Secretary, Department of Interior, Wellington, Letter to Rev. James N. Lambert, President N.Z. Mission of the Church of Jesus Christ of L.D.S. [sic], 11 February 1918, copied in New Zealand Mission, Manuscript History, 28 February 1918.

produced here. Still "it is enough to stir up the prejudice of some people."[75] When the film was shown in Hastings later, the MAC staff and students went in a body. "The picture was so grossly untrue that it was absurd and nobody took it seriously," Principal John Welch recorded.[76]

Preparations for the 1918 school year continued. A new music teacher, Franklin E. Stott, arrived on 22 January to replace Walter Smith. Stott, a nephew of Benjamin Goddard's wife, came "highly recommended" and was accompanied by his wife, Ida, and three little daughters. A new matron, Esther Kenneth, was engaged. Esther had nursed Annie Atkin during the last stages of pregnancy in April 1917 and had delivered the baby when the doctor did not arrive in time. The two women became close friends, and Nurse Kenneth began reading the Book of Mormon. In July, she asked Frank Atkin to baptize her. "We think so much of Mrs. Kenneth and are so proud and happy that she understands the gospel as we teach it in the Church of Jesus Christ [of Latter-day Saints] and wants to be one of us," wrote Annie Atkin. ". . . I will not complain more that I am useless in the Mission, because I feel [G]od had a mission here for me even if I couldn't get out among the people or make a speech worthy of the name."[77] Esther Kenneth, a widow with two daughters (one still of school age), saw her appointment as matron of the Maori Agricultural College as an opportunity to earn money with which to go to Utah. Gertie Kenneth joined the boys in the MAC schoolrooms and made good progress.

The school year began on Monday, 11 February 1918. Welch instituted a term prize for the tidiest dormitory, making regular inspections to give marks. The competition pleased the boys and dormitory tidiness improved dramatically. An election for student body president, vice-president, and secretary proved popular, the positions being won by Mafeking Pere, John Shortland, and Jack Clarke respectively. After the election, the staff gave the boys a surprise party. Within a month, Lambert, on a routine visit, noted a marked improvement in cleanliness and discipline.[78] Earl Francis, one of the two original Samoan students, was still enrolled at the college, and two more students had arrived from Samoa. Now President Lambert received a message from the Samoan Mission president that another five boys were on their way to the school.

The declining number of missionaries fluent in te reo (the Maori language) worried President Lambert, and he encouraged the missionaries to

---

75. Lambert, Journal, 3 January 1918, 420.
76. Welch, Journal, Vol. 2, 9 March 1918.
77. Annie M. Atkin, Journal, 29 September 1917.
78. New Zealand Mission, Manuscript History, 7 March 1918.

study the language.[79] While it appears that a large majority of Maori could both understand and speak English by this time, there were fewer who could read it; and still a few, especially in remote areas, who could neither speak nor understand English. Even those who were fluent in English were more comfortable with Maori and appreciated the concern that motivated the missionaries to learn their language.

In November 1916, President Lambert wrote to the First Presidency advising that the Maori edition of the Book of Mormon was out of print and recommending that it be republished together with a first Maori edition of the Doctrine and Covenants and Pearl of Great Price.[80] Lambert called Matthew Cowley, the best Maori speaker among the missionaries, to work on the revision of the Book of Mormon with the help of Wi Duncan and Stuart Meha. Elder Cowley, a grandson of early Australian missionary William Hyde and son of Apostle Matthias Cowley, was particularly intrigued with the assignment, as the first Maori edition had been largely the work of his father's cousin, Ezra Foss Richards.[81] The trio altered about 2,500 verses in the course of revising the Book of Mormon, before beginning on the other scriptures after a cable from Joseph F. Smith at the end of March 1918 authorised the translation of the Doctrine and Covenants and Pearl of Great Price.[82] "With all this work before me ... you can expect me home sometime during the millennium," Cowley quipped to his parents.[83]

The 1918 hui tau was held at Kiri Kiri, the Maori village where William Gardner had emerged from his overnight ordeal after being lost in the bush some thirty years earlier. "Today it contains some of the best Saints in the Church," wrote Principal Welch, who escorted a party of college pupils to the conference, held from 5 to 9 April.[84] A surprise visitor at hui tau was Louis G. Hoagland, who arrived on the *Makura* on 23 March 1918 with a special assignment to collect and organise Maori genealogical work in preparation for the opening of the Hawaii Temple. Hoagland spent a year touring New Zealand. During the conference, he was sustained as a special travelling elder for genealogical work.

---

79. Lambert, Journal, 18 June 1916, 47.
80. New Zealand Mission, Manuscript History, 12 November 1916; Lambert, Journal, 25 November 1916, 128.
81. Matthew Cowley, Letter to Mrs. Laura Brossard [his sister], 30 October 1932, also reproduced in Henry A. Smith, *Matthew Cowley: Man of Faith*, between pp. 54 and 55.
82. New Zealand Mission, Manuscript History, 30 March 1918.
83. Matthew Cowley, Letter to his parents, 18 April 1918, quoted in Smith, *Matthew Cowley*, 57.
84. Welch, Journal, Vol. 2, 4 April 1918.

New Zealand Mission Relief Society Conference, held in the newly completed chapel at Kiri Kiri, Thames District, during the 1918 hui tau. Courtesy LDS Church History Library.

Missionaries of the Reorganized Church of Jesus Christ of Latter Day Saints, who had been working in Dunedin, now began work in the Hawkes Bay District. Their mission president, an Elder Savage (first name not recorded), visited the MAC at the end of January 1918, where he was entertained and invited to address the Saints at sacrament meeting in the pa. "After meeting we showed him round the College, fed him a very good dinner and in general treated him the best we knew how," wrote Welch.[85]

At the end of March, President Lambert reported that "Reorganite" elders were working in Auckland. After an LDS street meeting on the corner of Pitt Street and Karangahape Road on 31 March 1918, the RLDS missionaries read aloud what they claimed to be LDS temple covenants, then mockingly challenged Elder Matthew Cowley to display his temple undergarments to the crowd. "I regret very much the coming here of these people but I think the spirit of contention they have will hurt them and if we can only 'hold our heads' and preach our own gospel, I think we will win out," wrote Lambert.[86] Lambert was disgusted when a Reorganized Church missionary told a street crowd in Auckland that he, Lambert, had brought his second wife to New Zealand and was living with her there.

---

85. Ibid., 27 January 1918.
86. Lambert, Journal, 31 March 1918, 488.

This was perfectly true: they simply omitted to mention that his first wife had died some time before his marriage to Edith Hunter.[87]

Matthew Cowley's three-year-term, the normal length of a foreign-language mission, was completed in November 1917; but owing to the shortage of missionaries and his new translation assignment, he agreed to extend his mission by a year to work on the Maori edition of the Doctrine and Covenants.[88] For much of this time, he lived in the Duncan home where a room was dedicated for the purpose, and no one else was permitted to enter it. He fasted and prayed often, especially when the work bogged down. "Now when I read these books I marvel that I was the one that was supposed to have done the translating," he told his sister some dozen years later. "The language surpasses my own individual knowledge of it. This was the great experience of my life and it will always remind me that God can and will accomplish his purposes through the human mind."[89]

Reporting assignments given to him at the April 1918 hui tau to his parents, Cowley wrote, "Last but not least, I was appointed in company with Brothers William Takana [Duncan] and Tuati [Stuart] Meha to translate the Doctrine and Covenants and Pearl of Great Price in the Maori language, a work which has never before been attempted."[90] Perplexingly, he misstated the facts, since his was not the first translation of the Doctrine and Covenants into Maori. It had previously been translated by other missionaries and published, section by section, in *Te Karere* over eight years, beginning in 1908 during Rufus K. Hardy's first term as mission president. President Hardy planned to keep the typeset pages so that when the project was completed, the book could be printed and bound at relatively little extra expense.[91] Publication of newly translated sections continued until at least the end of 1915.[92] Thus, portions of a Maori translation of the Doctrine and Covenants were still appearing in each issue of the mission paper when Matthew Cowley arrived in the New Zealand Mission in 1914. Elder Cowley soon contributed at least one article to the English edition of the paper, and as a Maori-speaking missionary he could not have been unaware of the project. The only explanation that appears feasible is that the piecemeal translation which appeared in *Te Karere*, the work of many different missionaries, was not authorised by the First Presidency. Elder Cowley's version was undoubtedly the first authorised

---

87. Ibid., 16 June 1918, 546.
88. Cowley to Laura Brossard, 30 October 1932.
89. Ibid.
90. Cowley to parents, 18 April 1918.
91. New Zealand Mission, Manuscript History, 5 February 1908.
92. *Te Karere*, 26 February 1908–22 December 1915.

translation of the Doctrine and Covenants into Maori, and the first to be published as a book.[93]

Meanwhile, as World War I continued, a cadet corps was formed at the college in 1917, drilled by New Zealand army officers from Hastings.[94] By 1918, more than twenty ex-MAC students had enlisted in the Army, and many of these were serving overseas. By May 1918, American males between the ages of twenty-one and thirty-one who were resident overseas were required to register for the American draft. This provision applied to the Mormon missionaries in New Zealand, but Winslow assured President Lambert that, as ministers of religion, they would probably be exempted from call-up. Lambert refused to worry. He reasoned that the administrative procedures involved in notification, obtaining medical reports, and serving notice to return to the USA would take months; and the war, he hoped (correctly), was drawing to a close.

Dismayed by the £125 annual rates levied on the college campus and farm, Welch and mission secretary C. William Birkinshaw consulted a Hastings solicitor in August 1918. The solicitor advised them to apply for exemption on the grounds that the college was a non-profit venture. Following his advice, Lambert challenged the rating in court. Counsel for the County Council produced several arguments that the Church counsel easily demolished, then finally submitted that even if the farm did not earn money for the Church at present, it might do so at some time in the future. On this somewhat specious argument, the Church lost the case.[95]

Far from making a profit, the school was in deep financial trouble. Few students paid their fees in full, and many not at all; in any case, the fees charged were obviously inadequate to fund the college. While a few ventures in buying lambs and raising them for sale were successful,[96] such profits came nowhere near compensating losses in other aspects. Welch cracked down on students whose fees were unpaid, refusing to advance them money to attend a big football game in Napier on the King's Birthday holiday in June 1918. "First time this year that any discrimination has been made in money matters," he wrote. "It certainly didn't take well, but I feel it is only just and right." By July 1918, the outstanding fees amounted

---

93. For a detailed evaluation of Matthew Cowley's work on the Doctrine and Covenants, see Newton, "Mormonism in New Zealand," chap. 6.

94. Welch, Journal, 23 April 1918; F. Earl Stott, "Educating the South Sea Islanders," *Improvement Era*, April 1921, 506–7.

95. New Zealand Mission, Manuscript History, 14 August 1918; Welch, Journal, Vol. 3: 16 September 1918; Vol. 4: 16 June, 10, 17 July, 21, 26 August 1919; Lambert, Journal, 17 December 1918, 694.

96. New Zealand Mission, Manuscript History, 19 September 1918.

to £992/16/- and Welch threatened legal action against parents if their accounts were not settled immediately.[97]

Welch continued the policy of having students gain leadership training in Sunday School and the Mutual Improvement Association. Students held the various offices for one term and were then rotated, so that as many as possible had the experience of organising programs and teaching classes.[98] In later years, it was the spiritual aspects that the students recalled as being the greatest benefit they gained from their years at the MAC.[99]

News of the Armistice signed at 11:00 A.M. on 11 November 1918 was confirmed by Prime Minister Massey on Tuesday, 12 November. Welch, who was out in the college paddocks, heard the bells and whistles in Hastings, seven miles away. After lunch, all the elders went to town in the white-top buggy or by bicycle and attended an open-air meeting. Welch thought the speeches were good but came home somewhat disgruntled. "One would think from the way they talk that the British Empire had fought and won the War alone," he wrote in his journal. "Not one word was mentioned of France or America but only of the Empire."[100]

The peace celebrations were severely limited. The "Spanish influenza" epidemic was raging in New Zealand, and indoor gatherings were forbidden. By 3 November 1918, all Auckland schools were closed. The Auckland Branch was hard hit. "One of our Saints, Sister Brown, died today," wrote President Lambert. "Her son died yesterday and her daughter the day before. Her husband is estranged from her and a big family is left." The Relief Society sisters met to discuss caring for the other children, and President Lambert told them to do what they could and the Church would help. "Elders Clark and Ercanbrack have been busy this week in burying people and visiting the sick," he wrote. At Sister Brown's funeral the following day, he heard that her son-in-law had also died. "This makes four in her immediate family and now several other members are lying at death's door," he wrote.

---

97. Welch, Journal, Vol. 2:3, 24, 27 June, 22 July 1918.
98. Ibid., Vol. 4: 9 June 1918; Vol. 2: 15 June 1919.
99. See the following interviews by Kenneth W. Baldridge, all in Kenneth Wayne Baldridge, Interviews, 1971–73: Tutu Waratini, 23 December 1971, Te Hauke, New Zealand, 4; Sid Crawford, 23 December 1971, Hastings, New Zealand, 3; Pita Edward, 23 December 1971, Hastings, New Zealand, 2; Kaiser Paerata, 24 December 1971, Tokomaru Bay, New Zealand, 3; Kelly Harris, 27 December 1971, Auckland, New Zealand, 3; James Joyce, 27 December 1971, Auckland, New Zealand, 3; Waimete Wihongi, 27 December 1971, Huntly, New Zealand, 2; Hixon Hamon, 29 December 1971, Ngahinapouri, New Zealand, 3; Simon Johnson, 31 December 1971, Hamilton, New Zealand, 4.
100. Welch, Journal, Vol. 3: 12 November 1918.

"The fact of the matter is that things are mighty serious."[101] Older doctors and nurses were brought out of retirement, and contingents of nurses were brought from the south to Auckland. "Because of so many doctors being at the Front the whole Dominion is short," Lambert commented.[102]

Auckland streets and stores were deserted, and the hospital refused to allow visitors. President Lambert reported that the railways were crippled and ships in the harbour were unable to sail as so many of their crew members were ill. Three of the mission office staff contracted the disease during the first week of November, and President Lambert himself fell ill a few days later.[103] Elsewhere in the mission the situation was even worse. Missionaries and members alike suffered from what was now being mistakenly identified as "bubonic plague."

The epidemic was particularly severe at Dannevirke, where there were many deaths. Eight were sick in the Duncan home, including all the missionaries. Wi Duncan rang the college to ask for Matron Kenneth's assistance; but as Welch's wife Lalia was pregnant and within a few weeks of delivery, he was reluctant to allow it.[104] Welch tried to engage a nurse for Duncan, who offered five guineas a week, but none were available at any price. Two young Maori men from Bridge Pa (Korongata) were buried on 22 November, one a former MAC student. So many ill Maori gathered there that the LDS primary school was turned into a makeshift hospital, and Welch sent over six mattresses from the college for extra bedding. "We decided we had better keep away unless absolutely necessary," Welch wrote. "It is reported that Maoris are dying like sheep all over the country and the Europeans are losing a great many as well."[105]

On 24 November, two college missionaries—Elders W. J. Wilson and Rudolph Church—volunteered to help at the pa. Next morning, they reported to Lambert that men, women, and children were lying on the floors of filthy houses. There had been two deaths that morning, one a baby, and the other a second ex-MAC student, Charlie Hapi. Welch officiated at their burials the same afternoon. Next day Hara Pomare, a young woman of thirty-five, died. "She and her husband [were] possibly the best Saints

---

101. New Zealand Mission, Manuscript History, 3, 7, 10 November 1918; Lambert, Journal, 3–6 November 1918, 650–55.

102. Lambert, Journal, 5 November 1918, 652.

103. Ibid., 5, 7, 8 November 1918, 652–54.

104. The baby, a son, was born on 24 January and died four days later.

105. Welch, Journal, Vol. 3: 20, 22, 23 November 1918. The Maori death rate during the epidemic was seven times that of Pakeha New Zealanders, more than 2,100 Maori dying. Michael King, "Between Two Worlds," in Geoffrey W. Rice, ed., *The Oxford History of New Zealand*, 287.

and most progressive people in the pa," wrote Welch. "Maoridom can ill afford to lose a young woman of her type." The elders dug the grave and officiated at the funeral. Next day another highly regarded former student, James Ihaia, and another baby died. "The old village is certainly being hit hard," wrote Welch.[106] Their coffins were made in the Manual Training rooms at the college.

In response to government appeals, Welch sent one of the large hui tents to be used as an emergency hospital in Taranaki. "We are all well at the College and certainly are thankful to our Heavenly Father that such is the case," he wrote.[107] Elder Rudolph Church wrote in his journal that President Lambert gave the missionaries a blessing and promised that if they helped care for the sick and dying, the Lord would bless them that they would not contract influenza but remain healthy. "This they did and the promise and blessing was fulfilled," he stated.[108]

Nevertheless, President Lambert reported to Benjamin Goddard that, by 25 November 1918, thirty-one missionaries had come down with influenza. On 17 November, genealogy missionary Louis G. Hoagland was visiting the sick down river from Huntly when he received a pencilled note from a stranger simply addressed to the "Mormon Elder" to say that another Mormon elder, Henry P. Rogers, was dying in hospital. Hoagland, who had recovered from a mild attack of the flu, had advised Lambert a few days earlier that Rogers had developed pneumonia. President Lambert had visited Rogers but found him improving and returned to Auckland the same day. Hoagland hastened to Rogers's bedside, reaching him the day before he died.[109]

A week later, President Lambert was advised of the death of Tamihana Te Awe Awe. Tamihana had been unofficially released from his full-time mission but had not returned to Utah, owing to complications in obtaining passports and visas for his mother and granddaughter. Although Tamihana had done little missionary work since the April hui tau, Lambert felt obliged to notify Church officials at home that a second missionary had died from influenza.

By the end of November, the epidemic started to wane, but on 1 December another of the long-time Maori Saints, Arepa Maaki, died at

---

106. Welch, Journal, 24–28 November 1918.
107. Ibid., 29 November 1918.
108. "Sketch of the Life of Bishop Rudolph Church," p. 2, in "Biographical Sketches of Bishops in Panguitch, Utah," c. 1977.
109. Because of the nature of the illness, Rogers's body was embalmed and buried immediately. It was not until 8 December 1919 that permission was given for the remains to be shipped home.

Korongata. Welch described Aripa, about seventy years old, as "one of the staunchest Latter-day Saints in the Mission ... exceptionally well versed in Maori tikanga." Welch also reported that he was one of the first translators of the Book of Mormon. Two small children of the Morgan family from the pa died the same day. The missionaries took the white-top buggy to collect the bodies from the emergency hospital while Welch and Elders Church, Lauritzen, and Harris dug their graves. Like all other public gatherings, tangi were forbidden by Health Department decree. Welch recorded the pitiful sight of Mariana Hakopa, grandmother of the two deceased children, sitting on the grass in front of her home holding a tangi all by herself during their burial.[110]

On 1 December 1918, Mere Whaanga, Apikara Pomare, Ihaiah Whaanga, Mere's grandson Sidney Christy, his wife, Kate, and their seven children returned from Utah to live in New Zealand. "They are among the best Maori Saints who ever joined the Church," said Benjamin Goddard, "and amongst the best immigrants who have ever come to Zion." All of them, he said, were great friends of President Joseph F. Smith. Sidney Christy had become a well-known basketball star in the United States, having played in the LDS University team that won third place at the World Series held as part of the St. Louis World Fair in 1904. He was also well known as a "Hawaiian" entertainer. A large farewell party planned for them had had to be cancelled owing to the influenza quarantine regulations in Utah.[111]

Because of influenza on board, their vessel was quarantined in Auckland, and no passengers were allowed to disembark for a week after arrival. When they were released from quarantine, President Lambert escorted them by train to the college, and from there to their family village of Nuhaka. "[Christy] retained his knowledge of the Maori language," noted President Lambert, 'though he went to America, nearly twenty-five years ago (and he was only eleven [years old] when he went)." However, his children did not speak Maori at all, though they understood it. Lambert was amused when he asked eight-year-old William Christy if he liked the Maori in Nuhaka, and William solemnly replied that he didn't know as he had not yet eaten any.[112] The Christy family remained in New Zealand, adding great strength to the mission. Mere Whaanga stayed for some years, but eventually returned to Utah in 1938 and died there in 1944.

---

110. Welch, Journal, Vol. 3: 1, 2 December 1918.

111. Benjamin F. Goddard, "Maori Returning to Native Land, Leave Many Friends Here," *Deseret News*, 2 November 1918, in Journal History, 2 November 1918, 2.

112. Lambert, Journal, 13 December 1918, 690.

Chapter 5

"...you will get a Temple"

It seemed to President James N. Lambert that the first year of peace opened with a declaration of war on Mormons. New Zealand newspapers reprinted a syndicated story on Mormon "white slavery" in England, alleging that 12,000 British girls were to be shipped to Utah for "Mormon business," the operation to be financed by a fund of £8 million. Most New Zealand editors printed rebuttals submitted by the missionaries; but within a week, police were investigating Mormon activities throughout New Zealand. The number of Mormons in each congregation was requested, but no reasons were given for the inquiry.

Within a few months, missionaries called to the New Zealand Mission were again being denied visas by the British ambassador. President Lambert made yet another visit to Wellington and secured promises from the relevant authorities that visas would be issued. At the 1919 hui tau at Nuhaka on 3–7 April, nine missionaries were released to return home, after periods ranging from one year (Louis G. Hoagland) to four-and-one-half years (Matthew Cowley). This meant that the missionary force was reduced to forty-one, the lowest number for many years. Six elders arrived in August, but President Lambert had to make yet another personal appeal in Wellington to secure visas for the next group of ten missionaries who arrived in October 1919.[1]

Seven students graduated from the MAC at the end of 1919. They were Earl Francis, Hone Karaki, Mafeking Pere, Mahenga Pere, John Peters, Pere Wihongi, and William Williams. Mafeking Pere and his brother were non-LDS students whose parents refused permission for them to be baptized. Mafeking excelled in student leadership and won

---

1. New Zealand Mission, Manuscript History, 6 June, 5 and 24 August, 22 October 1919.

MAC Thanksgiving Day picnic, 1919. MAC students enthusiastically helped their American teachers celebrate holidays such as July 4th and Thanksgiving Day. Courtesy Harold B. Lee Library, Brigham Young University, Provo, Utah.

a silver signet ring for scholarship in his final year. He was eventually baptized, and his family became strong Latter-day Saints; his son Baden became the first Maori mission president in LDS history.

A general election was held in New Zealand on 17 December 1919, and William Massey's Reform Party was reelected with a big majority. There was a concurrent poll on prohibition, and the Protestant Political Association campaigned strongly in its favour. For the first time in New Zealand history, the Mormon Church took a stand on political issues. Three missionaries stationed in Auckland (Sterling M. Ercanbrack, Leon Willie, and Graham H. Doxey) abandoned tracting during the last few weeks before the election and worked under the direction of a Congregationalist minister surnamed Warner directing the Protestant Political Association campaign in Auckland. On election day, they manned a polling booth. Prohibition almost won; only the postal votes of New Zealand troops still in Europe swung the result in favour of the "wets."[2]

After long construction delays, the Hawaii Temple was finished, but its dedication was postponed because of the illness of Church President Joseph F. Smith.[3] President Smith died in November 1918, a few days after the Armistice. Although President Lambert had been informally advised

---

2. Ibid., 17 December 1919; Keith Sinclair, *A History of New Zealand*, 232, 236; Len Richardson, "Parties and Political Change," 218–19. For a history of the Protestant Political Association, see H. S. Moores, "The Rise of the Protestant Political Association: Sectarianism in New Zealand Politics during World War I."

3. James Needham Lambert, Journal, 12 October 1918, 628.

that he and his wife, Edith, should invite ten Maori Saints to accompany them to the dedicatory services,[4] no official invitation was received. When the Hawaii Temple was finally dedicated by President Heber J. Grant on 27 November 1919, no one from the New Zealand Mission was present.

President Lambert was advised that the dedication had taken place and received instructions that "the native Saints from New Zealand who had been invited to attend the dedication services would now be expected to go there in April immediately after the hui tau." Lambert would be released at this time, and he and his family were to accompany the Saints to the temple on their homeward journey to Utah. President Lambert tentatively booked twenty-six berths on the April sailing of the *Niagara*.[5] "Now that it is definitely known about the Saints going to Hawaii, I am literally besieged with applications for people to go along," he wrote to Louis G. Hoagland, who was in Hawaii making advance preparations.[6]

President Lambert had difficulty helping some of the Saints understand and accept the stringent requirements of Word of Wisdom observance and chastity for temple recommends. A young Maori woman ran away with a young man at the very time when the temple party was being organised. With the aid of a court order, her father, a prominent and faithful Latter-day Saint, retrieved his daughter; but at the first opportunity, she returned to the young man. The father was devastated and told President Lambert that he was determined to get her back and take her to Hawaii to be sealed to him. When President Lambert explained that he could not now give the daughter a temple recommend but that he and his wife should go, the father showed signs of offence and suggested that they might not go either.[7]

Maori traditional marriages were still common, causing another—and enduring—problem for the mission presidents from this time on. Many of the Saints, some of whom were grandparents, were not willing to participate in a western marriage service after so many years. The First Presidency had, many years earlier, ruled that, while they should be encouraged to have such a ceremony performed, they were not to be excommunicated if they did not understand the necessity for it and exhibited fidelity in their marriages.[8] Temple attendance, not relevant when this counsel was given

---

4. Ibid., 1 April 1917, 208.

5. New Zealand Mission, Manuscript History, 14 November and 31 December 1919.

6. James N. Lambert, Letter to Louis G. Hoagland, 26 January 1920, in Hoagland Papers, Reel 4.

7. Ibid.

8. George F. Reynolds, Letter for the First Presidency, dated Salt Lake City, 19

in 1897, was now very relevant and a different matter altogether. The Hawaii Temple president, William M. Waddoups, remained adamant that even faithful Maori Saints in long-term customary marriages could not be admitted to the temple unless a "legal" marriage was performed first.[9]

There were still difficulties in obtaining enough missionaries, even though the war had been over for more than a year. President Lambert wrote to the prime minister again and received a curt reply stating that the government had considered his request but had decided not to relax the restrictions.[10] The American consul, Alfred A. Winslow, immediately wrote to Prime Minister William F. Massey, expressing his "great surprise" at Massey's letter to Lambert. He pointed out to Massey that, in March 1918, Massey had described the restrictions as a wartime measure. "I must enter a very strong protest against the statement that the restrictions are to be continued, unless some especially good reason is set forth," he continued.[11] He received a reply virtually identical to that sent to President Lambert and forwarded copies of the correspondence to the Secretary of State in Washington, asking for instructions.[12]

Meanwhile, MAC principal John S. Welch and his wife, Eulalia, were due to return home. Franklin Earl Stott was designated the new principal. The Welch family and four missionaries sailed on the *Niagara* on 9 March.[13] A contingent of eleven new missionaries, plus J. Howard Maughan, accompanied by his wife, Eldora, and three small children—seven-year-old Roy, five-year-old Helen, and three-year-old Erma—arrived on the *Makura* on 17 March 1920. Maughan, a qualified agronomist, was to take over the college farm. All eleven elders were sent to Tahoraiti to study Maori until the Easter hui tau at Tamaki.

This was President Lambert's last hui tau in New Zealand. About 1,200 people attended six Sunday services, three in English and three in

---

March 1897, received in New Zealand Mission office on 1 May 1897 but added to the New Zealand Mission, Manuscript History under 8 April 1897.

9. Marjorie Newton, "From Tolerance to 'House Cleaning': LDS Leadership Response to Maori Marriage Customs, 1890–1990," *Journal of Mormon History* 22 (Fall 1996): 72–91.

10. Sir Francis Bell, Letter for the Prime Minister, 24 February 1920, copied into New Zealand Mission, Manuscript History, 27–28 February 1920.

11. Alfred A. Winslow, Letter to W[illiam] F. Massey, 2 March 1920, in U.S. Department of State, Diplomatic Correspondence on Mormons and Mormonism, 1910–40.

12. Alfred A. Winslow, Letter to Secretary of State, Auckland, 6 April 1920, ibid.

13. New Zealand Mission, Manuscript History, 9 March 1920.

Maori. During the business session, the names of the first company going to the Hawaii Temple from the New Zealand Mission were announced. Those chosen to go were Wiremu Duncan, Hohepa Heperi, Eriata Nopera, Wiremu Karaka, Rahiri Harris, Waimate Anaru and their wives, plus Waitokorau Tamihana and Hui Hui Pera.[14] During the evening of 6 April 1920, the ninetieth anniversary of the organisation of the LDS Church, 120 testimonies were borne in an uplifting four-and-one-half-hour meeting.

Instead of announcing a new mission president to replace President Lambert, the First Presidency instructed him to appoint someone already in the mission to preside *pro tem*, a procedure that was not unusual. His choice fell on Elder Fred W. Schwendiman, a young married missionary who had arrived with his wife, Lillian, some months before and who was currently mission secretary. President Lambert made a last unsuccessful trip to Wellington to try to persuade government officials to lift the missionary quota. He and Elder Schwendiman then visited the consul and learned that the matter had been referred once again to the U.S. Secretary of State. As Lambert had already written again to Senator Smoot, there seemed nothing more that could be done.[15]

While the Lamberts and the Maori Saints were in Hawaii, two of the Maori party discovered a previously unknown connection between their pedigrees, several generations back. To the great interest of all, they also discovered that their Maori genealogy, the sacred whakapapa memorised and passed on from generation to generation, was identical with some Hawaiian ancestral genealogies from a point hundreds of years in the past. Mormon authorities in Hawaii accepted this overlap as evidence that the Maori were descended from Aikane, an ancestor of King Kamehameha, and that the traditional Maori place of origin, "Hawaiki," was in very fact Hawaii. The Maori party was feasted and feted by Hawaiian society, and major articles announcing this confirmation of the Semitic/Hebraic/American Indian theories of Polynesian origins appeared in both Honolulu and Auckland papers.[16]

The story was repeated in the *Deseret News* when five of the party (the Duncans, Noperas, and Waitokorau Tamihana) continued the journey to Salt Lake City with the Lamberts, leaving the rest of the Maori group in Hawaii. The party was met by Benjamin Goddard, now president of the New Zealand Missionary Society (successor of Zion's Maori Association),

---

14. Ibid., 6 April 1920.
15. Ibid., 15 April 1920.
16. "Another Racial Link between Maoris and Hawaiian Is Found," *Deseret News*, 31 July 1920, in Journal History, 23 June 1920, 5; and "Prominent Maoris Visiting in City," *Deseret News*, 3 July 1920, in Journal History, 3 July 1920, 3.

and welcomed by Church officials at an evening reception. During their short stay in Utah, Church President Heber J. Grant ordained Wiremu Duncan Sr. a high priest.[17] As there was neither a stake organisation nor a temple in New Zealand, this ordination was unprecedented, the purpose of which could only have been to honour the distinguished rangatira, who had first visited Salt Lake City in 1913.

In October, President Schwendiman heard that the British ambassador would visa only four passports for new missionaries. A large group of elders was due to leave Salt Lake City the following week, and a cable from Salt Lake City asked Schwendiman to get the Department of Internal Affairs to cable authorisation for their visas to the British ambassador. Schwendiman himself visited the capital and managed to convince the relevant officials that the mission was entitled to twenty-two new missionaries to reach the quota set by the government.[18]

The Maori Agricultural College was deeply in debt when President Lambert left. His representations to the First Presidency on arriving home bore fruit, and US$5,000 was sent to clear accumulated debts, and a $500 monthly allowance for the college was instituted. Schwendiman rejoiced over a temporarily low exchange rate, which netted the college nearly £400 more than it would have received at the customary exchange rate.[19] He was also pleased to welcome the new mission president, George S. Taylor, who arrived in Wellington with his wife, Ida, and daughters Miriam and Priscilla on 30 October 1920. They were accompanied by a party of seven missionaries, but the mission was still well below strength.

"Notwithstanding the fact that our school is run by Americans along American lines, and by Mormons at that—a most unpopular combination to the thinking of many people in New Zealand—yet we are becoming more and more widely known for the good we are doing; and the wall of prejudice is being battered down," wrote MAC Principal Stott to the editor of the *Deseret News*.[20] Stott stated that the college curriculum gave students as wide a variety of subject choices as any Utah high school. He was particularly impressed with the aptitude of Maori boys in penmanship, drawing, cartooning, woodwork, and music and was proud of the MAC Glee Club and concert party, which were frequently invited to participate in local benefit concerts. The cadet corps still functioned, drilled weekly by New Zealand army officers, and its rifle team won the district marksman-

---

17. New Zealand Mission, Manuscript History, 15 August 1920.
18. Ibid., 10–12 October 1920.
19. Ibid., 13 October 1920.
20. "'Mormon' Maori Agricultural College Doing Good Work," *Deseret News*, 5 March 1921 in Journal History, 21 January 1921, 6.

"... you will get a Temple" 161

MAC faculty and students, 1919. Courtesy Harold B. Lee Library, Brigham Young University, Provo, Utah.

ship trophy three years running. The school was becoming a mecca for Mormon youth in the islands. "We have Samoans, Tongans and Tahitians as well as Maoris at the school," wrote Stott.[21]

There was enormous excitement in the New Zealand Mission when it was announced late in 1920 that Apostle David O. McKay would tour the missions of the world the following year, "in order that there may be some one in the deliberations of the First Presidency and the Council of the Twelve thoroughly familiar with actual conditions."[22] David O. McKay, age forty-seven, was a professional educator who had been a member of the Quorum of the Twelve for fifteen years. He had been appointed Church Commissioner of Education in 1919 and, in this capacity, was ultimately responsible for the Maori Agricultural College among other Church schools and universities. His travelling companion, Hugh J. Cannon, age fifty-one, was a member of the Sunday School General Board and president of the Salt Lake Liberty Stake. He was a son of George Q. Cannon, a former Hawaiian missionary and apostle who had been counselor to four Church presidents.[23]

---

21. F. Earl Stott, "Educating the South Sea Islanders," *Improvement Era*, April 1921, 506–7.

22. Heber J. Grant, as quoted in "Two Church Workers Will Tour Missions of Pacific Islands," *Deseret News*, 15 October 1920, 5.

23. Brigham Young, John Taylor, Wilford Woodruff, and Lorenzo Snow.

The New Zealand Missionary Society held a farewell dinner for Elders McKay and Cannon at the Hotel Utah on 11 November 1920. President Heber J. Grant was present, as was Adam S. Bennion, whom Elder McKay had appointed superintendent of Church schools to replace the conservative Horace H. Cummings. President Grant and Elders McKay and Bennion shared an expansive view of the place of education in the LDS Church,[24] and Goddard and others of the New Zealand Missionary Society were well aware of this orientation. They took advantage of the occasion to raise several matters concerning the New Zealand Mission and the Maori Agricultural College with Elder McKay and President Grant.

Lambert stressed the character-building facets of the MAC and the great value of the school to the New Zealand Mission, even if fees could not be collected. He pointed out that the enrolment of non-LDS boys had resulted in conversion in nearly every case. Rufus K. Hardy, like Goddard, stressed that, despite the expenditure involved, the school "has already without doubt paid for itself by what it has done for the boys of New Zealand and other Islands" and urged the establishment of a parallel school for girls.[25]

Meanwhile, preparations went ahead in New Zealand for this exciting visit. Although members of the Quorum of the Twelve had visited the British and European missions at relatively frequent intervals for the past eighty years, no General Authority had ever visited the Pacific Missions. The Saints felt honoured and were full of anticipation. Hui tau was scheduled to be held at Puketapu, across the Waikato River from Huntly, during their visit. Mission President George S. Taylor was on the wharf in Wellington when the *Marama* docked on Thursday, 21 April 1921, with Apostle McKay and Elder Cannon on board. That afternoon, although Elder McKay was suffering badly with toothache, President Taylor took the visitors to meet Dr. Maui Pomare, Minister of Native Affairs, in his office at the Parliament buildings. "[Pomare] eulogised the M.A.C.," wrote Elder McKay, ". . . and praised the excellency of the results of Mormonism among the people, saying, 'I wish all the New Zealand Maoris were Mormons; if they were, they would all be good citizens.'"[26] Next, President Taylor took the two visitors to meet John Hislop, Under Secretary of the Department of the Interior, hoping they would be able to persuade him to

---

24. Gary James Bergera and Ronald Priddis, *Brigham Young University: A House of Faith*, 50–51.

25. New Zealand Missionary Society, "Book Prepared for David O. McKay and Hugh J. Cannon, 26 November 1920."

26. David O. McKay, "Journal of World Mission Tour, 1921," 21 April 1921, 17.

facilitate visas for the missionaries. However, Hislop explained that only the prime minister and cabinet could do this.[27]

The party left Wellington that evening by train for Huntly, a sixteen-hour journey. During the night, parties of Saints and missionaries joined the train at its scheduled stops. Next morning, President Taylor took the distinguished visitors through the train to greet the Saints, who gave Elder McKay his first experience of the hongi. From Huntly, they were driven to Puketapu. They showed great interest in the evident signs of autumn as they passed through fertile farmlands, in contrast to the signs of spring they were used to in April. Elder McKay was also intrigued to see his shadow on the "wrong" side of him, and to watch the sun set in the northwest instead of the southwest.[28]

On arriving at Puketapu, the visitors were given a traditional Maori mihi (welcome). Elders McKay and Cannon shook hands with about 200 Saints who stood in line to meet them. "Being pretty well filled with the Maori spirit," wrote Elder McKay, "we found ourselves not only shaking hands, but hongi-ing one by one and one after another. . . What an experience! What a variety of noses! You who think Maori noses are all alike, have never hongied a multitude!"[29] As was customary, the welcome ceremonies, including the tangi, were repeated as additional parties of conference visitors arrived during the day.

Two huge tents (each, Cannon noted in his journal, the size that held a three-ring circus at home) and several smaller ones were set up in a paddock at Puketapu,[30] about a mile outside Huntly, on a property belonging to Church members. One large tent was used for meetings by day and became a communal dormitory at night. The bedding doubled as seating for the daily conference sessions. "For the convenience of those people who like to sleep in Church, I recommend this combination scheme most highly," joked Elder McKay.[31] The other large tent was used as a dining room, holding eight tables which each seated forty people, a total of 320 per sitting; here the visitors ate their first meal at the conference. "It was evident that the cooks, the dish washers, and the waitresses were all thoroughly organized, for everything worked with army-like precision," wrote Elder Mc-

---

27. Ibid., 18.
28. Ibid., Friday, 22 April 1921, 19.
29. Ibid.
30. Today the name "Puketapu" seems to be remembered in Huntly only by the Puketapu Te Kohanga Reo childcare centre, situated next to the Kaitumu Marae at 212–214 Te Ohaki Road.
31. David O. McKay, "Hui Tau," *Improvement Era* 24, no. 9 (July 1921): 774.

Kay. "When we know that there were sometimes three sittings to a meal, we can begin to realize what it means to feed a hui tau for five days!"[32]

During the first afternoon, two elders of the Reorganized Church of Jesus Christ of Latter Day Saints appeared on the grounds. Mission president George Taylor invited them to eat dinner in the big tent but refused their request to speak for an hour at the scheduled priesthood meeting. When they began to argue about doctrine with some of the missionaries, President Taylor asked them to leave but was ignored. When they still refused to leave after the owner of the property ordered them off, James Elkington picked one of them up and dropped him over the fence. His companion was escorted off the property.[33]

Conference sessions began in the big tent at 10:00 A.M. on Saturday, 23 April. A table was placed in front of the congregation, with chairs for Elders McKay and Cannon, George S. Taylor, Fred W. Schwendiman (mission secretary), and Graham H. Doxey, another missionary, who recorded all of Elder McKay's sermons in shorthand. Also seated with the speakers were Maori leader Stuart Meha, who interpreted the sermons given in English into Maori. Sid Christy and Elder Gordon C. Young interpreted talks given in Maori to Elders McKay and Cannon respectively.

There was breathless interest when the apostle of the Lord stood to speak. "Everyone was so touched by the Spirit present that there was scarcely a dry eye in the assembly," wrote the mission clerk. Elder McKay began by expressing his heartfelt wish that he could speak to the congregation in their own language. "But since I cannot I am going to pray that while I speak in my own tongue, you may have the gift of interpretation and discernment. While you may not understand the words, the [S]pirit of the Lord will bear witness to you of the words that I give to you under the inspiration of the Lord."[34] These words became the foundation of an enduring Mormon legend, and the story of Elder McKay's prayer and its reputed fulfilment is still told today.[35]

---

32. McKay, "Journal of World Mission Tour, 1921," 22 April 1921, 19.

33. George Shepard Taylor, Private Journal, Book 2, 22 April 1921, 122–23.

34. George Shepard Taylor, "Report of Sermons of David O. McKay—Delivered at the Annual Conference of the New Zealand Mission of the Church of Jesus Christ of Latter-day Saints, Held at Huntly, April 23rd to 25th, 1921," 1. Taylor was the mission president; it was Elder Graham H. Doxey who actually recorded the sermons in shorthand, then transcribed them.

35. For a full discussion of this legend, which tells of a mass gift of interpretation of tongues for which no contemporary record exists, see Marjorie Newton, "Mormonism in New Zealand: A Historical Appraisal," chap. 6.

Elder McKay pleaded with the Saints for unity. "We have met here not as representatives from various tribes. We have met here as one body; members of the body of Christ. We do not meet here as 'Pakeha' or as Maori; we meet as brethren and sisters in the brotherhood of Christ. Let us forget our nationalities; let us forget our tribal superiorities, or accomodations [sic] more advantageous than others; let us drive from our midst every spirit of dissension."[36] When Elder McKay concluded his sermon, Stuart Meha arose and interpreted the main points in Maori.[37]

After dinner, the RLDS mission president, a Mr. Savage, and his companion, A. L. Loving, repeated their request for an hour in which to present the "true gospel" to the people, a somewhat undiplomatic appeal that President Taylor denied. When the afternoon session began, Savage and Loving sat quietly at the far end of the tent. Conscious of the presence of the RLDS missionaries, both Elders Cannon and McKay spoke on succession in the Church presidency and bore strong testimonies of the calling of Brigham Young. At the end of each talk, the mission history records, Stuart Meha again gave a short summary in Maori for the minority who did not understand English.

As soon as the meeting concluded, Loving approached Elder McKay with a view to arguing the succession question. Before he could begin, Elder McKay, a truly charismatic personality, took him by the hand and smiled at him. Loving became almost incoherent and, with tears in his eyes, said that he hoped "Zion would soon be built" whether by the LDS or RLDS Church. Elder McKay patted him on the back and advised him to go on his way, "building up his own house and not tearing other people's down, and he would perhaps be able to assist in building up Zion."[38]

On Sunday morning, at Elder McKay's request, the children sat on the ground at the front of the congregation. After the sacrament was administered, Elder McKay told the children a story, his remarks being interpreted briefly by Stuart Meha.[39] On Sunday afternoon, the apostle spoke yet again. He was still suffering with toothache, feeling bilious, and, to add to his discomfort, was coming down with a severe cold and losing his voice. More than 2,000 people were estimated to be on the grounds this day. About 700 crowded into the tent; the flaps were up, and the remainder

---

36. Taylor, "Report of Sermons of David O. McKay," 1.
37. New Zealand Mission, Manuscript History, Conference Minutes, 23 April 1921. The minutes explicitly state that on each occasion, Meha gave a brief interpretation only at the end of each sermon and at no point in the conference interpreted simultaneously, or even sentence by sentence, as McKay spoke.
38. Ibid.
39. New Zealand Mission, Manuscript History, 24 April 1921.

sat or stood around outside, hoping to hear despite the lack of any form of public address system. Elder McKay began by expressing doubts about the wisdom of his attempting to speak and apologised for his hoarseness. But as he spoke, his laryngitis disappeared and everyone was able to hear him, which he recorded in his journal as a miraculous answer to prayer. When he began to testify of the mission of Joseph Smith, Loving appeared in one of the open flaps of the tent and shouted, "Joseph Smith never did teach polygamy. I challenge you to prove it."[40] Indignant Maori Saints forcibly removed him from the tent, while Elder McKay reminded the congregation that at the Council in Heaven, "the devil came also," a witticism which drew instant laughter from the crowd. He then continued his sermon, telling the people, "When you find a man that is attacking others, that likes to live upon slander, on vilification, you will find a man that is not prompted by the Spirit of Christ."[41]

Despite his laryngitis, Elder McKay preached what many of those present reported to be an outstanding sermon. He spoke of the Book of Mormon, stating that it had never been disproved despite many attempts to do so. He spoke of Joseph Smith's prophecies about the Jews returning to the Holy Land, and of General Sir Edmund Allenby reclaiming Palestine from the Turks in 1917. "What did it mean? It meant the door was open for the return of the Jews to their own land. Isn't it significant that the Prime Minister of England said that the Holy Land should now be set apart for the stricken Jew?"[42] McKay looked forward to the time when there would be a Jewish president of a Jewish republic, "the first to preside over the Jewish Nation since the day of the Savior." As he closed, he recommended that Church members go and get their dinners and not get involved in the altercation which could be seen going on outside between the RLDS missionaries and the group which ejected them. "You know," he told them, "it [the Reorganization] is just a boil on the body of the Church and when you rub it, it gets sore, so let us not rub it, but just attend to our own business."[43]

The RLDS missionaries were apparently once again deposited over the paddock fence and this time left, making their way back to Huntly.[44] Elder McKay rewarded security man James Elkington (a former star of the MAC Rugby team) with a hug and recorded his distaste for the whole episode.

---

40. Taylor, "Report of Sermons of David O. McKay," 7.

41. Ibid., 7–8; McKay, "Journal of World Mission Tour, 1921," 24 April 1921.

42. On 24 October 1841, Apostle Orson Hyde, on assignment from Joseph Smith, stood on the Mount of Olives and dedicated the land of Palestine for the return of the Jews and other Israelites.

43. Taylor, "Report of Sermons of David O. McKay," 9.

44. McKay, "Journal of World Mission Tour, 1921," 24 April 1921.

Maori priesthood leaders at the 1921 hui tau with Apostle David O. McKay (centre, arms folded). Hugh J. Cannon is on his right (viewer's left) and Mission President George S. Taylor is on his left. Courtesy LDS Church History Library.

"We have treated them courteously and kindly as our guests, and they have violated every principle of good conduct . . . The whole affair tended to convince me that our best policy is to treat them with absolute indifference. In the future they are not invited to any meeting I attend," he wrote.[45]

Because of his illness, Elder McKay did not speak at the MIA conference session on Sunday night and took only a few minutes on Monday morning (Anzac Day) to invite the Saints, both Maori and Pakeha, who had served in the war or who had lost sons or husbands or brothers in the war, to speak of their feelings and bear testimony. A number of the Saints responded.

In the Monday afternoon session, Elder McKay was again the principal speaker and, during his talk, made a remarkable prophecy. He spoke movingly on the subject of Anzac Day, recalling the tears he shed when, several months before, he had read an account of the bravery of Maori soldiers at Gallipoli.[46] He spoke on life beyond the grave, giving comfort to

---

45. Ibid.
46. Approximately 100,000 New Zealanders served overseas in World War I, more than 10 percent of the population. Almost 17,000—one in sixty-five of the population—were killed, a higher death toll than that of Belgium whose population was six times larger and which was a battlefield. Total casualties including injuries equalled 58,000, one in seventeen of the population of New Zealand. Sinclair, *A History of New Zealand*, 227.

those who had lost relatives. He dwelt on the Mormon doctrine of vicarious ordinances of salvation in the temples and promised that there would be a temple in New Zealand as soon as the people were ready for it and could keep it busy. "I have no doubt in my heart, but what you will get a Temple," he prophesied. "You must be ready for it, however."[47]

A final public session was held on Monday night. Elder McKay expressed appreciation to all concerned with the organisation of the hui tau, his speech once again being interpreted at its conclusion by Stuart Meha. Next morning, Elder McKay spoke to the missionaries, telling them that they were not in New Zealand to preside over branches but to proselytise. Local men should be branch presidents, he said. "A time may come when there will be no elders from Zion," he stated prophetically. He spoke approvingly of the Maori Agricultural College. "I don't know any work the Church has ever done that is better than the establishment of that College," he said. "I don't know whether it is in the right place or not, but I do know the establishment of that college . . . is inspired of the Lord."[48]

After the most momentous hui tau ever held in the New Zealand Mission, Elders McKay and Cannon left to visit Tonga and Samoa. Before sailing, Elder McKay left an apostolic blessing on the New Zealand Mission, praying for its success and for blessings of wisdom, health, and strength on the missionaries.[49] He promised to return after visiting the islands.

Elder McKay arrived back in New Zealand on 18 July 1921 and in the next two weeks addressed a public meeting in the Auckland Town Hall and spoke at district conferences at Kaikohe and Porirua. In Dannevirke, Elders McKay and Cannon met with the mission hui tau committee and recommended that the annual conference should be changed to Christmas; there would be local advantages, such as missing the rainy season and ensuring excursion travel rates. As well, Elder McKay suggested, it might be possible for a General Authority to visit hui tau every year if the date no longer conflicted with the April general conference in Salt Lake City.[50]

The brethren travelled to the MAC where they inspected the college on Friday, 29 July 1921. Sixty students were enrolled: forty from New Zealand, thirteen from Samoa, four from Tonga, and three from Tahiti. Elder McKay, a professional educator, was pleased with their singing and general deportment but was critical of the English lessons. Although the MAC was intended to be a four-year secondary school, Elder McKay reported

---

47. Taylor, "Report of Sermons of David O. McKay," 12.
48. Ibid.
49. Taylor, Private Journal, 30 April 1921, 135; New Zealand Mission, Manuscript History, 30 April 1921.
50. New Zealand Mission, Manuscript History, 31 July 1921.

that more than half the students were in primary grades, with only twelve pupils in the first-year high school class, five in the second year, and four in each of third and fourth years.

On Saturday, Elders McKay and Cannon inspected the farm; and after attending district conference meetings on Sunday, Elders McKay, Cannon, and Taylor caught the overnight express back to Auckland. The travellers sailed for Australia on 2 August 1921.[51]

Travelling was still not easy for the New Zealand mission presidents. President Taylor recorded a journey to Gisborne on a heavily laden mail coach. The road was so muddy that he and three other men had to get out and walk two-and-a-half miles uphill, as the five horses could barely pull the coach. A month later, he travelled by coastal steamer to Tokomaru Bay. The sea was so rough that the vessel could not dock, and Taylor and other passengers were placed in a basket and swung over the side into a launch that took them to the wharf.[52]

But the Lord's work was progressing. Two new chapels were finished in 1922, one at Thames, built by the missionaries for a total of £764/11/10. This building, on McKay Street, was 22 by 45 feet, with cement foundations and walls, and an iron roof. The other new chapel was built by the Tamaki Branch at Tahoraiti, and President Taylor was pleased to contribute £75 from mission funds to help liquidate the debt of £172 on the building.[53] Both branches were composed almost entirely of Maori Saints. The branches were not segregated; but in practice, most of the European Saints lived in the cities and most of the Maori Saints in the country, so there were large majorities of one race or the other in most branches.

What was intended to be the last Easter hui tau was held at Otiria, in the Bay of Islands, on 15–18 April 1922. President Taylor spent some time during this conference discussing Tahupotiki Wiremu Ratana, the latest and most influential in the stream of Maori prophets. Although Ratana lacked many of the elements that brought success to his predecessors—he was not a rangatira, he had no tribal base or wealth or lands, and was not particularly charismatic—his identification of the Maori with ancient Israel and his faith-healing attracted many Mormon Maori, who could see little difference between Ratana's designation of them as Israelites and the Mormon identification of them as Lamanites.

---

51. McKay, "Journal of World Mission Tour, 1921," 2 August 1921, 150–51.

52. Taylor, Private Journal, Book 3, 9 August and 7 September 1921.

53. New Zealand Mission, Manuscript History, 12 February 1922; Taylor, Private Journal, Book 5, 12 and 20 February 1922.

Several Latter-day Saints had already consulted President Taylor about taking sick relatives to Ratana, a procedure Taylor discouraged.[54] However, hundreds of Saints saw no conflict in inscribing their names in Ratana's "Book of Life" and having them on Mormon records as well. Even Wiremu Duncan, ordained a high priest by President Heber J. Grant in Salt Lake City in 1920, confessed less than a year later that "his attitude over Ratana had not been just right."[55] President Taylor praised Ratana's condemnation of tohunga work but stressed that the LDS Church had the true priesthood, including authority to heal the sick.[56]

Leo B. Sharp, principal of the MAC, visited the Hon. James Parr, Minister of Education and Director of Education in Wellington, soliciting government financial aid for the college. Shortly after the 1922 hui tau, the government offered an annual grant of £300 for the upkeep of the MAC.[57] Despite earlier rejection of government subsidies, this was welcome news. When the MAC school year closed on 6 October, only one student (Apiata Meha) graduated. As usual, missionary teachers were reassigned to regular duties for the summer months.[58]

Missionary numbers gradually increased to fifty-seven. Although this figure was still eight under the quota, it was a big improvement on numbers in recent years. As suggested by Elder McKay, hui tau was held at Porirua on 22–26 December 1922.[59] On Christmas Eve, MAC principal Leo B. Sharp discussed the falling attendance of Maori pupils at the college. He reminded the Saints that, in its early years, seventy to eighty Maori boys had enrolled. When the school year closed in October 1922, there were fifty-two students enrolled, only thirty-seven of them Maori; the remaining fifteen were from the islands.[60] On Christmas Day, Sir Maui Pomare and Lady Pomare visited the conference. Pomare spoke briefly in English, commending the missionaries who, he said, were doing the Lord's work. He likened the different religious denominations to apple trees, which usually bore good-looking fruit; but the fruit did not always

---

54. Taylor, Private Journal, Book 4, 7 December 1921.
55. Ibid., Book 1, 7 March 1921, 75.
56. New Zealand Mission, Manuscript History, 15 April 1922.
57. Ibid., 28 April 1922.
58. Taylor, Private Journal, Book 7, 6 October 1922, 676.
59. As hui tau for 1922 had been held at Easter, this was regarded as the 1923 mission conference. In 1924, hui tau was held in February. Because of a polio epidemic, hui tau was not held in 1925, and the 1926 hui tau reverted to Eastertime, which the majority of the Saints preferred.
60. New Zealand Mission, Manuscript History, 24 December 1922.

taste as good as it looked. In the Mormon Church, he said, he had found the fruit was not only good to look at, but good to eat.[61]

Early in April 1923, news of President Taylor's release arrived; the incoming president was Angus T. Wright, who had served in the New Zealand Mission twice previously. President Wright, his wife, Martha, and three new missionaries arrived at the beginning of June; and a week later, the old and new presidents left for the traditional mission tour.

They called at Carterton to see John A. Jury (Te Whatahoro), whom Wright was commissioned to invite to Salt Lake City at the Church's expense. In recognition of his work on the Book of Mormon, Rufus K. Hardy had been commissioned several years earlier to obtain an oil portrait of Jury, which had been hung in the Salt Lake Temple.[62] But by 1915, Jury had fallen away from the Mormon Church. William Gardner, during his second term as mission president (1913–16), was pleased when Jury expressed a desire to come back.[63] In 1918, when Jury was about seventy-seven years old, he gave Louis G. Hoagland, then on a special genealogical mission in New Zealand, four large, leather-bound volumes of Maori genealogy and lore, part of a large collection of which he was custodian. As a young man, Jury had acted as scribe for Nepia Pohuhu and Moihi Te Matorohanga, writing down sacred genealogies and traditions as dictated by the two Maori elders between 1863 and 1865. Although the books into which he wrote had been copied and the copies sent to the Dominion Museum in Wellington in 1910, Jury had retained the originals. He had allowed noted ethnologist S. Percy Smith to use them extensively in his two-volume work, *The Lore of the Whare-Wananga*, published in 1913 and 1915[64] but had refused to hand them over to the government and guarded them jealously until he gave them to Hoagland. This gift was bestowed at Tiroa, Waikato, in October 1918. Hoagland had Jury sign a written statement in the front of each book that it was his personal property and that he was donating it to the Church of Jesus Christ of Latter-day Saints. Jury's signature was witnessed by the Waikato district president, Elder Wallace Campbell.[65] Mission president James N. Lambert had a fireproof

---

61. Ibid., 25 December 1922.

62. New Zealand Mission, Minutes, 23 April 1909. For some years, the portrait hung in the Manti Temple but was later hung in the Cannon Library, Brigham Young University-Hawaii campus.

63. William Gardner, Diaries, 7 November 1915.

64. D. R. Simmons, "Te Matorohanga, Moihi, fl. 1836–1865," *Dictionary of New Zealand Biography*.

65. Louis G. Hoagland, Letter to Angus T. Wright, dated Salt Lake City, 13 July 1925, in Hoagland Papers.

vault constructed in the basement of the Queen Street meetinghouse to safeguard these books, which he and Hoagland both rightly considered priceless, and other mission records.[66]

Jury wanted the books translated into English, urging that it should be done soon as he was now the only living Maori who knew the meaning of some of the obsolete terms used in the manuscripts.[67] Lambert and Hoagland tried to interest LDS Church authorities in the volumes and the projected translation, but without success. Eventually, Hoagland wrote to Apostle Joseph Fielding Smith, then serving as Church historian, outlining the story of the acquisition of the volumes, their contents, their inestimable value, and the need for them to be preserved in the Church archives.[68] Hoagland told Elder Smith that Jury was nearly eighty "and it was 'now or never' to get the translation." Elder Smith persuaded the First Presidency that, in view of Jury's long service to the Church, he should be invited to visit America, receive his endowment, and, with the help of returned missionaries, translate the books.[69]

Unfortunately, Major Brown (Hoani Paraone Tunuiarangi), an important non-LDS rangatira who had been present when Jury wrote the volumes and had stamped the Maori seal on each page as it was approved by the tohunga, heard of the proposal and persuaded government officials to refuse to allow either Jury or the books to leave the Dominion.[70] But in any case, the invitation to Jury had come too late. He was losing his memory and was too frail for such a journey.[71]

Moreover, Presidents Taylor and Wright discovered that the Whatahoro books were protected by the Maori Antiquities Act of 1908, which prohibited the removal of Maori artifacts from New Zealand.[72] A week after the Taylors had sailed from Auckland, President Wright visited Wellington and called on Sir Maui Pomare, asking for permission to send the books to the United States. Pomare advised Wright to leave the books

---

66. New Zealand Mission, Manuscript History, 3 September 1919; Hoagland to Wright, 13 July 1925.

67. Louis G. Hoagland, Letter to M. Charles Woods, dated Salt Lake City, 31 May 1937, in Hoagland Papers.

68. Louis G. Hoagland, Letter to Joseph Fielding Smith, dated Salt Lake City, 22 March 1923.

69. Hoagland to Woods, 31 May 1937.

70. Ibid.

71. Taylor, Private Journal, Book 10, 9 and 10 June 1923, 901–3; New Zealand Mission, Manuscript History, 26 June 1923.

72. Hoagland to Woods, 31 July 1937.

with him for examination by competent government officials.[73] President Wright did so, but the books were never returned to either the Church or the Jury family. Fifteen months later, Wright again spent a few days in Wellington, trying unsuccessfully to regain possession of the four volumes. Nothing had been done with them, but he was promised a report at a later date.[74] In 1927, mission president Howard Jenkins was still appealing unsuccessfully for the return of the books.[75]

Two building projects were begun during President Wright's term of office. The first was a large amusement hall for the Nuhaka Branch, which eventually cost $25,000, of which the Church paid $10,000. The First Presidency approved the allocation after learning from Wright that the Nuhaka chapel and an elders' home had been built without Church financial help. The latter had burned down, and the Nuhaka Saints had not only rebuilt it, but had also compensated the missionaries who lost belongings in the fire.[76] The second building begun by Wright was a third faculty home at the MAC. The first home had been destroyed by fire in November 1914, and its replacement was also gutted by fire on 12 December 1923. Now Wright supervised the building of a third Faculty Home for the MAC, this time built of cement blocks. It had ten rooms and was ready for occupancy within a few months.[77]

A second group of Saints from New Zealand sailed for Hawaii in March 1925 to visit the temple at Laie. There were five Maori couples: Hemi Witehira, Wilson Paewai, Nireaha Paewai, Hamiora Kamau, and Ratima Hakopa with their wives; two additional Maori women (Amohaere Anaru and Erana Paea); and one European Saint (Charles Spencer, president of the Auckland Branch). Nireaha and Wilson Paewai were both converts and graduates of the Maori Agricultural College. Charles Spencer, a manufacturing chemist educated at Oxford, was a colourful character who had joined the Church in January 1914 and was now in his sixties. "He wore a long frock coat all the time," reminisced Elder Julian R. Stephens. "The coat had pockets in the coat tails. In one he carried a Bible and in the other he carried a Book of Mormon and he would get them out

---

73. New Zealand Mission, Manuscript History, 17 July 1923; Hoagland to Woods, 31 May 1937.

74. New Zealand Mission, Manuscript History, 19 September 1924.

75. Ibid., 25 November 1927.

76. First Presidency, Letter to Angus T. Wright, 25 October 1923, copied into New Zealand Mission, Manuscript History, 23 November 1923.

77. New Zealand Mission, Manuscript History, 12 and 19 December 1923, 22 May 1924.

faster than a cowboy could get his gun. He was always ready to talk and argue about the gospel."[78]

Because of their poor health, Angus and Martha Wright were released in April 1925, before the scheduled end of their term. President Wright was instructed to return to the United States immediately, choosing a responsible missionary to preside *pro tem*. His choice fell on Elder Andrew Reed Halversen. Halversen, according to the mission clerk, was "the oldest Elder in point of service in the Mission, a fluent Maori linguist, industrious and discreet, and in every way a worthy and qualified person for his added responsibility."[79] The Wrights sailed on the *Aorangi* on 13 May 1925 and three months later the new mission president, J. Howard Jenkins, his wife, Cora, and four children—Barbara, Marion, Donna, and John—arrived on the *Aorangi*.

Missionary strength was still under quota, and President Jenkins visited John Hislop, Under Secretary for Internal Affairs, in Wellington on 29 September. Hislop agreed that the full quota of missionaries could be admitted, and President Jenkins wrote to the First Presidency, explaining that the mission was twenty under strength.[80] Meanwhile, local missionaries were called for six-month periods to augment the numbers.[81]

President Jenkins travelled from Wellington to Hastings to attend commencement at the MAC on 2 October 1925. Five students (Peter Kelly, Rupert Wihongi, James Heperi, Misitana Vili, and Samuela Fakatou) graduated. Before leaving the college, Jenkins helped the principal, Albert E. Sells, prepare the prospectus for the coming year. On 6 October, he and Sells were invited to be present when the governor-general, Sir Charles Fergusson, visited Hastings. President Jenkins and Sells felt somewhat slighted when they were the only visitors not introduced to the governor-general.[82]

For some time past, there had been little contact between the general Church Board of Education and the MAC. On 27 October 1925, President Jenkins wrote to the First Presidency and to the general superintendent of Church schools, Adam S. Bennion, asking for the MAC to be recognised as part of the Church school system. Aware of local concerns about low standards of scholarship, Jenkins pleaded with leaders in Salt Lake City to send qualified teachers to the New Zealand school.

---

78. Julian Rackham Stephens, "My Life's History Or a Reasonable Facsimile of It," 16; Lambert, Journal, 14 October 1916, 102; William Rosser Perrott, Oral History, 5–6.
79. New Zealand Mission, Manuscript History, 27 April 1925.
80. Ibid., 19 January 1926.
81. Ibid., 18–20 March 1926.
82. Ibid., 6 October 1925.

These appeals followed notification by the Maori Purposes Fund Control Board that grants from the Maori Secondary Schools Aid Fund were to be discontinued. President Jenkins assumed that the funding cut applied only to the MAC but was assured the cuts applied to all schools; these grants would be replaced by £10 grants made directly to Maori pupils earning government free places. "If you desire Government assistance you should apply to the Education Department that a number of the scholarships be made tenable at your school, and my Board will then be pleased to make each scholarship holder the grant of £10 above mentioned," wrote the secretary.[83] Efforts to get the MAC accredited for the award of the government scholarships and the consequent Maori Purposes Fund grants continued unsuccessfully for the remainder of the MAC's existence.

The Upper Queen Street site of the Auckland chapel, at first hailed as a wonderfully central location and good investment, was now proving a disadvantage. Motor traffic had increased enormously, and for some years electric trams had run up and down Queen Street. At times it was impossible for the congregation to hear the speakers in Church meetings. President Jenkins recommended to the First Presidency that the buildings (chapel and mission home) should be sold.[84] Permission to sell was given, but Auckland property values slumped and Jenkins withdrew the Church property from sale until the market picked up.[85] No more was heard of the plan to sell the Queen Street property until after World War II.

After missing a year because of a polio epidemic, the annual hui tau convened on 2–5 April 1926 at Nuhaka. The amusement hall, which seated 600, was the venue for conference sessions, while large tents provided dining and sleeping quarters. President Jenkins noted that the tents were in poor repair and would probably not last another year; they had already been patched and repaired as much as possible. The hui tau committee met as usual, discussing the difficulty of financing the annual conference. Luxford Peeti suggested that the annual gathering should cease. President Jenkins wanted hui tau to continue and suggested that the dining room should be run like an American cafeteria, with all meals being sold, a concept that ran counter to every Maori cultural tradition. However, Wi Duncan approved the idea, suggesting a price of one shilling and sixpence per meal. The idea of reverting to two conferences, northern and southern, was also considered.

---

83. J. Howard Jenkins, Letter to the Secretary, Maori Purposes Fund Control Board, 11 November 1925; H. R. H. Balneavis, Secretary, Letter to J. Howard Jenkins, 7 December 1925.

84. New Zealand Mission, Manuscript History, 4 March 1926.

85. Ibid., 13 November 1926.

Although it was intended that parties should travel to the Hawaii Temple every six months, only a handful of New Zealand members had actually made the pilgrimage by 1926. In 1921, David O. McKay had promised that a temple would be built in New Zealand when the members could keep it busy. The Laie temple had been built when Church membership in Hawaii was around 10,000. There were now about 6,000 Latter-day Saints in New Zealand; but Church members from Samoa, Tonga, Australia, and even Tahiti could reach New Zealand more quickly and cheaply than they could visit Hawaii. With President Jenkins's approval, a petition was addressed to the First Presidency asking permission to begin a building fund for a projected temple in New Zealand.[86] The fund was never started, and it was not until the 1950s that a temple was built in New Zealand.

On 1 October 1926, commencement exercises were once again held at the MAC, and President Jenkins presented graduation certificates to Bertie Brunt, Faafeu Tawa, and Ra Puriri. The following day, President Jenkins audited the college books, finding that it was costing the mission £56 per annum for each student.[87] President Jenkins was dismayed when he received a copy of the school's annual inspection report. "I have to draw your attention to [the school's] unfavourable character," wrote the Director of Education. "The results of the Proficiency Examination are very unsatisfactory and the report . . . draws attention to several weaknesses in the teaching. The Inspector recommends that more experienced and more capable teachers should be appointed, and the Department trusts that steps will be taken to carry out the recommendations of the Inspector." If the standard had not improved by the next inspection, he continued, "the Department will reluctantly be compelled to take into consideration the question of cancelling the registration."[88] Of twenty-eight MAC pupils who sat for the proficiency examination in 1926—taken at the end of primary schooling and technically necessary for admission to secondary school—only three had passed.[89] "Work in Standards 5 and 6 is by no means up to the standard usually found in Native Schools," wrote the inspector. "No stigma is meant to be cast upon the present assistants who, like most of

---

86. Ibid., 19 April 1926.
87. Ibid., 2 October 1926.
88. A. Bell, for Director of Education, Letter to the Principal, Maori Agricultural College, Hastings, 18 October 1926.
89. Only sixteen of the twenty-eight MAC candidates were actually enrolled in Standard Six; eight were enrolled in the first year secondary course; three in second year, and one in third year. Only two of the sixteen Standard Six candidates and one of the secondary school candidates passed.

the Mormon missionaries I have met are an earnest, well-meaning body of young men who would do excellent work under experienced direction." That the principal was expected to function also as farm manager and business manager was an impossible situation, wrote the inspector, pointing out that Te Aute College, with a similar enrolment, "has a principal, a farm manager, a business manager and three permanent assistant teachers on its staff besides several visiting teachers; and it is by no means liberally staffed."[90] President Jenkins once again repeated his plea to the First Presidency for qualified teachers.[91]

By the middle of February 1927, there had been no reply to Jenkins's request for qualified teachers; to make matters worse, the First Presidency cabled a release for the principal, Albert E. Sells, owing to the serious illness of his mother-in-law. President Jenkins wrote to Benjamin Goddard and Rufus K. Hardy, asking them to use their influence with the First Presidency to obtain both more missionaries and more help for the college.[92] By 12 March, only thirty students had enrolled for 1927, and President Jenkins was very discouraged.

The 1927 hui tau was held at Ngaruawahia. Princess Te Puea invited the Jenkins family to stay in her own home, and all accommodation for the conference was of a higher standard than usual. More than 500 Saints and friends enjoyed the program and meetings. During the annual meeting of the College Board of Education, President Jenkins intimated that he had heard unofficially (probably from Goddard or Hardy) that his request to have the college recognised as part of the Church Schools System was to be granted. This status would entitle the school to have paid, qualified teachers instead of missionaries. The board decided to write off old tuition debts amounting to £844 and also decided unanimously that, in the future, no pupil would be admitted unless his tuition was paid in full in advance.[93]

President Jenkins spent the last few months of 1927 attending district conferences, organising a new Maori hymn book, and printing a Maori edition of a popular LDS tract called "A Friendly Discussion." The tract had been translated a few years earlier and published in *Te Karere*. In November 1927, 10,000 copies of the pamphlet were printed; and early in 1928, Jenkins collected quotes for printing the new Maori hymnal. About 100 LDS hymns were translated by Eru Cooper, and the words were then

---

90. A. Bell to the Principal, 18 October 1926.
91. New Zealand Mission, Manuscript History, 23 October and 9 November 1926.
92. Ibid., 11 February 1927.
93. Ibid., 16 April 1927. Te Puea was the granddaughter of King Tawhiao.

A group of leading Maori brethren, c. 1927. Seated left: Wiremu Takana (Duncan) Sr. and Mission President J. Howard Jenkins. Standing left: Rahiri Harris, Dannevirke; Paul Hapi, Nuhaka; Luxford Peeti, Hastings; Wilson Paewai, Dannevirke; James Heperi, Bay of Islands; Eriata Nopera, Dannevirke; Ra White, East Coast; Stuart Meha, Waipawa. Courtesy Harold B. Lee Library, Brigham Young University, Provo, Utah.

fitted to their music by Elder Julian R. Stephens. The printers promised to have 500 copies ready for hui tau in April 1928.[94]

President Jenkins's last year as mission president followed the pattern of the previous two. His biggest concerns were the shortage of missionaries and the Maori Agricultural College. By now, the shortage of missionaries was not the fault of the government; though the quota was still set at sixty-five, Church authorities at home could not find nearly enough missionaries to keep the numbers at more than half of this figure. Only eleven arrived in 1926; and in 1927, the mission clerk recorded that the mission president "knew not what to do" to keep the districts staffed. What he did do was make extensive use of local Maori men called to short-term missions. This approach had been used in New Zealand since the late 1880s and, of course, in Europe, Australia, and other missions for a much longer period; but the numbers now called in New Zealand were greater than ever before. Contrary to earlier practice, President Jenkins did not call only older, experienced men. The lists of short-term missionaries are dotted with the

---

94. Ibid., 1 June, 22 September and 23 November 1927; 7 February 1928.

names of young men, many of them former students of the Maori Agricultural College.[95]

At President Jenkins's suggestion, Elder Stanley C. Kimball, acting principal of the MAC, launched an extensive campaign to tidy the college and its grounds. Jenkins was pleased with the look of the campus when the new principal, Ariel S. Ballif, arrived to take over in June 1927. A young college graduate, Ballif brought his wife, Artemisia Romney Ballif, and year-old son Ariel Smith Ballif Jr. The Ballifs were accompanied by another young married couple, Lawrence and Bernice Manwaring. Both wives were trained teachers, though their names are nowhere listed as members of the MAC teaching staff. Ballif was installed as president of the MAC Branch of the LDS Church on Sunday, 26 June 1927, and took over as principal of the school the following day.

Ballif instituted many reforms. Morale and discipline improved. The annual government inspection report, received soon after five boys—Robert Turnbull, Wi Pere Amaru, Tamata Mapuhi, Willie Shortland, and Puti Tipene (Steve) Watene—graduated in October 1927, reported some improvement but not enough. The Church was given one more year to improve the standard of teaching or its licence to run a school would be revoked.[96]

Altogether, President Jenkins must have felt more relief than sorrow when he was advised early in 1928 that his release was imminent. John Ephraim Magleby and his wife, Jennie, arrived on the *Aorangi* on 25 March 1928; it was Jennie Magleby's first visit to New Zealand, but her husband's third, and his second term as mission president. The two presidents, old and new, attended hui tau at Ngaruawahia, where once again every facility in Princess Te Puea's model pa on the banks of the Waikato was made available for the Mormon conference. "I am not a Mormon, but those people are doing great work among my people," she told a visiting reporter. "They are training our girls in the way in which women should be trained, in the home and in life generally. They are teaching thriftiness and to be of good repute and respectable citizens."[97] More than 2,000 "adherents of the faith" (as the reporter termed the Saints) attended the conference, most of them Maoris, but the paper reported a large number of Europeans present as well.

After hui tau, the old and new presidents set out to tour the mission together. President Magleby found the mission far more prosperous than

---

95. Ibid., 17 April and 19 July 1927; 8 and 9 April 1928.
96. Ibid., 7 and 20 October 1927.
97. "Mormon Conference—Gathering at Ngaruawahia," *Auckland Star*, 9 April 1928.

when he had left a quarter of a century earlier. Instead of constant financial embarrassment, the mission had a credit balance of $12,000, plus a well-furnished home and office, and more than $5,000 worth of books and tracts. "The work ... is much more systemised [sic] than when I was here before," he wrote. "Much more record keeping and report making."[98] The Saints had adopted the principle of tithing; while not all contributed, and not all were full tithe payers, the mission was in a better financial position than ever before. The college, however, continued to be a financial drain on both the New Zealand mission and the parent Church in Utah. "But money possibly can not be counted as against the souls of men," Magleby philosophised.[99]

President Magleby spent each weekend at a district conference, meeting many of his old friends and converts. He passed through towns and villages he had known on his two previous missions, and found some of them, such as Tokomaru, so "Europeanised" as to be almost unrecognisable.[100] At each conference, he made a point of holding special meetings with those who had visited the temple, on some occasions including those who intended to go. These meetings, he felt, were the most spiritual of each conference.[101]

At the end of July, Magleby was back at the MAC. After discussions with Ballif and the Board of Education, President Magleby decided that either they must change from crops to sheep raising (which would require capital outlay to begin but would be less labour-intensive), or lease the farmlands. They decided to put the alternatives to the First Presidency and await their reply.[102]

A few years earlier, Te Ao Wilson had written to President Heber J. Grant appealing for his support for those Latter-day Saints who interpreted some verses in the Book of Mormon referring to a future prophet as being fulfilled by Ratana. President Grant stated clearly that the specified verses did not refer to Ratana but to a prophet still in the future.[103] Despite this counsel, the growth and success of the Ratana movement was still causing dismay among LDS leaders, with up to two thousand Latter-day Saints by now either having "left" the LDS Church for Ratana or maintaining an uneasy foot in each camp. As there was still a shortage of missionaries, President Magleby decided on an innovation that simultaneously eased

---

98. New Zealand Mission, Manuscript History, 31 March 1928; John Ephraim Magleby, Journal, 28 March 1928, 11.
99. Magleby, Journal, 3 April 1928, 14.
100. Ibid., 21 May 1928, 37.
101. Ibid., 28 May 1928, 39.
102. Ibid., 22 and 24 July 1928, 69–70.
103. New Zealand Mission, Manuscript History, 24 September 1925.

this shortage and reduced Ratana's appeal. His solution was to appoint well-known rangatira as district presidents, freeing American missionaries for proselytising and incidentally providing a focal point in each area that helped regain the primary allegiance of many straying Latter-day Saints.

President Magleby began by ordaining Eriata Nopera a high priest and installing him as president of the Hawkes Bay District on 2 September 1928, with Stuart Meha as first counselor and Wilson Paewai as second counselor.[104] After explaining the shortage of missionaries worldwide, he stated that he felt the Maori Saints no longer needed to lean on the "Zion Elders" but should have the opportunity to gain executive experience. President Magleby announced that President Nopera's ordination as a high priest would take place with the permission of Church President Heber J. Grant. "All . . . felt the Spirit of God was present in rich abundance," wrote Stuart Meha. "We felt that if ever a man was inspired of God, President Magleby was on this occasion."[105]

On 23 September, Paora Hapi was sustained as president of the Mahia District with William Smith as first counselor and Iraparete Pomare second counselor. Three weeks later, in the Bay of Islands conference, Magleby's choice fell on Hohepa Heperi, with Hemi Witehira and Hirini Heremaia as counselors. On 21 July 1929, Turi Ruruku was sustained as president of the Wairau District. The fifth local district presidency, Whangarei, was organised on 22 March 1931 with Henere Pere Wihongi as president, and the sixth (Wairarapa) on 6 March 1932, the president being Eruera Taurau. All the district presidents were ordained high priests. President Magleby stressed that local leaders would stabilise the work of the districts, which would no longer be subject to sudden changes every time a missionary was transferred.[106] The First Presidency heartily approved of President Magleby's move to local leadership.[107]

---

104. Ibid., 2 September 1928; Meha, Reminiscences.

105. Meha, Reminiscences, 4. It should be noted, as Brother Meha pointed out, that while Brother Nopera was the first Maori district president, he was not the first Maori high priest. Wiremu Duncan Sr. had been ordained a high priest in Salt Lake City in 1920. The first Pakeha high priest in New Zealand was Charles Spencer of the Auckland Branch, ordained by President Magleby, with First Presidency permission, on 29 March 1931.

106. Magleby, Journal, 9 and 23 September, 14 October 1928, 87, 91–92, 100–101; New Zealand Mission, Manuscript History, 23 September and 14 October 1928.

107. Magleby, Journal, 9 October 1928, 98; New Zealand Mission, Manuscript History, 15 January 1929.

Between the Mahia and Bay of Islands conferences, President Magleby returned to Wellington and attended a meeting of the Maori Purposes Fund Control Board. He strenuously argued for financial aid from the board's funds, some of which were dedicated to secondary schooling for Maori boys. A few days later, the MAC school year closed; seven boys graduated, the largest number since the college had opened in 1913. Unfortunately, graduation meant only that the graduating pupils had attended the college for the requisite four years. It was not dependent on examination results or scholastic achievement.

President Grant gave permission for the college land to be either sold or leased according to President Magleby's judgment, though the First Presidency apparently favoured selling it.[108] Unable to sell at a reasonable price, Magleby and Ariel S. Ballif negotiated a ten-year lease of the college land to William J. Gimblett for $1,250 per year, with an option to buy after five years at £26 per acre.[109]

In a desperate effort to reverse the falling enrolment figures at the MAC, Magleby and Ballif placed a display advertisement in *The Dominion*, offering "the native boys of New Zealand the maximum of practical education at the minimum of expense." In the best tradition of salesmanship, they claimed that the MAC could not be surpassed "for development of initiative and leadership, and the maintenance of a high scholastic record."[110]

To President Magleby's great disappointment, the MAC was ruled ineligible for government free-place scholarships and, hence, for the additional grants from the Maori Purpose Fund Control Board. New Zealand's director of education, Thomas B. Strong, had commissioned a special report from John Porteous, senior inspector of native schools. While stressing that "sectarian considerations" should not influence the decision, Porteous reported that the majority of MAC students were grown men, including many from the Islands (Samoa, Tonga, and Tahiti), who had returned to school after considerable periods of time. He spoke of "the great difficulty" the college authorities appeared to experience "in bringing their system into line with New Zealand requirements," commenting particularly on the MAC's short school year and the unsatisfactory qualifications and teaching methods of the staff. He felt bound to report that "the quality of the work done at this college" did not justify the award of the scholarships; if additional scholarships were available, he would much prefer to

---

108. John. E. Magleby, Letter to L. G. Hoagland, 8 January 1929, in Hoagland Papers, Reel 4; Magleby, Journal, 9 October 1928, 98.

109. Ibid., 8 January, 18 May, and 25 June 1929.

110. Maori Agricultural College, display advertisement including photograph, *The Dominion*, 25 January 1929.

see them allotted to Te Aute, whose academic record was well established. The MAC pupils, Porteous suggested, would be much better off in the work-force rather than wasting time and money at the MAC.[111] While these comments were undoubtedly justified with regard to academic work at the MAC, the mission leaders were well aware that there was an extra dimension to the LDS Church school that could not be measured by purely secular standards.

In addition to this perpetual problem, President Magleby was still much concerned with the impact the Ratana movement was having on the Saints, estimating that up to two thousand Latter-day Saints—possibly up to 50 percent of the adult members—were affected. Both President Jenkins and President Magleby refrained from excommunicating the defectors. However, many were now returning to the LDS fold, and activity rates in the districts and branches, especially the districts with Maori leadership, had improved within months of the reorganisation.[112] After preaching against Ratana once or twice, Magleby decided it might be more politic to win Ratana's goodwill. Accordingly, on 21 January 1929, he visited Ratana's secretary at Ratana Pa near Wanganui and offered to present a program at Ratana's approaching birthday celebrations and conference. The offer was accepted; and the following Friday, 25 January (the first anniversary of the Ratana temple opening), an MAC group performed a Book of Mormon pageant and Magleby presented a Book of Mormon which was accepted by Ratana's secretary on his behalf.[113]

Hui tau 1929 was hosted on the college grounds by the MAC Old Boys Association. Meetings on Sunday, 31 March, celebrated the message of Easter. During the day, a Ratana official was allowed to speak and urged the Maori people to agree to the consolidation of all Maori lands. This question had been canvassed by Ratana followers for some time. "I was very glad indeed to have in my possession an answer to that question from

---

111. Magleby, Journal, 25 February 1929, 149; John Porteous, Senior Inspector of Native Schools, to T. B. Strong, Director of Education, 8 January 1929; T. B. Strong, Director of Education, to the Secretary [H. R. H. Balneavis], Maori Purposes Fund Control Board, 4 February 1929; H. R. H. Balneavis, Secretary, Maori Purposes Fund Control Board to the Principal [Ariel S. Ballif], Maori Agricultural College, 11 February 1929; the last three in New Zealand National Archives, Department of Education, E3 1947/1a Maori Agricultural College, Hastings, New Zealand National Archives, Wellington.

112. John E. Magleby, Letter to L. G. Hoagland, 8 January 1929, in Hoagland Papers; New Zealand Mission, Manuscript History, November 1928.

113. Magleby, Journal, 25 January 1929, 137–38; New Zealand Mission, Manuscript History, 29 January 1929.

the First Presidency," Magleby wrote. "This I read and commented. The letter stated that to consolidate land and people of Maoridom is not advisable and would likely lead to confusion. . . . After my remarks and advice not only our people were satisfied to keep out of the Ratana consolidation, but the Ratana man himself was in perfect accord, thanking me for what was said."[114]

Another group visit to the temple at Laie was being planned. Magleby was dumbfounded when he learned that, before the government would consider issuing passports, a deposit of £100 each must be lodged with the Department of Internal Affairs as security for the return of the Maori travellers. This meant a total deposit of £2,000 or US$10,000. He immediately protested, pointing out that such a deposit had not been required for any previous company. The mission solicitors advised Magleby that the demand was illegal and unconstitutional. The lawyers wanted to make a test case of it, but Magleby was not prepared to tolerate the time and expense.

Accompanied by a Wellington solicitor, Magleby finally saw the prime minister, Sir Joseph Ward, who raised the matter with the cabinet. Magleby was advised that passports would be issued if the Department of Internal Affairs was supplied with a complete list of the members of the party and if Magleby signed an undertaking binding the Church to be responsible for the party while in Honolulu and for their return on the scheduled date. As the Hawaii Mission had promised to feed and house the party in Hawaii, Magleby had no hesitation in signing the required document.[115]

By 2 May, five days before departure date, the passports had still not been issued. The Union Steamship Company refused to issue tickets unless they saw a valid passport for each intending passenger, while the government refused to issue passports unless its officials saw a return ticket. Magleby finally offered his personal surety for the cost of the tickets. This was accepted, and the steamship company assured the passport office that no single tickets would be issued to Maori passengers. Magleby finally received the passports for the normal fee of ten shillings each at almost the last minute.[116]

When enough qualified teachers failed to arrive from Utah, Magleby called Robert P. Hodge, an LDS schoolteacher in Auckland, to serve a mission at the college. As Hodge was a New Zealander who had trained and qualified in New Zealand, he was the first fully accredited teacher in the six-

---

114. Magleby, Journal, 31 March 1929, 162.

115. Copies of all correspondence in New Zealand Mission, Manuscript History, April 1929; Magleby, Journal, 6–20 April 1929, 165–72.

116. Ibid., 2 May 1929, 176–77.

"... you will get a Temple" 185

teen years of college history.[117] Magleby admitted to Louis Hoagland that he would feel a lot better when the school was better established and received government recognition. The Maori Saints, he told Hoagland, were becoming impatient with the low standards and lack of accreditation.[118]

Such statements make it clear that the guilt often felt by many Maori Saints who collectively take the blame for not supporting the school is unjustified and unnecessary. When the MAC opened in 1913, there was still little provision for secondary education for Maori boys. However, over the lifespan of the MAC, standards and opportunities improved; but unfortunately there was no corresponding improvement in the MAC. Without properly trained teachers who could prepare the students for the state examinations, parents with any other choice—and, as stated, by 1930 there were more options for the education of Maori youth—could scarcely be blamed for preferring them to the MAC. By 1960, LDS parents in New Zealand could send their children to CCNZ (the Church College of New Zealand), a Church school that offered both religious and secular education. Thirty years earlier, the MAC offered theology, character training, and Church service experience, plus music, football and some experience in different fields of agriculture—but all too often only unqualified and untrained teachers in academic subjects. While a few very bright young men were able to profit from even this standard of teaching, only a handful of such students obtained enough education to enable them to pass the most basic examinations or to obtain employment based on their education at the MAC.[119]

In his continual efforts to bring all the blessings of the Church to its members in far-away New Zealand, President Magleby asked President Heber J. Grant to appoint a patriarch for New Zealand and for an apostle to visit the South Pacific in 1930, the Church centenary year. President Grant replied that he would consider the matter of a patriarch but that no apostolic visit would take place.[120] No patriarch was appointed either.

The continued growth of the Ratana movement was unsettling to many of the Saints. Scenting a way to kill two birds with one stone, President Magleby visited Ratana in August 1929 and requested the privilege of again contributing to his birthday celebrations in January; he also asked Ratana to promote the MAC among his followers. A Mormon contingent, including President Magleby, again visited Ratana Pa for Ratana's birthday celebrations on 25 January 1930. President Magleby visited the Ratana

---

117. Ibid., 14 May 1929, 184.
118. Magleby to Hoagland, 8 January 1929.
119. For an in-depth evaluation of LDS schools in New Zealand, see Newton, "Mormonism in New Zealand," chaps. 4–5.
120. Magleby, Journal, 14, 22 August, 20 November 1929, 4:219, 221; 5:[39].

temple, describing it as the largest hall he had seen in New Zealand, decorated with carvings and paintings of the sun, moon, and stars. It was, he felt, a counterfeit of a Mormon temple. Shortly afterwards, Magleby wrote an article for the mission paper, advising the Saints not to sign the Ratana covenant, "signing land, home, body and spirit to Piri-wira-tua [a name Ratana had adopted] for ever and ever."[121]

The 1930 school year began on a desperate note. In a letter to Maori boys and their parents, Ariel S. Ballif appealed for renewed support. "Boys, we want you. We need you," he wrote. "Parents, you owe it to your boys to see that they get an education under the best influence that you can possibly obtain." He warned that unless more students enrolled, the school might close.[122] There were fifty-five in his first year as principal (1928), forty-five in 1929, but only thirty-five in 1930.[123] With these numbers, the school was simply not a viable financial proposition. In March 1930, the Minister of Education visited the MAC. "As a result of his report, the

---

121. Ibid., 6 February 1930, 76.

122. Ariel S. Ballif, "A Message from the College," *Te Karere* 24 no. 1 (20 January 1930): 26–27.

123. New Zealand Mission, *Catalogue and Announcement of the Latter Day Saints [sic] Maori Agricultural College*, 1929, 35–36; 1930, 32; New Zealand Mission, *Calendar and School Magazine of the Church of Jesus Christ of Latter Day Saints [sic] Maori Agricultural College*, 1931, 39. Each year's calendar listed the students enrolled the previous year, giving the figures quoted. While Brian W. Hunt, "The Maori Agriculture [sic] College," 16, states that the numbers fell to twenty in 1930, R. Lanier Britsch, *Unto the Islands of the Sea: A History of the Latter-day Saints in the Pacific*, states that there were "around eighty boys" enrolled at the MAC in 1930. Hunt's figure appears to have been taken from an item in "News of the Mission," *Te Karere* 24, no. 1 (January 1930): 32. This news item gives a total of 7,075 persons enrolled on the Mission membership records at 31 December 1929, and then lists the number of persons enrolled in each district of the mission. The enrolment of Church members at the MAC (20) at this date was given as though the MAC were a separate district such as the Whangarei District with an "enrolment" of 1,048. The 1929 school year had ended in October, and the 1930 school year not begun when this membership census was taken and the information published. The unmarried American missionaries teaching at the college were reassigned to regular mission duties during the long summer vacations. Only the married American faculty members and their families, plus some of the Samoan and Tongan students, would still have been at the MAC in December 1929. Britsch's statement that the MAC class of 1930 was "around eighty boys" is a figure he seems to have taken from his oral history interview with Ariel S. Ballif, several decades later. Ballif did not specify that this figure applied to the 1930 class and may have meant it to indicate an approximation of the total number of students for whom he was responsible at the MAC during his term as principal.

Inspector of Secondary Schools will pay us a visit on April 2nd to arrange for registration," the mission paper reported confidently.[124] However, it did not happen.

Despite later assertions to the contrary,[125] the MAC never became a registered secondary school. In April 1930, the mission history noted that mission president John E. Magleby "received word from Principal Ariel S. Ballif of the Maori Agricultural College that the Government man who inspected the College did not recommend them for regristration [sic] as a second grade [secondary] school, which was sad news. But 'we must work on—improving until we reach the standard required,' says Pres. Magleby."[126] An announcement that boarding scholarships were available to Maori students has been taken as evidence that the school was registered. But Robert P. Hodge, Ballif's successor, was merely alerting parents to the fact that government scholarships existed and was urging them to apply to have these scholarships made tenable at the MAC. These government scholarships for registered secondary boarding schools were available to any Maori student who obtained a primary school proficiency certificate and who did not live within reach of a secondary day school. They were non-competitive. In a final effort to divert LDS boys from the prestigious Anglican school, Te Aute, LDS parents were promised that any boy with a proficiency certificate from his local school would be given a Church scholarship worth £40 (two years' dormitory fees) at the MAC.[127]

A party of seventeen Maori Saints sailed for the Hawaii Temple in May, including David Smith and Mary Ruruku, the first young couple from New Zealand to be married there, chaperoned by the bride's parents. President Magleby had to certify that each of the party was an LDS adherent and that he or she was going to Hawaii for religious purposes before passports were issued. Sailing at the same time was Wi Pere Amaru, a former MAC student who was going to Brigham Young University in Provo, Utah.[128] Two other MAC graduates, Joe Hapi and Tom Clarke, followed

---

124. "Nga Whakaaturanga," *Te Karere* 24, no. 3 (19 March 1930): 86.

125. Hunt, "The Maori Agriculture College," 17; Brian W. Hunt, *Zion in New Zealand: A History of the Church of Jesus Christ of Latter-day Saints in New Zealand, 1854–1977*, 51; Britsch, *Unto the Islands of the Sea*, 307.

126. New Zealand Mission, Manuscript History, 15 April 1930.

127. R. P. Hodge, Principal, Maori Agricultural College, "Maori Scholarships," *Te Karere* 24, no. 8 (August 1930): 331–32; New Zealand Mission, *Catalogue and Announcement of the Latter Day Saints' Maori Agricultural College*, 1930, 8. The school catalogue specified that the scholarship covered two consecutive years of dormitory fees.

128. Magleby, Journal, 3, 4, and 31 May 1930, 112, 124.

Amaru to BYU a few months later.[129] All three were given scholarships at President Magleby's request. Magleby asked the New Zealand Missionary Society to look after these young men.[130]

Ariel and Arta Ballif had now been at the MAC for three years and were anxious to return home for family reasons. New Zealand schoolteacher Robert P. Hodge was appointed to succeed Ballif as principal at a salary of £250, to be increased if the school achieved secondary registration.[131] On 5 July 1930, ten days before sailing, Ballif baptized a young man from Tokomaru Bay who had graduated with honours from the MAC the previous October. He was Sid Crawford, later to become the third president of the Hawkes Bay Stake. Crawford credited the MAC with giving him the foundations that led to the establishment of a successful business career as well as his conversion to Mormonism.[132]

The school was taking up more and more of President Magleby's time. The buildings needed painting, and new lavatories were needed. An accumulation of bills from local provision merchants had to be paid. President Magleby wrote a long letter to the First Presidency on 17 August. Their reply, received in November, questioned the feasibility of keeping the school open past 1931.[133]

In a letter to Louis G. Hoagland, President Magleby lamented the passing of the Maori language. Few of the current missionaries learned Maori. "Nor does it seem possible for them to do so," Magleby reasoned. "Even the old Maori people themselves, I find are half-casting their language or *korero*." Hoagland had suggested the need for missionaries to continue to learn and speak Maori, hinting at future needs (probably the translation of the temple ceremonies into Maori). "Yourself, Rufus Hardy, Matt Cowley and some others who have a knowledge of the Maori language will need to retain it for the purposes mentioned in your letter," President Magleby replied, "for we shall not be able to produce any more such Maori students."[134] As more and more Maori spoke, read, and wrote English, the need for Maori-speaking missionaries was decreasing; and as Magleby said, it was becoming difficult

---

129. New Zealand Mission, Manuscript History, 8 August 1930; "Maori Boys in America," *Te Karere* 25, no. 1 (January 1931): 14.

130. John E. Magleby, Letter to Louis G. Hoagland, 19 September 1930, in Hoagland Papers.

131. Magleby, Journal, 30 June 1930, 138.

132. Sid Crawford, Oral History, interviewed by Kenneth W. Baldridge, 23 December 1971, in Hastings, New Zealand.

133. New Zealand Mission, Manuscript History, 17 August 1930; Magleby, Journal, 19 November 1930, 219.

134. Magleby to Hoagland, 19 September 1930.

to find pure Maori spoken. However, within another decade, a resurgence of the Maori language began; far from disappearing, the nation of Aotearoa/New Zealand today is officially bilingual.

The 1930 annual report showed that there were 7,256 Latter-day Saints in New Zealand, organised into fifteen districts. Only twenty-nine missionaries, including three sister missionaries, were in New Zealand at the end of 1930, the lowest number in living memory. The Great Depression was biting in Utah; twenty-four missionaries had been released, but only seven had arrived. "At the close of this year we will be down to 16 Zion Elders," President Magleby wrote to Hoagland, adding, only half-jokingly, "Are you run out[?]"[135]

The Maglebys went to Madsen, French Pass, on 31 January 1931 to visit the Ruruku and Elkington families and attend district conference. They arrived back in Wellington early on the morning of Wednesday, 4 February, and were stunned to see newspaper placards announcing that a major earthquake and subsequent fires the previous day had devastated the Hawkes Bay/Poverty Bay region and caused great loss of life.[136]

The MAC school year was calendared to begin with registration on Monday, 2 February 1931. It is difficult to tell how many students had arrived when the earthquake struck just before 11:00 A.M. on Tuesday morning, 3 February 1931. No one at the college was injured. Jim Southon later said that most of the students had already registered; there may not have been many, as there had been only thirty-five the previous year. Although it remained standing, the MAC dormitory, pride of the complex, was severely cracked and structurally unsound, while the front of the chapel/assembly hall had caved in.[137]

By Wednesday, the death toll in the district was estimated at 640 (though this figure was far in excess of the final official death toll of 246[138]); thousands were injured, and there were shortages of food and water. Troops, medical supplies, doctors, and nurses were rushed to the area. The trunk railway line between Auckland and Wellington was cut, and many roads were impassable. Napier was a shambles, with the dead and dying still trapped in the wreckage of shops, offices, and homes. After-shocks continued for a few days, and fires raged out of control so that a pall of smoke hung over the stricken cities of Napier and Hastings.

---

135. John E. Magleby, Letter to L. G. Hoagland, 13 March 1930, in Hoagland Papers.

136. Magleby, Journal, 2, 3, and 4 February 1931.

137. James Southon, Oral History, interviewed by Roger Tansley, 27 December 1971.

138. J. G. Wilson, et al., *History of Hawke's Bay* [sic], 451.

The town of Hastings, seven miles from the MAC, after the 1931 earthquake which caused the closing of the Church school. Courtesy Harold B. Lee Library, Brigham Young University, Provo, Utah.

Unable to travel directly to Hastings from Wellington, President Magleby made his way to Dannevirke as quickly as he could. Wi Duncan had already inspected the afflicted area and reported that both the MAC and Te Aute College buildings were unsafe. "So it looks like school days in N[ew] Z[ealand] for the Church are over," Magleby wrote in his journal. He immediately cabled the First Presidency: "Elders unhurt, Saints quite secure in earthquake areas; College buildings standing, worthless; dangerous."[139] On Thursday, 5 February, Duncan drove the mission president to Hastings and on to Bridge Pa where Magleby inspected the damage to the college and faculty home. Magleby realised that the college buildings would have to be razed, forcing a decision about whether to rebuild or abandon the school.[140]

It is commonly believed that President Magleby had prophesied that an earthquake would destroy the college because the Maori Saints were not supporting it.[141] There is no contemporary record of such a specific

---

139. Magleby, Journal, 4 February 1931, 35–36; "L.D.S. Members Escape in Quake," *Deseret News*, 5 February 1931 in Journal History, 5 February 1931, 2.
140. Magleby, Journal, 5 February 1931, 36–37.
141. Kaiser Paerata, Oral History, interviewed by Kenneth W. Baldridge, 24

prophecy, but both President Magleby and Principal Ballif had certainly warned the Saints that they would lose the college if it were not better patronised. What the mission president and principal had in mind, of course, was not an earthquake but that the First Presidency was considering closing the school in any case.

Moving on to Nuhaka, President Magleby was relieved to find that the new amusement hall, completed at so much expense, was not even cracked as a result of the earthquake. That weekend, 21–22 February 1931, he reorganised the Mahia district presidency as a result of the recent death of Paora (Paul) Hapi. Wi Smith was sustained as district president and, by permission of the First Presidency, was ordained a high priest the following year.[142] "The Mahia District and especially the Nuhaka Branch is [sic] going ahead just fine," wrote Magleby. "I think Nuhaka is our model and leading branch of the Church in New Zealand."[143] Not everyone in Utah had approved President Magleby's action in calling Maori district presidents and ordaining them high priests.[144] But despite criticism from some former mission presidents active in the New Zealand Missionary Society, he remained convinced of the wisdom of his actions and rightly refused to be influenced by others who, though remaining interested in the mission, had no ecclesiastical jurisdiction over it.

Easter 1932 fell at the end of March. Hui tau was held the following week, as the Church of England had booked the Nuhaka marae for Easter. It rained heavily all Easter weekend but was fine for the Mormon conference, which President Magleby considered a special blessing. "No one can say God is not with us," he wrote.[145] The 1,200 assembled Saints enjoyed the conference, as did Magleby, who realized it was his last hui tau. During the conference, President Magleby released his wife, Jennie, from the presidency of the mission Relief Societies, and appointed Polly Duncan, the first New Zealand woman to head the New Zealand Mission Relief Society. Two local women, Olive Edwards and Muriel Hay, were appointed as presidents of the mission Young Ladies' Mutual Improvement Association and Primary Association respectively, but American missionaries continued to preside over the Young Men's Mutual Improvement Association and the Sunday School.

Following cabled instructions from the First Presidency, President Magleby and Principal Hodge had offered the ten-acre college campus to

---

December 1971, in Tokomaru Bay.
    142. Magleby, Journal, 5 January 1932, 173.
    143. Ibid., 21–22 February 1931, 48–49.
    144. Ibid., 14 February 1932, 196.
    145. Ibid., 7 April 1932, 16.

the government if it would agree to keep the school open. The New Zealand government declined the Church's offer.[146] The First Presidency never gave any serious consideration to rebuilding. Students and staff dispersed, the missionaries were reassigned, and the printing shop for *Te Karere*, the mission paper, was transferred back to Auckland. The Gimblett family already leased 200 acres of the farm; the remaining forty acres and the faculty home were now taken on a seven-year lease by William J. Gimblett and his sons John and William, for £2/10/- per acre. The little graveyard in one corner of the college grounds was fenced off and remained Church property.

The MAC lives on in the collective memory of the Saints of the New Zealand Mission. While its academic standards were extremely poor and its teaching staff almost totally unqualified, the students who spent from one to four years there all remembered it fondly. While most later admitted that their college years did not qualify them academically, they enjoyed the music, football, and taste of American life.[147] But its main benefit to the New Zealand Mission was undoubtedly the gospel training and Church service experience received by the pupils and the benefit they gained from close association with fine role models in the American missionaries who served there. In later years, students recalled their experience with gratitude and attributed much of the strength of the New Zealand Mission in later decades to the "old boys" of the Maori Agricultural College.

---

146. Ibid., 3 March 1931, 59; 10 October 1931, 132.

147. See, for example, Eruha Kawana and George Nepia, interviewed by Kenneth W. Baldridge, 21 December 1971, in Masterton, New Zealand; Tipi Kopua, interviewed by Kenneth W. Baldridge, 23 December 1971, in Tokomaru, New Zealand; Nephi Wharemahihi, interviewed by Kenneth W. Baldridge, 21 December 1971, in Hamilton, New Zealand; Heteraka Anaru and Rupert Wihongi, interviewed by Kenneth W. Baldridge, 27 December 1971, in Huntly, New Zealand; John Ormsby, interviewed by Kenneth W. Baldridge, 28 December 1971, Hastings, New Zealand; and Daniel Williams, interviewed by Roger Tansley, 29 Deember 1971, in Hastings, New Zealand.

Chapter 6

"...we need buildings, buildings and more buildings..."

Soon after hui tau 1932, President John E. Magleby received a cable from President Heber J. Grant announcing his release and instructing him to leave a capable missionary in charge.¹ Magleby appointed Elder Harold T. Christensen mission president *pro tem* and then booked berths on the *Aorangi*, sailing 3 May 1932, for himself, his wife, Jennie, and a group of returning missionaries and Saints en route to the temple in Hawaii. "Our leaving New Zealand, no doubt never to see the country or people again is no easy task," President Magleby wrote. "My Mission has been as Pres[ident] Grant promised the crowning feature of my life."²

John Ephraim Magleby died in 1939 at the age of seventy-seven. His name deserves wider recognition among the Saints of New Zealand. He was a fluent Maori speaker, regarded by many as the best missionary speaker of Maori ever. It was said that non-LDS Maori hearing him could not tell that it was a Pakeha speaking.³ His love for the Maori people was deep and genuine, untinted by any hint of racism or patronage. He understood the vast cultural differences involved and was unfailingly tolerant when Maori Saints fell short of the high standards expected by most American Mormons. Magleby was not blind to the sins of backsliders but obviously felt that little lasting good was accomplished by severe Church discipline and rarely excommunicated anyone.

President Magleby was not the only missionary to return to preside twice in New Zealand, but both his terms as mission president saw many

---

1. John E. Magleby, Journal, 14 April 1932, Reel 3, 4:20.
2. Ibid., 3 May 1932, Reel 3, 4:29.
3. Ariel S. Ballif, Oral History, interviewed by R. Lanier Britsch, 20 July 1973, 19.

innovations that affected the course of the New Zealand Mission for half a century. His overriding desire was to give the New Zealand Saints the opportunity to experience the gospel and Mormon life as available in Utah. If the Maori Saints were not permitted to gather there, then all the blessings of the Church should be made available to them in their homeland. Not all his ideas became a reality while he was in New Zealand, but most did, and others came to fruition under the mission presidents who succeeded him. During his first term as mission president (1900–1902), he organised the first Maori Relief Societies; he began street meetings in the Pakeha cities; he started to persuade the government to officially recognise the Church of Jesus Christ of Latter-day Saints and then to officially recognise LDS marriage celebrants; he developed the foundations of the mission paper; he tried to get Church authorities to consider a "colony" in New Zealand for the Maori Saints; and he tried his best to get occasional visits from General Authorities.

During his second term as mission president (1928–32), he set apart local men as district presidents, ordaining them high priests, and called local women to preside over mission auxiliaries; he tried to persuade the First Presidency to appoint a patriarch for the New Zealand Mission; he instituted regular "temple meetings" as a part of the quarterly district conferences; and at one particularly spiritual hui tau session at Nuhaka even spontaneously led the congregation in the "Hosanna Shout," somewhat sheepishly recording in his journal his doubts about the propriety of this action.[4]

The appointment of a serving missionary as acting mission president was not without precedent, but such an appointment usually lasted for only two or three months until a new mission president could organise his affairs at home and travel to New Zealand. Harold Thomas Christensen served as acting mission president for just under fifteen months, from Magleby's departure on 3 May 1932 to the arrival of a new mission president, Rufus K. Hardy, on 14 July 1933. I have found no record explaining the delay in appointing a new president. Possibly the Great Depression, which was making it difficult to send enough missionaries to the worldwide missions, was also making it difficult to find mission presidents in a position to leave their affairs at home for three years in such stressful economic times.

President Magleby had left a sound foundation, which Elder Christensen appreciated and endeavoured to build on. Because of the depression, the average number of missionaries in the New Zealand Mission during 1932 was only eleven, the smallest number in half a century, and

---

4. Magleby, Journal, 4 April 1931, Reel 2, 3:77–78.

Beloved mission president John Ephraim Magleby (left), Elder Harold T. Christensen, and Sister Jennie Magleby outside the Duncan home toward the end of President Magleby's second term as mission president (1928–32). Courtesy Harold B. Lee Library, Brigham Young University, Provo, Utah.

not one single new elder arrived during the fifteen months that Christensen presided. By the time Christensen was replaced in July 1933, only eight American missionaries remained. President Magleby had partially compensated for the shrinking number of missionaries by releasing those who were serving in district presidencies in six districts and appointing local priesthood holders to serve instead. (See chap. 5.) As it happened, Elder Christensen was one of those released district presidents, having served as president of the Wairarapa District.

President Christensen now followed President Magleby's example and released missionaries from the presidencies of another three districts. He called Henry Hamon as district president in Poverty Bay but left the Wellington and South Islands districts without district organisations. So by hui tau 1933, seven districts (Hawkes Bay, Mahia, Bay of Islands, Wairau, Whangarei, Wairarapa, and Poverty Bay) had local Saints serving in their district presidencies, and all mission auxiliary boards except the YMMIA now had local leaders.[5] President Christensen also organised the first Mission Genealogical Committee, setting apart Stuart Meha as its president on 15 December 1932.[6] Meha and his wife, Ivory (Ivy), had been

---

5. New Zealand Mission, Manuscript History, 1933 Hui Tau Report.
6. New Zealand Mission, Manuscript History, Report of Officers, 8 February 1933; ibid., 1933 Hui Tau Report; "News Briefs: Mission and Church," *Te Karere* 27, no. 1 (January 1933): 45; Harold T. Christensen, "The New Zealand Mission

called to spend time at the Hawaii Temple learning genealogical work, policies, and procedures.[7] The mission helped pay their passage, indicating how much mission finances had improved since the turn of the century.

President Magleby had increased the number of local part-time missionaries to eighteen, most of whom served short-term missions of six months. At hui tau 1933, President Christensen set apart twenty-eight young men and six young women, adding four more male and four more female missionaries over the next few weeks. By the time he left New Zealand, more than fifty part-time missionaries were helping fill the void left by the scarcity of "Zion elders."[8]

Far from suffering because of having a young, inexperienced acting president, the New Zealand Mission prospered under Christensen. At the end of 1931, there were 7,498 Latter-day Saints in the New Zealand Mission; by the end of 1932, there were 7,810. In 1931, there were 237 baptisms in the mission (121 convert baptisms and 116 children); in 1932, despite the now-critical shortage of American missionaries, there were 338 baptisms of which 194 were converts and 144 children of record. "Strange to say the number of Zion elders in this mission for the greater part of last year numbered 11, as compared to 27 at the end of 1931—a decrease of over one hundred per cent, and yet did the work decrease accordingly? No! The number of converts increased as the figures above show," proclaimed the mission paper.[9] Elder Christensen acknowledged that he was greatly helped by a combination of factors: President Magleby's sound foundation, frequent supportive letters from the First Presidency, the support of the local Church members, and much prayer and fasting.[10] By contrast, there were still fewer than 1,500 members in the parent Australian Mission.[11]

Rufus K. Hardy arrived in Auckland on the *Monterey* on 14 July 1933 to succeed President Christensen.[12] President Hardy had served his first mission in New Zealand and had also served a prior term as mission president (1907–09). He had maintained a keen interest in the New Zealand Mission and had become its chief spokesman in Salt Lake City after the death of Benjamin F. Goddard in December 1930.

---

during the Great Depression: Reflections of a Former Acting President," *Dialogue: A Journal of Mormon Thought* 24, no. 3 (Fall 1991): 69–76.

7. Magleby, Journal, 13 December 1931, 4 March 1932, Reel 3, 3:157, 208.

8. Christensen, "The New Zealand Mission during the Great Depression," 74.

9. "News Briefs: Mission and Church," 45.

10. Christensen, "The New Zealand Mission during the Great Depression."

11. W. Lynn Roberts, "Australian Mission," *Improvement Era* 35, no. 7 (May 1932): 398.

12. New Zealand Mission, Manuscript History, 14 July 1933.

President Hardy was warmly welcomed by old friends wherever he went. After the Waikato district conference at Huntly on 30 September–1 October, Hardy travelled to the South Island and visited Dunedin, Invercargill, and Christchurch. Although there were Latter-day Saints in each city, only Dunedin had a branch functioning at this time. He arrived back in Auckland in time to help compile the annual reports.[13] These showed a membership total of 8,146.[14]

Plans for disposing of the college land at Korongata had been discussed for some time. Now it was subdivided into thirty-two allotments; and in August, President Hardy conducted a two-hour meeting in which Saints from the Korongata Branch took part in a draw or ballot to decide who got which lot. Although Hardy intended that the area would be known as "Atareta Pa," it continued to be known as Bridge Pa. John Gimblett surrendered seven acres for the new pa in return for the lease of nine acres where the college buildings had stood. Formalities were completed on 1 October, and separate title deeds were organised to facilitate the arrangements.[15]

On 7 October 1934, President Hardy received a lengthy cable from Salt Lake City, informing him that, owing to the death of President Anthony W. Ivins, David O. McKay had been called as a counselor in the First Presidency at the general conference being held that weekend and that he himself had been sustained as a member of the First Council of the Seventy. He was instructed to return to Utah as soon as possible.[16] While Hardy did not preside very long, the New Zealand Mission felt his impact. A keen Maori linguist himself, he insisted that missionaries once again learn Maori; and by the time he left New Zealand, every American missionary in New Zealand could speak "te reo" to some extent.[17] Such facility was not strictly necessary by the 1930s, but it was a good policy. Elder Robert L. Simpson, who arrived in the New Zealand Mission just three years after President Hardy left, also learned Maori as a young missionary. "Most Maoris spoke English quite well," he commented many years later, "and the only real need for the Maori language was to help us gain their confidence and to let them know that we were really interested in them and to talk to some of the older people who didn't really know the English language that well."[18]

---

13. Ibid., October–November 1933.
14. "News Briefs: Mission and Church," *Te Karere* 28, no. 2 (February 1934): 93–94.
15. New Zealand Mission, Manuscript History, 1 October 1934.
16. Ibid., 7 October 1934.
17. "Homeward Bound," *Te Karere* 28, no. 11 (November 1934): 501–3.
18. Robert L. Simpson, Oral History, Interviewed by Gordon Irving, 1978, 4.

Elder Alvin T. Maughan, who had arrived in the mission the previous December with his wife, Evelyn Going Maughan, and their three children, was chosen as acting mission president[19] until Moroni Charles Woods, accompanied by his wife, Elline, and two daughters, Charlene and Janet, arrived to take over the mission presidency in March 1935. Both Maughan and Woods attended the forty-seventh hui tau at Nuhaka 28 March–1 April 1935. Soon afterwards, a party of fifteen Saints sailed on a temple trip, the first to go to the Hawaii Temple since 1932. While in Hawaii, group members met Church President Heber J. Grant and his counselor J. Reuben Clark Jr., who were in Hawaii to form its first stake.[20]

One of the first problems with which President Woods had to deal was the expense of the annual hui tau. A Hui Tau Board, with representatives from each district, had been established in 1921, the original board members being set apart by David O. McKay. Originally, the branch "calling" the hui had borne the entire cost; then the district assumed responsibility, with all branches in the district helping. Even this was too much for some of the smaller, poorer districts. Next it was decided that all districts should contribute to the cost each year, the amounts payable being set by a kind of poll tax based on the number of active Maori Church members in each district. However, many families were unable or unwilling to contribute; consequently, in several areas, a small number of Saints ended up paying most of their district's assessment.

Various alternatives, such as expecting each conference participant to pay for his or her kai (food) had been tried; but these schemes seemed inhospitable to visitors and went against deeply ingrained Maori tradition and practice. Now President Woods called a meeting of the mission Hui Tau Board to discuss the growing financial burden of the annual conference. It was decided to charge for attendance at hui tau. A season ticket would cost six shillings and would admit the bearer to all meals, dances, functions, and sports. Those without tickets (except special guests) would be charged one shilling per meal plus admission charges to all events except actual conference sessions.[21] This did not work either, as revenue raised from ticket sales was insufficient to cover costs.

Missionary numbers gradually increased again, and there were thirty-two present at Tamaki, near Dannevirke, for the 1936 hui tau. It had become evident that no tent would ever again be large enough to accommodate the conference sessions, and the idea of a permanent tabernacle had

---

19. "Our New President," *Te Karere* 28, no. 12 (December 1934): 542.
20. "News Briefs: Mission and Church," *Te Karere* 29, no. 7 (July 1935): 282.
21. "Important: Hui Tau Special Notice," *Te Karere* 29, no. 11 (November 1935): 420–21.

"... we need buildings, buildings and more buildings ..." 199

Tent city erected for hui tau at Tamaki, near Dannevirke, 1936. Courtesy of LDS Church History Library.

been mooted the previous year.[22] However, the 1937 hui tau scheduled for Nuhaka had to be cancelled because of an epidemic of infantile paralysis (poliomyelitis)[23] and nothing more was done about building a permanent tabernacle for hui tau.

President Woods, an architect and builder, decided that all LDS chapels and elders' homes should be renovated and painted, and actively lent a hand himself whenever possible. He used the weekend of the cancelled 1937 hui tau to remodel the basement of the Auckland chapel, dividing it into two storerooms, a tool room, and an office and print shop for *Te Karere*.[24]

President Woods was concerned about the neglect of missionary work among the Pakeha, and felt it was time that a major effort should be made to proselytise among the Europeans in New Zealand's cities. He realised that tracting and street meetings were not as effectual as they used to be and decided that the MIA (Mutual Improvement Association), which sponsored drama, music, dance, public speaking, and sport, was one of the best missionary tools available.

Newsreels screening in New Zealand cinemas were arousing keen interest in basketball. Quick to seize the opportunity, President Woods

---

22. New Zealand Mission, Manuscript History, 31 May 1935.
23. Ibid., 16–25 March 1937.
24. Ibid., 23 March 1937.

approached the YMCA and suggested organising a basketball league in Auckland. The missionaries played several exhibition games, at one of which the spectators included the governor-general. An American Basketball League was subsequently organised in Auckland, and later replicated in other cities, with missionaries coaching most teams. As the elders served on all the committees of the league, acted as coaches and referees, and fielded a representative team, they began to make friends with many people, inviting them to MIA and Sunday meetings.[25] In September 1937, a missionary basketball team that included Elder Robert L. Simpson (later to become a General Authority and the first Pacific Area President) toured the North Island.[26] As summer approached, the basketball season ended and the missionaries turned their attention to baseball and softball.[27]

At the same time that President Woods began to urge more work among the Pakeha population, he appealed to the First Presidency to call former missionaries who spoke Maori to return to New Zealand. The quarterly report explained:

> There are still a few primitive groups of Maoris in the bush country of N.Z. who have not had a chance to hear the Gospel. Recently two Elders visited several of these villages. They report that the field is ready for harvest, and that many of the old Maori Priests or Tohungas have died and the people are now ready to listen to the Gospel. The Elders who did missionary work among the Maoris many years ago are needed to help carry on this work. They knew the Maori people in their more primitive state and understood Maori tikanga or customs which have only been maintained in these villages in the bush country. The Elders in the field now seldom have the privilege of seeing the natives in their primitive surroundings.[28]

Nevertheless, the young missionaries of the 1930s did learn the language and found great joy and satisfaction in serving in the Maori branches. The experience of Elder Simpson (1937–40) was typical. "We were expected to learn the Maori language as well as we could and spend most of our time traveling amongst the people seeing that the branches were organized, auxiliaries were functioning properly, collecting tithing, seeing that babies were blessed. It was almost like being a bishop, more than a proselyting missionary," he recalled in later years. "It was not uncommon for those district missionaries working amongst the Maori to . . . be gone for four to

---

25. Ibid., 31 May 1937.
26. Ibid., 6 and 23 September 1937.
27. Ibid., 30 November 1937.
28. Ibid., 31 May 1937.

six weeks from their mission headquarters as they traveled from branch to branch doing all these things. It was a real joy to come back after four to six weeks and read all your mail and have your clothes cleaned up again. Then after a week or so we were ready to go again and make the circuit."[29]

Early in 1938, President Woods, who had been ill, was advised that Matthew Cowley had been appointed his successor. President Cowley, his wife, Elva, and their daughter, Jewell, arrived on the *Mariposa* on 18 February 1938. Also on board the vessel were Apostle George Albert Smith (future president of the Church), and Elder Rufus K. Hardy of the First Council of Seventy. They were the first General Authorities to visit the South Pacific since Elder David O. McKay's 1921 tour. Leaving the Cowley family in Auckland, the two General Authorities continued on to Australia on the *Mariposa,* planning to return to New Zealand in time for hui tau.

The Woods family sailed for home on 7 March; two months later, the mission was shocked to learn of the death of President Moroni Charles Woods in Ogden, Utah, from a cerebral haemorrhage.

Back in New Zealand, preparations for hui tau went ahead rapidly. Anticipation was high because two General Authorities of the Church would be present. Elder Smith and Elder Hardy arrived back in New Zealand on 4 April 1938. They toured Rotorua and visited Maori branches of the Church at Opotiki, Gisborne, Nuhaka, Wairoa, Hastings, and Korongata. From Bridge Pa they moved on to Opapa, Waipawa, Tahoraiti, and Dannevirke and then to Wellington. Here they met the American consul and government officials as well as local Saints, both Maori and Pakeha. They drove back to Auckland via Palmerston North before returning to the Waikato for hui tau.

About 2,500 people attended the forty-ninth hui tau on 13–17 April 1938 at Ngaruawahia, where Princess Te Puea turned her entire pa over to the Mormons. A traditional Maori mihi or welcome ceremony was conducted for the visitors on Thursday, with 250 men performing the haka. During the ceremonies, Elder Smith, Elder Hardy, and President Cowley sat on the carved porch of the King's reception house. On Sunday afternoon, Radio 1ZB broadcast a forty-five minute program of conference highlights from the King's house, during which musical numbers were presented by the winning choir (Korongata), and Apostle Smith (who served on the advisory board of the National Council of Boy Scouts of America and was an ardent supporter of Scouting) spoke to the radio audience about Boy Scout work throughout the world. Between meetings, President Cow-

---

29. Simpson, Oral History, 3.

ley photographed a group of forty-seven mothers, who among them had 605 children; thirteen of the group had more than fifteen children each.[30]

Back in Auckland, Elder Smith met local Boy Scout officials and addressed a final meeting in the Auckland chapel on 1 May. He had recently lost his wife and was unwell when he commenced his long journey from America. Elder Hardy had been sent to look after him, but, ironically, it was Hardy who became ill. While he was hospitalised, Elder Smith sailed for Tonga without him.

Church President Heber J. Grant was pleased with Elder Smith's report of his visit to the South Pacific missions and promised to have General Authorities of the Church visit Australia and New Zealand more often.[31] It had been seventeen years since Elder McKay's visit; certainly such a long period never again elapsed before a General Authority visited New Zealand. But World War II intervened, so it was 1947 when the next General Authority visited New Zealand—Matthew Cowley, as a newly ordained apostle.

Meanwhile, after hui tau 1938, Matthew Cowley, as the new president of the New Zealand mission, visited each district as often as he could. At a Bay of Islands conference at Kaikohe, held 13–14 January 1939, President Cowley ordained Percy S. C. Going a high priest, the second European to be ordained a high priest in New Zealand; the first, Charles Spencer, had died a few years earlier.[32] Missionary numbers were increasing and there were fifty-nine American elders in New Zealand by February 1939. President Cowley continued President Woods's emphasis on European work; and with more missionaries, he was able to do this without neglecting Maori work. A good Maori linguist himself, Cowley, like Rufus K. Hardy, insisted that his missionaries learn Maori. He urged missionaries to find opportunities to use radio as a proselytising tool, and many MIA programs were broadcast.[33]

The fiftieth hui tau was held 6–10 April 1939, once again at Ngaruawahia. The conference began with a missionary meeting in the King's reception house. Not since before World War I had so many missionaries been in New Zealand. During the conference, President Cowley reorganised the MAC Old Boys' Association that had lapsed for some years; Jim Elkington was reelected president, with George Randell and Eru Cooper

---

30. "49th Annual Hui Tau of the New Zealand Mission, at Ngaruawahia, 13–17 April, 1938," typescript, fd. 15, Cowley Collection.

31. First Presidency, Letter to the Members of the General Hui Tau Board, 18 May 1938, *Te Karere* 32, no. 7 (July 1938): 203.

32. New Zealand Mission, Manuscript History, 14–15 January 1939.

33. Ibid., 28 February 1939.

"... we need buildings, buildings and more buildings ..." 203

as counselors. Cowley was pleased to encourage the Old Boys' Association. During his mission tours, he was reported to be "more than thrilled to observe that the majority of the former L.D.S. Maori College boys [were] the leaders in the Mission today."[34]

A novel feature at this jubilee hui tau was a sunrise choral service on Easter Sunday. On Easter Monday, the sports began with a grand parade led by the "Zion" elders, who were followed by the "pioneers" of the LDS Church in New Zealand and then competitors dressed in their branch and district colours. The traditional program included competitions in tennis, haka, poi dances, wood-chopping, tug-of-war, basketball, and track and field events. Missionaries played exhibition games of basketball and baseball and demonstrated horseshoe pitching. Floorshows were featured at the closing ball. When points for all competitive events were totalled, Tamaki Branch won the cup for the highest aggregate. Overall attendance was estimated at between 2,500 and 3,000. Special tents housed missionary exhibitions of Church literature and auxiliary work. Other competitions included cooking and preserving, needlework, knitting, quilting, and traditional Maori taniko work; these entries were also on display.

Among the distinguished visitors were King Koroki (nephew of Princess Te Puea), Judge Frank O. V. Acheson of the Native Land Court, and Princess Te Puea herself. Prime Minister Michael J. Savage was invited but sent greetings and apologies, as did other prominent politicians. Despite the sale of tickets, profits from a store set up on the ground, and donations from the districts, the hui tau committee still reported a loss of nearly £100 on the conference.[35]

Threatening clouds over Europe cast only small shadows on the New Zealand Mission. Isolated by distance and preoccupied with Church affairs, President Cowley and his missionaries continued their rounds of tracting, teaching, and meetings, playing basketball and baseball as the last months of peace slipped away. An Auckland Latter-day Saint wrote an article for the mission paper in which he suggested that Herr Adolf Hitler was fulfilling prophecy by causing German citizens to search their ancestry for Jewish blood. Latter-day Saints, he thought, might come to be grateful for this research, as so many had German ancestry.[36] Just five months later, after war had begun, another article in *Te Karere* referred to Hitler in less

---

34. Ibid., 31 August 1938.
35. New Zealand Mission, Manuscript History, Quarterly Historical Report, 31 May 1939.
36. "Is the Lord behind the Headlines?" *Te Karere* 33, no. 6 (June 1939): 201–3.

flattering terms as one who had "arrogated himself [sic] the God of the German people."[37]

The declaration of war on 3 September 1939 was noted in the mission history purely because of its effect on the American missionaries, who were now required to register as aliens at their local police station, a procedure they had to repeat on each transfer.[38] The war was not mentioned again in the mission history until March 1940 but made more impact in the pages of the mission paper. Local members who enlisted were assured that the Church supported their cause. "Although it is a sin to force war upon anyone, President Joseph F. Smith once said that it is both righteous and just to defend our lives, liberties, and homes with the last drop of our blood," wrote Elder Demar V. Taylor. "The brethren in this mission who are called to service in the war will be complying with the teachings of the Gospel in every respect."[39]

Elaborate preparations were being made for New Zealand's centennial celebrations in 1940. A special centenary exhibition opened in Wellington on 8 November 1939 and included an LDS booth designed and largely built by a young missionary, Elder George R. Biesinger, the first but by no means the last building job he was to do for the Mormon Church in New Zealand. The LDS exhibit featured models of the Salt Lake Temple and Tabernacle, with background music provided by recordings of the Mormon Tabernacle Choir. Tracts and literature were given away.[40] By April 1940, 6,000 people had signed the visitors' book, and 22,000 tracts and 9,000 Articles of Faith cards had been given away.[41]

In February 1940, President Cowley's *Te Karere* editorial featured the Waitangi Centennial. "The descendants of the noble chiefs who affixed their signatures to this momentous document will assemble on the occasion and in voices vibrant with racial pride will extol the ancestral virtues," he wrote. "... At the Waitangi centennial celebration the Maori chief [sic] of 1940 will with song, dance, speech and story, praise the fathers who in 1840 consummated an act intended to preserve unto their posterity the land of their inheritance. They will do well," he concluded, "on this memo-

---

37. Elder Demar V. Taylor, "War and the Gospel," *Te Karere* 33, no. 11 (November 1939): 400.

38. New Zealand Mission, Manuscript History, Quarterly Historical Report, 30 November 1939, entry dated 4 September 1939.

39. Taylor, "War and the Gospel," 401.

40. New Zealand Mission, Manuscript History, Quarterly Historical Report, 30 November 1939.

41. Matthew Cowley, "The Wellington Exhibit," *Te Karere* 34, no. 4 (April 1940): 131.

rable occasion to pledge themselves to acquire within the years ahead as much as possible of that heritage."[42]

A few years earlier, Rufus K. Hardy had suggested that the Saints in Bridge Pa use materials salvaged from the MAC to build an amusement hall. It was later decided to build a new chapel for the Korongata Branch instead, and plans were drawn by President Woods. After many delays, construction began on 2 June 1938, supervised by a Hawkes Bay building contractor, Joseph J. Powick. Aided by a small army of volunteers, including missionaries and a group of Maori boys aged between eleven and fifteen—perhaps the original labour missionaries (see chap. 7)—the work progressed. Four Maori carpenters were sent by the New Zealand government (such help was available on application for projects for Maori causes), and Relief Society women provided meals and whatever additional help they could. The building was finished in October 1938; President Cowley dedicated it on 4 February 1940.

The fifty-first hui tau was held at Nuhaka on 21–25 March 1940; it was dedicated to all New Zealand servicemen.[43] A concert organised by the revitalised MAC Old Boys' Association was attended by over a thousand people. Five former college matrons were honoured: Hiria Katerina McKay of Nuhaka; Ani Kamau of Korongata; Ida Smith of Auckland; Ka Kariana Tiwai of Korongata, and A. George of Auckland. At this hui tau, Elva Cowley introduced the first Singing Mothers chorus in New Zealand, a worldwide feature of Relief Society work. Proceeds of the Gold and Green Ball and associated queen competition raised more than £700, which was donated to the national Patriotic Fund.[44]

Later in 1940, President Cowley dedicated another chapel, this time at Maromaku, in Whangarei, home of the Going family. The Going family had been staunch members of the LDS Church since 1893; by 1940, four of their children had immigrated to the United States. Family members had long dreamed of a chapel in Maromaku. President Cowley reported their long years of faithful membership and full tithe paying to the First Presidency, who then offered to pay for the building. However, a giant kauri on the Going property was felled, its timber sawn, and the entire chapel built from this one tree. Branch members supplied labour, and all that the Church finally paid for was the plumbing and electrical work.

---

42. Matthew Cowley, "Waitangi 1840–1940," *Te Karere* 34, no. 2 (February 1940): 58–59.

43. Elder Warren S. Ottley, "A Remnant of the House of Israel Meets in Conference," *Te Karere* 34, no. 5 (May 1940): 166.

44. Ibid., 166–69; Matthew Cowley, "Support Your Hui Tau," *Te Karere* 35, no. 3 (March 1941): 595.

Top left: Percy Stanley Connorton Going (1868–1940) and (right) Gertrude Cutforth Going (1869–1936), pioneer LDS converts in the Bay of Islands District. Below: A giant kauri log from the Going property supplied all the timber needed to build the Maromaku Chapel in 1940. Photos courtesy Pamela Going White.

Percy Stanley Connorton Going died on 12 May 1940, before the building was finished; his wife Gertrude Cutforth Going had died a few years earlier. The new chapel, which featured a plaque to their memory, was dedicated on 6 October 1940.[45]

As more and still more LDS men enlisted in the New Zealand armed services, the branches began to feel their loss. The war effort dominated the thoughts and lives of most New Zealanders. On 16 June 1940, President Cowley received a cable from the First Presidency advising that no more missionaries would be sent to either Australia or New Zealand for the duration of the war. The following day the *Niagara*, a veteran of the trans-Pacific run that had transported hundreds of Mormon missionaries between North America and Australia and New Zealand, was sunk by a mine off the east coast of New Zealand a few hours after sailing from Auckland. Auckland Harbour was closed to shipping; and the *Mariposa*, due to dock a week later, bypassed New Zealand. The realities of war were coming very close. Petrol rationing was already in force, and President Cowley travelled by train instead of driving to visit the more distant districts.

By August 1940, there were thirty-three fewer missionaries in New Zealand than at the same time the previous year, and President Cowley's hardest task was deciding how to make best use of those he had.[46] As in World War I, there was some antagonism over America's non-involvement in the war. Some New Zealanders resented seeing these young American men playing basketball and baseball while their own men were facing death and danger. Able-bodied men not in the services were expected to do war work of some kind; accordingly, most of the missionaries stationed in Auckland became air raid wardens and took some training in civil defence.[47] Elva Cowley became very involved in the New Zealand war effort; she joined the Auckland Red Cross and stood on street corners collecting for wounded servicemen.[48] As the war progressed, she and her daughter, Jewell, also worked in a Red Cross canteen and participated in many other Red Cross activities.

---

45. "Dedication of Maromaku Chapel," *Te Karere* 34, no. 11 (November 1940): 438; Elva Eleanor Taylor Cowley, Autobiography, 150, Box 6, fd. 6, Cowley Collection.

46. New Zealand Mission, Manuscript History, 27 August 1940, in Quarterly Historical Report, 31 August 1940.

47. Glen L. Rudd, "Evacuation of Zion Missionaries from the South Pacific during World War II," 1.

48. Matthew Cowley, Letter to "Father and Aunt Luella" [Matthias F. Cowley and Luella Smart Parkinson Cowley], 11 June 1940, Box 1, fd. 10, Cowley Collection.

Matthew Cowley believed that the Allied cause was righteous and was impatient for the United States to declare war on Germany. "It looks like the U.S. is finding it more difficult every day to maintain its neutrality during this war," he wrote to his father in June 1940. "After all the conflict is resolving itself in to a struggle between democracy and totalitarianism. If the allies win the U.S. will be a beneficiary of the war and if they should lose our country will not evade the consequences. We must do everything in our power to aid the allied cause and the sooner we do it the better it will be for all the right-thinking people of the world."[49]

On 14 October 1940, a cable from the First Presidency ordered all missionaries still in the Pacific to return to the United States on the first available transport; mission presidents were to remain until further notice, and their family members were permitted to choose whether to stay or return home.[50] To many of the Saints, it seemed as if the Church must fall apart without the help and guidance of the beloved "Zion elders."

Mission secretaries James V. Haslam and Glen L. Rudd immediately began work to obtain departure permits for the thirty missionaries still in New Zealand. Elder Rudd (later to serve as both mission and area president) booked thirty berths on the return voyage of the *Mariposa*, then on its way to Australia and due back in New Zealand on 22 October. Sure that President Cowley couldn't manage all the necessary reports and paper work without them, Elders Rudd and Haslam persuaded him to allow them to stay an extra month till the next vessel sailed for North America. The two elders managing and editing *Te Karere* also received Cowley's permission to stay another month; all four intended to train local Saints to take over their work. However, when President Cowley read newspaper reports that the *Mariposa* might be the last passenger vessel to cross the Pacific for many months, he withdrew his permission and these four elders sailed with the rest.

The missionaries were scattered across New Zealand and were not easy to contact, but by Saturday night, 19 October, all were gathered in the mission home.[51] Haslam and Rudd worked day and night getting reports up-to-date and making sure President Cowley understood the bookwork so he could train a local Church member to take over. They averaged three or four hours' sleep each night and did not get to bed at all the last night.[52]

---

49. Ibid.
50. Rudd, "Evacuation of Zion Missionaries," 2; Elva Cowley, Autobiography, 175.
51. Rudd, "Evacuation of Zion Missionaries," 3.
52. Ibid., 3–4.

Mission president Matthew Cowley (left) on a pastoral visit with his driver and companion, Mission Secretary Elder Glen L. Rudd, c. 1940. Courtesy Elder Glen L. Rudd.

On Tuesday, 22 October 1940, President Cowley interviewed each missionary for the last time. The luggage was sent to the wharf by noon, and then the elders left, too. The four office missionaries were the last to go. They left their mission president sweeping the floor, too distressed to watch the sailing.[53] The Australian Mission elders were already on board the *Mariposa* when it arrived in Auckland, though those travelling by train from Perth in Western Australia had not reached Sydney in time and had to wait for another boat. With the addition of the New Zealand contingent, the ship was carrying sixty-seven Mormon missionaries when it arrived in Pago Pago and collected the Samoan and Tongan missionaries.[54] The Tahitian missionaries, who should also have been picked up at Pago

---

53. Elva Cowley, Autobiography, 176; Rudd, "Evacuation of Zion Missionaries," 4.
54. Rudd, "Evacuation of Zion Missionaries," 5.

Pago, missed the connection when one of their number had an emergency appendectomy. Faced with the possibility of having to wait six months for another passenger liner, the Tahitian mission president chartered a schooner, and his missionaries travelled under sail to Hawaii.[55]

Once in Hawaii, those missionaries who had served twenty-two months or longer were released; the remainder were reassigned to the California and Northwestern States missions, though a few remained in the Japanese Mission in Hawaii. Those returning to the mainland sailed on the *Mariposa*'s sister ship, the *Monterey*, and were welcomed in San Francisco by President David O. McKay of the First Presidency.[56]

Two former editors of *Te Karere*, Kelly Harris and Hohepa Meha, took over the journal again, and the printing was done commercially. Members were assessed a small sum to help pay the printer's bill for the magazine, which contained each month's Primary, Sunday School, MIA, and genealogy lessons. More than ever, President Cowley pushed for subscriptions to *Te Karere*. This was not just an effort to make the paper pay its way. Cowley realised that he could not single-handedly keep contact with more than 8,000 members scattered over both North and South Islands; the mission paper had a vital role to play, and he was determined to get it into the homes of as many Saints as possible. Subscription campaigns continued throughout the war; while the price of an annual subscription remained fixed at five shillings, costs increased 100 percent. Income from subscriptions raised only about one third of the costs of the paper.[57]

The 1941 hui tau was dedicated to the memory of all "Zion" missionaries, not just those who had recently been evacuated. "To the men and women, numbering more than one thousand, who, during the past sixty years, have come to New Zealand from their homes in America to serve God by serving their fellow-men, this Hui Tau programme for 1941 is respectfully dedicated," proclaimed President Cowley. "For the first time in the history of the Mission a Hui Tau will be convened without the attendance of Zion elders.... God bless their memory."[58]

Held at Nuhaka, hui tau was as successful as ever despite somewhat lower attendance figures. During the conference, George Watene was sustained as mission secretary and Kelly Harris as editor of *Te Karere*. Ten local district presidents were sustained: Hohepa Heperi (Bay of Islands);

---

55. R. Lanier Britsch, *Unto the Islands of the Sea: A History of the Latter-day Saints in the Pacific*, 60–61.
56. Rudd, "Evacuation of Zion Missionaries," 5.
57. "*Te Karere* and Its Future," *Te Karere* 39, no. 10 (October 1944): 249.
58. 1941 Hui Tau Program, copy microfilmed with *Te Karere* 35, no. 4 (April 1941), inserted between pp. 626 and 627.

Polly (Pare) Duncan, the first New Zealand woman to serve as mission Relief Society president (1932–53). Courtesy Harold B. Lee Library, Brigham Young University, Provo, Utah.

Henare P. Wihongi (Whangarei); William R. Perrott (Auckland); Henry S. Marshall (Waikato); Mane Taurau (Manawatu-Wairarapa); Toke Watene (Hauraki); Eriata Nopera (Hawkes Bay); Hirini (Sidney) Christy (Mahia); Henare Hamon (Poverty Bay), and Turi Ruruku (Wairau). Hohepa Meha was placed in charge of mission Sunday Schools; Pare Takana (Polly Duncan) continued as mission Relief Society president; Wi Duncan presided over the YMMIA and Una Thompson over the YWMIA, with Stuart Meha continuing to preside over the mission genealogical committee. Elva Cowley was sustained as mission Primary president.[59]

The First Presidency was kept aware of conditions in New Zealand by President Cowley and wrote encouraging messages back. "We have no doubt but that the stalwart native Elders of the Church in New Zealand will loyally support you in the present crisis," they wrote in March 1941, "and will carry on the work ably, as the Lord will give them strength and guidance."[60] This they did.

Certainly local leaders responded well to the challenge, feeling that to continue the work was "a living and workable memorial to the Zion Elders who have laboured in this land."[61] President Cowley was delighted. "You

---

59. "News from the Field," *Te Karere* 35, no. 4 (April 1941): 640.
60. "Message from the First Presidency," *Te Karere* 35, no. 5 (May 1941): 655.
61. Tipi Kopua, "Poverty Bay District," *Te Karere* 35, no. 3 (March 1941): 605.

would be inspired to see how the local Priesthood has taken hold of things since the exodus of the Elders," he wrote to one former missionary.[62]

As the grim months of 1941 passed, *Te Karere* pages contained reports of Saints wounded, killed, or missing in action. The Manawatu-Wairarapa District proudly reported that Ngahuka Love of Otaki had five sons serving in the armed forces.[63] President Cowley was touched when his old friend, Rangikawea Puriri of Korongata, slipped away from his daughter's home one day and travelled to Wellington by train to enlist as a chaplain for Mormon servicemen overseas. "He returned home in a very sad mood because he had not been accepted," wrote President Cowley. Puriri, already a veteran of three wars, died peacefully at home a year later at the age of 102. He was accorded a full military funeral.[64]

On 7 December 1941, Japanese planes bombed the American military base at Pearl Harbor. The United States entered the war, and the Cowley administration of the LDS Mission in New Zealand entered another phase.

For only the third time in half a century, hui tau had to be suspended in 1942; food and petrol rationing, travel restrictions, and the long hours worked by those in essential services made it quite impracticable.

By mid-1942, there were so many American troops in the South Pacific that New Zealanders, President Cowley reported, were "beginning to feel like strangers in their own country."[65] American LDS servicemen, either training in New Zealand or on leave from the battle zones farther north, found their way to the mission home.[66] The mission paper listed more than 125 servicemen who visited the Auckland Branch in one month in 1943, while the Wellington Branch reported twenty American marines at one Sunday service in 1943.[67]

"It is inspiring the way some of these chaps come in to pay their tithing and partake of the sacrament," wrote Cowley. "Others to be adminis-

---

62. Matthew Cowley, Letter to David A. Harris, 19 July 1942, Box 1, fd. 10, Cowley Collection.

63. "News from the Field," *Te Karere* 35, no. 6 (June 1941): 704.

64. Matthew Cowley, Letter to Wilford E. Smith, 31 July 1942, Box 1, fd. 10, Cowley Collection; "News from the Field," *Te Karere* 36, no. 9 (September 1942): 269.

65. Matthew Cowley, Letter to "Ellis and Virginia" (Mr. and Mrs. Ellis W. Barker), 19 January 1943, fd. 11, Cowley Collection.

66. "Visitors to Headquarters," *Te Karere* 36, no. 9 (September 1942): 270; "General Mission News," *Te Karere* 36, no. 7 (July 1942): 214.

67. "General News," *Te Karere* 38, no. 6 (June 1943): 160–61; "News from the Field," *Te Karere*, 37 no. 4 (April 1943): 103. N.B. There was an editorial error in numbering the volumes of *Te Karere*, jumping from 37, no. 4 (April 1943) to 38, no. 5 (May 1943).

tered to.... One nineteen year old called on us one night before Christmas [1942]. He was here only for the one night but he wanted to spend his time visiting Church members. He was the only L.D.S. in his outfit and it was really touching to hear him tell how he would shut himself up in his cabin on Sunday, bless a bit of bread and a bit of water and partake of the sacrament. He said as long as he could do this the other men would not influence him away from his ideals."[68]

Jewell Cowley had been a twelve-year-old schoolgirl when she arrived in New Zealand in 1938. Her adolescence could not have been easy, living in the mission home and helping run what her mother described as a small hotel, with missionaries and Church members constantly coming and going, and always, it seemed, invited for dinner. Jewell suffered severe culture shock when she enrolled at Auckland Girls' Grammar School and, for the first time, had to wear a uniform—tunic, blazer, hat, black bloomers, and black stockings. The American missionaries teased her unmercifully; and her self-esteem, according to her mother, dropped several notches. Later, she transferred to St. Cuthbert's College where she was happier, finding a friend and compatriot in the daughter of the American consul. Jewell worked hard to help her parents, running a small Primary for Auckland Branch children on Saturday mornings at age fifteen, writing occasional short articles for *Te Karere*, serving in the Red Cross canteen, and helping to care for her adopted baby brother Tony.

Despite Elva Cowley's initial reluctance, in 1940 she and Matthew Cowley began adoption proceedings for an eleven-month-old part-Maori boy.[69] Tony was a beautiful child, one whom passers-by turned to look at in the street. He was self-willed, independent, and something of a handful as he grew up. As Tony developed from a baby to a determined small

---

68. Cowley, Letter to "Ellis and Virginia."

69. Tony's birth was registered by his biological mother with the Registrar of Births, Deaths and Marriages in Wellington, New Zealand. After the adoption was finalised, the baby was officially re-registered as Duncan Meha Cowley. However, because he was already known to everyone, including the Cowley family, as Tony, he continued to be known by this name. When Tony's photograph appeared on the cover of *Te Karere* in January 1941, he was identified by the editor as "Nopera Takana Meha Kauri, better known as 'Tony.'" *Te Karere*, February 1941, 553. "Kauri" is the Maori transliteration of "Cowley," and "Takana" is the Maori transliteration of "Duncan." It is not known when "Nopera" was unofficially added, but Eriata Nopera, Wiremu Duncan (Takana), and Stuart Meha were three great Maori Mormon leaders with whom Cowley was closely associated; and Brother Nopera presided at a formal meeting at which the baby was handed over to the Cowleys by his birth mother. Elva Cowley, Autobiography, 154.

boy, Jewell passed through adolescence to young womanhood. After leaving school, she attended business college classes as well as taking some courses at Auckland University. She was sixteen in 1942 when American servicemen began to frequent the Auckland LDS Mission home. Unlike the missionaries, the servicemen were not forbidden to show interest in the opposite sex, and Jewell had frequent dates for the movies and dances held in wartime Auckland. Her mother later reported that Jewell often saw the same movie five or six times with different escorts, as the lonely servicemen begged her to go with them and the programs were changed only once a week. In 1944, at the age of eighteen, Jewell fell in love with an LDS naval officer, Val Sheffield, who spent a week in the mission home. The romance continued by mail, and Jewell returned to the States to be married in the Salt Lake Temple.[70]

Meanwhile, most of the eighty-plus branches of the Church in New Zealand continued to hold services,[71] though the columns of *Te Karere* indicate that attendance at meetings was low in many areas. Local part-time missionaries, most of them women, were called in several areas. A new missionary endeavour began when a young, newly married couple, Samoan-born Fritz Bunge Krueger and his Maori wife, Moririki, went to Rarotonga in the Cook Islands where Krueger opened a bakery business. President Cowley set Krueger apart as a missionary; and within weeks he baptized Samuel Glassie and his wife, blessed their two daughters, Moe and Ngai, and baptized a sixteen-year-old woman named Mii Henry. Matthew Cowley was unaware that Elder Noah Rogers had visited the Cook Islands as early as 1845 or that missionaries from the French Polynesia Mission had spent four-and-one-half years there, unsuccessfully, from 1899 to 1903. He delightedly termed Krueger the first-ever LDS missionary in the Cook Islands. Although Kreuger was not the first to preach the Mormon gospel there, he *was* the first to find success. There were nearly forty Latter-day Saints in the Cook Islands by 1946.[72]

---

70. Matthew Cowley, Letter to Rulon N. Smith, 18 July 1942, fd. 10; Letter to J. Martell Bodell, 13 April 1944; Letter to Patty Miller, 3 August 1944, all in fd. 11, Cowley Collection; Elva Cowley, Autobiography, 135, 139–40, 205; K[elly] H[arris], "Jewell Cowley," *Te Karere* 39, no. 10 (October 1944): 248–49.

71. "Sunday Schools in the Missions [sic]," *Te Karere* 37, no. 1 (January 1943): unnumbered page.

72. "News from the Field," *Te Karere* 36, no. 11 (November 1942): 325; "News from the Field," *Te Karere* 37, no. 1 (January 1943): 25; Kelly Harris, "Rarotonga's Missionaries," 38, no. 10 (October 1943): 246–47; Britsch, *Unto the Islands of the Sea*, 10, 34, 332–33.

Late in 1942, President Cowley organised the Maori Battalion Branch, with Pera Tengaio as president, Ephraim Prime and Benjamin Christy as counselors, and J. H. Elkington as class leader.[73] There were numerous Latter-day Saints in the Maori Battalion, which gave distinguished service in North Africa and Italy. The branch organisation allowed these LDS men to hold sacrament meetings and run such programs as battlefront conditions made possible. A year later, one of Cowley's former missionaries, Lieutenant Robert L. Simpson, finished basic Air Force training and was sent to San Francisco, widely recognised as the embarkation point for the Pacific war zone. Simpson was pleased. "I just knew that I was going to be able to go back to New Zealand and help Brother Cowley because all the missionaries had been evacuated," he recalled years later. "'I'll be sent down there and help Brother Cowley during my off duty hours. I knew the military would probably send me there, because of my knowledge of the Maori language being an asset to . . . help them in some of the liaison work."

The American military, of course, did nothing so sensible; a few days before Simpson was due to embark for the South Pacific, he and a few others of his unit were suddenly shipped across the Atlantic. "I didn't understand how this would happen to me, when I was so sure that I was going to be able to go back to New Zealand," he relates:

> When I arrived at my final destination, it was Egypt, of all places. But I found a whole Maori battalion at the New Zealand base there in Egypt, not more than twenty miles from my American air base. During the next eighteen months or so that I was stationed there, I was able to go over to the New Zealand base and hold Church meetings—priesthood and sacrament meetings and MIA and other meetings—with the troops, and it was just like being on a mission again. I'd known most of these young men as a missionary in New Zealand just a few years before. And the Maori language helped, because many of these young men, even though they spoke English, whenever they got in trouble and wanted to confess their problems, they wanted to do it in Maori.

The Maori Battalion had been through the North African campaign and was resting before leaving for Italy. "These Maori boys kept rotating, some coming and some going," commented Simpson, "but there was [sic] always a few hundred there, forty or fifty of whom would be LDS boys."[74]

---

73. "News from the Field," *Te Karere* 36, no. 11 (November 1942): 325.
74. Simpson, Oral History, 13–14.

Truly, the Lord moves in mysterious ways, and one of His servants found himself able to serve both his country and his church in time of war.

Having cancelled the 1942 hui tau, President Cowley was determined to hold one in 1943 and decided to make it a fund-raising effort for the regional Patriotic Committees. After obtaining government consent (a necessity in wartime), he scheduled hui tau for Easter (23–26 April) at the Tomoana Show Grounds in Hastings, and began advertising it in the pages of the mission paper, although he urged those in essential work not to attend the hui without leave. Travel restrictions were still in force, but President Cowley negotiated with relevant officials and obtained permission for limited numbers to travel from each district.

More than 2,000 attended, some from every LDS district in the North Island and even some from the Wairau District in the South Island. Sir Apirana Ngata and Bishop Frederick A. Bennett of the Church of England both addressed the conference. Ngata and Algernon Rainbow, the mayor of Hastings, spoke at a sacred concert held in the Municipal Theatre on Friday night. An Anzac Day march and service were held after morning conference on Sunday, 25 April, and another sacred concert was held in the evening, commemorating both Easter and Anzac Day. As the Saints left for home on Tuesday, 27 April, the northern contingent began a testimony meeting on the train, a meeting that continued without pause for more than 200 miles. Nearly £14,000 was raised at hui tau, more than half of it coming from the queen competition.[75]

In July 1943, President Cowley spoke sternly to local priesthood members about abuse of authority. A local elder had been charged and fined for illegally demanding a fee for witnessing a signature on a social security document. Cowley was horrified. "He was not only violating the law of his country pertaining to the attesting of such applications, but he was flagrantly transgressing the doctrine of the Church that the Priesthood of God is not for hire," he wrote in *Te Karere*. President Cowley was not even certain that local branch and district presidency members were legally entitled to witness such signatures. Henceforth, he decreed, only those who were gazetted marriage celebrants should witness any legal document. He also worried about reports that some local priesthood officers were receiving extra petrol for pastoral visits but using it for personal purposes. "If any branch or district officer is receiving petrol to be used for Church work and he is using it for his own pleasure . . . he is liable to prosecution by the Government and disciplinary action by the Church," he warned. "The

---

75. "Patriotic Hui Tau," *Te Karere* 38, no. 6 (June 1943): 134–36.

Church will not tolerate infractions of the Oil-fuel Regulations by any of the Elders or others who may be acting in the name of the Church."[76]

By 1943, scarcely an LDS family was untouched as the war ground on through its fourth long year and into the fifth. "The Maori boys have been doing a great job overseas," wrote President Cowley to a former missionary, "and when the history of the war is written, their deeds will be recorded in bold letters."[77] A Mormon soldier, George Katene of Porirua, won the Military Medal, becoming the first Maori to be decorated in World War II, before being killed in action.[78] Sid Christy's son, Benjamin Goddard Christy, an officer of the Maori Battalion, won the Military Cross.

Twenty members of the Uawa Branch (sixteen men and four women) had enlisted; by the end of 1943, four had been killed in action, two invalided home, and one was a prisoner of war. There were thirty-two members of the Nuhaka Branch in the services by 1943. In the little Rotorua/Horo Horo branch, David Moore had six sons overseas and three in the Home Guard. Two of his nephews and his wife's three brothers were also overseas.[79]

In September 1944, as the war entered its sixth year, President Cowley received news that another former New Zealand missionary, A. Reed Halversen, had been called as his successor and would sail as soon as berths were available for him and his family.[80] Months passed with no word of the Halversens' arrival. President Cowley continued travelling, visiting most of the North Island branches frequently and those in the South Island once or twice a year.

In June 1944, President Cowley announced the establishment of the MAC Old Boys' Scholarship Fund. "The M.A.C. has really been appreciated more since it was discontinued than when it was in operation," commented Cowley wryly. "The Old Boys, especially, wish that there was such a school to which they could send their own sons.... It is to be hoped, and we are all praying for it, that sometime in the not too distant future the Church authorities will be inspired to establish another school in New Zealand for the youth of the Mission, for both young men and young women."[81]

---

76. "The President's Page," *Te Karere* 38, no. 7 (July 1943): 170–71.
77. Matthew Cowley, Letter to David M. Evans, 20 July 1942, fd. 10, Cowley Collection.
78. "News from the Field: Porirua Branch," *Te Karere* 41, no. 5 (May 1946): 128.
79. Wi Pere Amaru, "Uawa Branch at War," *Te Karere* 39, no. 2 (February 1944): 48; Rangi Davies, "Rotorua-Horo Horo Branch at War," *Te Karere* 39, no. 4 (April 1944): 104.
80. George Albert Smith, Letter to Matthew Cowley, 9 August 1944, fd. 11, Cowley Collection; "New Mission President Appointed," *Te Karere* 39, no. 9 (September 1944): 225.
81. Matthew Cowley, "The President's Page," *Te Karere* 39, no. 6 (June 1944): 138–39.

In October 1944, the New Zealand government sponsored a conference on Maori welfare that was attended by four hundred representatives of the thirty principal Maori tribes. The conference was held in the Ngati Poneke Hall in Wellington and was addressed by the Prime Minister, the Rt. Hon. Peter Fraser, and by government and Church leaders, including Matthew Cowley.[82] Cowley urged the Christian denominations to unite in the cause of Maori welfare. To prolonged applause, he stated, "Maori blood, regardless of Church affiliation, has been spilled and mingled as one on foreign soil in this war. Let not us, home here, separate that oneness." Speaking in Maori, as an "honorary" Maori, he continued, "We . . . do not wish to be considered as a race to be humoured. We want to be considered as a race to be given responsibility."[83] Seconded to one of the select committees, Cowley was given a stenographer and commissioned to write up the resolutions of his particular committee. He drew heavily on the LDS Church Welfare program for his suggestions. At the end of the conference, Father Reardon, the Roman Catholic Church representative at the conference, offered President Cowley a blessing, which he gratefully accepted.[84] A day or two later, Maori Member of Parliament the Hon. E. T. Tirikatene attended the Porirua LDS branch conference. Invited to speak, he urged President Cowley to remain in New Zealand, accept a government appointment, and continue his work for the Maori people.[85]

The April 1945 issue of the mission paper featured the obituary of Rufus K. Hardy, former missionary, twice mission president in New Zealand, and then a member of the First Council of the Seventy. During President Hardy's first term as mission president, the Auckland chapel and mission home were built, and land acquired for the now-defunct Maori Agricultural College (the latter a more controversial purchase). In recent years, Rufus K. Hardy dreamed of the Church building a magnificent carved whare wananga at Nuhaka. "He wanted this building to be the finest of its kind in New Zealand," wrote Matthew Cowley. "God grant that this wish of his may be fully realised."[86]

At least three LDS students won university scholarships in this period. Nitama Paewai qualified in medicine at the University of Otago and

---

82. "Maori Welfare," *Evening Post* (Wellington), 18 October 1944, 6.
83. Kelly Harris, "Maori Conference," *Te Karere* 39, no. 12 (December 1944): 309.
84. Elva Cowley, Autobiography, 180.
85. "News from the Field: Porirua Branch," *Te Karere* 39, no. 12 (December 1944): 327.
86. Matthew Cowley, "Death of President Hardy," *Te Karere* 40, no. 4 (April 1945): 83.

became an intern at the Auckland Hospital. His cousin, Luxford Peeti Walker, followed him to Knox College, Dunedin, two years later and studied dentistry, while another Maori LDS student studied law at Auckland University. At a time when there were relatively few Maori university students, President Cowley was proud of the LDS record. Now Kelly Harris, Maori editor of *Te Karere*, urged the Saints to have their children work towards secondary school scholarships. "If they are to live with the Pakeha under the Pakeha environment of future economic life, then we Maori people must of necessity learn as much of the Pakeha way of doing things. We must learn it the Pakeha way—at the Pakeha schools and from the Pakeha himself."[87]

Almost a year after his appointment was announced, President A. Reed Halversen was finally able to obtain berths on the *Ruahine* and arrived in Wellington on 24 July 1945. He was accompanied by his wife, Luana, and four children. Many of the Saints remembered Halversen from his service at the MAC and his term as acting mission president in the 1920s. "He comes like an older brother bringing his bride back to the family hearth," wrote Kelly Harris in *Te Karere*.[88]

President Cowley had presided in New Zealand for seven and one half years, longer than any other president in the history of the mission. He had now spent a total of twelve years—one quarter of his life—in New Zealand. Both missions coincided with world wars, and both were extended long past the usual period. There were sorrowful farewells, and New Zealand Latter-day Saints agreed then and now with Kelly Harris: "When the history of the New Zealand Mission is finally written for these past war years, there will be told that President Matthew Cowley, Sister Elva Taylor Cowley, and their daughter Jewell, with their Maori son, 'Toni' Nopera Takana Meha Cowley, were the right people in the right place at the right time."[89] The transfer of mission authority was effected in a few hectic days; and on 30 July 1945, Matthew, Elva, and Tony Cowley sailed from New Zealand as passengers on a U.S. naval vessel.[90] The war in the Pacific ended during their journey home.

Matthew Cowley was called to serve in the Quorum of the Twelve at the October 1945 general conference in Salt Lake City.[91] There was

---

87. "Scholarships for Maori Students," *Te Karere* 40, no. 8 (August 1945): 178.
88. "Our Mission Presidents: Matthew Cowley, Farewell; A. Reed Halversen, Welcome," *Te Karere* 40, no. 9 (September 1945): 203–5.
89. Ibid.
90. New Zealand Mission, Manuscript History, 30 July 1945.
91. "President Matthew Cowley Appointed Member of the Quorum of the Twelve Apostles," *Te Karere* 40, no. 11 (November 1945): 242.

great rejoicing but little surprise in the New Zealand mission as this news spread. Some months earlier when Maori Saints were mourning the death of Elder Rufus K. Hardy of the Seventy, their spokesman in Church leadership councils, Rahiri Harris told them not to worry: when Matthew Cowley returned home, he would fill the first vacancy in the Council of the Twelve, and the New Zealand Mission would still have a representative among the General Authorities of the Church.[92] Elder Cowley's call came within weeks of his return. He was sustained on 5 October 1945, filling the vacancy caused by the death of Church President Heber J. Grant and the ordination of George Albert Smith as the new prophet.

Joyful welcomes were given to returning servicemen and repatriated prisoners-of-war in each branch of the New Zealand Mission. An almost equal joy was felt when the first "Zion" missionaries since 1940 arrived in Auckland on the *Monterey* on 8 February 1946. The first to come were Elders Norman V. Larsen and Ray H. Lloyd from Idaho, and Elders J. Clifford French, Joseph Talmage McMurray, and Leonard V. McKee from Alberta, Canada. All were assigned to the Auckland District.[93] "The coming of these five Elders is the answer to the prayers of the people," wrote Kelly Harris.[94] Two more, Elders Guy Foote and Wayne Leavitt, arrived on 29 March 1946.

The first day of hui tau, Friday, 19 April 1946, was dedicated to honouring the Maori Battalion with speeches, receptions, a banquet, and entertainment. Over 100 servicemen were present, as were Sir Apirana Ngata, Turi Carroll, and other non-LDS Maori leaders. About 1,500 attended this, the first hui tau since 1943. The program followed the usual course, except that, at President Halversen's suggestion, most competitive sports were eliminated in favour of activities in which all could participate. The honour of being the first "Zion missionary" to speak at hui tau since 1940 went to Elder Joseph Talmage McMurray, son of Joseph McMurray, a former New Zealand missionary, and his wife, Helena Harriet Weaver McKenzie McMurray, who had been born in New Zealand.[95]

After hui tau, President Halversen assigned his small missionary force to district work (where they could cover a larger geographical area than if assigned to a particular branch), calling local men to serve six-month missions as companions for each "Zion elder." Six more "Zion missionaries" arrived on 28 June 1946. Among them were two women, Sisters Meryl

---

92. Elva Cowley, Autobiography, 225.
93. New Zealand Mission, Manuscript History, 8 February 1946; "Elders from Canada and America aboard 'Monterey,'" *Te Karere* 41, no. 3 (March 1946): 72.
94. "Zion Elders," *Te Karere* 41, no. 3 (March 1946): 58–59.
95. Kelly Harris, "Hui Tau, 1946," *Te Karere* 41, no. 7 (July 1946): 170–71.

Reber and Rose Marie Wegener, the first single women called to serve as full-time missionaries in New Zealand, apart from the service given by daughters of earlier presidents.[96]

Fritz and Moririki Krueger returned to New Zealand, leaving a small branch in the Cook Islands. In June 1946, two Church officers from Salt Lake City, Elders Alma Burton and Frank J. Fulmer, called at Rarotonga during a survey of Church building needs in the Pacific. While there, they ordained Samuel Glassie and Harry T. Strickland to the Melchizedek Priesthood. Now New Zealander Trevor Hamon and his Canadian wife, Mildred, were called to serve as full-time missionaries in the Cook Islands. They sailed on the *Maui Pomare* on 6 September 1946.[97] Once in Rarotonga, Brother Hamon was sustained as branch president, with Glassie and Strickland as counselors; the auxiliaries were reorganised and the branch began reporting to *Te Karere*.[98]

President Halversen released some of the local district presidents who had given long and faithful service, replacing them with "Zion" elders.[99] As more missionaries arrived from America, they were assigned to the South Island, the Bay of Islands, and other districts that had not seen missionaries since 1940.[100] In November, President Halversen organised a branch in Nelson, with Ben Hippolite as branch president, and then travelled on to Dunedin for a branch conference. He was pleased to see that attendance figures were building up. Before the advent of the missionaries, the Dunedin Branch had held only one meeting each month during the war; now the branch held both Sunday School and sacrament meeting each Sunday. Within three months, the Christchurch Branch had also revived.[101]

There were fifty "Zion missionaries" at the 1947 hui tau in Korongata. Despite severely curtailed rail services owing to coal strikes, more than two thousand people arrived by car, bus, and truck. The New Zealand Army loaned four trucks to transport members from Auckland and Wellington, and freight companies came to the rescue of others. Large numbers arrived on-site in cov-

---

96. New Zealand Mission, Manuscript History, 29 April, 19 May, 15, 28, 30 June 1946.

97. New Zealand Mission, Manuscript History, 22 July 1946; Meryl Reber, "New Missionaries for Rarotonga," *Te Karere* 41, no. 10 (October 1946): 259.

98. "News from the Field: Rarotonga Branch," *Te Karere* 41, no. 12 (December 1946): 341.

99. New Zealand Mission, Manuscript History, 19 May 1946.

100. Ibid., 14, 17, 18 October 1946.

101. "News from the Field," *Te Karere* 42, no. 1 (January 1947): 33, and no. 4 (April 1947): 122.

ered trucks reminiscent, Kelly Harris thought, of the covered wagons whose arrival in the Salt Lake Valley 100 years earlier was being commemorated.[102]

Of twelve district presidents sustained at the 1947 hui tau, four were now missionary elders. The thirteenth district, Hawkes Bay, was without a president owing to the death of veteran Maori leader Eriata Nopera on 9 February 1947. On Easter Sunday in the early morning hours, MAC "old boys" and their families made a pilgrimage to the college site. Here they picked their way among the rubble and broken bricks and cement till all were assembled within the remains of the college chapel, where a memorial service was held for the school and for those of its former students who had served in two world wars.

With hui tau over for another year, Reed and Luana Halversen left Auckland by Sunderland flying boat for Rarotonga where they held meetings in the little "home-made" thatched-roof chapel at Muri Enua that had been built by the Saints and the Hamons. Fund-raising for this meetinghouse was started by the Kruegers, who, before they left Rarotonga, helped the small group of Saints gather coral to make lime. Timber was cut and carted, and the main building erected in just nine days at a total cost of £16/12/6. Two "Zion missionaries," Elders Donlon P. Delamere and John L. Sorenson, were also in Rarotonga. Besides the branch at Muri Enua, a home Sunday School and a Primary were meeting at Avarua, with a neighbourhood Primary at Black Rock. The Halversens flew out a few days later, decked with leis and bead necklaces, symbols of the love the little group of Latter-day Saints felt for the first mission president to visit them.[103]

In December 1946, the First Presidency assigned Elder Matthew Cowley of the Quorum of the Twelve to preside over all the Pacific Missions of the Church, the first such since Apostle Parley P. Pratt in 1851.[104] After visiting Hawaii and Sydney, Elder Cowley arrived in New Zealand on 23 May 1947 and was warmly welcomed by everyone in the mission. He spent the weekend in Auckland, then with President Halversen visited the Whangarei and Bay of Islands districts. In Kaikohe, they inspected land for a new church building. Elder Cowley recommended an all-purpose building which could be used for dances and basketball as a means of pro-

---

102. "President's Page: Hui Tau Thoughts," *Te Karere* 42, no. 5 (May 1947): 132; Kelly Harris, "Our Recent Hui Tau," ibid., 143–45.

103. New Zealand Mission, Manuscript History, 18–23 April 1947; "President's Page: The Church in Rarotonga," *Te Karere*, 42, no. 6 (June 1947): 164–65; Elder T. C. Hamon, "A New Chapel in Rarotonga," ibid., 170.

104. "Elder Cowley Given New Assignment over Missions," *Church News*, 7 December 1946, 1; "New Assignment for Matthew Cowley," *Te Karere* 42, no. 2 (February 1947): 45.

viding wholesome recreation for the Maori youth; more than 50 percent of the local Maori population, he reported, were under the age of twenty.

They then travelled to the Waikato District conference at Te Kuiti, where Elder Cowley was troubled because most of the Saints slept on straw placed on the damp ground inside tents while he and President Halversen sheltered from the bitterly cold weather at an hotel. "What inconveniences these people will submit themselves to in order that they may attend conference," he wrote. "We need buildings, buildings and more buildings." Moving south, they visited Porirua and Wellington, then Tahoraiti and Korongata, where Elder Cowley recalled the happy days he had spent in the Duncan and Puriri homes respectively.[105] The return trip included the Mahia District Conference on 7 and 8 June.[106] During his travels, Elder Cowley promised the MAC "old boys" that he would do everything in his power to get another Church school in New Zealand.[107]

Elder Cowley left New Zealand for the islands, including Rarotonga (where he dedicated both the new chapel and the island group for the preaching of the gospel), on 14 June.[108] When he returned home, he carried with him a report signed by President Halversen, but undoubtedly concocted with Elder Cowley's help, to be used as ammunition for Elder Cowley to fire in leadership councils in Utah. Its recommendations were staggering in breadth and expense; it is a measure of Elder Cowley's influence, persuasiveness, and devotion to the New Zealand Mission that, within a decade, most of them had become a reality.

The recommendations included: the purchase of a new, larger mission home in a more desirable locality; the erection of a new chapel and recreation hall for the Auckland Branch to be partly financed by selling the present Upper Queen Street property; the purchase of property for another secondary school for Maori boys, of higher academic standing than the old MAC, with consideration to be given later to provision of a similar school for Maori girls; new chapels for most mission branches; a recreation hall for the Kaikohe Branch; another Maori edition of the Book of Mormon; and a plea for a small temple in New Zealand to serve the Saints of the South Pacific, from Tahiti to Australia.[109]

---

105. Matthew Cowley, Diary, 31 May 1947, Box 1, fd. 6, Cowley Collection.

106. New Zealand Mission, Manuscript History, 23 May–14 June 1947; "Elder Cowley Returns," *Te Karere* 42, no. 7 (July 1947): 207.

107. "Appeal to Old M.A.C. Boys," *Te Karere* 43, no. 2 (February 1948): 56.

108. "News of the Field: Rarotonga Branch," *Te Karere* 42, no. 9 (September 1947): 285–86.

109. A. Reed Halversen, Letter to Elder Matthew Cowley, 12 June 1947, Box 1, fd. 12, Cowley Collection.

Soon after Elder Cowley's departure, the Auckland Branch was divided by the formation of the Rangitoto Maori Branch, at the request of the many Maori Saints who were among the marked Maori drift to the cities during and after the war. The Maori Saints wanted their own Maori-speaking branch, rather than being part of the English-speaking Auckland Branch. The Rangitoto Branch grew and flourished.

At the end of June 1947, President Halversen visited Wellington. Here he asked the relevant government officials to either raise or remove the quota of sixty-five LDS missionaries allowed in New Zealand, a quota that had been in effect since World War I. On 9 July 1947, Halversen was advised that the minister had directed that "American born missionaries of the Church who are wholly of European race and color will be admitted to New Zealand without restriction as to number, provided they comply with usual customs formalities."[110] For the first time since the early years of the century, there was to be no restriction as to number. The "race and colour" restrictions reflect immigration policies then in force in both Australia and New Zealand.

President Halversen followed the same busy schedule of visits and meetings as his predecessors. During February 1948, a typical month, he visited Wellington, Christchurch, Dunedin, Blenheim, French Pass, Wellington again, Porirua, Awarua, Palmerston North, and Wellington for a third time. Everywhere he inspected existing Church buildings and planned new ones, looking into land titles and talking to government officials about building permits. Post-war scarcity of materials was the biggest problem. He frequently visited Nuhaka to review progress on the carved house at last being built there. By August 1948, the foundations were partly laid, and some of the walls were rising.[111]

In March 1948, Apostle and Sister Cowley arrived in Auckland. It was Elder Cowley's second visit as a member of the Quorum of the Twelve and as president of the Pacific Missions of the LDS Church. A highlight of their visit was attending the fifty-sixth hui tau at Korongata.[112] By Thursday, 25 March 1948, Latter-day Saints were pouring onto the marae. Hundreds of tents and tons of straw provided sleeping accommodation, and a huge marquee was the venue for conference sessions and concert programs. It was estimated that more than two thousand Latter-day Saints thronged the grounds; those who could not get into the marquee stood by

---

110. New Zealand Mission, Manuscript History, 25 June and 9 July 1947.
111. Ibid., Mahia District Quarterly Report, 31 August 1948.
112. New Zealand Mission, Manuscript History, 9–24 March 1948.

the rolled-up flaps to see and hear Apostle Cowley speak, just as the Saints had done a quarter of a century earlier to hear Apostle David O. McKay.

After hui tau, the Halversens drove back to Auckland while the Cowleys travelled to the South Island. Here they visited the Dunedin and Christchurch branches before flying back to Auckland. In Auckland, Elder Cowley set apart two missionaries as counselors for President Halversen, the first such organisation of a mission presidency in New Zealand.[113] The Cowleys then flew to Tonga via Fiji on 18 April. Two days later, the Halversens, accompanied by Dr. Nitama Paewai, a Latter-day Saint, sailed for Rarotonga where they spent ten days. William Tailby, the resident commissioner, agreed to admit two more elders in June, as Trevor and Mildred Hamon would be released in August.

President Halversen arrived back in Auckland to find several missionaries ill with yellow jaundice (hepatitis A), apparently contracted during hui tau.[114] A month later, another missionary, Rex E. Arthur, was diagnosed with infantile paralysis, which had reached epidemic proportions in the North Island a few months previously, causing schools, Sundays Schools, and all gatherings of children under sixteen to be prohibited. All the sick missionaries recovered, though Elder Arthur had to be flown home after several months in a Wellington hospital.[115]

President Halversen's term as mission president was drawing to a close. In July 1948, his successor, President Gordon C. Young, arrived with his wife, Virginia, and their two youngest children.[116] LDS Church membership in New Zealand had grown to nearly 12,000, making it one of the largest LDS missions in the world.[117]

Gordon Claridge Young was a great-grandson of Brigham Young, and his wife was a granddaughter of Wilford Woodruff, the fourth president of the LDS Church. Young was proud of their ancestry and mentioned it frequently. He had been a young New Zealand missionary when Apostle David O. McKay, now a counselor in the First Presidency, visited New

---

113. "Mission Presidency Organised," *Te Karere* 43, no. 5 (May 1948): 152.
114. New Zealand Mission, Manuscript History, 18 April–10 May 1948.
115. "Here and There in the Mission: Elder Arthur Flies Home," *Te Karere* 44, no. 1 (January 1949): 24.
116. New Zealand Mission, Manuscript History, Quarterly Historical Report, 31 August 1948,
117. Marvin S. Wright, "Parting Words to the Halversens," *Te Karere* 43, no. 8 (August 1948): 222. In 1948, membership of the British Mission was approximately 6,000. Louis B. Cardon, "War and Recovery, 1939–1950," in *Truth Will Prevail: The Rise of The Church of Jesus Christ of Latter-day Saints in the British Isles, 1837–1987*, edited by V. Ben Bloxham, James R. Moss, and Larry C. Porter, 392.

Zealand in 1921. He was an able Maori speaker and had interpreted for Hugh J. Cannon when he and President McKay attended hui tau. Later, when Elders McKay and Cannon toured New Zealand, Elder Young was appointed to travel with them as translator and interpreter.

The Youngs found the mission home very run down after the long war years when there had been neither materials nor workmen available. Postwar austerity conditions still prevailed. However, within weeks of his arrival, President Young had purchased a fourteen-room home on Remuera Road in Remuera, an upper-class suburb overlooking Waitemate Harbour. This house too was run down; and because wartime price controls were still operating, the Church was able to buy the property for £12,500, about one third of what President Young considered its real value. Elder Cowley had recommended the purchase of a new mission home, and the search for a new, larger home had been ongoing for well over a year. It seems likely that Elder Cowley and President Halversen had already inspected the property and begun preliminary negotiations and that President Young consummated its acquisition for the Church.[118]

Exciting news soon came from Salt Lake City, when the First Presidency approved construction of another school for Maori youth. Elder Cowley made a flying visit to New Zealand in September 1948 to begin the search for a suitable site.[119] He and President Young drove through Hamilton and Te Kuiti to Dannevirke to visit Wi Duncan Jr., then north to Nuhaka where Elder Cowley inspected progress on the carved house and attended the Mahia district conference. They then drove south again to Hastings and visited the Puriri and Southon families before Elder Cowley flew home.

The new school was to be a fully accredited, co-educational high school. Above all, it was to be centrally located. It was to begin in a small way but have sufficient land to produce food and enable additional build-

---

118. New Zealand Mission, Manuscript History, 1 September 1948; "Here and There in the Mission: Purchase of Mission Home," *Te Karere* 43, no. 9 (September 1948): 272; Gordon Claridge Young, Oral History, interviewed by Lauritz G. Petersen, 28 August 1972, 30. During this interview, Young stated that he found the property. However, it is difficult to see how he could have located it, obtained approval from the First Presidency and the Church Committee on Expenditures, and concluded the purchase (except for land court approval) between his arrival in New Zealand on 23 July 1948 and the announcement of the new home in the September 1948 issue of *Te Karere*.

119. "Here and There in the Mission: New Zealand Church Schools," *Te Karere* 43, no. 10 (October 1948): 309.

ings to be erected in future years.[120] President Young visited government leaders in Wellington a few weeks later and begged for American building materials to be admitted duty free.[121] He also asked the First Presidency to send two cement-block-making machines and wood-working machines. Similar machines had recently been supplied to the Tongan Mission for construction of a Church school there.[122]

During September 1948, the mission lost two of its most stalwart Maori leaders when Turi Ruruku and Henare Pere Wihongi, both former branch and district presidents, died.[123] Now President Young decided to release other long-serving district and branch officers so that others could have leadership training opportunities.[124] A few weeks after Wihongi's death, Young released William R. Perrott, who had served as Auckland Branch president since 1925 and concurrently as district president since 1940.[125] Brother Perrott had also been a member of the Church Trust Board in New Zealand since 1938 and was retained in this capacity. Despite his avowed purpose of wanting to train more local leaders in case the American missionaries were again removed, when it came to the point, President Young replaced the remaining local district presidents with missionary elders. By the end of February 1949, all of the districts had missionaries as presidents except Mahia and Hawkes Bay. Young also created two new districts, Bay of Plenty and King Country, carved out of the Hauraki and Waikato districts respectively.

At the end of October 1948, Church Architect Edward O. Anderson flew into Auckland to inspect possible building sites. First stop was Ngaruawahia, where Princess Te Puea offered to sell 400 acres to the Church for the proposed college. Elder Anderson later stated that, on this visit, he inspected the Hamilton site that the Church later purchased for the college.[126] Brother Anderson then flew to Hastings to inspect another possible college site before leaving for Tonga.

---

120. "Here and There in the Mission: College for New Zealand," *Te Karere* 43, no. 11 (November 1948): 344.

121. New Zealand Mission, Manuscript History, 6 October 1948.

122. Gordon C. Young, Personal Monthly Report to First Presidency, 30 November 1948, in New Zealand Mission, Manuscript History.

123. "Here and There in the Mission: Death of Two Local Church Leaders," *Te Karere* 43, no. 11 (November 1948): 345.

124. "The President's Page: Church Government in the Mission," *Te Karere* 43, no. 10 (October 1948): 292.

125. New Zealand Mission, Manuscript History, 17 October 1948; Elder Charles E. Pearce, "William R. Perrott," *Te Karere* 44, no. 1 (January 1949): 21.

126. Edward O. Anderson, Letter to Richard M. Cyert, 16 June 1973.

President Young left on the same plane, en route for Rarotonga. There were now four American missionaries and sixty-five local members in the Cook Islands, but no functioning branch organisation; the members were widely scattered with little transportation available. Despite the strength of the London Missionary Society (LMS) in the islands, there was great interest in the Mormon message, and President Young felt that Rarotonga was a field rich in potential converts.[127] He thought that the Cook Islands should be a separate mission with a Maori or Tahitian mission president and at least ten elders to cover the islands. He wanted the Church to buy a small plantation where all the converts could live together, have a chapel and recreation hall, and participate more fully in Church programs.

President Young was proud of the new mission home in Remuera, Auckland, and of the new Mercury automobile (purchased by the Church) that he had brought with him to replace the worn-out mission car. New cars were rare in the post-war austerity conditions prevailing in New Zealand, and the bright red Mercury attracted attention wherever Young went, so that in later years President Young claimed that it was the best missionary New Zealand ever had.[128]

Like Elder Cowley, President Young wanted to see the Maori people reestablished on the land. "Keep your land," he urged through the columns of the mission paper. "You who haven't any, try to get a section large enough to grow the food necessary for yourself and family. . . . Work the land, it will give you healthful exercise and keep you occupied, giving less time to be spent in places where no good can come."[129]

President Young continued President Halversen's search for an alternative site for the Auckland chapel. When Apostle Cowley arrived at the mission home in March 1949 for his fourth apostolic visit, President Young told him that he had found the ideal spot. He then took Elder Cowley outside and demonstrated how a new chapel could be built on the existing site, with its frontage to Scotia Place to avoid traffic noise that would disturb meetings. His plan was adopted at a subsequent district conference.

Although Nuhaka had been chosen to host hui tau 1949, the venue was changed to Korongata. Elder Cowley's presence was a drawcard. "Leaning on his carved Maori stick, he chatted in such a way that each of us felt that he was talking directly to us individually," reported *Te Karere*. A high wind blew dust everywhere, even into the marquee. Cowley told the

---

127. "Here and There in the Mission: President Young's Rarotongan Visit," *Te Karere* 44, no. 1 (January 1949): 22.

128. Young, Oral History, 13.

129. "The President's Page," *Te Karere* 44, no. 3 (March 1949): 80.

congregation that they had gathered as God's people to be instructed and guided by Him and that they had a right to ask Him for better weather. "Pray when you return to your tents that the weather might be improved for tomorrow's sessions," he told the assembled Saints on Friday evening. "Pray that the wind will cease and that the dust may be settled." During the night, the wind dropped, gentle rain settled the dust, and the Saints awoke to sparkling blue skies and warm sunshine, which continued for the rest of hui tau. More than 3,600 dinners were served at one meal when visitors from surrounding towns and villages crowded onto the marae and stood around the marquee listening to Elder Cowley's Easter Sunday sermon.[130]

The Nuhaka carved house was intended to help preserve traditional Maori crafts and teach them to a new generation. This necessitated setting up a training school for carvers, for which Sir Apirana Ngata sent qualified instructors. Work had begun during Halversen's term as mission president but ceased when government regulations forbade the use of building materials for non-essential purposes. Sidney Christy now proposed that the carved house should be dedicated as a Kahungunu War Memorial, and his proposal was adopted, thus exempting it from these regulations. There were still protracted construction delays and other problems: The carving instructor quit, and costs reached something like three times the original estimates. Still, the building was dedicated during a special hui on 25-28 August 1949. Prime Minister the Rt. Hon. Sir Peter Fraser, Turi Carroll, and Sir Apirana Ngata were just a few of the distinguished speakers at the opening.

On the last day of the hui, President Young released Sid Christy from the office of district president and installed an American missionary instead.[131] Stuart Meha, last of the local district presidents, was replaced by an American missionary on 2 October 1949.[132] President Young then called four of the released district presidents as local missionaries. Hohepa Heperi, Rahiri Harris, Stuart Meha, and Sidney Christy were assigned to travel around New Zealand, visiting and teaching wherever opportunity offered. "Those men did more good than all our missionaries had among the Maoris...," President Young recalled later. "They were respected, they were all highly born men. They'd go into any place they cared to and the red carpet was out and the Maoris came to listen to them."[133]

---

130. "Report on Hui Tau," *Te Karere* 44, no. 6 (June 1949): 203–5.

131. Mahia District Report, New Zealand Mission, Manuscript History, 31 August 1949; Elder Elliott A. Fairbanks, "Carved Meeting House Completed," *Te Karere* 44, no. 10 (October 1949): 368–71.

132. Hawkes Bay District Report, New Zealand Mission, Manuscript History, 31 December 1949.

133. Young, Oral History, 19.

Missionary arrivals and departures were still delayed by post-war transport difficulties. Some missionaries worked in California for as long as six months before obtaining passage to Australia or New Zealand.[134] Those due to go home sometimes found their missions extended as they waited for a berth. On 17 September 1949, a Pan American clipper chartered by the Church brought new missionaries for the South Pacific, including fourteen for New Zealand and fifteen for Australia, the first ever to arrive by air. Rulon G. Craven, a future Area President, was one of seventeen New Zealand missionaries who flew home on the chartered plane's return trip. Fourteen New Zealand Saints sailed for the United States or Canada on the *Aorangi* on 27 September 1949, joining a mini-exodus of Latter-day Saints from Australia and New Zealand.[135] While this belated "gathering" of the New Zealand and Australian Saints weakened some branches in both countries, many of those who left returned later with experience that would prove invaluable when the first stakes were organised in the South Pacific a decade later.

---

134. "Here and There in the Mission: New Arrivals," *Te Karere* 44, no. 10 (October 1949): 372.

135. "Here and There in the Mission: 'Charter Plane Brings, Takes Missionaries' and 'More Saints Gather to Zion,'" *Te Karere* 44, no. 11 (November 1949): 408–10.

Chapter 7

"... two great strains of the house of Israel ..."

Finding land for the new school was difficult, but the Lord's hand was over the project. Under the Servicemen's Settlement and Land Sales Act, land prices were frozen at the values current on 15 December 1942, the restrictions to apply until five years from the end of the war, which would not be until August 1950.[1] Accordingly, few people were willing to sell land in 1949, as they expected prices to rise the following year. In any case, returned servicemen were legally entitled to first option on any rural land offered for sale, so it seemed as though building the new college would have to be postponed indefinitely. However, the right site was found and the land obtained for the Church by President Gordon C. Young.

Although the actual date when he found the Church College land is not recorded in either the mission history or his journal, President Young frequently told the story in later years. One day in May 1949, President Young drove from Auckland to Hamilton to call on local real estate agents. In one agency, which he had visited fruitlessly four times previously, he was told of a dairy farm on Tuhikaramea Road, past Frankton Junction, that might be suitable. According to President Young, the agent (a Mr. Collins) knew the farm was not for sale and simply wanted an excuse for a ride in the mission's American car, a Mercury. However, when they pulled up in the road beside the farm, President Young states that he saw the college in vision. Following this prompting, he insisted on speaking to the owner, Bert Meldrum. Meldrum didn't want to sell, but he did want to exchange his 215-acre farm for a smaller property, which President Young could not provide. When Young promised Meldrum he could stay on his farm until a suitable replacement property was found, Meldrum agreed to sell if the land court approved

---

1. Jane Thomson, "The Policy of Land Sales Control: Sharing the Sacrifice," *New Zealand Journal of History* 25, no. 1 (April 1991): 3–17.

the sale.[2] The court did so, setting a price of £4,900. In October 1949, the Church Committee on Expenditures approved its purchase.[3]

President Young also gave much thought to the need for branch meetinghouses. Most branches had building funds of £200 to £300. Young pleaded with the First Presidency (George Albert Smith, J. Reuben Clark Jr., and David O. McKay) to allocate a similar sum to each branch, so that each could build a small chapel. He used as an example the Matakowhai Branch of 147 members who met, with great difficulty, in a member's home. They owned a building lot, could provide timber, and were willing to do the labour themselves, but needed financial help to purchase nails, hardware, and roofing materials. President Young pointed out that there was some heartburning in the mission over the carved house at Nuhaka. Members of other branches felt it unfair that the Church should spend $80,000 building the carved house at Nuhaka when that branch already had both a large recreation hall and a chapel, while other branches needed only two or three thousand dollars to build a basic meetinghouse.[4]

The First Presidency expressed interest in President Young's ideas and suggested that specific proposals should be submitted to Apostle Cowley.[5] As a result, in December 1949 the Church Committee on Expenditures approved not only the purchase of a concrete-block machine for the construction of the school, but also the allocation of sums ranging from £200 to £1,000 for five small chapels in the New Zealand Mission.

Church Architect Edward O. Anderson, who was designing the new college, advised President McKay and President Young that he intended to use the California building code to ensure that, unlike the old MAC, the new college buildings would be earthquake resistant. President McKay advised Anderson to consult George R. Biesinger, who was not only an experienced builder and construction contractor but had served his mission in New Zealand and was familiar with conditions there.

---

2. Stanley E. Richards, "New Zealand Sets the Pace," *Te Karere* 45, no. 9 (September 1951): 307, 311, and no. 10 (October 1951): 339–40, 342; Gordon C. Young, "Tena ra Koutou e Hoa Ma," *Te Karere* 51, no. 12 (December 1957): 415–19. Young told several versions of the story, differing in details but consistent in essentials.

3. First Presidency, Letter to Gordon C. Young, 29 October 1949, Gordon Claridge Young Papers.

4. Gordon C. Young, Letter to First Presidency, [18 June 1949], fd. 2, Young Papers. The First Presidency's reply refers to this letter as dated 20 June 1949. There is no date on the carbon copy of the letter, but staff at the LDS Church History Library checked the original and found the date handwritten by President Young on the typed letter.

5. First Presidency, Letter to Young, 29 October 1949, ibid, fd. 8.

Anderson did so and advised President Young that he would like Brother Biesinger to represent the Church Building Department in New Zealand to see that the buildings were of a high standard of construction and would be durable. Earthquakes were not the only hazard, Anderson explained. Moisture and termites had destroyed many Church buildings in the South Pacific, and he knew they must be very careful in the future.[6]

Meanwhile, the regular work of the mission continued. The Rangitoto (Maori) Branch, which had been organized by President Halversen on 15 June 1947, met in a rented hall on Karangahape Road. President Young convinced the two Auckland branch presidents that they should share the chapel on Queen Street, staggering meeting times. This arrangement served the double purpose of saving the rental money and giving the Maori Saints the privilege of meeting in a dedicated chapel. Both branches had grown steadily through President Halversen's term as mission president and grew still further under Young. Much of the growth in Auckland between 1945 and 1949 resulted not only from the return of the American missionaries but also from a large number of "move-ins" as Maori Saints joined the prevailing drift to the cities in search of work and education. Even using the vacated mission home and the house next door (4 Scotia Place, which President Cowley had bought in 1942), the three buildings were inadequate to accommodate the numbers now attending.[7] In April 1949, Young commented to Elder Cowley that the Auckland chapel was so packed the walls needed to be pushed out; Cowley replied that if they had just one or two more attending the walls *would* be pushed out.[8]

In February 1950, President Young received Church approval for a new chapel in Auckland. The estimated cost was £86,100, of which the Church would contribute 70 percent, or £60,270; local members were to raise the rest, either in cash or donated labour credited at an hourly rate. President Young was dismayed when he learned that the planned new chapel would seat only 220 and told President David O. McKay that, with more than 150 attending one branch and about 120 the other, a chapel

---

6. Edward O. Anderson, Letter to Gordon C. Young, 17 February 1950, ibid., fd. 9.

7. Activity reports are not available to researchers. However, news reports in *Te Karere* for the year preceding Young's arrival make it clear that both Auckland branches flourished during Halversen's presidency. For example, in May 1948 the Rangitoto Branch reported that not only was the MIA fully organised, but that every MIA class and most Sunday School classes had presidencies and secretaries. This would have been quite impossible to achieve with an average attendance of thirty-five, which was Young's recollection a quarter of a century later. See "News of the Field: Rangitoto Branch," *Te Karere* 43, no. 7 (July 1948): 212.

8. "News of the Field: Auckland Branch," *Te Karere* 44, no. 5 (May 1949): 184.

seating fewer than 400 would be a mistake.⁹ A compromise was reached and the new chapel eventually seated 375.

President Young, who still needed government permission to build the college and the new chapels and to import building materials, cultivated the acquaintance of influential politicians including Labor Prime Minister Peter Fraser. Fraser promised Young that he would exempt the proposed college land from the provisions of Section 51 of the Servicemen's Settlement and Land Sales Act.¹⁰ In 1949, Sir Sidney Holland, leader of the National Party, became Prime Minister, and President Young managed to meet him on 21 February 1950.¹¹ By putting pressure on a reluctant Polly Duncan, he also obtained a personal introduction to Deputy Prime Minister Keith Holyoake, a neighbour of the Duncans in Dannevirke, whom he thereafter referred to as a personal friend.¹² However, when President Young importuned Holyoake over building matters, he was told that he must see the relevant ministers of the Departments of Works, Finance, and Maori Affairs.

Holyoake did agree to set up appointments with these men for President Young, who flew to Wellington for the meetings. The Minister of Works, the Hon. William S. Goosman, bluntly reminded Young that there had been a war and, consequently, neither building materials nor skilled labour were available. Young insisted that he could provide both if he was given permission to build and to import material paid for by Church headquarters, which would not deplete New Zealand's limited dollar reserves.

President Young then urged the Church architect to specify concrete-block construction, arguing its advantages over timber in the prevailing climate. He wanted to put a small joinery on the college land to produce windows and doors not only for the college buildings but also for new chapels wherever they might be built. As there were young men in the mission anxious to work in advance for their tuition at the new school, Young suggested to President McKay that temporary accommodation might be built on the college site so that these young men could work there under supervision. They would learn building trades, take gospel classes, and operate "under a sort of missionary discipline" while the building was constructed.¹³ This plan seems to have been the genesis of the labour missionary program in New Zealand.

---

9. Gordon C. Young, Letter to President David O. McKay, 4 March 1950, fd. 3, Young Papers.

10. Gordon Claridge Young, Oral History, interviewed by Lauritz G. Petersen, 28 August 1972, 24.

11. Young to McKay, 4 March 1950.

12. Young, Oral History, 28.

13. Young to McKay, 4 March 1950.

President Young suggested planting vegetables on part of the college land; with milk, cream, and butter from the existing dairy herd, much of the labourers' food would be supplied. President Young favoured Biesinger's appointment, but he also wanted New Zealander Lionel Going called back from his current residence in California. He wanted one of these men to supervise the construction of the Auckland chapel and the other the school.[14] Instead, Brother Going was sent to Tonga to build the Liahona College (now known as Liahona High School), and Brother Biesinger was given responsibility for both major works in New Zealand (some eighty miles apart) as well as a school in Samoa.

President Young was dismayed when George and Audrey Biesinger and their three small children arrived unexpectedly a week after the 1950 hui tau at Nuhaka.[15] Audrey Biesinger's fourth child was born shortly after their arrival. No one had advised Young that the Biesingers were on their way, and no preparations had been made for housing the family. Their arrival was premature, as nothing could be done until title deeds to the college land were obtained, plans drawn in Salt Lake City and approved by relevant New Zealand authorities, permission to build granted by the government, and materials obtained, either locally or from the United States.

President Young wrote to Church Architect Edward Anderson in May 1950, suggesting that Biesinger should go to Samoa until he could begin building in New Zealand. "Things don't move in this country quite like they do in America," he told Anderson, "due to Governmental red tape, but they are very fair, and in their own time, I am sure we will be able to accomplish everything we desire."[16] Two weeks later he wrote to President David O. McKay, asking him to spell out George Biesinger's status in the mission.[17] The First Presidency replied that Brother Biesinger was not called as a missionary but was a paid employee whose expenses would be paid by Church headquarters.[18] In mid-August 1950, George and Audrey Biesinger and their two youngest children sailed for Samoa for a stay of several months. Young arranged for their two boys (three and four years old) to be cared for by Church members in New Zealand. On the same ship were two New Zealand LDS tradesmen going to Tonga to help with

---

14. Ibid.

15. Gordon C. Young, Letter to Edward O. Anderson, 25 May 1950, fd. 3, Young Papers.

16. Ibid.

17. Gordon C. Young, Letter to President David O. McKay, 12 June 1950, fd. 9, Young Papers.

18. First Presidency, Letter to Young, 18 July 1950, ibid.

the Church building program there: James Hapeta, a carpenter, and Leslie Clarke, an electrician.

Once President Young received verbal approval in Wellington for the Auckland chapel and the college building project to go ahead (conditional on the plans being passed by local authorities), he engaged Auckland architect Thomas Haughey to make detailed drawings from the plans Anderson sent from Utah.[19] On 2 October 1950, Young wrote to the Auckland City Building Controller requesting permission to build a chapel and recreation hall on the corner of Queen Street and Scotia Place, assuring them that the new church would be an asset to the city of Auckland.[20] Two weeks later the permit was issued.[21]

There were only sixty-five full-time missionaries at the 1950 hui tau compared with 104 in 1948. Of the sixty-five, ten were New Zealanders and four were Australians. For some months, missionary departures had exceeded arrivals. When the Korean War broke out a few months later in June 1950 and American draft laws came into operation, the situation became critical. It is not clear, however, why numbers were falling before the Korean War. By January 1951, the supply was drying up. Elder Cowley wrote to President Young telling him there would be few replacements, as the draft boards would not allow men of military age to be called on missions.[22]

Membership numbers in Rarotonga increased to nearly 250, and eight missionaries laboured there. In April 1950, President Young found three acres of land facing the sea at Avarua and, by a combination of persuasion and bribery, secured a lease that he negotiated at £10 per year for thirty years, with a further thirty-year option. Twenty years later he confessed to feeling remorseful about this transaction because of the low price paid. He also had qualms of conscience about the low price Bert Meldrum had received for the college land, a price far below its true value. He even suggested to the Church Building Committee during the late 1960s that Meldrum should receive additional compensation.[23]

During the last quarter of 1950, three acres of college land were cleared of swamp logs by missionaries and Saints working with a bulldozer and the farm tractor. The Waikato District conference was held on the grounds on

---

19. Gordon C. Young, Letter to Edward O. Anderson, 16 August 1950, ibid., fd. 4.

20. Gordon C. Young, Letter to Building Controller, 2 October 1950, ibid.

21. E. B. Corbett, Minister of Maori Affairs, telegram to Gordon C. Young, 12 October 1950, fd. 9, Young Papers.

22. Matthew Cowley, Letter to Young, 15 January 1951, fd. 10, Young Papers.

23. New Zealand Mission, Manuscript History, Annual Report 1950; Young, Oral History, 39–41.

9–10 December. A stage was built for the speakers, and the congregation sat on the hillside. Various tents housed a canteen, a Relief Society handicrafts display, and the mission bookstore. A large hole was dug and lined with canvas, and six people were baptized in this improvised font.[24]

On 1 January 1951, President Young instructed William Perrott, whom he had installed for a second term as Auckland District president, to amalgamate the Auckland and Rangitoto Branches with Matthew Chote as branch president. Young had never been happy with the segregated branches, even though they had been organised by President Halversen at the request of Auckland's Maori Saints. The Rangitoto Branch now also included numerous Samoan and Tongan Saints who had immigrated to New Zealand.[25]

Demolition of the old house in Scotia Place began a week later, although Presidents Young and Perrott had still not found a temporary meeting place for the newly reconstituted Auckland Branch. When President Young received a cable from Utah asking if he could get 5,000 bags of cement admitted to New Zealand duty free, he flew to Wellington. Prime Minister Sidney Holland was on his way to England, but Young hoped to persuade Acting Prime Minister Keith Holyoake, whom he regarded as a personal friend, to intercede on the Church's behalf. However, either Holyoake's probity was proof against the demands of friendship, or the friendship was not as firm as Young believed, for Young was unsuccessful.[26]

In mid-January a dispute erupted over organising the 1951 hui tau scheduled for Nuhaka. The Nuhaka Saints wanted to run the program, but the Mission Hui Tau Board members felt that they should run it as they had done for many years. President Young threatened to cancel hui tau if agreement was not reached. He was not in favour of hui tau in any case, feeling that it was entirely too expensive, though he was willing to consider the option of making the new college grounds a permanent venue.[27]

By 20 January, the house at 4 Scotia Place was almost down and the demolition crew under George Biesinger (who had returned from Samoa in mid-December) was getting ready to tear down the old mission home at 2 Scotia Place. Next day the combined branch met in the Druids Hall. "Not Maoris, Samoans, Tongans, or Europeans, but LATTER-DAY SAINTS," reported Young with satisfaction, capitalizing "LATTER-DAY

---

24. New Zealand Mission, Manuscript History, Waikato District Report, quarter ending 31 December 1950.
25. Young, Oral History, 19.
26. Young, Diary, 1 and 8 January 1951, fd. 1, Young Papers.
27. Gordon C. Young, Letter to Bessie Whiteri, 22 January 1951, Young Papers.

SAINTS" to emphasise his point when he repeated the sentiment in the mission paper. There were 295 people at Sunday School that day.[28]

Another twenty missionaries arrived in January 1951; but because of the Korean War, Young did not expect any more unless they came from Canada. Some months later, the First Presidency asked the seventies' quorums to provide a thousand older, married men to make up the worldwide shortfall. "This will just be a drop in the bucket when divided among all the missions," commented Elder Cowley in a letter to President Young. "The situation is very disheartening."[29]

For the first time in seventy years, a New Zealand Mission president decided to direct the major part of the mission's proselytising efforts towards the Pakeha. "There wasn't a Maori in New Zealand who hadn't heard the gospel time and time again and here were 1,750,000 Europeans who didn't even know anything about the Church," Young said later. He felt that this move was necessary to further the work of the Lord but described the action as making him unpopular with Maori Church members and the missionaries alike.[30] Young told President McKay (newly sustained as Church President) that he was working "among nearly two million Europeans" not just the "75,000 Maoris." He continued, "I love the Maoris as much as any President, but feel they must now begin to take more initiative themselves. They have leaned on the Elders so long they have not developed their own potentialities."[31] Considering that President Magleby had successfully installed Maori district and branch presidencies twenty years earlier and that it was first Halversen and then Young himself who dismantled these local organisations, these strictures seem unjustified. However, the decision to do more Pakeha work was a wise and necessary one, because the European population of New Zealand also needed the opportunity to hear the restored gospel.

Several New Zealand couples visited temples in "Zion" during President Young's mission, among them Henry and Rangi Davies (who sold their home to finance their visit), Joseph and Muriel Going Hay, and Norman and Myra Going Mason. In Wellington in late February 1951, Mick Stinson (son-in-law of former MAC matron Esther Kenneth) asked President Young his attitude towards Latter-day Saints moving permanently

---

28. Young, Diary, 20 and 21 January 1951; Gordon C. Young, "The President's Page," *Te Karere* 45 no. 3 (March 1951): 84.

29. Matthew Cowley, Letter to Gordon C. Young, 9 August 1951, fd. 9, Young Papers.

30. Young, Oral History, 17–18.

31. Gordon C. Young, Letter to President David O. McKay, 15 May 1951, fd. 6, Young Papers.

to the States. Young advised him to go and receive his temple ordinances but then return to serve in the mission. President Young reported to the First Presidency that he was discouraging immigration to America[32] and was assured that this policy accorded with instructions given by the First Presidency to all presidents of foreign missions.[33] The literal phase of the Mormon gathering was over, and the missions needed to grow and gain strength in the nations of the world.

In April a dock strike crippled New Zealand. The expected 5,000 bags of cement were on board the *Sierra*, which was waiting to unload. Excavation of the Queen Street property was complete, and the cement was needed for footings and foundations. Because of the strike, the *Sierra* sailed for Noumea and Australia without unloading. President Young and Brother Biesinger arranged to "borrow" cement from an Auckland firm and repaid the quantity from the Church consignment on the *Sierra* when it finally arrived. The footings were poured on 19 April 1951.

President Young resolutely refused to give in to Maori, Samoan, and Tongan members of the Auckland Branch who still regretted the loss of their defunct Rangitoto Branch. There can be little doubt that a Maori-speaking branch was not necessary at this time, but the Polynesian Saints preferred their own branch organisation, even though they had plenty of leadership opportunities in the combined branch. Because he was opposed to racial segregation, President Young refused to allow even a Maori class in the branch Sunday School, but he did encourage the Rangitoto (Maori) Choir to continue. The choir brought good publicity to the LDS Church in New Zealand, performing at the opening of the British Empire Games (now the Commonwealth Games) in Auckland in February 1950, and also at Auckland's birthday celebrations. The choir was also featured in a world-release Fitzpatrick's Travelogue feature film on New Zealand. Young even considered renting an Auckland theatre for a Sunday night program where he could lecture on Mormonism and have the Rangitoto Choir perform, though apparently nothing came of this idea.[34]

Volunteers from other branches travelled to Auckland every Saturday to work on the new chapel. Workers from as far away as Rotorua, Nuhaka, Hamilton, and even Porirua frequently outnumbered the local Saints. Six carpenters from Porirua spent their three-week annual vacation on the Auckland building site, one of them not even a member of the LDS

---

32. Gordon C. Young, Letter to President David O. McKay, 13 November 1950, fd. 4, Young Papers.

33. First Presidency, Letter to Gordon C. Young, 8 December 1950, fd. 9, Young Papers.

34. Young, Diary, 29 May 1951.

Church.³⁵ Nuhaka Branch sent four carpenters for three months as well as a truckload of food to sustain them.³⁶ Men of five nationalities (New Zealanders, Samoans, Tongans, Cook Islanders, and Americans) worked together. In July the concrete-block machine was taken to the Hamilton college site, and an experienced block-maker, Otto Buehner, whose son was just finishing a mission in New Zealand, was sent from America to teach New Zealanders how to use it. With construction of the college officially started, President Young held a meeting with the MAC Old Boys' Association to discuss a name for the new school. Young was adamant that it would not be named after the old Maori Agricultural College. He wanted a name that would be more comprehensive, not limiting the college to either Maori students or to agriculture.³⁷

By mid-1951, President Young was afraid that his wife, Virginia, was on the verge of a nervous breakdown and cabled the First Presidency (David O. McKay, Stephen L Richards, and J. Reuben Clark Jr.) asking permission for her to go home for a few months. They consented, and she sailed on the *Aorangi* on 10 July with the two children. In Vancouver, she learned that her return booking had been cancelled. She telephoned this news to Young, who hurried to the Union Steamship office in Auckland and found that the bookings had, indeed, been cancelled by the Church. "So it looks like I'm slated for home also," he wrote.³⁸ He had, after all, already completed the usual three years of a mission president's term.

Now that his release was imminent, President Young was filled with a desire to see the building projects to completion. He conceived the idea of going home for a month to discuss problems relating to the buildings, particularly finance, with the General Authorities and cabled this request on 29 August 1951. The following day, he received a cable announcing his release. For undisclosed reasons, President Young paid a flying visit to Australia early in October. He was back in his own mission when the new mission president, former MAC teacher Sidney J. Ottley, accompanied by his wife, Alice, and teenage son Jerold (later conductor of the Mormon Tabernacle Choir) arrived on the *Aorangi* towards the end of October.

Under New Zealand law, all goods had to be transported internally by rail. Consignments of building materials for the College were therefore loaded onto Church trucks at the Auckland wharves, driven a short distance to the Auckland railway freight depot, unloaded from the trucks

---

35. "Porirua Carpenters Donate Labour," *Te Karere* 45, no. 7 (July 1951): 233.
36. "New Zealand Sets the Pace," *Te Karere* 46, no. 1 (January 1952): 19.
37. Young, Diary, 17 July 1951.
38. Ibid., 9 August 1951.

and reloaded on to a goods train that transported them eighty miles to Frankton Junction. Here they were unloaded from the train, reloaded on to the same trucks that had been driven, empty, from Auckland to Frankton, and then driven to the building site. President Young pulled every possible string to have the Church trucks licensed to collect the consignments at the wharf and drive them straight to the college site. While introducing Ottley to various cabinet ministers and reserve bank officials in Wellington, Young raised the transport question and received assurances of sympathetic consideration. "It has opened President Ottley's eyes the way I am accepted and treated," he confided in his diary.[39]

Certainly President Young never missed an opportunity to introduce himself to anyone whom he thought important or worth knowing, always, he insisted, with a view to preaching Mormonism and making the Church known in New Zealand. "The Lord has opened the way for us to meet some of the finest men in this country," he wrote in one of his last messages in the mission paper. "Men of prominence and influence. We have tried to turn these blessings toward helping build the Kingdom in this land."[40]

Aspects of culture conflict, largely dealt with in a low-key fashion by both Saints and mission presidents for half a century, came close to erupting during his presidency, as he set about "house-cleaning" the LDS Church in New Zealand. Unlike some of his predecessors, President Young felt that the Maori people had had more than enough time in which to leave behind those aspects of their traditional culture and customs that in any way conflicted with Mormon and even American ideals. As the Church expanded in subsequent years throughout the world, it became necessary to stress a universal, "celestial" culture that would replace local and national cultures. President Young was in the forefront of this movement. While most mission presidents who preceded and succeeded him recognised that fundamental cultural change took many generations, Young was sure that the Maori people had already had enough time. With hindsight, he became convinced that his reforms, particularly in forbidding Maori customary marriages and refusing to allow some traditional facets of the tangihanga, had been inspired to prepare the Maori Saints for the organisation of stakes and the building of a temple among them. Both developments occurred within a decade of his release. Young was not a popular mission president, but many Maori leaders among the Saints later paid tribute to his wisdom and foresight. He left New Zealand on 13 November 1951.

---

39. Ibid., 29 October 1951.
40. Gordon C. Young, "The President's Page," *Te Karere* 45, no. 10 (October 1951): 332.

While President Ottley took over the reins of the mission, George Biesinger continued to promote the building program. He was enthusiastic about the block-making machine and optimistically (but unrealistically) thought that the college could be finished by April 1953. A further shipment of 3,000 bags of cement followed the first 5,000 bags, plus a consignment of reinforcing iron. The timber shortage was most critical; accordingly, the Church bought its own stand of forest land and a timber mill at Kaikohe. The block-making plant, which Otto Buehner set up, began by producing about 250 concrete blocks per day; by the end of 1951 an eight-man crew was producing 2,850 blocks each day. These were stockpiled for the college buildings and three projected chapels.

Hui tau was held at Korongata from 11–14 April 1952, and President Ottley devoted one session to explaining the proposed labour missionary program. A model of the college was displayed; and James Elkington, who had helped build the Church college in Tonga, described how the system worked there. Workmen were needed; they would be set apart as labour missionaries, and their home branches would provide food and £1 per week pocket money for each missionary, all of whom would be trained in various trades. After this explanation, the proposition was put to the vote of the assembled Saints who unanimously agreed to support the project. A number of men left for Tuhikaramea straight from hui tau. By the end of August, forty-five "Project Missionaries" had been set apart for periods ranging from three months to three years.[41] Excitement and enthusiasm built up as the New Zealand Mission entered a period of unprecedented growth and development. All were conscious that the work of the Lord was moving forward.

At the college site, volunteers were organised into crews. They broke ground for bunkhouses for the single men and huts or cabins for families, and for a cookhouse; drains and even roads were laid out. By October, foundations and walls of the joinery were finished and a start was made on roofing the building. Two permanent homes, later to be used as faculty homes, were nearly completed and others were begun. The original farmhouse up on the hill was moved down to the labourers' camp, overhauled, painted, and used as a recreation centre. Another American builder, William Child, arrived in August to supervise the masonry work for the main college buildings.

---

41. "Featuring the Districts' News: News from the College," *Te Karere* 46, no. 8 (August 1952): 292; Sidney J. Ottley, "The President's Page," ibid., 46, no. 11 (November 1952): 380, 384.

Although, as President Ottley reported, "the whole Mission [was] looking towards the Waikato," progress on the Auckland chapel also continued. When Ottley arrived in New Zealand in October 1951, the new Auckland chapel was still just a framework. A year later, it was nearing completion and the new baptismal font was already in use. "Much favorable publicity has been given the church by reason of curiosity and interest aroused by the construction of this building," Ottley reported. "The missionaries have capitalized on this curiosity and have taught the gospel very consistently to the bringing of many into the fold."[42] Demolition of the original Auckland chapel, which until now had been used as a construction storage building, began on 6 October 1952.[43]

Meanwhile, at Tuhikaramea, the joinery building was finished except for its roof. The first permanent home was finished and the Biesinger family moved into it on Christmas Eve. Eight more homes, destined for college faculty, were in various stages of construction. These houses were the focus of much attention from government officials, the public, and the media, as the concrete-block construction cost considerably less than comparable homes provided by the government housing scheme.

As well as the joinery, three barracks for workmen were finished and another was under construction. Also under construction were eight huts for families, communal shower and toilet blocks, a kitchen, and a communal dining room where the food was served cafeteria style. Slaughtering facilities and stock from the farm provided meat, which was stored in deep freezers. Several miles of fencing had been built and similar miles of drainage dug. An orchard was being planted, and bores were drilled to augment the water supply. Foundations and heating ducts were in place for the first of the college classroom blocks, and footings were in place for a second.

The home branch or district undertook to provide £2 per week for each labour missionary, £1 to cover food and £1 for the missionary's pocket money and entertainment outside the project.[44] Movies, meetings, choir practices, football, and council meetings kept them amused and occupied outside work hours. As the project workers were now swamping the lo-

---

42. New Zealand Mission, Manuscript History, Mission President's Annual Report, 1952; see also "Mormon Chapel May Be Ready by End of Year," *New Zealand Herald*, Auckland, 17 April 1952.

43. "Here and There in the Mission," *Te Karere* 46, no. 11 (November 1952): 410.

44. The actual amount of "pocket money" that the labour missionaries received varied at different times from ten shillings to eighteen shillings to £1 (twenty shillings) per week. Married couples received more.

cal Hamilton Branch of the Church, a College Branch, complete with all auxiliaries, was organised on 26 April 1953.[45]

By mid-1953, foundations were laid for three classroom blocks, and one was bricked to the square. The joinery, with floor space equal to all the hui tau tents combined, was operating. There were seven married couples and twenty children in the married quarters and eighty-three men in barracks.[46] Although none were permanent residents, they nevertheless formed the embryo that would become the Mormon town of Temple View, the nearest approach to Hoagland's "Mormon colony" that New Zealand was to know. As author David Cummings has pointed out, George Biesinger's assignment was to build a college, but he also built a town.[47]

The new Auckland Chapel was opened on 26 July 1953 with a district conference to which the whole mission was invited. More than 1,200 attended, representatives coming from almost every North Island LDS district. Among the guests were the mayor of Auckland, Sir John Allum, and the architects and sub-contractors. On the following Sunday, the building was open for inspection by the public, and more than 600 visitors toured the facilities.[48]

Once the new chapel was opened, the mission office was moved from the Remuera mission home into the new building. A self-contained flat was fitted out for the office missionaries, including *Te Karere* staff, as the Upper Queen Street location was more convenient for running the mission than suburban Remuera.[49] In June 1954, President Ottley reported that, as rooms in the mission home were no longer needed as offices and bedrooms for office missionaries, a smaller mission home, situated at 17 Orakei Road, had been purchased and the Remuera property listed for sale.[50]

Two more chapels were under construction, both smaller than that in Auckland but larger than any other LDS meetinghouses yet built in New Zealand. These were at Porirua (near Wellington), and Kaikohe in the Bay of Islands. By September 1953, the Porirua foundations were ready; and in October a crew of "brickies" from the college, under American supervisor

---

45. "Featuring the Districts," *Te Karere* 47, no. 7 (July 1953): 252.
46. Ibid.
47. David W. Cummings, *Mighty Missionary of the Pacific: The Building Program of the Church of Jesus Christ of Latter-day Saints—Its History, Scope, and Significance*, 29.
48. W. M. Burge, "The New Auckland Chapel and Mission Headquarters Opened," *Te Karere* 47, no. 9 (September 1953): 317, and "Featuring the Districts," ibid., 322.
49. "In New Quarters," *Te Karere* 47, no. 11 (November 1953): 384–85.
50. New Zealand Mission, Manuscript History, Quarterly Report 30 June 1954.

William Child, swooped down on the site and completed all block work for the walls in two weeks.[51] Construction at Kaikohe began in April 1953, with Jim Elkington supervising.

President Ottley continued the mission president's round of visits, now including Niue, where a new field was opened in 1952, as well as the Cook Islands.[52] During a mid-year circuit of the islands, President Ottley organised an LDS Sunday School in Suva while his ship lay over in Fiji. During this trip, he also took the opportunity to visit the two new LDS schools—Liahona College in Tonga and a new building for the LDS elementary school at Pesega in Samoa. Both were now open, with enrolments of 300 and 1,000 respectively.[53]

Missionary success in New Zealand fluctuated with rising and declining missionary numbers that were, in turn, still affected by the Korean War. In April 1953, all districts except Auckland had missionary elders presiding over them; by the end of the year, twelve of the eighteen districts once again had local members as district presidents.[54]

Other problems sometimes hampered the regular work of the Church. In rural districts, such as Hawkes Bay and the Wairarapa Valley, Church activity virtually ceased for three or four months every year during the shearing season from October till after Christmas, and this interruption had occurred for the better part of fifty years. Missionaries in the Wairarapa district reported that 90 percent of LDS families there depended on shearing for a sizable part of their yearly income.[55] In October 1953, President Ottley published an urgent plea that men and youths working as building missionaries on the college should not be recalled to go shearing.[56]

With the Auckland chapel completed, attention focused on the college and the need for more chapels. Another chapel, for Te Hapara Branch at Gisborne in the Poverty Bay district, was begun on 3 October 1953.[57] The college site was flooded during the winter of 1953, only the married couples' housing escaping. An additional 700 acres of land were purchased

---

51. "Building in Porirua," *Te Karere* 47, no. 10 (October 1953): 341, and "Featuring the Districts," ibid., no. 11 (November 1953): 399.

52. "Here and There in the Mission," *Te Karere* 46, no. 11 (November 1952): 404–5; Elder Basil DeWitt, "A Visit to Niue or Savage Island," ibid., 47, no. 5 (May 1953): 168–69.

53. "The President's Page," *Te Karere* 47, no. 8 (August 1953): 264.

54. New Zealand Mission, Manuscript History, 31 December 1953.

55. Ibid., Wairarapa Historical Report, 31 December 1953.

56. "Only Sheep Shearers Read This!!" *Te Karere* 47, no. 10 (October 1953): 338.

57. "Featuring the Districts," *Te Karere* 47, no. 11 (November 1953): 396.

in mid-1953, increasing the value of the Church property but also the work of the farm crews, especially when lambing began.

By the time winter was over and conditions on the building site more tolerable, President Ottley faced serious financial problems as well as a continual manpower shortage. The original two-year building missionaries were nearing the end of their missions. Some agreed to stay, and Ottley appealed for replacements for those who were leaving. The difficulty of obtaining materials had been largely overcome by acquiring forest land, a timber mill, and a quarry at Whata Whata, seven miles from the college site; but manpower could not be bought. "All the cement and timber in New Zealand is [sic] not of any value without men to use it," he wrote, "and the finest farm will not handle itself without labour and a great deal of it."[58] He reminded the Saints and their leaders that they had pledged their support before the project began.

Financial support also lagged. Each district was assessed monthly cash amounts to support the workmen. "Some [districts] stand well and others stand *very poorly*," President Ottley wrote. "The total figure is staggering. Here it is: You, the members of the Mission, who have pledged yourselves to support your missionary labourers to the extent of two pounds per week, are a thousand pounds behind right now. Men cannot eat and do missionary work on that basis." He issued the ultimate threat. "Brethren, if you don't support them, the work will have to stop. It can't run on promises."[59]

LDS meetinghouses are not dedicated until they are paid for. It is therefore significant that the Auckland chapel was dedicated on 15 December 1953, only six months after its opening. Apostle LeGrand Richards was assigned to dedicate the building, and there was great excitement in the expectation of the visit of a fourth apostle to New Zealand, following David O. McKay (1921), George Albert Smith (1938), and Elder Cowley's four visits as an apostle (1947–49). However, Elder Richards arrived on Monday, 14 December 1953, to find the New Zealand Mission in mourning. News had just been received of the death of Polynesia's beloved apostle, Matthew Cowley. With other General Authorities, Elder Cowley had attended the laying of the Los Angeles Temple cornerstone on Saturday, 12 December 1953. He died peacefully in his sleep in the early hours of Sunday, 13 December 1953 (14 December New Zealand time). His death cast gloom over the chapel dedication ceremony, which nevertheless proceeded as scheduled.

---

58. "Bulletin: To District and Branch Presidents and Members All Over the Mission," *Te Karere* 47, no. 11 (November 1953): 376.

59. Ibid. Emphasis in original.

While Latter-day Saints all over the Pacific grieved, the Maori people were devastated. Matthew Cowley was "their" apostle, their beloved "Tumuaki"—a title simply meaning leader or president and used for every mission president during his term of office but never relinquished for Cowley even after his release. Cowley loved the Maori people. "He was very forgiving," said Elder Robert L. Simpson, himself a "Cowley missionary" and later a New Zealand mission president and then Pacific Area President. "He saw in these people their Christlike attributes, in spite of their shortcomings and imperfections, and they appreciated that sincere trust and belief in them and they responded to what he asked of them as a result."[60] Now they were inconsolable. "A great and noble 'Kauri' [the Maori transliteration of "Cowley," and coincidentally the name of New Zealand's greatest tree] has fallen in the physical forest of mankind," wrote President Ottley to Elva Cowley.[61]

At a meeting in Apia, Samoa, on 18 July 1954, between Howard B. Stone (president of the Samoan Mission), D'Monte Coombs (president of the Tongan Mission), and Sidney J. Ottley (president of the New Zealand Mission), the Niue Island District of the New Zealand Mission was transferred to the Tongan Mission, and its Cook Islands District and Suva Branch to the Samoan Mission. New Zealand Mission presidents had to travel through both the Samoan and Tongan Missions to visit these districts, and the difficulties of obtaining transport and connections meant that presidents were away from their Auckland office for long periods. Now all three districts could be visited quarterly.[62] As Niue Islanders are closely related to Tongans, this move was timely and sensible. But while the Cook Islands were physically closer to Samoa than to New Zealand, they were a New Zealand protectorate. Despite the seeming advantages of the 1954 transfer to the Samoan Mission, it was not to be permanent.

Momentous things were happening in the LDS Church in the South Pacific. Wendell B. Mendenhall, who had served in the New Zealand Mission from December 1927 to August 1930, was president of the Stockton California Stake more than twenty years later when his son Paul was called to serve in the New Zealand Mission. Towards the end of Paul Mendenhall's mission, his parents visited New Zealand (in January–February 1953); while there, Wendell Mendenhall spent some time with George R. Biesinger, whom he had known in California. A large-scale building

---

60. Robert L. Simpson, interviewed by Gordon Irving, 1978, 3.
61. Sidney J. Ottley, "New Zealand's Message of Love to Sister Cowley & Family on the Passing of Our Loved One," *Te Karere* 48, no. 2 (February 1954): 47–48.
62. New Zealand Mission, Manuscript History, 30 September 1954.

contractor, Mendenhall became very interested in the building program in New Zealand.⁶³

A year after this visit, when it was announced that Church President David O. McKay and his wife, Emma Ray Riggs McKay, intended to visit the Pacific missions early in 1955, Brother Mendenhall volunteered to accompany them at his own expense. Instead, he was given a special assignment to precede them and look into the extent and viability of the college project.⁶⁴

On 6 January 1955, Wendell and Wealtha Mendenhall arrived in New Zealand to make advance preparations for this first-ever visit of a Church president to New Zealand. Mendenhall also audited costs of the building program, especially the college. There was considerable disquiet in Church offices in Salt Lake City over the escalating costs of the project (already in the vicinity of US$1.5 million⁶⁵), and it was suggested that it might be necessary to cut back the ambitious plans for the college. President McKay also asked Brother Mendenhall to help President Ottley make a preliminary, confidential search for a suitable temple site in New Zealand.⁶⁶

The McKays, accompanied by Church transportation agent Franklin J. Murdock (a great-grandson of John Murdock, first president of the Australasian Mission), arrived on 24 January 1955 and were given a Maori welcome at the college site that evening. Next morning, President McKay inspected the college project, then moved on to visit Tauranga, Gisborne, Nuhaka, and Hastings, holding meetings in each area. At each succeeding meeting, the congregation was swollen as members from other areas followed the official party. Stops at TeHauke, Pukehou, Dannevirke, Palmerston North, and Wellington followed.

In Wellington, President McKay was received by Deputy Prime Minister Keith Holyoake and a group of cabinet ministers; this meeting was followed by a press conference. That evening (Thursday, 27 January), the Prophet spoke in the Porirua chapel before flying back to Hamilton next morning. After general and business meetings there, the party proceeded to Auckland where more than 1,000 people attended a special conference. For

---

63. Cummings, *Mighty Missionary of the Pacific*, 37. Cummings's statement that Mendenhall assisted Biesinger in the purchase of the forest and sawmill is inaccurate as both were functioning twelve months before Mendenhall's 1953 visit to New Zealand.

64. Ibid., 50; New Zealand Mission, Manuscript History, 31 March 1955.

65. "Mormons' Progress among Maoris," *Northern Daily Mail*, Manchester, England, 26 May 1955, clipping pasted in New Zealand Mission, Manuscript History.

66. Cummings, *Mighty Missionary of the Pacific*, 50.

the first time in mission history, closed-circuit television was used to convey proceedings to overflow crowds downstairs and in a marquee in the grounds. Next day, nearly 500 people from all over New Zealand bade farewell to the Church president at the airport when his party left for Australia.[67]

As a result of this visit, great things happened. President McKay was impressed by his inspection of the Church College site. Instead of cutting back on the project, as intended, he decided to expand it.[68] The Matthew Cowley Administrative Building and the David O. McKay Building (containing an auditorium, an indoor swimming pool, and a gymnasium) were added to the campus, at an estimated additional cost of US$3.5 million.[69] But this was not all.

During their visit to the college site, President McKay, Brother Mendenhall, President Ottley, and George Biesinger, the building supervisor, also agreed on the ideal site for a temple: a hill overlooking the college project. As the new temple was to serve all the South Pacific, the sensible location was Auckland for the convenience of Saints travelling from Samoa, Tonga, Tahiti, and Australia. "[B]ut we always came back and looked at that dairy farm on the hill. That looked like the place to us," said President Ottley later. "I kept coming back to that one piece of property."[70] While not actually announcing the temple, President McKay strongly hinted at it during his final talk in New Zealand on Sunday afternoon, 30 January.[71] The official announcement that a temple would be built in New Zealand was made on 17 February 1955, a few days after McKay's return to Salt Lake City, following a meeting between the First Presidency and Council of the Twelve.[72] In 1921, David O. McKay, as an apostle, had prophesied that there would one day be a temple in New Zealand. Now this prophecy was to be fulfilled.

During his New Zealand visit, President McKay gave Wendell Mendenhall another informal assignment—that of overseeing the whole con-

---

67. "We Thank Thee O God for a Prophet," *Te Karere* 49, nos. 2–3 (February–March 1955): 41–78.

68. Cummings, *Mighty Missionary of the Pacific*, 51; "New Zealand Church College Carries on Tradition of 'Old M.A.C.,'" *Church News*, 12 October 1963, 20.

69. "Mormons Progress among the Maoris," *Northern Daily Mail*, 26 May 1955.

70. Sidney J. Ottley, Oral History, interviewed by Kenneth W. Baldridge, 10 August 1972, 10–11.

71. Cummings, *Mighty Missionary of the Pacific*, 54. See also, "Pres. McKay Suggests South Pacific Temple," *Church News*, 12 February 1955, 3.

72. "Church Will Build New Zealand Temple," *Church News*, 19 February 1955, 12.

struction of the college and temple in New Zealand. After the McKays left, Mendenhall and Biesinger toured the mission together, drumming up enthusiasm and recruiting more workers for the college construction.[73] Purchase of the temple site, bringing Church-owned land on Tuhikaramea Road to 1,300 acres, was announced at hui tau in April 1955. The temple, to cost $1.5 million, was to be built with the help of 230 labour missionaries in an estimated construction time of two years. Events began to move to a climax.

Early in 1955, it was announced that Ariel S. Ballif, former principal of the MAC, would succeed Sidney J. Ottley as mission president. On 6 February 1955, the first elders' quorum in the New Zealand Mission was formed in Auckland, with Frederick M. P. Danielson as president, and Thomas Ivan Reid and William Roberts as his counselors.[74] Another eight elders' quorums were organised during the next few weeks (in the Waikato, Hawkes Bay, Whangarei, Bay of Islands, the combined Hauraki, King Country and Taranaki districts, Mahia and Poverty Bay, Bay of Plenty and Manawatu districts), the majority with Maori leadership.[75] This was an important administrative step in preparing the mission, not just for a temple, but for the organisation of autonomous stakes, and was obviously suggested by President McKay during his visit. There were now 13,000 Latter-day Saints in New Zealand, of whom 90 percent were Maori.

The Ballifs arrived by air on 28 March 1955, and they and the Ottleys toured much of the mission before hui tau, which was held on the college grounds from 7 to 12 April with between 2,500–3,000 present. Although full-time missionary numbers had declined to forty-five during the Korean War, there were now 120, including the American building supervisors and also their wives.[76] By the end of the year, there were 137 full-time missionaries in New Zealand.[77]

Following purchase of the temple land, Church architect Edward O. Anderson arrived in New Zealand on 1 June to inspect the site before preparing preliminary drawings. The temple was to be built to the same floor plan as the temple under construction in Berne, Switzerland, but of course, had to be adapted to the contours of the site and to New Zealand building regulations. Anderson was accompanied by Brother Mendenhall, who was acting in his capacity as consultant and adviser to both the mission presi-

---

73. New Zealand Mission, Manuscript History, District Quarterly Reports, 31 March 1955.
74. Ibid., Auckland District Historical Report, 31 March 1955.
75. Ibid., District Quarterly Reports, 31 March 1955.
76. Ibid., Historical Report, 30 June 1955.
77. Ibid., 31 December 1955.

dency and the First Presidency on the New Zealand building program.[78] In July 1955, less than two months after this visit, Wendell B. Mendenhall was officially appointed chairman of the reconstituted Church Building Committee, responsible for Church building construction worldwide,[79] a full-time position he held for the next ten years.

At the college site, great progress was being made by Biesinger's team of fourteen American tradesmen and 150 building missionaries. Total population of the construction village was now 235. Engagements, weddings, and births began occurring in the new community. By September 1955, the last of the first batch of faculty homes was finished, and several motel units (for the use of long-distance visitors to the temple) were begun. A medical clinic, dental clinic, canteen, and barber shop were under construction; five classroom blocks were almost finished, and the boys' and girls' dormitories were ready for roofing.[80] Women living on the project were organised into support teams, assigned to the laundry, kitchen, gardens, sick bay, etc., and acting as guides to the increasing number of sightseers who stopped to look over the project. Children of the building missionary families were driven to school by bus, which also took the women to Hamilton for shopping excursions.

Wendell B. Mendenhall returned to New Zealand on 5 December 1955 to attend the groundbreaking ceremony for the temple, inspect progress on the college site, and to look at land for other chapels. The temple groundbreaking ceremony was held on 21 December, and more than 600 Latter-day Saints from every district in the mission attended, including fifteen of the sixteen district presidents. During the service, Wendell B. Mendenhall presented Brother Biesinger with a cheque for US$1,000 from the New Zealand Missionary Society, as a contribution to the temple building fund. Another cheque for US$500 for the building fund arrived from the Magleby family. Samoan Relief Society sisters raised over £1,000 towards the cost of temple clothing, and this cheque was presented to Arta Ballif, who had already organised a committee that began producing a stock of white temple clothing. After prayers (offered by Alex Wishart representing the Saints in Tonga and Oliver Ahmu representing those in Samoa) and speeches, Elders Ballif, Mendenhall, and Biesinger symbolically turned the first sod. As the closing prayer of the service concluded,

---

78. Ibid., 30 June 1955.
79. "Church Construction Chief: Pres. Mendenhall Building Chairman," *Church News*, 23 July 1955, 7.
80. "Featuring the Districts: LDS College," *Te Karere* 49, no. 9 (September 1955): 298–99; "A Birdseye View of the College," ibid., no. 10 (October 1955): 309–11.

heavy earth-moving equipment moved in and began excavating.[81] The first concrete foundations were poured on 15 January 1956.

Erick Albert Rosenvall, a successful American building contractor, was called to supervise building the temple. He sold his home, closed his business, and arrived in New Zealand on 16 June 1955 with his wife, Vernice, and sons, Lynn and James. As well as supervising the temple construction, Brother Rosenvall was one of a nine-man committee in charge of all LDS Church building projects in New Zealand. By 1956, there were thirty-six American building supervisors and their families in New Zealand, either working with particular "crews" or supervising the building of particular chapels.[82]

By the end of June 1956, the temple walls were visible in Hamilton, five miles away. The David O. McKay Building and Matthew Cowley Auditorium at the college next door were also under construction.[83] The block-making machine produced enough concrete blocks for all LDS construction projects in New Zealand, and between fifty and seventy-five tons of blocks were shipped to Samoa each month, with the capacity to produce another 200 tons for the islands had shipping space been available.[84]

Early in June 1956, President Ballif reorganised the mission presidency, releasing his counselors, Joseph Hay and George Biesinger. They were replaced by two missionary elders, one with responsibility for the proselytising missionaries, the other to supervise the work of branch and district officers.[85] The mission was still growing, and many new branches were organised. The Auckland Branch was divided on 15 November 1956,[86] and land for another chapel was bought on Auckland's north shore. A new chapel was already under construction at Tamaki in the Auckland District and was opened on 1 September 1957.

On 22 December 1956, Elder Hugh B. Brown, then an Assistant to the Quorum of the Twelve, laid the cornerstone of the temple in the presence of 1,520 assembled Latter-day Saints, including all proselytising mis-

---

81. New Zealand Mission, Manuscript History, 31 December 1955; "Ground Breaking Services Held on Temple Hill," *Te Karere* 50, no. 2 (February 1956): 42–46.

82. Erick Albert Rosenvall, Oral History, interviewed by Bruce Blumell, 23 October 1973, 2.

83. New Zealand Mission, Manuscript History, 30 June 1956.

84. Ibid., Waikato District, College Branch historical report, 30 September 1956; Barbara Baigent, "A Church Builds a Village," *Church News*, 21 September 1957, 3, reprinted from New Zealand periodical *Women's Choice*.

85. New Zealand Mission, Manuscript History, 30 June 1956.

86. Ibid., 31 December 1956.

sionaries. Among the speakers were faithful "old-timers" Hohepa Heperi (age eighty-seven), the only survivor of Magleby's original high priests, and Polly Duncan.

The tempo of work increased, and public interest grew also. Over the weekend of 20–21 October 1956, for example, 600 visitors toured the site, guided by volunteers from the project families. A year later, there were as many as 2,000 visitors each week; missionary elders acted as guides during the week, while college personnel took over on weekends.[87]

By mid-January 1957, the temple walls reached the third storey; the college cafeteria was roofed, and the gymnasium was far enough advanced to make it possible to plan to hold April hui tau sessions there. The classrooms and girls' dormitories were almost finished. A new timber mill was being built on a two-acre site at Kaikohe; at full capacity, it employed twenty-nine men.[88]

The new mission home that President Ottley had purchased proved far too small to accommodate the Browns and Mendenhalls when they visited for the cornerstone laying in December. With a temple being built, more General Authority visitors could be expected, and Elder Mendenhall suggested building a specially designed mission home. A site was purchased at the end of March.[89] Land was also bought for a chapel in Mount Roskill, an Auckland suburb where the Church had owned land several decades earlier.[90]

Hui tau 1957 (18–22 April) was the biggest ever, with nearly 4,000 attending one or more sessions. Held at the college, meetings were conducted in the shells of the David O. McKay and Matthew Cowley buildings. To President Ballif's satisfaction, less time was spent on food preparation, so that everyone was able to attend the conference sessions.[91]

By the middle of 1957, the basic temple structure was finished. President Ballif called a meeting on 15 June 1957 to plan both temple and college dedications. About forty people, including all district presidents and members with special expertise in various Polynesian cultures, began to prepare a spectacular welcome for Church President David O. McKay, who was expected to dedicate both facilities the following year.[92]

---

87. Ibid., Waikato District Report, 30 September 1957; Fern Lyman, "The Crossroads of the South Pacific," *Te Karere* 51, no. 10 (October 1957): 354–57.

88. New Zealand Mission, Manuscript History, Bay of Islands District Report, 31 December 1956.

89. Ibid., 31 March 1957.

90. "1957–A Year of Progress," *Te Karere* 52, no. 1 (January 1958): 20.

91. New Zealand Mission, Manuscript History, 30 June 1957.

92. Ibid.; "Meeting Held to Plan Programme for Dedication," *Te Karere* 51, no.

Left: E. Albert Rosenvall, temple building supervisor and first president of the New Zealand Temple; George R. Biesinger, New Zealand Construction Supervisor; Wendell B. Mendenhall, chairman of the world-wide Church Building Committee; and Edward O. Anderson, temple architect, on the steps of the almost-completed New Zealand Temple, 8 March 1958. Courtesy LDS Church History Library.

With the growth of LDS Church assets and real-estate holdings in New Zealand (for example, the buildings at the temple and college site were now estimated to be worth US$3 million),[93] changes had to be made to the Church Trust Board. These developments necessitated having the New Zealand Parliament pass a private member's bill. Through the influence of Joseph Hay, the bill was introduced by the Minister of Internal Affairs, Hon. Sidney W. Smith; and the Church of Jesus Christ of Latter-day Saints Trust Board Empowering Act became law in August 1957, establishing the Church in New Zealand on a sound legal footing.[94]

One journalist visited the Frankton construction site regularly. "What I like so much about it all is the evident happiness of the voluntary work-

---

8 (August 1957): 264.

93. Baigent, "A Church Builds a Village."

94. New Zealand Mission, Manuscript History, 30 June 1957; "1957–A Year of Progress," 21.

ers," she wrote, stating that, in all her wandering around the site, she had never heard a cross word. "They don't walk along a plank wheeling a wheelbarrow—they run. And work there is not easy—there is no 40-hour week." She finally concluded, "They must like it, or they wouldn't keep on doing the work."[95] The labour missionary force was augmented all through the project by short-term volunteers from LDS branches around New Zealand. Buses transported groups from Auckland for Saturday work on the site; others came from more distant branches for a day, a long weekend, or to spend their annual vacations helping.[96]

Meanwhile, as college and temple approached completion—the temple spire was erected on 26 August 1957—school policies were being hammered out in Utah. With high schools in Tonga and Samoa as well as New Zealand to be administered, the First Presidency on 21 June 1957 appointed a Board of Education for the South Pacific under the chairmanship of Wendell B. Mendenhall.[97] This move effectually removed the schools from the sole jurisdiction of already overworked mission presidents, avoiding problems like those that had surfaced during the life of the MAC.

The board selected Dr. Clifton D. Boyack, an experienced school principal from Berkeley, California, to head the new secondary school in New Zealand,[98] which was officially named the Church College of New Zealand, the Church of Jesus Christ of Latter-day Saints.[99] (In New Zealand and Australia, private high schools are usually designated "colleges.") Opening day was set for 10 February 1958.

Meetings with local education authorities were held, and formal application for registration was lodged with the Department of Education in Wellington.[100] Provisional registration was granted for the first year, continuance to depend on inspectors' reports once the school was operating.[101] Principal Boyack visited local high schools, observing methods and procedures. The college prospectus was mailed to potential students and their parents by the end of November 1957. Enrolment of boarders was somewhat limited for the first term, as the college dormitories were being

---

95. Baigent, "A Church Builds a Village."
96. "Editorial," *Te Karere* 51, no. 10 (October 1957): 341.
97. "The Board of Education for the South Pacific Islands," *Te Karere* 51, no. 8 (August 1957): 262.
98. "New Headmaster Formulating Plans for College," *Te Karere* 51, no. 10 (October 1957): 358.
99. "From the College," *Te Karere* 51, no. 12 (December 1957): 424.
100. "From the College," *Te Karere* 51, no. 11 (November 1957): 383.
101. "A Dream Comes True," *Te Karere* 52, no. 1 (January 1958): 17.

used by a considerable number of labour missionaries, previously housed in temporary barracks, who were now completing the temple construction.[102]

An advisory committee was set up on 21 November 1957, consisting of George R. Biesinger, Stanford W. Bird (treasurer and purchasing agent of the building program in New Zealand), and three local Latter-day Saints (Sidney Crawford, William Roberts, and Selu Fruean), as well as mission president Ariel S. Ballif. Despite President Gordon C. Young's insistence as early as 1951 that "we must not make the same mistake we did before, in going ahead with our own American ideas,"[103] Brother Boyack wanted to run the college like an American high school. His observation of New Zealand schools had not impressed him.

The New Zealand education system worked towards preparation for two competitive external examinations, held countrywide at the end of each academic year—the School Certificate and Higher School Certificate. Candidates were required to pass three-hour written examinations in each subject, which usually required several long essays for each paper. American methods, promoting exploration of topics by discussion and multiple-choice type examinations, did not help students memorise the large body of facts needed for the New Zealand examinations. Nor did these methods give them practice in writing several well-planned and reasoned essays in the three-hour time limit set for most papers.

President Ballif, drawing on his experience at the old MAC, insisted that preparation of students for the New Zealand School Certificate, Higher School Certificate, and Matriculation Examinations must take first priority. He knew that students had to pass these examinations to get employment or to enter tertiary institutions in New Zealand, and that parental support would be lost if the college curriculum and teaching did not clearly promote examination success, just as had happened at the old MAC. Local board members supported President Ballif; but in practice after the college opened, Boyack still tried to achieve examination passes using American methods, despite limited success.

Owing to a teacher shortage in New Zealand, the Church hired American teachers who arrived with their families on the *Mariposa* on 11 January 1958, with only a few short weeks to acclimatise, settle into the faculty homes, and learn what they could about the New Zealand education system. Initially, there were only four New Zealand teachers on the staff.

---

102. "From the College," *Te Karere* 51, no. 10 (December 1957): 424, 434.
103. Gordon C. Young, Letter to Edward O. Anderson, 7 July 1951, fd.6, Young Papers.

By now there were 15,600 Latter-day Saints in the New Zealand Mission.[104] There were seventy-two branches, only a minority of which had modern chapels. In November 1957, Mendenhall and Ballif announced that the building program would continue after the completion of the temple and college. Districts would still be expected to supply and support building missionaries; but without the two huge projects at Frankton to be manned, the contribution rate would drop by about 50 percent.[105]

Preparations continued for the opening of the temple. Stuart Meha was appointed by the First Presidency to go to Hawaii and translate the temple ceremonies into Maori. Meha did so, then travelled to Salt Lake City, where a committee of Maori-speaking returned mission presidents and missionaries (A. Reed Halversen, Gordon C. Young, and Paul Mendenhall) met with Meha in an upper room of the Salt Lake Temple and reviewed his work. Dr. Nitama Paewai (son of early MAC graduate Niki Paewai and the first Mormon Maori to graduate in medicine) was in the United States doing postgraduate studies at the University of Utah. Paewai also checked the final draft, while his wife Hineapa (daughter of Stuart and Ivory Meha) acted as stenographer to the committee.[106]

On 9 February 1958, the existing College Branch, which served the building community, was renamed Temple View Branch and a new Church College Branch was organized for faculty, domestic and clerical staff, and students.[107] Next day, the school opened with a special assem-

---

104. "*Te Karere*' in Retrospect," *Te Karere* 51, no. 11 (November 1957): 392.

105. "A Dream Comes True," 18–19, and "1957–A Year of Progress," 21; New Zealand Mission, Manuscript History, 31 December 1957.

106. During his oral history interview in 1972, Gordon C. Young stated that Meha could not do the translation because he was too old. He also stated that, despite having forgotten the Maori he himself had learned as a missionary in 1920–21, it miraculously came back to him and that in eight days he and Halversen were able to complete the translation. Young also stated in this interview that he had spoken no Maori during his term as mission president, a statement that his own diaries and the mission history clearly contradict. Further, he said there were no Maori-speaking elders in the 1950s, but the inclusion of young returned missionary Paul Mendenhall on the review committee indicates otherwise. Young, Oral History, 6–7. It would therefore appear that Young's memory was at fault, and there is no reason to doubt that it was Stuart Meha who actually translated the temple ceremonies into Maori; Meha reported this mission in a lucid and well-written article in the mission paper shortly after his return to New Zealand. Stuart Meha, "Mission to Hawaii and the U.S.," *Te Karere* 52, no. 2 (February 1958): 44–45, 63. It seems likely that the committee, including President Young, merely checked Meha's work.

107. New Zealand Mission, Manuscript History, 31 March 1958; "Here and

The David O. McKay Auditorium at the Church College of New Zealand, Temple View, near Hamilton, New Zealand, in 1960. Courtesy LDS Church History Library.

bly. Approximately 300 boarding students and forty-seven day pupils were welcomed by mission president Ariel Ballif and college "president" (principal) Boyack. The new turquoise and grey uniform was modelled, and the school song (a revised version of the old MAC school song originally written by Walter Smith) was sung. After the assembly, work began in the superbly equipped classrooms, science laboratories, and homecraft rooms, all a far cry from facilities of the old MAC.[108]

Now work on the temple accelerated. An additional 100 full-time building missionaries and all full-time proselytising missionaries were recruited to ensure that it was completed in time for the dedication scheduled for 20 April 1958, and work continued, literally around the clock. The First Presidency announced on 22 February 1958 that F. Albert Rosenvall,

---

There in the Mission," *Te Karere* 52, no. 3 (March 1958): 111.

108. New Zealand Church members faced the end of an era when the Church College of New Zealand finally closed its doors in November 2009. For a fine discussion of the college, its place in the wider Church education system, and the reasons for the closure, see Scott C. Esplin, "Closing the Church College of New Zealand: A Case Study in Church Education Policy," *Journal of Mormon History* 37, no. 1 (Winter 2011): 86–114.

supervisor of the temple construction crew, would be the first president of the New Zealand Temple and that his wife, Vernice, would serve as temple matron.[109] This appointment was a popular one, as the Rosenvalls had endeared themselves to New Zealand Latter-day Saints during the previous three years. In turn, President Rosenvall could not speak highly enough of the faith of the Polynesian Saints.[110]

The Maori culture program for the dedicatory celebrations was under the direction of Arta Ballif and the mission MIA board. During planning sessions, it quickly became evident that tribal loyalties were still of vital importance to Maori Latter-day Saints. Every New Zealand iwi (tribe) traced its whakapapa or ancestry back to one of the traditional canoes in the Great Fleet. Each canoe group felt that its story was the one that should be acted out in haka, waiata (song), and poi dances during the welcome ceremonies for the Church prophet. Long discussion hammered out points on which there was general consensus, and tribal representatives eventually accepted a syncretised program of Maori culture items that were practised in the districts and put together in final massed rehearsals.

It is interesting to note that the haka was included in the program. While of relatively minor importance compared with marriage and funeral customs, the ambivalent attitudes of successive mission presidents towards the haka in many ways illustrate a whole range of cultural tensions as Maori Saints endeavoured to become worthy Latter-day Saints as well as honouring their heritage. Frequently regarded as a war dance, the posture dance or haka was actually far more complex and was a feature of ceremonial Maori welcomes. Several early Mormon missionaries described the haka, which was extremely exotic to them. "The one who can come nearest to making his tongue touch his ear, his eyes jump from their sockets and shout the loudest is considered the leading man," wrote John T. Smellie in 1889. "They also cause their bodies to twist and take peculiar shapes evidently with the intention of frightening people away rather than bid them welcome."[111] Until World War II, the haka was, in some years, one of many competitive events at the annual hui tau, while in other years it was forbidden, depending on the views of the incumbent mission president. Numerous American missionaries learned the haka and performed it

---

109. "Elder Rosenvall Named N.Z. Temple President," *Church News*, 22 February 1958, 7.

110. Rosenvall, Oral History, 6, 11.

111. John T. Smellie, Letter to the Editor, 15 April 1889, printed as "The Australasian Mission: Proceedings of the Annual Conference at Te Hawke," *Deseret News*, 17 May 1889, [3].

at fund-raising concerts and reunions once home in the United States.[112] Some mission presidents, however, made ineffectual attempts to prohibit or at least curtail all performances of the haka, not only by missionaries but also by Maori.

For instance, John E. Magleby, whose genuine love for the Maori cannot seriously be doubted, nevertheless disapproved of the haka. During a visit to Parihaka in 1902, he described the ceremonial haka as "a rude affair at the best—rather tending to vice and evil."[113] Efforts to omit the haka from Church conferences met with some success over the next few years. Reporting the 1907 hui tau, when Louis G. Hoagland was serving as mission president, the mission paper commended the various amusements and competitions of the conference, congratulating the people "on the absence of the offensive Maori haka."[114]

This absence was not permanent, and mission president Orson D. Romney raised a storm of protest when he prohibited the haka from the annual hui tau of 1913 at Korongata, the occasion of the dedication of the MAC. Principal John Johnson recorded that "some strong language was used on both sides. . . . [I]t was finally decided that [the haka] should be discouraged everywhere, and put entirely down at all conferences where the [S]aints are in charge."[115]

President Romney's edict was found to be unenforceable, and both haka and poi dances were performed during the ceremonial welcome extended to Apostle David O. McKay in 1921. Elder McKay was captivated by the poi dances, which were repeated next day at his request. Although less enthusiastic about the haka, he registered no disapproval, merely some apprehension in case he should be expected to reciprocate in kind.[116] Elder George Albert Smith, the second Mormon apostle to visit New Zealand (1938) enjoyed the haka, according to his travelling companion, Elder Rufus K. Hardy.[117] However, in the early 1950s President Gordon C. Young prohibited the haka, not only for missionaries but for all endowed members.[118]

---

112. "New Zealand Missionaries Hold 'Hui Nui' in Inglewood: Elder Matthew Cowley Attends," *California Inter-Mountain News*, 10 July 1951, in Journal History, 10 July 1951, 5.

113. John Ephraim Magleby, Journal, 18 June 1902, Book 13.

114. "General Conference, 1907," *Te Karere* 1, no. 6 (15 April 1907): 56.

115. John Johnson, Journal, 20–21 March, 5 April 1913.

116. David O. McKay, "Hui Tau," *Improvement Era* 24, no. 9 (July 1921): 770–71, 774.

117. Rufus K. Hardy, "With Church Leaders in New Zealand," *Deseret News*, 25 June 1938, in Journal History, 25 June 1938, 8.

118. Young, Diary, 27 March 1951; Rangi Davies, Letter to Gordon C. Young,

Nevertheless, the haka was featured when the ceremonial welcome to President David O. McKay was planned. Two years later, in 1960, Apostle Spencer W. Kimball was entertained by Maori haka and poi dances during his visit to New Zealand. Like President McKay, he was obviously entranced with the graceful, intricate poi dances of the women but, unlike President McKay, Elder Kimball was somewhat offended by the haka. "Elder Kimball wondered ... whether the Maori Saints ought not to relegate the wild war dances and songs to an annual festival, held for the purpose of perpetuation, and substitute their peaceful, beautiful dances for more frequent use at Church entertainments," his biographers wrote later.[119] Such ingenuous suggestions, of course, completely overlooked the important role of the haka in Maori ceremonial welcomes, but the changing fortunes of the haka provide an interesting illustration of the ambivalence of leadership direction in dealing with underlying cultural tensions experienced by many of the Maori Saints.[120]

Three weeks before the dedication, the temple was opened for public inspection. Almost 113,000 people, three times the population of Hamilton (the nearest city), filed through the multi-million dollar, seven-storey, seventy-five-room building during the twenty-three days it was open.[121] After dedication, LDS temples are open only to recommend-holding Church members. As the dedication dates of college and temple approached, ships and chartered planes also brought many former American missionaries and New Zealand expatriates from the United States. More than 5,000 visitors were estimated to be in Hamilton and the surrounding district, 1,000 of them from overseas, as Latter-day Saints converged on the new temple from all parts of New Zealand, from Australia and from the Islands.[122]

The greatest week in the history of the New Zealand Mission began when President David O. McKay and two apostles (Elders Delbert L. Stapley and Marion G. Romney) flew into Auckland on Thursday, 17 April 1958. All three men were accompanied by their wives. The visitors received a great welcome at the airport from many of the Saints, including a Samoan brass band. On Saturday, the official party was driven to the tem-

---

Auckland, 11 January 1953, fd.11, Young Papers.

119. Edward L. Kimball and Andrew E. Kimball Jr., *Spencer W. Kimball: Twelfth President of the Church of Jesus Christ of Latter-day Saints*, 327.

120. For a fuller discussion of Mormon leadership response to Maori culture, see Newton, "Mormonism in New Zealand," chap.7.

121. Cummings, *Mighty Missionary of the Pacific*, 76.

122. "Culmination of Huge £2,500,000 Church Project Attracts 5000 Visitors," *Waikato Times* (Hamilton, New Zealand), 18 April 1958.

262   *Tiki and Temple*

More than 113,000 people lined up to visit the New Zealand Temple during the twenty-three days it was open for inspection before its dedication on 20 April 1958. Courtesy LDS Church History Library.

ple and college site where, that evening, with an audience of 5,000, they watched an outdoor ceremonial welcome and Polynesian culture program presented by 1,000 Maori, Samoan, and Tongan Saints. The New Zealand Temple, the thirteenth temple in this dispensation, was dedicated the next morning, Sunday, 20 April. The first session was attended by mission, district, branch, and elders' quorum presidencies of the Pacific missions and their wives. The session was repeated that afternoon for temple and college building missionaries and their families. In the following days, President McKay spoke and read the dedicatory prayer in another six sessions to accommodate the New Zealand, Australian, Samoan, and Tongan Saints. It was a time of great rejoicing. Truly, as Elder Gordon B. Hinckley (newly sustained as an Assistant to the Twelve) wrote of the temple dedication, here were mingled "two great strains of the house of Israel—the children of Ephraim from the isles of Britain, and the children of Lehi from the isles of the Pacific."[123]

---

123. Gordon B. Hinckley, "Temple in the Pacific," *Improvement Era* 61, no. 7 (July 1958): 509.

On Thursday, President McKay dedicated the Church College of New Zealand in a service attended by nearly 3,000 people. Prominent visitors included the Governor-General, Lord Cobham; Prime Minister the Right Hon. Walter Nash; the American ambassador to New Zealand, the Hon. Francis H. Russell; Dame Hilda Ross, Member of Parliament for Hamilton; the Right Hon. Keith J. Holyoake, former Prime Minister; Her Majesty Queen Salote Tupus of Tonga, and Their Royal Highnesses Prince Tungi and Princess Mata-aho. Several New Zealand and Pacific Island education officials attended the dedication, as well as LDS mission presidents from Australia and the Polynesian islands and former mission president, Gordon C. Young. Featured speakers included Prime Minister Nash, Dame Hilda Ross, and Auckland District Schools Superintendent L. le F. Ensor.[124]

Next day, the Church leaders inspected the college facilities before attending an emotional missionary meeting in the evening where 185 labour missionaries were released after periods ranging from two to eight years of service. President McKay and party returned to the mission home in Auckland on Saturday, 26 April, and the following day the Prophet dedicated the Tamaki chapel in suburban Auckland.[125] At dinner that night in the mission home, President McKay announced that a stake would soon be organised in New Zealand, and that the mission itself would be divided.[126] This final announcement concluded what most Church members agreed was "the most outstanding event in the history of the New Zealand Mission."[127]

At lunch next day, President McKay told Apostle Romney that he wanted the mission division and stake organisation to proceed quickly. He would present the two proposals to the Twelve as soon as he returned to Utah; and obviously expecting their approval to be a mere rubber-stamping, he suggested that the business could be carried out before Elder Romney left New Zealand. President McKay nominated George R. Biesinger as stake president, by-passing the usual lengthy interviewing procedure. In a special meeting on the following Thursday, 1 May, with Elder Romney, President Ballif, and Elder Mendenhall, he repeated these instructions, and it was decided that the Auckland Stake should be organised on Sunday, 18 May 1958. President McKay personally called George R. Biesinger

---

124. Ric Morehouse, "The Establishment of Church Education in New Zealand," 47.

125. Rulon H. Tingey, secretary to President David O. McKay, "New Zealand Dedication Trip by President David O. McKay and Sister McKay," 3, copy in New Zealand Mission, Manuscript History, April 1958.

126. Marion G. Romney, Diary, 27 April 1958, 8.

127. Tingey, "New Zealand Dedication Trip," 3.

to be stake president later that day before flying home via Fiji and Honolulu.[128] President McKay's counselors and the Twelve were obviously presented with a *fait accompli* on his return to Salt Lake City on 10 May.

After visiting North and South Island branches, Elder Romney and mission president Ariel S. Ballif (who happened to be Elder Romney's brother-in-law), visited the Geographical Names Board in the Department of Internal Affairs and applied to have the name of the LDS village, variously referred to as being at Tuhikaramea, Frankton, or Hamilton, officially renamed "Templeton." As there was already a Templeton in New Zealand (also a Templebarn, Temple College, and Temple Peak), this was not allowed, so they settled for "Temple View," a name that had already been given to the reorganised College Branch in February.[129] Elder Romney and President Ballif next visited the Postmaster General's Department, where they were assured that a post office would be established in the town without delay.

Official authorisation for the formation of the new stake arrived on Friday, 16 May, barely in time.[130] George R. Biesinger had already been called to serve as stake president by President McKay. Following this precedent, it became the usual practice, as the first stakes were organised in other countries outside the United States and Canada, that expatriate Americans were called to preside over them in almost every case, with the expectation that they would train local leaders to take over. Thus, it remained only for Elder Romney to call counselors for President Biesinger to complete the proposed stake presidency. He spent Friday and Saturday, 16 and 17 May, interviewing prospective counselors, as well as calling high councilors and bishoprics for the new wards to be created on Sunday. Following President McKay's advice, Elder Romney invited President Ballif and Elder Mendenhall to assist in the interviewing process.

The new Auckland Stake, the 264th in the Church, was duly formed on 18 May with George Ross Biesinger as president, New Zealander William Roberts as first counselor and American Stanford W. Bird, treasurer of the building program, as second counselor. Five wards in Auckland and three wards and an independent branch (Huntly) in the Waikato area, comprised the new stake.[131]

A week later, the Ballif family moved into the new mission home, built, ironically enough, in Remuera, where President Ottley had sold the

---

128. Romney, Diary, 28 April 1958, 9.
129. Ibid., 29 April 1958, 10.
130. New Zealand Mission, Manuscript History, 30 June 1958.
131. Ibid.; "Auckland Stake Formed in New Zealand Mission," *Church News*, 24 May 1958, 5.

large home bought during Gordon C. Young's administration. The mission office staff moved into the old mission home in Orakei Road, leaving their former offices in the Queen Street chapel for the new stake presidency and high council.[132]

The final step was the mission division, which became effective at the end of August 1958. Robert L. Simpson arrived to take over as president of the New Zealand Mission; and a few days later, Alexander P. Anderson, a Salt Lake City jeweller, arrived to preside over the new New Zealand South Mission. The New Zealand Mission now consisted of the Bay of Islands, Whangarei, Bay of Plenty, Hauraki, and King Country districts, a total of 5,380 members. The New Zealand South Mission, with 6,271 members, contained the Hawkes Bay, Mahia, Manawatu, Otago, Poverty Bay, Taranaki, Wairarapa, Wairau, and Wellington Districts.[133] Church population may have been divided more or less evenly, but geographically all the South Island and half the North Island were in the New Zealand South Mission, with the dividing line roughly crossing New Zealand through Lake Taupo. The population of New Zealand was also roughly divided, as one third of the country's population lived in Auckland.[134] Geographically, the Auckland Stake was located entirely within the New Zealand Mission boundaries, but the pastoral care of the Latter-day Saints living in the stake boundaries was now the responsibility of the stake officers rather than the mission president.

Both new mission presidents were called and set apart in Salt Lake City. President Anderson was originally called to preside over the New Zealand Mission and President Simpson to preside over the newly created New Zealand South Mission. However, as David O. McKay prepared to set President Simpson apart, he reversed the callings because President Simpson, a former "Cowley missionary," spoke Maori, and the majority of Maori-speaking Saints lived in the area of the northern Mission.[135] Historian Glen M. Leonard, who served as President Simpson's mission secretary, felt the change was inspired. "President Simpson had to guide the mission through a crucial period," he recalls. "The Church wanted to change the image of the Mormon Church in New Zealand from that of

---

132. New Zealand Mission, Manuscript History, 30 June 1958.

133. New Zealand Mission, Manuscript History, 30 September 1958; "First Presidency Announces Division of N.Z. Mission," *Church News*, 31 May 1958, 14.

134. Simpson, Oral History, 5.

135. "New President Appointed for the N.Z. Mission," *Deseret News-Telegram*, 23 July 1958, B-1, clipping pasted in New Zealand Mission, Manuscript History; "Californian Named to Serve As New Zealand Mission Head," *Church News*, 26 July 1958, 4; Simpson, Oral History, 19.

a Maori Church. The Maori members loved Elder Simpson and accepted some difficult changes from him which they might not have taken well from anyone else."[136] These changes were to include the termination of the annual mission-wide hui tau and of the mission paper, *Te Karere*, both symbols of the Maori image of the LDS Church in New Zealand. Deeper changes also occurred, as the Maori Saints saw leadership positions in the new stakes initially go to Pakeha members in an inverse proportion to the ratio of Maori to Pakeha Saints. "[The Church] was becoming broader and didn't have the cozy little feeling that [the Maori Saints] were used to," said Elder Simpson.[137]

Although the name "New Zealand Mission" was retained until 1970 (when it became known as the New Zealand North Mission, and was changed again in 1974 to the New Zealand Auckland Mission), in reality the days of the New Zealand Mission ended with the first mission division in May 1958. Suddenly, there were three Church administrative units—two missions and a stake—giving pastoral care to the New Zealand Saints. The changes were far-reaching, and the old-time Maori Saints must often have longed for the old days. By the end of 1960, the two beloved institutions of the New Zealand Mission, hui tau and the mission paper, *Te Karere*—were only a memory. But the Saints were faithful, and the Church in New Zealand grew. That same year saw the Auckland Stake divided into the Auckland and Hamilton Stakes, and a third stake organised from the Hawkes Bay District. Mature and capable local priesthood leaders, Maori and Pakeha, took over the administration of these stakes.

From this point, the story of the Church of Jesus Christ of Latter-day Saints in New Zealand continues to be one of growth, stability, and development. But the story becomes increasingly fragmented and complex as the Church grew from 17,000 members in 1958 to nearly 100,000 fifty years later. There was much to be done. Cultural issues had to be resolved. Most Maori Saints gradually relinquished ways that Church leaders found incompatible with gospel teachings. One and all, Maori and Pakeha Saints, the "two great strains of the house of Israel," rejoiced as they witnessed the growth that began to take place, growth built on the foundation of the sacrifice and devotion of the pioneer missionaries and members of the New Zealand Mission.

---

136. Glen M. Leonard, interviewed by Marjorie Newton, Upper Canada Village, Ontario, Canada, 21 June 1995; notes in my possession.

137. Simpson, Oral History, 5–7, 16, 55.

Glossary of Maori Words

Aotearoa	Maori name for New Zealand
haka	ceremonial posture dance
haakari	feast, funeral feast
hongi	salute, greet by pressing noses
hui	ceremonial meeting or formal assembly
hui pariha	quarterly district conference
hui tau	annual LDS mission conference
iwi	tribe
kai	food
kainga	village
karakia	prayers, prayer meeting
karere	messenger
kaumatua	tribal elders; male Mormon missionaries
Kotahitanga	nineteenth-century Maori parliament
mana	authority, influence, prestige, power
Maoritanga	Maori culture, way of life
mihi	greeting, welcome ceremony
mihinare	missionary (transliteration)
Mihinare Church	Church of England (Church Missionary Society)
moko	tattoo
muru	plunder
noa	ordinary, the opposite of *tapu*
pa	originally a fortified village, now any village
Pakeha	foreign, non-Maori
pariha	district, branch or local unit of the Church
piupiu	fringed waist-band
poi	small woven ball on string
puhi	ceremonially dedicated
rangatira	chief, noble, gentleman
raupo	rushes

reo	Maori language
taha Maori	Maori world view
tangata	man, human being
tangata whenua	people of the land, original inhabitants
tangi	cry
tangihanga	funeral customs
tapu	sacred; under ceremonial religious restriction
taumau	betrothed
te	the
tikanga	customs
tiriti	treaty
tohunga	priest, expert
tumuaki	president
utu	payment, satisfaction
waiata	song, songs
whakapapa	genealogy, oral recitation of ancestry
whare	house
whare karakia	prayer house
whare raupo	rush-walled house
whare wananga	house for instruction in Maori lore

Appendix A

New Zealand Mission Presidents, 1851–1958

The Australasian Mission of the Church of Jesus Christ of Latter-day Saints began on 31 October 1851 with the arrival in Sydney of the first missionaries from Utah. In 1897 (effective 1 January 1898), the Australasian Mission was divided to form the Australian Mission and the New Zealand Mission. In 1958, the New Zealand Mission was divided to form two missions. The New Zealand Mission, responsible for the whole of New Zealand, therefore virtually ended at this date, although the northern mission retained the name until 1970.

Australasian Mission Presidents

John Murdock	1851–52
Charles Wesley Wandell	1852–53
John Jones *(pro tem)*	1853
Augustus A. Farnham	1853–56
Absalom P. Dowdle	1856–57
Andrew J. Stewart	1857–58
Thomas Ford (pro tem)	1858–62
William Broadbent (acting)	1862–[unknown]
No mission president	[unknown]–1869
Robert Beauchamp	1869–74
William Geddes	1874–75
Job Welling	1875
Isaac Groo	1875–77

Fred J. May*	1878
Thomas A. Shreeve*	1878
Elijah F. Pearce	1878–80
George Batt *(pro tem)*	1880–81
William M. Bromley	1881–83
William T. Stewart	1883–86
William Paxman	1886–89
Angus T. Wright	1889–90
John S. Bingham	1890–91
William T. Stewart (second term)	1891–93
William Gardner	1893–96
Ezra F. Richards	1896–

*According to the Manuscript History of the Australian Mission, May and Shreeve were sustained as joint mission presidents at a conference in New Zealand on 15 September 1878. To date, no evidence has been found that either was officially appointed mission president. According to "The Story of the New Zealand Mission from the Journal of Elder Thomas A. Shreeve, 1878–1880," 4, at the September 1878 conference they were sustained as "Presiding Elders over the Australian Mission," Shreeve presiding in New Zealand and May presiding in Australia.

From 1878, all presidents of the Australasian Mission made their headquarters in New Zealand.

New Zealand Mission Presidents 1898–1958

Ezra F. Richards	–1898
Ezra T. Stevenson	1898–1900
John E. Magleby	1900–1902
Charles B. Bartlett	1902–05
Louis G. Hoagland	1905–07
Rufus K. Hardy	1907–09
George Bowles	1909–11
Orson D. Romney	1911–13
William Gardner (second term)	1913–16
James N. Lambert	1916–20

Fred W. Schwendiman (*pro tem*)	1920
George S. Taylor	1920–23
Angus T. Wright (second term)	1923–25
A. Reed Halversen (*pro tem*)	1925
J. Howard Jenkins	1925–28
John E. Magleby (second term)	1928–32
Harold T. Christensen (*pro tem*)	1932–33
Rufus K. Hardy	1933–34
Alvin T. Maughan (*pro tem*)	1934–35
M. Charles Woods	1935–38
Matthew Cowley	1938–45
A. Reed Halversen	1945–48
Gordon C. Young	1948–51
Sidney J. Ottley	1951–55
Ariel S. Ballif	1955–58

Appendix B

LDS European Branches in New Zealand, 1855–1900

Branch	Date Organized
Auckland	6 June 1880
Alford Forest	16 June 1879
Carterton	20 February 1881
Christchurch	1876
Dunedin	6 August 1882
Invercargill	25 July 1882
Kaiapoi	3 December 1867
Karori	April 1855
Le Bons Bay	12 March 1882
Makarewa	31 December 1882
Mangapai	2 June 1886
Maromaku	5 January 1889
Napier	17 October 1880
Norsewood	12 December 1880
Opuawhanga	2 June 1886
Owaka	11 April 1893
Papanui	18 March 1877
Palmerston North	11 December 1892
Prebbleton	15 September 1878

Rama Rama	26 September 1897
Rangiora	
Ruatangata	
Sydenham	4 January 1880
Thames	
Timaru	28 September 1879
Wanganui	3 April 1881
Wellington	
Wreys Bush	4 November 1883

Appendix C

First Maori District Presidents

Installed by John E. Magleby:

1. Hawkes Bay District Eriata Nopera 2 September 1928
2. Mahia District Paora Hapi* 23 September 1928
3. Bay of Islands District Hohepa Heperi 14 October 1928
4. Wairau District Turi Ruruku 21 July 1929
5. Whangarei District Henere Pere Wihongi 22 March 1931
6. Wairarapa District Eruera Taurau 6 March 1932

Installed by Harold T. Christensen:

7. Poverty Bay District Henry Hamon 22 January 1933

*Paora Hapi died 27 December 1930 and was succeeded by Wi Smith.

Bibliography

Note: Letters and newspaper articles are also cited in full in the notes.

Shortened Citations

Ancestral File. Genealogical Society of Utah, Salt Lake City. www.familysearch.org

Church News. Weekly (Saturday) tabloid-sized insert into *Deseret News*, focusing on news of the LDS Church.

Journal History. Journal History of the Church of Jesus Christ of Latter-day Saints. Chronology of typed entries and newspaper clippings, 1830-present. LDS Church History Library.

LDS Church History Library. Library and Archives, History Department, Church of Jesus Christ of Latter-day Saints, Salt Lake City.

Perry Special Collections. L. Tom Perry Special Collections, Harold B. Lee Library, Brigham Young University, Provo, Utah.

Citations

"An Address to the Aboriginals of New Zealand." *Zion's Watchman* 1, nos. 24–25 (15 December 1855): 200.

Alexander, Thomas G. *Mormonism in Transition: A History of the Latter-day Saints, 1890–1930*. Urbana: University of Illinois Press, 1986.

———. *Utah: The Right Place*. Salt Lake City: Gibbs Smith, 1995.

Allen, James B., and Glen M. Leonard. *The Story of the Latter-day Saints*. 2d ed. rev. and enl. Salt Lake City: Deseret Book, 1992.

Allington, Henry. Letter to Albert Carrington, Esq., dated Karori, 27 March 1870. *Millennial Star* 32, no. 22 (31 May 1870): 346–47.

———. Letter to President Albert Carrington, dated Karori, 30 July 1870. *Millennial Star* 32, no. 41 (11 October 1870): 649.

———. "From New Zealand." Letter dated Karori, 20 March 1885. *Millennial Star* 47, no. 20 (18 May 1885): 319.

Amaru, Wi Pere. "Uawa Branch at War." *Te Karere* 39, no. 2 (February 1944): 48.

"Among the Passengers by the *Colima*." *Daily Southern Cross* (Auckland), 15 December 1875.

"Amongst the Mormons." Reprinted from *Manawatu Evening Standard*. Date not given. *The Messenger* 8, no. 3 (11 February 1914): 28.

Anaru, Heteraka. Transcript of Oral History Interview. In Kenneth Wayne Baldridge, Interviews, 1971–73.

Anderson, Charles. "The New Zealand Mission, 3 December 1884, Waotu." *Deseret Evening News*, 9 February 1885, [4].

———. Letter to YMMIA (Young Men's Mutual Improvement Association) of Elsinore. "Correspondence: Interesting Letter from New Zealand." *Deseret Evening News*, 28 April 1885, [4].

———. "Correspondence: New Zealand Letter to Editor, dated 5 August 1885, Auckland." *Deseret Evening News*, 11 September 1885, [1].

Anderson, Edward O. Letter to Richard M. Cyert, dated Salt Lake City, 16 June 1973. Edward O. Anderson, Correspondence. MS 7926. LDS Church History Library.

———. Letter to Gordon C. Young, 17 February 1950. In Gordon Claridge Young, Papers, 1948–72. MS 4016, fd. 9. LDS Church History Library.

"Annual Conference of the Church of Jesus Christ of Latter-day Saints, in Australasia. Held in the Old Assembly Rooms, King Street, Sydney, on April 1st, 1855." *Zion's Watchman* 1, nos. 32–33 (12 April 1855): 257.

Annual Statistical Reports (Form EE) for New Zealand Mission, 1907–21. Microfilm. LDS Church History Library.

"Another Mormon Hunt." *The Star* (Christchurch), 30 September 1901.

"Another Racial Link between Maoris and Hawaiians Is Found." *Deseret News*, 31 July 1920. In Journal History, 23 June 1920, 5.

"Anti-'Mormon' Mobocracy." *Deseret News*. In Journal History, 2 December 1901, 2.

"Appeal to Old M.A.C. Boys." *Te Karere* 43, no. 2 (February 1948): 56.

"An Appreciated Gift." *The Messenger* 9, no. 24 (1 December 1915): 282.

Arrington, Leonard J. *Great Basin Kingdom: An Economic History of the Latter-day Saints, 1830–1900*. Cambridge, M.A.: Harvard University Press, 1958.

Asmussen, Carl C. Letter to President F. D. Richards, dated Copenhagen, 31 August 1867. *Millennial Star* 29, no. 41 (12 October 1867): 653.

Atkin, Annie M. New Zealand Mission Journal. In William Frank Atkin, Papers. MS 341, fd. 11, Perry Special Collections.

Atkin, William Frank. Papers and New Zealand Mission Journals, 1903–06, 1916–18. MSS 341. Perry Special Collections.

Atwood, Leslie. Death Certificate, 21 July 1902. New Zealand Registry of Births, Deaths and Marriages, Wellington.

"Auckland Stake Formed in New Zealand Mission." *Church News*, 24 May 1958, 5.

Auckland Weekly Star. Article, n.d. Reprinted in *Millennial Star* 52, no. 26 (30 June 1890): 414.

Australasian/Australian Mission. Minutes, 1851–1955. Microfilm. MS 10870, Series 11. LDS Church History Library.

Baigent, Barbara. "A Church Builds a Village." *Church News*, 21 September 1957, 3. Rpt. from New Zealand periodical *Women's Choice*.

Baldridge, Kenneth Wayne. Interviews, 1971–73. MS 4231. LDS Church History Library.

———. "The Maori Agricultural College: An Experience in Rural Education." Photocopy of typescript, n.d. Church College of New Zealand Library, Temple View.

Ballara, Angela, and Keith Cairns. "Te Potangaroa, Paora, ?–1881." *Dictionary of New Zealand Biography*. Updated 7 April 2006. http://www.dnzb.govt.nz/ (accessed 18 January 2009).

Ballara, Angela, and Mita Carter. "Te Maari-o-te-rangi, Piripi, 1837?–1895." *Dictionary of New Zealand Biography*. Updated 7 April 2006. http://www.dnzb.govt.nz/ (accessed 18 January 2009).

Ballif, Ariel Smith. "A Message from the College." *Te Karere* 24, no. 1 (20 January 1930): 26–27.

———. Oral History. Interviewed by R. Lanier Britsch, Provo, Utah, 1973. Typescript. OH 154. LDS Church History Library.

Balneavis, H. R. H., Secretary, Maori Purposes Fund Control Board. Letter to the Principal [Ariel S. Ballif], Maori Agricultural College, 11 February 1929. Carbon copy of typescript. Department of Education, E3 1947/1a, Maori Agricultural College, Hastings. National Archives of New Zealand, Wellington.

———. Letter to J. Howard Jenkins, 7 December 1925. Typescript. Maori Affairs, Series 21, Box 7. National Archives of New Zealand, Wellington.

Barber, Ian G. "Between Biculturalism and Assimilation: The Changing Place of Maori Culture in the Twentieth Century New Zealand Mormon Church." *New Zealand Journal of History* 29, no. 2 (October 1995): 142–69.

Barker, Ian R. "The Connexion: The Mormon Church and the Maori People." M.A. thesis, Victoria University, Wellington, 1967.

Barlow, Cleve. *Tikana Whakaaro: Key Concepts in Maori Culture*. Auckland: Oxford University Press, 1991.

Bartlett, Charles Bart. Journals, 1895–97, 1902–5. MS 6846. LDS Church History Library.

———. "The New Zealand Mission." *Millennial Star* 66, no. 32 (11 August 1904): 499.

———. Letter to W. Frank Atkin, 24 November 1904. In William Frank Atkin Papers.

———. Letter to Louis G. Hoagland, dated At Sea, 13 August 1905. In Louis Gerald Hoagland, Papers, 1905–1938, Reel 1.

Batt, George. "Correspondence." Letter dated Timaru, 25 February 1881. *Deseret Evening News*, 8 April 1881, [4].

———. "Correspondence: Interesting from New Zealand." Letter from George Batt to the Editor, 7 October 1880. *Deseret Evening News*, 6 November 1880, [2].

———. "Correspondence: Interesting from New Zealand." [Letter from] George Batt to the Editor, 6 December 1880. *Deseret Evening News*, 11 January 1881, 831.

———. Letter dated Christchurch, 27 March 1880. *Deseret Evening News*, 3 May 1880, [4].

———. "Sad Occurrence." Letter. *Deseret Evening News*, 29 June 1881, [2].

———. "The Work in New Zealand." Letter dated Auckland, September 10, 1880. *Deseret Evening News*, 27 October 1880, 821.

Beauchamp, Robert. Letter to President A. Carrington, dated Karori, 30 April 1870. *Millennial Star* 32, no. 27 (5 July 1870): 425–26.

———. Letter to President B. Young, jun., dated Melbourne, 26 August 1866. *Millennial Star* 28, no. 44 (3 November 1866): 701–3.

———. Letter to President Carrington, dated Maiden Town, 4 December 1869. *Millennial Star* 32, no. 8 (22 February 1870): 123.

———. Letter to President Albert Carrington, dated Kaiapoi, 25 May 1871. *Millennial Star* 33, no. 41 (10 October 1871): 653.

Bell, A., for Director of Education. Letter to the Principal, Maori Agricultural College, Hastings, 18 October 1926. Carbon copy of typescript. Department of Education, E 3 1947/1a. National Archives of New Zealand, Wellington.

Bergera, Gary James, and Ronald Priddis. *Brigham Young University: A House of Faith*. Salt Lake City: Signature Books, 1985.

Biggs, Bruce. *Maori Marriage: An Essay in Reconstruction*. Wellington: The Polynesian Society, 1960.

Binney, Judith. *The Legacy of Guilt: A Life of Thomas Kendall*. Christchurch: Published for the University of Auckland by Oxford University Press, 1968.

"A Birdseye View of the College." *Te Karere* 49, no. 10 (October 1955): 309–11.

Bishop, Nelson Spicer. New Zealand Mission Diaries. Perry Special Collections.

Bloxham, V. Ben, James R. Moss, and Larry C. Porter, eds. *Truth Will Prevail: The Rise of the Church of Jesus Christ of Latter-day Saints in the British Isles, 1837–1987*. Solihull, England: Church of Jesus Christ of Latter-day Saints, 1987.

"The Board of Education for the South Pacific Islands." *Te Karere* 51, no. 8 (August 1957): 262.

Bowen, L. J. Letter to W. Frank Atkin, dated Kato, 19 December 1903. In William Frank Atkin, Papers.

Britsch, R. Lanier. "Maori Traditions and the Mormon Church." *New Era*, June 1981, 37–46.

———. *Unto the Islands of the Sea: A History of the Latter-day Saints in the Pacific*. Salt Lake City: Deseret Book, 1986.

Bromley, William Michael. "Introduction of the Gospel to the Maories." *Juvenile Instructor* 22, no. 1 (1 January 1887): 6–7, 26–27, 45–46; and no. 4 (15 February 1887): 57.

———. Journals and Notebook, 1871–1911. Microfilm of holograph. MS 1913, 1–6, LDS Church History Library.

Buck, Sir Peter (Te Rangi Hiroa). *The Coming of the Maori*. Wellington: Maori Purpose Fund Board and Whitcoulls, 1977.

Buick, T. Lindsay. *The Treaty of Waitangi: How New Zealand Became a British Colony*. New Plymouth, New Zealand: Thomas Avery & Sons, 1936.
"Building in Porirua." *Te Karere* 47, no. 10 (October 1953): 341.
"Bulletin: To District and Branch Presidents and Members All Over the Mission." *Te Karere* 47, no. 11 (November 1953): 376.
Burge, W. M. "The New Auckland Chapel and Mission Headquarters Opened." *Te Karere* 47, no. 9 (September 1953): 317.
Burnett, William. Letter to President F. D. Richards, dated New Zealand, 4 September 1867. *Millennial Star* 29, no. 48 (30 November 1867): 764–65.
———. Letter to President F. D. Richards, dated Kaiapoi, Canterbury, [New Zealand], 3 December 1867. *Millennial Star* 30, no. 8 (22 February 1868): 125.
———. Letter to President F. D. Richards, dated Canterbury, [New Zealand], 1 January 1868. *Millennial Star* 30, no. 14 (4 April 1868): 220–21.
———. Letter to President Albert Carrington, dated Kaiapoi Island, Canterbury, 20 March 1870. *Millennial Star* 32, no. 22 (31 May 1870): 346–47.
———. Letter to President Albert Carrington, dated Kaiapoi, 25 May 1870. *Millennial Star* 32, no. 32 (2 August 1870): 486–87.
"Californian Named to Serve As New Zealand Mission Head." *Church News*, 26 July 1958, 4.
Cardon, Louis B. "The First World War and the Great Depression, 1914–39." In *Truth Will Prevail: The Rise of the Church of Jesus Christ of Latter-day Saints in the British Isles, 1837–1987*. Edited by V. Ben Bloxham, James R. Moss, and Larry C. Porter. Solihull, England: Church of Jesus Christ of Latter-day Saints, 1987, 335–60.
———. "War and Recovery, 1939–1950." In *Truth Will Prevail: The Rise of the Church of Jesus Christ of Latter-day Saints in the British Isles, 1837–1987*. Edited by V. Ben Bloxham, James R. Moss, and Larry C. Porter. Solihull, England: Church of Jesus Christ of Latter-day Saints, 1987, 361–93.
Chapman's New Zealand Almanac for the Year 1862. Auckland, New Zealand: George T. Chapman, 1862.
Christensen, Harold T. "The New Zealand Mission during the Great Depression: Reflections of a Former Acting President." *Dialogue: A Journal of Mormon Thought* 24, no. 3 (Fall 1991): 69–76.
"Church Construction Chief: Pres. Mendenhall Building Chairman." *Church News*, 23 July 1955, 7.
"The Church in New Zealand." *Millennial Star* 34, no. 2 (9 January 1872): 24–26.
"The Church in New Zealand." *Deseret News*, 15 August 1883, 476–77.
"Church Will Build New Zealand Temple." *Church News*, 19 February 1955, 12.
"College Activities." *The Messenger* 8, no. 6 (25 March 1914): 68.
"College Notes." *The Messenger* 9, no. 21 (20 October 1915): 246–47.
"College Notes." *The Messenger* 9, no. 26 (29 December 1915): 306.
"College Notice." *The Messenger* 9, no. 4 (24 February 1915): 45–46.

Corbett, E. B., Minister of Maori Affairs. Telegram to Gordon C. Young, 12 October 1950. Gordon Claridge Young, Papers, 1948–72, MS 4016, fd. 9. LDS Church History Library.

"Correspondence: Elders Arrested by Maories [sic], Progress of the Work, Curious Customs." Letter to the Editor from Edward Cliff, dated Hastings, Hawkes Bay, 15 July 1886. *Deseret Evening News*, 12 August 1886, [2].

"Correspondence: Interesting from New Zealand—[Letter from]'Miles' Boy' to Editor, Auckland, December 6, 1880." *Deseret News*, 26 January 1881, 831.

"Correspondence: New Zealand Mission: 'Frater.'" Letter dated Mayfield, Utah, 17 January 1881. *Deseret News*, 2 February 1881, 843.

"Correspondence: Wm. Paxman. Letter to President Geo. Teasdale, dated Hastings, New Zealand, 29 April 1889," *Millennial Star* 51, no. 28 (15 July 1889): 436–38.

Cowan, Richard O. "Church Growth in England, 1841–1914." In *Truth Will Prevail: The Rise of the Church of Jesus Christ of Latter-day Saints in the British Isles, 1837–1987*. Edited by V. Ben Bloxham, James R. Moss, and Larry C. Porter. Solihull, England: Church of Jesus Christ of Latter-day Saints, 1987, 199–235.

Cowie, William Garden. *Our Last Year in New Zealand: 1887*. London: Kegan Paul, Trench & Co., 1888.

Cowley, Elva Eleanor Taylor. Autobiography. N.d. In Cowley Collection, MSS 1470, Box 2, fd. 6, Perry Special Collections.

Cowley, Matthew. "Death of President Hardy." *Te Karere* 40, no. 4 (April 1945): 83.

———. Letter to J. Martell Bodell, 13 April 1944. In Cowley Collection, MSS 1470, Box 1, fd.11, Perry Special Collections.

———. Letter to Mrs. Laura Brossard [his sister], dated Salt Lake City, 30 October 1932. In Cowley Collection, MSS 1470, Box 1, fd. 10, Perry Special Collections.

———. Letter to "Ellis and Virginia" (Mr. and Mrs. Ellis W. Barker), 19 January 1943. In Cowley Collection, MSS 1470, Box 1, fd. 11, Perry Special Collections.

———. Letter to David M. Evans, 20 July 1942. In Cowley Collection, MSS 1470, Box 1, fd. 10, Perry Special Collections.

———. Letter to "Father and Aunt Luella," 11 June 1940. In Cowley Collection, MSS 1470, Box 1, fd. 10, Perry Special Collections.

———. Letter to David A. Harris, 19 July 1942. In Cowley Collection, MSS 1470, Box 1, fd. 10, Perry Special Collections.

———. Letter to Patty Miller, 3 August 1944. In Cowley Collection, MSS 1470, Box 1, fd. 11, Perry Special Collections.

———. Letter to Rulon N. Smith, 18 July 1942. In Cowley Collection, MSS 1470, Box 1, fd. 10, Perry Special Collections.

———. Letter to Wilford E. Smith, 31 July 1942. In Cowley Collection, MSS 1470, Box 1, fd. 10, Perry Special Collections.

———. Letter to Gordon C. Young, 15 January 1951. In Gordon Claridge Young, Papers, 1948–72. MS 4016, fd. 10. LDS Church History Library.

———. Letter to Gordon C. Young, 9 August 1951. In Gordon Claridge Young, Papers, 1948–72. MS 4016, fd. 9. LDS Church History Library.

———. "Maori Chief Predicts Coming of L.D.S. Missionaries." *Improvement Era*, September 1950, 696–98, 754–56.

———. "Miracles." *Ensign*, October 2004, 44–46.

———. New Zealand Mission Journals, 1914–19, 1938–44, and Correspondence. In Cowley Collection, MSS 1470, Perry Special Collections.

———. "The President's Page." *Te Karere* 39, no. 6 (June 1944): 138–39.

———. "Support Your Hui Tau." *Te Karere* 35, no. 3 (March 1941): 595.

———. "Tribute to Prest. Gardner." *Deseret Evening News*, 7 October 1916, Section 3, 8.

———. "Waitangi 1840–1940." *Te Karere* 34, no. 2 (February 1940): 58–59.

———. "The Wellington Exhibit." *Te Karere* 34, no. 4 (April 1940): 131.

Cox, Samuel. Letter to *Relief Society Magazine*, dated Pocatello, Idaho, 13 March 1957. Copy inserted in New Zealand Mission, Manuscript History, following entry for 22 June 1880.

Cox, Thomas L. "The Work Is Spreading." Letter dated Milton, Otago, 12 April 1894. *Deseret News Weekly*, 9 June 1894, 770–71.

Crawford, Sidney. Transcript of Oral History Interview. In Kenneth Wayne Baldridge, Interviews, 1971–73.

"Culmination of Huge £2,500,000 Church Project Attracts 5000 Visitors." *Waikato Times* (Hamilton, New Zealand), 18 April 1958.

Cummings, David W. *Mighty Missionary of the Pacific: The Building Program of the Church of Jesus Christ of Latter-day Saints—Its History, Scope, and Significance*. Salt Lake City: Bookcraft, 1961.

Cutler, Heber S. "In Maori Land." Letter to his parents, 27 November 1889. *Deseret News Weekly*, 4 January 1890, 52–54.

———. "The Australasian Mission." Letter dated 12 January 1890. *Deseret News Weekly*, 1 March 1890, 325–26.

———. "Letter from New Zealand." Dated Whangaroa, Bay of Islands, 11 November 1890. *Deseret News Weekly*, 3 January 1891, 153–55.

———. "The Australasian Conference." *Deseret News Weekly*, 17 August 1889, 254.

Dalley, Julia Amussen. "Carl Christian Asmussen (Amussen)." In Daughters of Utah Pioneers Lesson Committee, comp. *An Enduring Legacy*. 12 vols. (Salt Lake City: Daughters of Utah Pioneers, 1978–89) 4: 217–33.

Davies, Rangi. "Rotorua-Horo Horo Branch at War." *Te Karere* 39, no. 4 (April 1944): 104.

———. Letter to Gordon C. Young, dated Auckland, 11 January 1953. In Gordon Claridge Young, Papers, 1948–72. MS 4016, fd. 11. LDS Church History Library.

"A Death." [Charles Hardy]. *The Messenger* 8, no. 2 (28 January 1914): 19–20.

"Death of a Distinguished Maori." *Deseret Evening News*, 17 June 1886, [1].

"Dedication of Church Facilities in Provo and Argentina." *Ensign*, June 1994, 74.

"Dedication of Maromaku Chapel." *Te Karere* 34, no. 11 (November 1940): 438.

DeWitt, Basil. "A Visit to Niue or Savage Island." *Te Karere* 47, no. 5 (May 1953): 168–69.

"A Dream Comes True." *Te Karere* 52, no. 1 (January 1958): 17.

"Doings at the College." *The Messenger* 7, no. 7 (26 March 1913): 79.

The Dominion. 25 January 1929. Display advertisement.

Douglas, Norman. "The Sons of Lehi and the Seed of Cain: Racial Myths in Mormon Scripture and Their Relevance to the Pacific Islands." *Journal of Religious History* 8, no. 1 (June 1974): 90–104.

Douglass, William Jr. Journal Notes of William Douglas [sic] Jr, While on a Mission to New Zealand. Genealogical Society of Utah. Microfilm 180430. Incorrectly catalogued under William Douglas Jr.

Dunstall, Graeme. "The Social Pattern." In Geoffrey W. Rice, ed. *The Oxford History of New Zealand*, 2d ed. Auckland: Oxford University Press, 1992, 451–81.

"Editorial." *Te Karere* 51, no. 10 (October 1957): 341.

"Editorial and General Intelligence." *Zion's Watchman* 2, no. 1 (15 May 1855): 12.

Edward, Pita. Transcript of Oral History Interview. In Kenneth Wayne Baldridge, Interviews, 1971–73.

"Elder Cowley Given New Assignment over Missions." *Church News*, 7 December 1946, 1.

"Elder Cowley Returns." *Te Karere* 42, no. 7 (July 1947): 207.

"Elder Rosenvall Named N.Z. Temple President." *Church News*, 22 February 1958, 7.

"Elders' Correspondence: Extracts of a Letter from Augustus A. Farnham to Brigham Young." Dated Newcastle, New South Wales, 12 January 1855. *Deseret News*, 6 June 1855, 100.

"Elders' Correspondence: Extracts of a Letter from Elder John Murdock, 5 February 1852." *Deseret News*, 24 March 1852, [74].

"Elders from Canada and America aboard 'Monterey.'" *Te Karere* 41, no. 3 (March 1946): 72.

Ellsworth, S. George. *The Journals of Addison Pratt: Being a Narrative of Yankee Whaling in the Eighteen Twenties, a Mormon Mission to the Society Islands, and of Early California and Utah in the Eighteen Forties and Fifties.* Salt Lake City: University of Utah Press, 1990.

Embry, Jessie L. "LDS Sister Missionaries: An Oral History Response, 1910–1970." *Journal of Mormon History* 23, no. 1 (Spring 1997): 100–139.

Esplin, Scott C. "Closing the Church College of New Zealand: A Case Study in Church Education Policy." *Journal of Mormon History* 37, no. 1 (Winter 2011): 86–114.

Fairbanks, Elliott A. "Carved Meeting House Completed." *Te Karere* 44, no. 10 (October 1949): 368–71.

Farnham, Augustus A. "Extracts of a Letter from Elder Augustus A. Farnham to Brigham Young, 14 August 1853." *Deseret News*, 8 December 1853, [96].

———. Letter to Brother F. D. Richards, dated Sydney, 26 January 1855. *Millennial Star* 17, no. 18 (5 May 1855): 283.

———. Letter to President F. D. Richards, dated Sidney [sic], 31 May 1855. *Millennial Star* 17, no. 37 (15 September 1855): 591.
"Featuring the Districts." *Te Karere* 47, no. 7 (July 1953): 252.
"Featuring the Districts." *Te Karere* 47, no. 9 (September 1953): 322.
"Featuring the Districts." *Te Karere* 47, no. 11 (November 1953): 399.
"Featuring the Districts: LDS College." *Te Karere* 49, no. 9 (September 1955): 298–99.
"Featuring the Districts: News from the College." *Te Karere* 46, no. 8 (August 1952): 292.
Ferris, John Solomon. "Correspondence: Opotiki." Letter. *Deseret Evening News*, 10 November 1881, [4].
———. Journals, 1880–82. MS 1435. LDS Church History Library.
First Presidency. Letter to Prest. W. T. Stewart, dated New Zealand, 14 October 1893. Photocopy of typescript in William Thomas Stewart, 1853–1935, Papers. MS 2198, LDS Church History Library.
———. Letter to President William Paxman, February 1895. Copied into William Gardner, Diary, 2 April 1895.
———. Letter to the Members of the General Hui Tau Board, 18 May 1938. *Te Karere* 32, no. 7 (July 1938): 203.
———. Letter to Andrew Smith Jr., 28 October 1897. Journal History, 28 October 1897, 10–11.
———. Letter to Gordon C. Young, 20 October 1949. In Gordon Claridge Young, Papers, 1948–72, MS 4016, fd. 8. LDS Church History Library.
———. Letter to Gordon C. Young, 18 July 1950. In Gordon Claridge Young, Papers, 1948–72, MS 4016, fd. 9. LDS Church History Library.
———. Letter to Gordon C. Young, 8 December 1950. In Gordon Claridge Young, Papers, 1948–72, MS 4016, fd. 9. LDS Church History Library.
"First Presidency Announces Division of N.Z. Mission." *Church News*, 31 May 1958, 14.
"49th Annual Hui Tau of the New Zealand Mission, at Ngaruawahia, 13–17 April, 1938." Typescript. In Cowley Collection, MSS 1470, Box 1, fd. 15. Perry Special Collections.
Fritzen, Mary Jane. *History of George Brunt and Elizabeth Susan Burnett Brunt Family*. Salt Lake City: George Brunt/Elizabeth Susan Burnett Brunt Family Organization, 1978.
"From the College." *Te Karere* 51, no. 10 (December 1957): 424, 434.
"From the College." *Te Karere* 51, no. 11 (November 1957): 383.
Gardner, Eldon J., and Alice Gardner, eds. "Day Journal of John W. Gardner in New Zealand LDS Mission, 17 July 1901 to 23 January 1904." [n.p.]. Photocopied and bound typescript. M279.31 G227 d 1980. LDS Church History Library.
Gardner, William. Diaries, 1884–1916. Microfilm. MS 2884, items 1–8. LDS Church History Library.
Gardner, William. Papers, 1886–1915. Microfilm. MS 2884 9. LDS Church History Library.

Gardner, W. J. "A Colonial Economy." In Geoffrey W. Rice, ed. *The Oxford History of New Zealand*, 2d ed. Auckland: Oxford University Press, 1992, 57–86.
"General Conference, 1907." *Te Karere* 1, no. 6 (15 April 1907): 56.
"General Intelligence." *Zion's Watchman* 1, nos. 4–5 (12 November 1853): 40.
"General Intelligence." *Zion's Watchman* 1, nos. 30–31 (15 March 1855): 247.
"General Mission News." *Te Karere* 36, no. 7 (July 1942): 214.
"General News." *Te Karere* 38, no. 6 (June 1943): 160–61.
Goddard, Benjamin. "Australasian Conference." *Deseret News Weekly*, 14 June 1895, 818–21.
_____. "Distant Maoridom." *Deseret News Weekly*, 27 January 1894, 172–73.
_____. "In Far Off New Zealand." *Deseret News Weekly*, 15 July 1893, 107–8.
_____. "In Maoridom," *Deseret News*, 13 October 1894, 516–17.
_____. "In the Antipodes: An Annual Conference of the Australasian Mission." *Deseret Evening News*, 19 May 1894, 11.
_____. "Letter from New Zealand." Dated Palmerston North, 11 July 1892. *Deseret News Weekly*, 9 August 1892, 7.
_____. "Letter from New Zealand." Dated Palmerston North, 6 September 1892. *Deseret News Weekly*, 8 October 1892, 494–95.
_____. "Letter from New Zealand, 19 April 1893." *Deseret News Weekly*, 27 May 1893, 706–7.
_____. "Maori Returning to Native Land, Leave Many Friends Here." *Deseret News*, 2 November 1918. In Journal History, 2 November 1918, 2.
_____. "New Zealand Conference." *Deseret News Weekly*, 28 May 1892, 710–12.
Going, Cyril. Transcript of Oral History Interview. In Kenneth Wayne Baldridge. Interviews, 1971–73.
Greenwood, Alma. "Cause of Truth in New Zealand: Alma Greenwood to Mrs F. M. Greenwood, dated Taonoke, Hawkes Bay, 14 May 1884." *Deseret Evening News*, 2 July 1884, [2].
_____. Diary and Scrapbook, 1882–88. MSS 336. Perry Special Collections.
_____. "Gospel Work among the Maoris." *Deseret Evening News*, 15 October 1884, in Journal History, 22 August 1884, 4.
_____. Quoted in "Return from New Zealand: The Australasian Mission Prospers." *Deseret Evening News*, 6 December 1884, [3].
_____. "My New Zealand Mission." *Juvenile Instructor* 20, no. 14 (15 July 1885): 222–23, and no. 16 (15 August 1885): 251.
"Ground Breaking Services Held on Temple Hill." *Te Karere* 50, no. 2 (February 1956): 42–46.
Gudmansen, Ray [Re]. Letter to L[ouis] G. Hoagland, dated Nuhaka, 23 May 1906. In Louis Gerald Hoagland, Papers, MS 4693, Reel 2.
Haeata, Tiaki. Transcript of Oral History Interview. In Kenneth Wayne Baldridge. Interviews, 1971–73, 6.
"Half-Yearly Conference of the Church of Jesus Christ, of Latter-day Saints [sic]. Held in the Old Assembly Rooms, King Street, Sydney, Sunday, October 1st, 1854." *Zion's Watchman* 1, nos. 20–21 (14 October 1854): 156.

Halls, F. W. "New Zealand Conference." *Deseret Evening News*. In Journal History, 28 October 1911, 4.
Halversen, A. Reed. Letter to Elder Matthew Cowley, 12 June 1947. In Cowley Collection, MSS 1470, Box 1, fd. 12. Perry Special Collections.
Hamon, Hixon. Transcript of Oral History Interview. In Kenneth Wayne Baldridge, Interviews, 1971–73.
Hamon, Trevor C. "A New Chapel in Rarotonga." *Te Karere* 42, no. 6 (June 1947): 170.
Hardy, Charles. "Interesting in New Zealand." *Deseret Evening News*, 23 June 1886, 6.
Hardy, Rufus K. Letter to L[ouis] G. Hoagland, dated Kamo, 1 July 1908. In Louis Gerald Hoagland, Papers, MS 4693, Reel 3.
———. "With Church Leaders in New Zealand." *Deseret News*, 25 June 1938, in Journal History, 25 June 1938, 8.
Harris, Kelly. "Hui Tau, 1946." *Te Karere* 41, no. 7 (July 1946): 170–71.
———. "Jewell Cowley." *Te Karere* 39, no. 10 (October 1944): 248–49.
———. "Maori Conference." *Te Karere* 39, no. 12 (December 1944): 309.
———. "Our Recent Hui Tau." *Te Karere* 42, no. 5 (May 1947): 143–45.
———. "Rarotonga's Missionaries." *Te Karere* 38, no. 10 (October 1943): 246–47.
———. Transcript of Oral History Interview. In Kenneth Wayne Baldridge, Interviews, 1971–73.
He Poropititanga Enei: Na nga Poropiti Maori o nga wa o mua. Korongata, New Zealand: Te Karere Press, 1927. LDS Church History Library.
"Here and There in the Mission." *Te Karere* 46, no. 11 (November 1952): 404–5, 410.
"Here and There in the Mission." *Te Karere* 52, no. 3 (March 1958): 111.
"Here and There in the Mission: College for New Zealand," *Te Karere* 43, no. 11 (November 1948): 344.
"Here and There in the Mission: Death of Two Local Church Leaders." *Te Karere* 43, no. 11 (November 1948): 345.
"Here and There in the Mission: Elder Arthur Flies Home." *Te Karere* 44, no. 1 (January 1949): 24.
"Here and There in the Mission: Charter Plane Brings, Takes Missionaries." *Te Karere* 44, no. 11 (November 1949): 408–10.
"Here and There in the Mission: More Saints 'Gather to Zion.'" *Te Karere* 44, no. 11 (November 1949): 408–10.
"Here and There in the Mission: New Arrivals." *Te Karere* 44, no. 10 (October 1949): 372.
"Here and There in the Mission: New Zealand Church Schools," *Te Karere* 43, no. 10 (October 1948): 309.
"Here and There in the Mission: President Young's Rarotongan Visit." *Te Karere* 44, no. 1 (January 1949): 22.
"Here and There in the Mission: Purchase of Mission Home." *Te Karere* 43, no. 9 (September 1948): 272.
Hinckley, Gordon B. "Temple in the Pacific." *Improvement Era* 61, no. 7 (July 1958): 506–9, 538.

"Hirini Whaanga, the Maori Chief." *San Francisco Examiner*, 15 July 1894, reprinted in *Deseret Weekly News*, 19 February 1898, 313. Accessed digitally 20 June 2009.

Hiroa, Te Rangi. *See* Sir Peter Buck.

History of Kiri Kiri Branch. New Zealand Mission, Manuscript History.

History of Mahia Conference. New Zealand Mission, Manuscript History.

Hoagland, Louis Gerald. "In Distant New Zealand." *Deseret News Weekly*, 8 October 1893, 494–95.

———. Letter to Joseph Fielding Smith, 22 March 1923. In Louis Gerald Hoagland, Papers, 1915–41.

———. Letters to M. Charles Woods, 11 May 1937, 31 May 1937, 31 July 1937. In Louis Gerald Hoagland, Papers, 1915–41.

———. Letter to Angus T. Wright, 13 July 1925. In Louis Gerald Hoagland, Papers, 1915–41.

———. Papers, 1905–38. Microfilm. MS 4693. LDS Church History Library.

———. Papers, 1915–41. Microfilm. MS 6545. LDS Church History Library.

Hodge, R. P. "Maori Scholarships." *Te Karere* 24, no. 8 (August 1930): 331–32.

Hodson, Fred Bromley. *None Shall Excel Thee: The Life and Journals of William Michael Bromley*. Yorba Linda, Calif.: Shumway Family History Services, 1990.

"Homeward Bound." *Te Karere* 28, no. 11 (November 1934): 501–3.

Howells, David P. Letter to President L[ouis] G. Hoagland, Wednesday [27 March 1907]. In Louis Gerald Hoagland, Papers, MS 4693, Reel 3.

Hui Tau Program, 1941. *Te Karere* 35, no. 4 (April 1941), inserted between pp. 626 and 627.

Hunt, Brian William. "The Maori Agriculture [sic] College." Paper for Graduate Religion Class 544, Brigham Young University, Provo, Utah, 1969. Photocopy of typescript. LDS Church History Library.

———. *Zion in New Zealand: A History of the Church of Jesus Christ of Latter-day Saints in New Zealand, 1854–1977*. Hamilton, New Zealand: Church College of New Zealand, 1977.

Hurst, Floyd Harris. "Australian Converts and Missionaries." Typescript. Photocopy in my possession, courtesy of Floyd Harris Hurst.

Hurst, Samuel H. and Ida, comps. *Diary of Frederick William Hurst*. N.p.: privately printed, 1961.

"Important: Hui Tau Special Notice." *Te Karere* 29, no. 11 (November 1935): 420–21.

"Impressions of Utah." Reprinted from the *Dannevirke Evening News* of 12 November 1913 in *The Messenger* 7, no. 26 (17 December 1913): 309–11.

"In New Quarters." *Te Karere* 47, no. 11 (November 1953): 384–85.

"In the Antipodes." *Deseret News Weekly*, 19 May 1894, 680–82.

Irwin, James. *An Introduction to Maori Religion: Its Character before European Contact and Its Survival in Contemporary Maori and New Zealand Culture*. Bedford Park, S.A.: Australian Association for the Study of Religions, 1984.

"Is the Lord behind the Headlines?" *Te Karere* 33, no. 6 (June 1939): 201–3.

Jenkins, J. Howard. Letter to the Secretary, Maori Purposes Fund Control Board, 11 November 1925. Typescript. Maori Affairs, Series 21, Box 7, item 36. National Archives of New Zealand, Wellington.

Jensen, Elwin W. Papers, [n.d.]. MS 6429. LDS Church History Library.

Jensen, Richard L. "The British Gathering to Zion." In *Truth Will Prevail: The Rise of the Church of Jesus Christ of Latter-day Saints in the British Isles, 1837–1987*. Edited by V. Ben Bloxham, James R. Moss, and Larry C. Porter. Solihull, England: Church of Jesus Christ of Latter-day Saints, 1987, 199–235.

Jenson, Andrew. "Jenson's Travels: Letter No. 34." *Deseret News Weekly*, 4 April 1896, 498–99.

———. "Jenson's Travels: Letter No. 61." *Deseret News Weekly*, 18 April 1896, 562–64.

Johnson, John. Journals, 1893–1925. Microfilm. MS 1333. LDS Church History Library.

———. "Dedication of the Maori Agricultural College." *Millennial Star* 75, no. 24 (12 June 1913): 369–73.

———. "Over in Maoriland." Letter dated 23 January 1896. *Deseret News Weekly*, 9 May 1896, 644.

———. "Annual Conference of the New Zealand Mission: Dedication of Maori Agricultural College." *The Messenger* 7, no. 9 (23 April 1913): 107.

Johnson, M. N. "New Zealand." *Deseret Evening News*, 10 June 1911. In Journal History, 29 March 1911, 4.

Johnson, Simon. Transcript of Oral History Interview. In Kenneth Wayne Baldridge, Interviews, 1971–73.

Joyce, James. Transcript of Oral History Interview. In Kenneth Wayne Baldridge, Interviews, 1971–73.

Karori Branch Record of Members. Genealogical Society of Utah. Microfilm 128889, item 21.

Kawana, Eruha. Transcript of Oral History Interview. In Kenneth Wayne Baldridge, Interviews, 1971–73.

Kimball, Edward L., and Andrew E. Kimball Jr. *Spencer W. Kimball: Twelfth President of the Church of Jesus Christ of Latter-day Saints*. Salt Lake City: Bookcraft, 1977.

King, James. Letter to Louis G. Hoagland, 6 November 1906. In Louis Gerald Hoagland, Papers, 1905–38. Microfilm. MS 4693, Reel 3. LDS Church History Library.

King, Michael. "Between Two Worlds." In Geoffrey W. Rice, ed. *The Oxford History of New Zealand*, 2d ed. Auckland: Oxford University Press, 1992, 285–307.

Kirkham, Francis Washington. Papers, 1896–1916. MS 7427. LDS Church History Library.

Kopua, Tipi. "Poverty Bay District." *Te Karere* 35, no. 3 (March 1941): 605.

———. Transcript of Oral History Interview. In Kenneth Wayne Baldridge, Interviews, 1971–73.

Lambert, James Needham. Diaries, 1895–98. Microfilm of holograph. MS 9426. LDS Church History Library.

———. Journals, 1916–19. Microfilm of holograph. MS 6457. LDS Church History Library.

———. Letter to Louis G. Hoagland, 26 January 1920. In Louis Gerald Hoagland, Papers. 1905–38. Microfilm. MS 4693, Reel 4. LDS Church History Library.

"Latest from Parihaka." *Auckland Evening Star*, 18 June 1881.

"The Latter Day Saints." *The New Zealand Spectator and Cook Strait Guardian*, Wellington, 13 December 1854, 1.

"L.D.S. Members Escape in Quake." *Deseret News*, 5 February 1931. In Journal History, 5 February 1931, 2.

Leonard, Glen M. Conversation at Upper Canada Village, Ontario, Canada, 21 June 1995. Notes in my possession.

Lineham, Peter J. "Meha, Stuart, 1878–1963." *Dictionary of New Zealand Biography*. Updated 7 April 2006. http://www.dnzb.govt.nz/ (accessed 10 March 2007).

———. "The Mormon Message in the Context of Maori Culture." *Journal of Mormon History* 17 (1991): 62–93.

———. "The Mormons and Karori." *Stockade* 24 (1991): 4–13.

———. "Whaanga, Hirini Te Rito, 1828–1905." *Dictionary of New Zealand Biography*. Updated 7 April 2006. http://www.dnzb.govt.nz/ (accessed 18 January 2009).

Lyman, Fern. "The Crossroads of the South Pacific." *Te Karere* 51, no. 10 (October 1957): 354–57.

McCune, H[enry] F[rederick]. Autobiography and Diaries, 1919–24. Typescript. MS 2267. LDS Church History Library.

McDonnel, William John. "The Start of the Mission among the Maoris." Typescript. [n.d.] MS 4169. LDS Church History Library. Catalogued under "McDonnell."

McKay, David O. "Hui Tau." *Improvement Era* 24, no. 9 (July 1921): 770–71, 774.

———. "Journal of World Mission Tour, 1921." Typescript by Clare Middlemiss. Photocopy in possession of Lavina Fielding Anderson, Salt Lake City, Utah.

McLachlan, William. Letter to the Editor, dated Christchurch, 8 February 1876. *Juvenile Instructor* 11, no. 5 (1 March 1876): 59.

———. Letter to the Editor, dated Christchurch, 28 June 1876. *Juvenile Instructor* 11, no. 15 (1 August 1876): 172–73.

———. Letter to the Editor. *Juvenile Instructor* 11, no. 17 (1 September 1876): 202.

———. "A Religious Phenomenon[:] New Zealand Missionaries." Letter to George Goddard, 10 January 1876. *Deseret Evening News*, 5 March 1876, [3, 5].

———. Reminiscences and Journal, 1863–86. Microfilm of holograph. MS 1514. LDS Church History Library.

Magleby, John Ephraim. "Among the Maoris, Funeral of a Chief—Queer Native Customs." *Deseret News*, 30 November 1887, [2].

———. Journal. In John Ephraim Magleby, Papers, 1885–1937. Microfilm of holograph. MS 1557. LDS Church History Library.

_____. Letters to Louis G. Hoagland, 8 January 1929, 13 March 1930, 19 September 1930. In Louis Gerald Hoagland, Papers, 1905–38. Microfilm. MS 4693, Reel 4. LDS Church History Library.

_____. Letter to George Reynolds, 25 April 1902. In New Zealand Mission, Minutes.

Mangum, Diane L. "The First Sister Missionaries." *Ensign*, July 1980, 62–65.

Manihera, R. H. "Account of Missionary Work in N. Z. in 1880s." Microfilm of typed copy of holograph given to Louis G. Hoagland in August 1918. In Elwin W. Jensen, Papers, [n.d.]. MS 6429. LDS Church History Library.

Manuscript History of the New Zealand Mission. Cited as New Zealand Mission, Manuscript History. LDS Church History Library.

Maori Agricultural College. Catalogues, 1913–14, 1914, 1918–26, 1929–31. Microfiche. LDS Church History Library.

Maori Agricultural College. Correspondence and Reports. Education Department. National Archives of New Zealand, Wellington.

"Maori Boys in America." *Te Karere* 25, no. 1 (January 1931): 14.

"Maori Chief Returns Home." *Deseret Evening News*, 13 May 1899, 17.

Maori Purposes Fund Control Board. Letter from the Secretary to the Principal, Maori Agricultural College, 11 February 1929. Carbon copy of typescript. Maori Affairs. National Archives of New Zealand, Wellington.

"Maori Welfare." *The Evening Post* (Wellington). 18 October 1944, 6.

Marsden, Samuel. "Journal of Proceedings at New Zealand, 29 July 1819–19 October 1919." Holograph copy made in New South Wales, signed by Samuel Marsden ("II New Zealand Journal"). Hocken Library, University of Otago. Quoted in Judith Binney, *The Legacy of Guilt: A Life of Thomas Kendall*. Christchurch: published for the University of Auckland by Oxford University Press, 1968.

"Meeting Held to Plan Programme for Dedication." *Te Karere* 51, no. 8 (August 1957): 264.

Meha, Tetuati [Stuart]. Letter to Francis W. Kirkham, dated Waipapa, 14 March 1961. MS 7956. LDS Church History Library.

_____. "Mission to Hawaii and the U.S." *Te Karere* 52, no. 2 (February 1958): 44–45, 63.

_____. "A Prophetic Utterance of Paora Potangaroa." *Te Karere* 43, no. 10 (October 1948): 298–99.

_____. "A Request Talk for Sunday Evening the 15th April, 1962." Photocopy of typescript provided courtesy of Robert P. Manookin.

Meihana, Otene. "Brother Otene's Letter, 4 December 1884." *Deseret News*, 14 January 1885, 820.

Meikle, R. G. "New Zealand Conference." *Deseret News Weekly*, 25 March 1893, 429.

Meldrum, Jeff, and Trent D. Stephens. *Who Are the Children of Lehi? DNA and the Book of Mormon*. Salt Lake City: Greg Kofford Books, 2007.

"Message from the First Presidency." *Te Karere* 35, no. 5 (May 1941): 655.

The Messenger [Te Karere]. New Zealand Mission paper, 1907–58. At first published under *The Elders' Messenger* for English section, with Maori pages under *Te Karere;* then as *The Messenger,* later still *Te Karere* only.

Metge, Joan. *The Maoris of New Zealand: Rautahi.* London: Routledge & Kegan Paul, 1976.

Millennial Star. Published monthly as *The Latter-day Saints' Millennial Star* by the British Mission of the Church of Jesus Christ of Latter-day Saints, Liverpool and London, 1840–1970.

Miller, Jacob Royal, and Elna Miller, eds. *Journal of Jacob Miller.* Salt Lake City: Mercury, 1967.

"Mission Fields: Letters from Hirini Whaanga." *Deseret Evening News,* 7 January 1899, 15.

"Mission Notes." *The Messenger* 7, no. 17 (13 August 1913): 198–99.

"Mission Notes." *The Messenger* 7, no. 24 (19 November 1913): 283.

"Mission Notes." *The Messenger* 8, no. 2 (28 January 1914): 19.

"Mission Presidency Organised." *Te Karere* 43, no. 5 (May 1948): 152.

"A Mission to the Antipodes: Elder McCune Returns." *Deseret News,* 10 February 1886, 62.

"Missionaries among the Maoris of New Zealand." *Millennial Star* 56, no. 13 (26 March 1894): 205.

"Missionary Work in New Zealand." *Deseret Evening News,* 11 December 1884, [2].

Moores, H. S. "The Rise of the Protestant Political Association: Sectarianism in New Zealand Politics during World War I." M.A. thesis, University of Auckland, 1966.

Morehouse, Ric. "The Establishment of Church Education in New Zealand." B.A. Independent Study, Brigham Young University, 1983.

"The Mormon and the Maori." *The Messenger* 7, no. 10 (7 May 1913): 109–11.

"Mormon Chapel May Be Ready by End of Year." *New Zealand Herald* (Auckland), 17 April 1952.

"Mormon Conference—Gathering at Ngaruawahia." *Auckland Star,* 9 April 1928.

"'Mormon' Maori Agricultural College Doing Good Work." *Deseret News,* 5 March 1921. In Journal History, 21 January 1921, 6.

"Mormons in Canterbury." *Millennial Star* 42, no. 9 (1 March 1880): 133.

"Mormons Progress among the Maoris." *Northern Daily Mail* (Manchester, England), 26 May 1955. Clipping in New Zealand Mission, Manuscript History.

Murdock, John. Autobiography [includes Journal of Australian Mission 30 January 1851–2 June 1852]. Microfilm of holograph. MS F822. LDS Church History Library.

Murdock, John. "Elders' Correspondence; Extracts of a Letter from Elder John Murdock, 5 February 1852." *Deseret News,* 24 March 1852, [74].

Nepia, George. Transcript of Oral History Interview. In Kenneth Wayne Baldridge, Interviews, 1971–73.

"New Assignment for Matthew Cowley." *Te Karere* 42, no. 2 (February 1947): 45.

"New Headmaster Formulating Plans for College." *Te Karere* 51, no. 10 (October 1957): 358.

"New Mission President Appointed." *Te Karere* 39, no. 9 (September 1944): 225.
"New President Appointed for the N.Z. Mission." *Deseret News-Telegram*, 23 July 1958, B-1.
"New Zealand." *Millennial Star* 32, no. 35 (30 August 1870): 552.
"New Zealand." *Millennial Star* 34, no. 25 (18 June 1872): 394.
New Zealand Auckland Mission. General Minutes. LR 6048-11. LDS Church History Library.
New Zealand Auckland Mission. Presidents' Correspondence, 1967–75. LR 6048 Series 25. LDS Church History Library.
"New Zealand Church College Carries on Tradition of 'Old M.A.C.'" *Church News*, 12 October 1963, 20.
"New Zealand Conference." *Deseret News Weekly*, 28 May 1892, 746–47.
New Zealand Gazette. Department of Internal Affairs, New Zealand Government, Wellington, New Zealand.
"The New Zealand Mission." *Deseret Evening News*, 23 March 1886, [2].
New Zealand Mission. *Calendar and School Magazine of the Church of Jesus Christ of Latter Day [sic] Saints Maori Agricultural College, 1931*. Microfiche. LDS Church History Library.
New Zealand Mission. *Catalogue and Announcement of the Latter Day [sic] Saints Agricultural College, First Year 1913–1914*. Auckland: Abel Dykes Ltd., 1913. Microfiche. LDS Church History Library.
New Zealand Mission. *Catalogue and Announcement of the Latter Day [sic] Saints Maori Agricultural College, 1929*. Microfiche. LDS Church History Library.
New Zealand Mission. Manuscript History. CR MH 6048. LDS Church History Library.
New Zealand Mission. Minutes, 1891–1915. LR 6048, Series 11. LDS Church History Library.
New Zealand Mission. Presidents' Correspondence, 1897–1900. LR 6048, Series 23. LDS Church History Library.
"New Zealand Missionaries Hold 'Hui Nui' in Inglewood: Elder Matthew Cowley Attends." *California Inter-Mountain News*, 10 July 1951. In Journal History, 10 July 1951, 5.
New Zealand Missionary Association. Maori Hymnal, 1910. No title page. Copy in Perry Special Collections.
New Zealand Missionary Society. "Book Prepared for David O. McKay and Hugh J. Cannon, 26 November 1920." MS 6830. LDS Church History Library.
"New Zealand Sets the Pace." *Te Karere* 46, no. 10 (October 1951): 339–40, 342.
"New Zealand Sets the Pace." *Te Karere* 46, no. 1 (January 1952): 19.
"News Briefs: Mission and Church." *Te Karere* 27, no. 1 (January 1933): 45.
"News Briefs: Mission and Church." *Te Karere* 28, no. 2 (February 1934): 93–94.
"News Briefs: Mission and Church." *Te Karere* 29, no. 7 (July 1935): 282.
"News from New Zealand." *Deseret Evening News*. In Journal History, 8 October 1901, 4.
"News from the Field." *Te Karere* 35, no. 4 (April 1941): 640.
"News from the Field." *Te Karere* 35, no. 6 (June 1941): 704.

"News from the Field." *Te Karere* 36, no. 9 (September 1942): 269.
"News from the Field." *Te Karere* 36, no. 11 (November 1942): 325.
"News from the Field." *Te Karere* 37, no. 1 (January 1943): 25.
"News from the Field." *Te Karere* 37, no. 4 (April 1943): 103.
"News from the Field." *Te Karere* 42, no. 1 (January 1947): 33.
"News from the Field." *Te Karere* 42, no. 4 (April 1947): 122.
"News of the Field: Auckland Branch." *Te Karere* 44, no. 5 (May 1949): 184.
"News from the Field: Porirua Branch." *Te Karere* 39, no. 12 (December 1944): 327.
"News from the Field: Porirua Branch." *Te Karere* 41, no. 5 (May 1946): 128.
"News of the Field: Rangitoto Branch." *Te Karere* 43, no. 7 (July 1948): 212.
"News from the Field: Rarotonga Branch." *Te Karere* 41, no. 12 (December 1946): 341.
"News of the Field: Rarotonga Branch." *Te Karere* 42, no. 9 (September 1947): 285–86.
Newton, Marjorie. "'From Tolerance to House Cleaning': LDS Leadership Response to Maori Marriage Customs, 1890–1990." *Journal of Mormon History* 22 (Fall 1996): 72–91.
_____. "Mormonism in New Zealand: A Historical Appraisal." Ph.D. thesis, University of Sydney, 1998. Forthcoming from Greg Kofford Books.
_____. "Nineteenth-Century Pakeha Mormons in New Zealand." In *Proclamation to the People: Nineteenth-Century Mormonism and the Pacific Basin Frontier*. Edited by Laurie F. Maffly-Kipp and Reid L. Neilson. Salt Lake City: University of Utah Press, 2008, 228–254.
_____. *Southern Cross Saints: The Mormons in Australia*. Laie, Hawaii: The Institute for Polynesian Studies, 1991.
"Nga Whakaaturanga." *Te Karere* 24, no. 3 (19 March 1930): 86.
"1957–A Year of Progress." *Te Karere* 52, no. 1 (January 1958): 20.
"Officiating Ministers for 1903." *The New Zealand Gazette*, no. 56 (9 July 1903): 1571.
Oliver, Steven. "Potae, Henare, 1895." *Dictionary of New Zealand Biography*. Updated 17 April 2006. http://www.dnzb.govt.nz/ (accessed 18 January 2009).
Olpin, W. J. "Passed to the Great Beyond." *The Messenger* 9, no. 21 (20 October 1915): 245.
"Only Sheep Shearers Read This!!" *Te Karere* 47, no. 10 (October 1953): 338.
Ormsby, John. Transcript of Oral History Interview. In Kenneth Wayne Baldridge, Interviews, 1971–73.
Ottley, Sidney James. Diary, 1951–52. MSS 1826, fd. 3. Perry Special Collections.
_____. Transcript of Oral History Interview. In Kenneth Wayne Baldridge, Interviews, 1971–73.
_____. "New Zealand's Message of Love to Sister Cowley & Family on the Passing of Our Loved One." *Te Karere* 48, no. 2 (February 1954): 47–48.
_____. "The President's Page." *Te Karere* 46, no. 11 (November 1952): 380, 384.
Ottley, Warren S. "A Remnant of the House of Israel Meets in Conference." *Te Karere* 34, no. 5 (May 1940): 166.
_____. Transcript of Oral History Interview. In Kenneth Wayne Baldridge, Interviews, 1971–73.

"Our New President." *Te Karere* 28, no. 12 (December 1934): 542.
"Our Mission Presidents: Matthew Cowley, Farewell; A. Reed Halversen, Welcome." *Te Karere* 40, no. 9 (September 1945): 203–5.
Paerata, Kaiser. Transcript of Oral History Interview. In Kenneth Wayne Baldridge, Interviews, 1971–73.
Panek, Tracey E. "Life at Iosepa, Utah's Polynesian Colony." *Utah Historical Quarterly* 60 (Winter 1992): 64–77.
Parsons, M. J. "Jury, Hoani Te Whatahoro, 1841–1923." *Dictionary of New Zealand Biography*. Updated 7 April 2006. http://www.dnzb.govt.nz/ (accessed 18 January 2009).
"The Past Three Months in and around the M.A.C." *The Messenger* 8, no. 2 (28 January 1914): 20.
"Patriotic Hui Tau." *Te Karere* 38, no. 6 (June 1943): 134–36.
Paxman, William. "Correspondence." Letter to Pres. Geo. Teasdale, dated Hastings, New Zealand, 29 April 1880. *Millennial Star* 51, no. 28 (15 July 1889): 436–38.
Pearce, Charles E. "William R. Perrott." *Te Karere* 44, no. 1 (January 1949): 21.
Perkins, John. Diary, December 1853–November 1854. LDS Church History Library.
Perrott, William Rosser. Interviewed by R. Lanier Britsch. Auckland, NZ, 1974. Typescript. OH 335. LDS Church History Library.
Phelps, W. W. "We accidentily [sic] came across . . ." *The Evening and the Morning Star* 1, no. 6 (November 1832): 44.
Pierce, P. W., comp. *The Melbourne Commercial Directory, including Collingwood and Richmond, and Almanac for the Year 1853*. Melbourne: James Shanley, Bookseller.
"Porirua Carpenters Donate Labour." *Te Karere* 45, no. 7 (July 1951): 233.
Porteous, John, Senior Inspector of Native Schools. Letter to T. B. Strong, Director of Education, dated Wellington, 8 January 1929. Typescript. Maori Affairs. National Archives of New Zealand, Wellington.
Pratt, Addison. Letter to Elder W. W. Phelps, dated Ship *Timoleon*, Pacific Ocean, 25 April 1844. *Times and Seasons* 5, no. 21 (15 November 1844): 710.
Pratt, Parley Parker. *Autobiography of Parley P. Pratt*. Edited by Parley P. Pratt Jr. 1878. Rpt., Salt Lake City: Deseret Book, 1980 printing.
"Pres. McKay Suggests South Pacific Temple." *Church News*, 12 February 1955, 3.
"President Matthew Cowley Appointed Member of the Quorum of the Twelve Apostles." *Te Karere* 40, no. 11 (November 1945): 242.
"The President's Page." *Te Karere* 38, no. 7 (July 1943): 170–71.
"The President's Page." *Te Karere* 44, no. 3 (March 1949): 80.
"The President's Page." *Te Karere* 47, no. 8 (August 1953): 264.
"The President's Page: Church Government in the Mission." *Te Karere* 43, no. 10 (October 1948): 292.
"President's Page: The Church in Rarotonga." *Te Karere* 42, no. 6 (June 1947): 164–65.
"President's Page: Hui Tau Thoughts." *Te Karere* 42, no. 5 (May 1947): 132.

"Prominent Maoris Visiting in City." *Deseret News*, 3 July 1920. In Journal History, 3 July 1920, 3.

"Quarterly Conference of the Australasian Mission of the Church of Jesus Christ of Latter-day Saints, Held at the Old Assembly Rooms, King Street, Sydney, 7 January 1855." *Zion's Watchman* 1, nos. 26–27 (15 January 1855): 204.

Re. *See* Gudmansen, Ray.

Reber, Meryl. "New Missionaries for Rarotonga." *Te Karere* 41, no. 10 (October 1946): 259.

"Reception for Visiting Maoris." *Deseret Evening News*, 4 June 1913. In Journal History, 3 June 1913, 2.

"Religion of Soldiers." *Auckland Star*, 18 September 1918.

"Report on Hui Tau." *Te Karere* 44, no. 6 (June 1949): 203–5.

"Return from New Zealand: The Australasian Mission Prospers." *Deseret Evening News*, 6 December 1884, [3].

"Revolutionary Thinking on Evolution Forces Rethink on Species." *Sydney Morning Herald*, 29–30 June 2006.

Rice, Geoffrey W., ed. *The Oxford History of New Zealand*. 2d ed. Auckland: Oxford University Press, 1992.

Richards, Ezra Foss. Papers, 1885–1927. Microfilm. MS 4739. LDS Church History Library.

Richards, Stanley E. "New Zealand Sets the Pace." *Te Karere* 45, no. 9 (September 1951): 307, 311, and no. 10 (October 1951): 339–40, 342.

Richardson, Len. "Parties and Political Change." In Geoffrey W. Rice, ed. *The Oxford History of New Zealand*, 2d ed. Auckland: Oxford University Press, 1992, 201–29.

Roberts, W. Lynn. "Australian Mission." *Improvement Era* 35, no. 7 (May 1932): 398.

Rodley, Chris. "Time Lord: The Work of 25-Year-Old Researcher Simon Ho Is Overturning Established Ideas about the Pace of Evolution and Human Development." *Sydney [University] Alumni Magazine*, Winter 2006, 10–11.

Romney, Marion G. Diary, April–June 1958. MS 5347. LDS Church History Library.

Rosenvall, Erick Albert. Oral History. Interviewed by Bruce Blumell, Salt Lake City, 23 October 1973. Typescript. OH 134. LDS Church History Library.

Rudd, Glen Larkin. Interviewed 1992–93 by Ronald G. Watt. Typescript. OH 1192. LDS Church History Library.

———. "Evacuation of Zion Missionaries from the South Pacific during World War II." October 1979. Typescript. Photocopy in my possession courtesy of Elder Glen L. Rudd.

Russon, Leo W. Letter to Mr. and Mrs. M. F. Huffaker, dated Auckland, 27 October 1972. New Zealand Auckland Mission, Presidents' Correspondence, 1967–75, fd. 21, 2.

"A Sad and Sorrowful Homecoming." *Deseret Evening News*, 29 August 1902, 8.

Sanders, Sondra Jr., Journals, 1861–1934. Microfilm. MS 807. LDS Church History Library.

———. "Conference in New Zealand." Letter dated Uawa, 19 August 1885. *Deseret Evening News*, 8 October 1885. [4].

"Scholarships for Maori Students." *Te Karere* 40, no. 8 (August 1945): 178.

Scott, Patricia Lyn. "Sarah Ann Sutton Cooke: 'The Respected Mrs. Cooke.'" In *Worth Their Salt, Too: More Notable but Often Unnoted Women of Utah*. Edited by Colleen Whitley. Logan: Utah State University Press, 2000, 1–27.

Shreeve, Thomas Arthur Gladman. "The Story of the New Zealand Mission from the Journal of Elder Thomas A. Shreeve [1880]." Typescript. MS 5876. LDS Church History Library.

Simmons, D. R. "Te Matorohanga, Moihi, fl. 1836–1865." *Dictionary of New Zealand Biography*. Updated 7 April 2006. http://www.dnzb.govt.nz/ (accessed 18 January 2009).

Simpson, Robert Leatham. Interviewed by Gordon Irving, Salt Lake City, 1978. James Moyle Oral History Program. Typescript. LDS Church History Library.

Sinclair, Keith. *A History of New Zealand*. Harmondsworth, England: Penguin Books, 1960.

"Sketch of the Life of Bishop Rudolph Church, including Mission to NZ, 1917–1920." In "Biographical Sketches of Bishops in Panguitch, Utah, ca. 1977. MS 2735/469. LDS Church History Library.

Smellie, John T. "Australasian Mission." *Deseret News Weekly*, 25 September 1889, 678.

———. Letter to the Editor, 15 April 1889, printed as "The Australasian Mission: Proceedings of the Annual Conference at Te Hawke." *Deseret News*, 17 May 1889, [3].

Smith, George Albert. Letter to Matthew Cowley, 9 August 1944. In Cowley Collection, MSS 1470, Box 1, fd. 11, Perry Special Collections.

Smith, Henry A. *Matthew Cowley: Man of Faith*. Salt Lake City: Bookcraft, 1954.

Smith, Walter. "A Brief History of the Church of Jesus Christ of Latter-day Saints in New Zealand from 1854 to 1941." Photocopy of typescript, Church College of New Zealand Library, Temple View, New Zealand.

———. "'From the Leaves of an Old Family Bible': The First Maoris to Emigrate to Zion." *Te Karere* 35, no. 5 (May 1941): 658–60. Condensed from "The First Maoris to Emigrate to Zion."

Smoot, Reed. Letter to Secretary of State, 9 October 1917. In United States Department of State, Diplomatic Correspondence on Mormons and Mormonism, 1910–40.

Solomon, R. H. "New Zealand: Traveling in the Mission." Letter 30 March 1902. *Deseret Evening News*, 10 May 1902, 22.

Sorensen, John Peter. New Zealand Mission Diaries, 1879–81. MS 8627, LDS Church History Library.

Sorrenson, M. P. K. "Maori and Pakeha." In Geoffrey W. Rice, ed. *The Oxford History of New Zealand*. 2d ed. Auckland: Oxford University Press, 1992, 141–66.

Southern Provinces Almanac, Directory, and Year Book for 1861, 1862, 1863. Lyttelton, New Zealand: Lyttelton Times.

Southerton, Simon. *Losing a Lost Tribe: Native Americans, DNA, and the Mormon Church*. Salt Lake City: Signature Books, 2004.

Southon, James. Transcript of Oral History Interview. In Kenneth Wayne Baldridge, Interviews, 1971–73.

Spring-Rice, Cecil. Letter to Senator Reed Smoot, 24 July 1917. In United States Department of State, Diplomatic Correspondence on Mormons and Mormonism, 1910–1940.

Steed, Thomas. Diaries, 1875–77. MS 1548. LDS Church History Library.

Stephens, Julian Rackham. "My Life's History or a Reasonable Facsimile of It." 1981. Microfilm. MS 9245. LDS Church History Library.

Stevenson, Ezra T. "Among the Maories [sic]: Conference in New Zealand—Labors among the Natives." *Deseret Evening News*, 24 October 1888, [4].

———. Letter to Wilford Woodruff, 9 June 1898. New Zealand Mission, Presidents' Correspondence.

———. Letter to George Reynolds, Secretary to First Presidency, 11 January 1899. New Zealand Mission Presidents' Correspondence.

Stewart, William Thomas. Papers, 1878–93. MS 2198. LDS Church History Library.

———. Letter to the editor, dated Papawai, 22 April 1884. *Millennial Star* 46, no. 24 (16 June 1884): 378–79.

———. Letter to Elder Franklin D. Richards. In Journal History, 12 March 1886.

Stott, F. Earl. "Educating the South Sea Islanders." *Improvement Era*, April 1921, 506–7.

Strong, T. B., Director of Education. Letter to H. R. H. Balneavis, Secretary, Maori Purposes Fund Control Board, 4 February 1929. Carbon copy of typescript. Maori Affairs, National Archives of New Zealand, Wellington.

"Sunday Schools in the Missions [sic]." *Te Karere* 37, no. 1 (January 1943): unnumbered page.

"Tamihana Te Awe Awe Dies in New Zealand." *Deseret Evening News*. In Journal History, 28 November 1918, 4.

Taylor, Demar V. "War and the Gospel." *Te Karere* 33, no. 11 (November 1939): 400.

Taylor, George Shepard. Private Journal, 1920–24. MSS 167. Perry Special Collections.

———. "Report of Sermons of David O. McKay Delivered at the Annual Conference of the New Zealand Mission of the Church of Jesus Christ of Latter-day Saints, held at Huntly, 23–25 April 1921." Typescript. MS 5919. LDS Church History Library.

Te Karere. New Zealand Mission, Paper. 1907–58. See also *The Messenger* and *Elders' Messenger*.

"*Te Karere* and Its Future." *Te Karere* 39, no. 10 (October 1944): 249.

"'*Te Karere*' in Retrospect." *Te Karere* 51, no. 11 (November 1957): 392.

Te Rangi Hiroa. See Sir Peter Buck.

Thomson, Jane. "The Policy of Land Sales Control: Sharing the Sacrifice." *New Zealand Journal of History* 25, no. 1 (April 1991): 3–17.

Tingey, Rulon H. "New Zealand Dedication Trip by President David O. McKay and Sister McKay." Copy in New Zealand Mission, Manuscript History, April 1958.

"To Parents and Students of M.A.C." *The Messenger* 9, no. 25 (15 December 1915): 297.

"A Tribute to President Romney." *The Messenger* 8, no. 6 (25 March 1914): 69.
"Two Church Workers Will Tour Missions of Pacific Islands." *Deseret News*, 15 October 1920, 5.
United States Bureau of the Census. Utah 1880. www.familysearch.org (accessed 3 May 2004).
United States Department of State. Diplomatic Correspondence on Mormons and Mormonism, 1910–40. [U.S.] National Archives. MS 12130. Microfilm copy in LDS Church History Library.
Victoria District Record of Members, 1868–1906. Genealogical Society of Utah. Microfilm 105322, item 3, p. 247.
"Visitors to Headquarters." *Te Karere* 36, no. 9 (September 1942): 270.
Wairarapa Standard. Clippings of letters not individually dated. In Journal History, 2 January 1884.
Walton, W. D. Letter to Louis G. Hoagland, 8 January 1906. In Louis Gerald Hoagland, Papers. 1905–38. Microfilm. MS 4693, Reel 1. LDS Church History Library.
Wandell, Charles Wesley. Letter to Prests. B. Young, H. C. Kimball, and W. Richards, dated Sydney, 11 February 1852. *Deseret News*, 27 November 1852.
Waratene, Tutu. Oral History Interview. In Kenneth Wayne Baldridge, Interviews, 1971–73.
"We Thank Thee O God for a Prophet." *Te Karere* 49, nos. 2–3 (February–March 1955): 41–78.
Welch, John Shaw. New Zealand Missionary Journals, 1917–20. Utah Historical Society, MSS A 1524, Salt Lake City.
Wharamahihi, Nephi. Oral History Interview. In Kenneth Wayne Baldridge, Interviews, 1971–73.
Whitley, Colleen, ed. *Worth Their Salt, Too: More Notable but Often Unnoted Women of Utah*. Logan: Utah State University Press, 2000.
Wihongi, Rupert. Oral History Interview. In Kenneth Wayne Baldridge, Interviews, 1971–73.
Wihongi, Waimete. Oral History Interview. In Kenneth Wayne Baldridge, Interviews, 1971–73.
Williams, Daniel. Oral History Interview. In Kenneth Wayne Baldridge, Interviews, 1971–73.
Wilson, J. G., et al. *History of Hawkes Bay*. Dunedin, New Zealand: A. H. and A. W. Reed, 1939.
Winslow, Alfred A. Letter to W[illiam] F. Massey, 2 March 1920. United States Department of State, Diplomatic Correspondence on Mormons and Mormonism, 1910–40.
———. Letter to Secretary of State, Auckland, 6 April 1920. United States Department of State, Diplomatic Correspondence on Mormons and Mormonism, 1910–40.
Within These Hallowed Walls. Dedication program for the Auckland Chapel of the Church of Jesus Christ of Latter-day Saints, 1953. LDS Church History Library.

Woods, Moroni Charles. 6 April 1938. The One Hundred Eighth Annual Conference of the Church of Jesus Christ of Latter-day Saints, April 1938. *Conference Report*, 90.

Woolley, W. Wallace. "A Letter from Zion." *The Messenger* 7, no. 1 (1 January 1913): 2.

"The Work in New Zealand." Reprinted from *Auckland Weekly News* in *Millennial Star* 52, no. 26 (30 June 1890): 414.

Wright, Angus Taylor. Journals, 1875–90. Microfilm. MS 1520. LDS Church History Library.

_____. Letter to the editor, dated Auckland, 3 October 1890. *Millennial Star* 52, no. 46 (17 November 1890): 731.

Wright, Marvin S. "Parting Words to the Halversens." *Te Karere* 43, no. 8 (August 1948): 222.

Young, Gordon Claridge. Oral History. Interviewed by Lauritz G. Petersen, 28 August 1972. OH 24. Typescript. LDS Church History Library.

_____. Journal. In Gordon Claridge Young, Papers, 1948–72. Microfilm. MS 4016. LDS Church History Library.

_____. Letter to First Presidency, [20 June 1949]. In Gordon Claridge Young, Papers, 1948–72. Microfilm. MS 4016. LDS Church History Library.

_____. Letter to Building Controller, 2 October 1950. In Gordon Claridge Young, Papers, 1948–72, fd. 4. Microfilm. MS 4016. LDS Church History Library.

_____. Letter to Edward O. Anderson, 25 May 1950. In Gordon Claridge Young, Papers, 1948–72, fd. 3. Microfilm. MS 4016. LDS Church History Library.

_____. Letter to Edward O. Anderson, 16 August 1950. In Gordon Claridge Young, Papers, 1948–72, fd. 4. Microfilm. MS 4016. LDS Church History Library.

_____. Letter to Edward O. Anderson, 7 July 1951. In Gordon Claridge Young, Papers, 1948–72, fd. 6. Microfilm. MS 4016. LDS Church History Library.

_____. Letter to President David O. McKay, 4 March 1950. In Gordon Claridge Young, Papers, 1948–72, fd. 3. Microfilm. MS 4016. LDS Church History Library.

_____. Letter to President David O. McKay, 12 June 1950. In Gordon Claridge Young, Papers, 1948–72, fd. 9. Microfilm. MS 4016. LDS Church History Library.

_____. Letter to President David O. McKay, 13 November 1950. In Gordon Claridge Young, Papers, 1948–72, fd. 4. Microfilm. MS 4016. LDS Church History Library.

_____. Letter to President David O. McKay, 15 May 1951. In Gordon Claridge Young, Papers, 1948–72, fd. 6. Microfilm. MS 4016. LDS Church History Library.

_____. Letter to Bessie Whiteri, 22 January 1951. In Gordon Claridge Young, Papers, 1948–72. Microfilm. MS 4016. LDS Church History Library.

_____. "The President's Page." *Te Karere* 45, no. 3 (March 1951): 84.

_____. "The President's Page." *Te Karere* 45, no. 10 (October 1951): 332.

_____. "Tena ra Koutou e Hoa Ma." *Te Karere* 51, no. 12 (December 1957): 415–19.

"Zion Elders." *Te Karere* 41, no. 3 (March 1946): 58–59.

Zion's Watchman. Published monthly by the Australasian Mission of the Church of Jesus Christ of Latter-day Saints, Sydney, 1853–56.

Photograph References

Chapter 1

1. Advertisement for Carl Asmussen's Christchurch business. *The Southern Provinces Almanac, Directory, and Year Book for 1861*, [202]. Courtesy Wellington City Libraries.
2. William Michael Bromley, PH 1700 5127, Courtesy of Church of Jesus Christ of Latter-day Saints, LDS Church History Library.
3. Thomas and Hannah Cox, PH 262, fd. 1, item 3, LDS Church History Library.

Chapter 2

1. Moroni and Georgiana Marriott, PH 1700 4428, LDS Church History Library.
2. John A. Jury, PH 1700 633, LDS Church History Library.
3. Missionary group, New Zealand Mission Diaries of Nelson Spicer Bishop, BX 8670 .1 .B54, p. 16. L. Tom Perry Special Collections, Harold B. Lee Library, Brigham Young University (hereafter Perry Special Collections).

Chapter 3

1. Hirini Whaanga, PH 2000, Box 28, fd. 1850, item 6, LDS Church History Library.
2. Whaanga grave in the Salt Lake City Cemetery (S-36. 5. 1E), photograph taken November 2010. Courtesy of Patricia Lyn Scott.
3. Drawing of the First Auckland Chapel, *Te Karere* (*The Messenger*), 8, no. 24 (2 December 1914): 284. LDS Church History Library.

Chapter 4

1. Maori Agricultural College opening 1913, Sidney and Ernest Ottley Album Collection, MSS 3734, Scrapbook 2, Perry Special Collections.
2. Maori at the Salt Lake Temple, Peeti Family and New Zealand Missionary Photographs, PH 3373, fd. 2, LDS Church History Library.
3. Maori Agricultural College Parade, Ottley Album Collection, MSS 3734, Box 1, fd. 3, Perry Special Collections.

4. James N. Lambert and wife, Edith in New Zealand, ca. 1919. PH 7868, fd. 4, item 12, LDS Church History Library.
5. Relief Society Conference 1919, New Zealand Photographs, PH 3311, fd. 3, item 4. LDS Church History Library.

Chapter 5

1. Maori Agricultural College Thanksgiving, Sidney and Ernest Ottley Album Collection, MSS 3734, Box 2, fd. 5, Perry Special Collections.
2. Maori Agricultural College student body, Ottley Album Collection, Box 2, fd. 5, Perry Special Collections.
3. David O. McKay, Hugh J. Cannon, and George S. Taylor with Maori Leaders at hui tau, PH 7868, fd. 2, item 1, LDS Church History Library.
4. Leading Maori, Stark Family Collection, MSS 2357, Box 3, fd. 6, Perry Special Collections.
5. Hastings after earthquake, Harold T. Christensen Photographs, MSS 1529, Box 55, fd. 1, envelope 15, Perry Special Collections.

Chapter 6

1. Magleby and Christensen, Christensen Photographs, MSS 1529, Box 54, Perry Special Collections.
2. Tent City, PH 3258, item 10, LDS Church History Library.
3. Polly Duncan, Christensen Photographs, Box 54, fd. 5, Perry Special Collections.

Chapter 7

1. Rosenvall, Biesinger, Mendenhall, and Anderson, PH 399, fd. 1, item 7, LDS Church History Library.
2. McKay Auditorium, PH 148, fd. 1, item 2, LDS Church History Library.
3. Crowds lined up to tour the New Zealand Temple, New Zealand Photographs, PH 399, fd. 1, LDS Church History Library.

Index

Notes: Town names without a country specified are in New Zealand. Photographs and maps are in bold

A

Acheson, Frank O. V., 203
administration to sick, 106, 112
Ahmu, Oliver, 251
Aikane, 159
Alford Forest Branch, 24, 32, 273
Allenby, Edmund, 166
Allington family, 64
Allington, Elizabeth, 15
Allington, Ellen Reading, 15, 17, 19
Allington, Henry, 13–17, 45
Allred, Rodney C., 124–25, 128
Allum, John, 244
Amaru, Wi Pere, 179, 187
American Basketball League, 200
Americans
    servicemen, at New Zealand branches, 212
    work on Auckland Chapel, 240
Anaru, Amohaere, 173
Anaru, Waimate, 159
Anderson, Alexander P., 265
Anderson, Charles, 45, 46
Anderson, Edward O., 227, **254**
    and Church College of New Zealand, 232, 235–36
    and New Zealand Temple, 250, 254
Anderson, James H., 88
Anderson, Lavina Fielding, xv
Anglican Church Missionary Society (CMS), 36, 46, 47, 123 note 10
Anglican college. *See* Te Aute College.
Anglicans. *See* Church of England.
anti-Mormonism, 141, 143–46, 155

Anzac Day, 167–68
Aorangi (ship), 174, 193, 230, 240
Apiata Kuikainga (prophet), 42
apostolic visits, requested, 94–95, 185
Arama Toiroa (prophet), 42
Arani, Eruiti (chief)
    baptized, 101
    on Word of Wisdom, 105
    supports boys' school, 100–101
    supports mission newspaper, 109
Arawa, Maori at, 24
Arthur, Rex E., 225
Articles of Faith, translated into Maori, 53
Ash, J. W., 112
asthma, missionaries suffer from, 112
Ashurst, missionary work at, 76
Asmussen/Amussen, Carl Christian
    advertisement, **11**
    conversion and missionary work of, 10–13
    gathers to Utah, 13, 17
Atareta Pa. *See* Bridge Pa.
Atkin, Annie, 137, 141, 146
Atkin, W. Frank
    missionary activities, 101, 109, 137, 146
    on boils, 112–13
Atwood, Leslie C., 93–94
Auckland, missionary work in, 25, 32
Auckland Branch, 27, 29, 32. *See also* mission headquarters.
    emigration from, 30
    meetinghouse(s), 115, **116**, 119, 199, 233–34, 243–44
    members in, 26–27, 45

306   *Tiki and Temple*

organization/reorganization, 85–86, 133, 224, 237, 252, 273
   Spanish flu, impact on, 151
Auckland Girls' Grammar School, 213
Auckland University, 219
Austral Star, 110, 119
Australasian Mission, 3 and note 6, 86–87, 269
Australia (ship), 30
Australian Mission
   and joint mission newspaper, 109
   first meetinghouse (1904), 72
   missionary visas for, 142
   number of members, 118, 196
Avarua, missionary work in, 222, 236. *See also* Cook Islands.
Awapuni, hui tau at, 121
Awarua, LDS school at, 118

B

Baldridge, Kenneth, 123
Ballance, John, 49–50
Ballif, Ariel Smith, Sr.
   and Church College of New Zealand, 258
   and Maori Agricultural College, 179, 182, 186–87 and note 123, 188, 191, 256
   and organization of Auckland Stake, 263–64
   as mission president, 250–64, 271
Ballif, Ariel Smith, Jr., 179
Ballif, Artimisia Romney, 179
   and temple clothing, 251
   returns to Utah, 188
Baring Bank failure, 79 note 142
Barker, Ian, 60
Barratt, William, 14 note 45
Bartlett, Charles B.
   and Maori education, 100
   and mission newsletter, 101
   and official Church recognition, 98
   as mission president, 98–104, 107, 270
   attitude toward Maori, 99
   debate with minister, 104
   new reporting system, 99
Barrett, William. *See* Barratt, William.
baseball, as missionary activity, 200, 203
basketball, as missionary activity, 200, 203
Batt, George
   as mission president, 270
   as missionary, 25–29

   on Maori and the gospel, 41
   returns to Utah, 30
Bay of Islands, Mormons in, 63, 74, 88
Bay of Plenty
   confiscation of land, 23
   establishment of LDS district, 227
   missionary work in, 38, 41
Beauchamp, Robert, 93, 269
   Australasian Mission president, 13–16, 20, 87
   released, 18
   reorganizes Karori Branch, 35 note 136
Belgian relief, 135
Bennett, Frederick A., 216
Bennion, Adam S., 162, 174
Benson, Ezra Taft, 13
Benson, Flora Amussen, 13
Best, W. O., 85
Biesinger, Audrey, 235
Biesinger, George Ross, **254**
   and Auckland Chapel construction, 237
   and Church College of New Zealand, 232–33, 235, 237, 239, 242–44
   and exhibit for 1940 centenary, 204
   and temple site/construction, 249, 251, 254
   as Auckland Stake president, 263–64
   consults with Wendell Mendenhall, 247–48 and note 63, 250
   in mission presidency, 252
   in Samoa, 235
   on college advisory committee, 256
Bingham, John S., 74, 270
Bird, Stanford W., 256, 264
Birkinshaw, C. William, 150
Bishop, Nelson, **66**
   administers to horse, 112
   living conditions, 44, 113
   missionary activities, 61, 63–64
   on funeral customs, 62
   on John A. Jury, 70
   on Kate Paxman and Georgiana Marriott, 54–55
   on Maori emigration, 77
   on Maori testimony meetings, 68
   on Word of Wisdom, 71
Blythe, John L., 14 note 45
boils, missionaries suffer from, 112
Book of Mormon
   and eruption of Mount Tarawera, 52
   as Sunday School course, 68

first distributed 1889, 63–64
   king wants Book of Mormon translation, 32
   new Maori edition, 223
   presented to Ratana, 183
   prophecies about gathering Israel, 78 and note 139
   reprinted, 147
   role in conversions, 14
   translation into Maori, 53–60
Bowles, Christine, 116
Bowles, George, 116–18, 270
Bowles, George, Jr., 116
Boy Scouts of America, 201
Boyack, Clifton D., 255–56, 258
branch presidencies. *See* local members.
Bridge Pa, 152, 197. *See also* Korongata.
Brigham Young University—Provo, xv, 131
Brigham Young University—Hawaii, xv
Brimhall, George, 131
Brisbane (Australia) meetinghouse, 118
British–born members. *See* Europeans.
Britsch, R. Lanier, xiii, 42
Broadbent, William, 269
Bromley, Michael William, **28**
   as mission president, 27–28, 32–35, 270
   on Maori prophecies, 41–42
   proselytizing among Maori, 27 note 102, 29
bronchitis, missionaries suffer from, 112
Brown, Ernest P., 91–93
Brown, Hugh B., 252
Brown, Major. *See* Tunuiarangi, Hoani Paraone.
Brunt, Bertie, 176
Brunt, George, 10 note 26, 13
Buck, Peter, 67
Buehner, Otto, 240, 242
Burnett family, gathers to Utah, 24
Burnett, Catherine Jane, 10
Burnett, Fanny Fairbrother Orchard, 10, 12, 21
Burnett, James, 10, 12–13, 16–18, 21, 29
Burnett, Mary Ann Denham, 10–11, 24 note 89
Burnett, Susan, 10
Burnett, William, 10–11, 13, 15
Burton, Alma, 221

C

California Mission, 210, 230

Cambridge–Huntly area, Mormons in, 34, 35
Campbell, Wallace, 171
Cannon, George Q., 78, 161
Cannon, Hugh J., 161–69, **167**, 226
Canterbury District, emigration from, 24
Carrington, Albert, 17
Carroll, James, 97, 110, 118
Carroll, Lady, 126
Carroll, Turi, 220, 229
Carter, Harry. *See* Te Katere, Hare.
Carterton Branch, 28–29, 32, 35, 58, 61, 171, 273
carved house at Nuhaka, 226, 229
   Reed Halversen supervises, 224
   resentment over, 232
   Rufus K. Hardy encourages, 218
centenary exhibit (1940), LDS participation in, 204
chapels. *See* meetinghouses *and* individual branches.
chastity, required for temple recommend, 157
Chatham Islands, 85
Child, William, 242, 245
Chote, Matthew, 237
Christchurch
   mission conference in, 32
   mission headquarters at, 27 note 103
   missionary work in, 19–20, 27, 92
   Mormons at, 13, 15, 24
Christchurch Branch, 32, 221, 273
   impact of emigration on, 85
Christensen family (of Carterton), 35
Christensen, Harold Thomas, 195
   as mission president, 193–95, 271
   installs local district president, 275
Christy, Benjamin Goddard, 215, 217
Christy, Kate, returns to New Zealand, 154
Christy, Sidney (Hirini Whaanga Hirihiti)
   and carved house, 229
   as home missionary, 229
   gathers to Utah and returns, 81, 154
   interprets for McKay and Cannon, 164
   president of Mahia District, 211
Christy, William, 154
Church Building Committee, 251
Church College of New Zealand
   closed in 2009, 258 note 108
   compared to Maori Agricultural College, 185
   construction of, 227, 242–44, 246, 251–52

308   *Tiki and Temple*

Matthew Cowley seeks site, 226
visitors to, 251, 253
Church Missionary Society. *See* Anglican Church Missionary Society.
Church of England, 15, 48, 73, 81
Church of Jesus Christ of Latter-day Saints. *See* members, New Zealand Mission, missionaries *and* individual branches.
Church of Jesus Christ of Latter-day Saints Trust Board Empowering Act, 254
Church, Rudolph, 152–54
Church Trust Board in New Zealand, 227
City of Sydney (ship), 30
Clark family, emigrates from Christchurch, 85
Clark (missionary), during flu epidemic, 151
Clark, George ("Gus"), 17
Clark, J. Reuben, 198
Clark, Louisa Holder, 7, 15, 17
Clarke, Jack, 146
Clarke, Leslie, 236
Clarke, Tom, 187
Cobham, Lord (governor-general), 263
Colima (ship), 18
College Branch, 244
college. *See* Maori Agricultural College *and* Church College of New Zealand.
Collins (real estate agent), 231
Colonia Juarez, as possible Maori gathering site, 109
Colyton, missionary work at, 76
Commonwealth Games. *See* Empire Games.
concrete block machine, 227, 232, 240, 242, 252
Cook Islands
as Eastern Polynesian culture, 19 note 68
assigned to Samoan Mission, 247
members in, 228
members work on Auckland Chapel, 240
missionary work in, 85, 221, 245
Cook, Florence, 137
Cook, Lashbrook L., 137
Cook, Mabel, 137
Cooke, Sarah Ann, 4
Cooke, William
as missionary, 7, 13, 15, 17, 26

converted, 4–5
Coombs, D'Monte, 247
Cooper, Eru, 177, 202
Cowie, William, 103
Cowley, Duncan Meha (Tony), 213–14 and note 69, 219
Cowley, Elva Taylor
and war work, 207
as mission Primary president, 211
condolences from Sidney Ottley, 247
in New Zealand, 201, 219, 224
introduces Relief Society Singing Mothers, 205
Cowley, Jewell
comes to New Zealand, 201
during World War II, 213–14
farewell to, 219
Cowley, Matthew
and Book of Mormon second edition, 147
and Maori prophecies, 42
and *Te Karere*, 210
apostolic visits, 222–24, 246, 228–29
as mission president, 201–5, 207–20, **209**, 271
as missionary, 134, 155
blessing from Catholic priest, 218
called as apostle, 219–20
death of, 246–47
Doctrine and Covenants translation, 149
encouraged to retain Maori language, 188
encourages Church College of New Zealand, 223
on Maori Agricultural College, 217
on Maori faith, 106
on Maori welfare, 218
on William Gardner, 137–38
suffers from fleas and boils, 113
support for World War II, 208, 209, 216–17
Cowley, Matthias, 134 note 38, 147
Cox, Hannah, 32–34, **33**
Cox, Samuel, 33 and note 126
Cox, Thomas, **33**, 32–35
Craven, Rulon G., 230
Crawford, Sidney, 188, 256
cultural conflict
funerals, 62
sexual morality, 62–63
haka, 259–61
hongi, 163

missionary observations on, 65, 90, 105
traditional vs. "legal" marriages, 63, 157–58
Cummings, David, 244
Cummings, Horace Hall, 122, 162
Curtis, Asa L., 100
Cutler, Heber S., 65, 68, 70, 74

D

Dairy Flat, 51
Danielson, Frederick M. P., 250
Dannevirke, 26, 27
David O. McKay Auditorium, 249, 252, 253, **258**
Davies, Henry, 238
Davies, Rangi, 238
Davis, David Elmer, 98, 100
deaths. *See also* missionaries, illness.
   from Spanish influenza, 151–54 and note 105
   of American missionaries, 112
   of Mormon converts, 30
Deering, donates agricultural implements, 122
Delamere, Donlon P., 222
demographics. *See* members *and* missionaries.
Dillingham, Frank, 92
diphtheria, missionaries suffer from, 112
disillusioned Mormons, return to New Zealand, 19–20
DNA research. *See* Polynesian origins.
Doak, Agnes, 24
Doctrine and Covenants, Maori edition, 147, 149
Dolling. *See* Beauchamp, Robert.
Dominion Museum, 171
Donnelly, J. P., 100–101, 110
Douglass, William, 44
Dowdle, Absalom P., 269
Doxey, Graham H., 156, 164
Dryden family, 15, 19
Dryden, Mary Ann, 19 note 70
Dryden, Robert, 19 note 70
Duke of York, 91
Duncan (of Christchurch), 94
Duncan family (of Tahoraiti), 223
Duncan, Polly (Pare), 191, **211**, 234, 253
Duncan, William Jr. (also Wi), 226
   as mission YMMIA president, 211
   Matthew Cowley visits, 226
   on earthquake damage, 190
Duncan, Takare, 129–30, 141, 159–60
Duncan, William Sr. (also Wi/Wiremu Tanaka) **178**
   and Book of Mormon, 147
   and Doctrine and Covenants, 149
   and Maori Agricultural College, 101
   and Spanish influenza, 152
   and wife, 159
   as home missionary, 132
   debate with minister, 104–105
   first Maori high priest, 160, 181 note 105
   in first New Zealand company to Hawaii Temple, 159
   on hui tau, 175
   on New Zealand gathering, 140
   on Ratana, 170
   visits Utah, 129–30, 159–60
Dunedin, street meetings, 92
Dunedin Branch, 32, 197, 221, 273
Dunford, Ida, 56

E

Eagle, Hannah, 19 note 70
earthquakes, 134, 189–90, 233
East (first name not recorded), threatens missionaries, 21
East Coast Maori tribes, 24
Easter, hui tau coincides with, 170 note 59. *See also* hui tau *and* specific locales.
Edmunds, George F., 92
Edwards, Olive, 191
Elders' Messenger, 110–11. *See The Messenger*.
Elkington family, 189
Elkington, James, 135, 164, 166, 202, 242, 245
Elkington, James H., 215
emigration. *See* gathering.
Empire Games, 239
Ensor, L. le F., 263
Ercanbrack, Sterling M., 151, 156
Esplin, Ronald K., xv
Europeans. *See also* members.
   LDS success among, 38–39
   numbers of LDS converts, 39
Evans family, gathers to Utah, 17
Evans, Emma, 5
Evans, Francis, 5

Evans, John S., 105
Evening and the Morning Star, The, 1

F

Fakatou, Samuela, 174
Farnham, Augustus A.
   on preaching to Maori, 4, 7
   missionary work in New Zealand, 5–7, 41
   as mission president, 87, 269
   interest in Maori translations, 53
Fawcett family, 35
Fawcett, William, 15, 20
Fergusson, Charles (governor–general), 174
Ferris, John S.
   as missionary, 27, 30–32, 76
   mental instability, 32
   on Maori prophecies, 41–42
Fielding, missionary work at, 76
Fiji Islands, 85, 245
"firsts" in New Zealand
   conference broadcast by closed–circuit television, 249
   convert baptized in Australasian Mission, 14 and note 45
   convert baptized in New Zealand, 7
   elders' quorums, 250
   fully accredited teacher at Maori Agricultural College, 184
   LDS branch in Auckland, 25
   LDS branch in New Zealand, 7, 273
   LDS Maori Branch, 34
   LDS meeting in Napier, 25
   LDS primary school (Nuhaka), 47
   LDS stand on political issues, 156
   local mission Relief Society president, 191, **211**
   Maori baptized, 30
   Maori decorated in World War II, 217
   Maori mission president, 156
   Maori ordained to Melchizedek Priesthood, 36
   Maori Relief Society, 95, 194
   Maori to gather, 53, 81
   Maori woman missionary, 104
   marriage solemnized by a Mormon, 98
   mission presidency in New Zealand, 225
   Mission Genealogical Committee, 195
   missionary work in Scandinavian settlements, 25
   missionaries to arrive by air, 230
   Mormon pamphlet printed, 19
   New Zealand converts to gather, 17
   non–LDS woman called on mission, 132
   preaching to Maori, 17–18
   Primary, 132
   Relief Society, 24, 95
   tract in Maori, 29
   visit of Church president (1955), 248–49
   young couple to go to temple to be married, 187
First Presidency. *See also* individual presidents.
   authorizes meetinghouses, 232
   discourages Maori gathering, 77–79, 84, 94
   discourages all gathering, 79–80, 84, 94, 239
   during World War II, 207–8, 211
Fitzpatrick's Travelogue feature, 239
fleas, missionaries suffer from, 112
flu. *See* Spanish influenza.
Foote, Guy, 220
Ford, Thomas, 269
Forest Dale Ward (Salt Lake City), 117
Fox, William (premier), 16
Francis, Earl, 133, 146, 155
Fraser, Peter (prime minister), 218, 229, 234
Freece, Hans P., 141
French, Clifford, 220
French Polynesia, 2–3
Frost, Burr, 5, 14
Fruean, Selu, 256
Fulmer, Frank J., 221
funeral customs. *See* tangi/tangihanga.

G

Gardner, John W., 93, 96, 100
Gardner, William, **66**
   and John A. Jury, 171
   as mission president, 80, 84–87, 131, 137, 147, 270
   as missionary, 52
gathering
   Colonia Juarez, as possible site, 109
   First Presidency discourages, 78–79, 84, 94, 239
   gathering place in New Zealand, 140, 194
   impact on branches, 16, 39
   Maori interest in, 76–80
   to Utah, 5, 7, 13, 30, 94, 112, 132
Geddes, Hugh S., 123
Geddes, William, 18, 269

genealogies as sacred, 88
Geographical Names Board, 264
George, A., 205
George V (king), 142
Gimblett, John, 197
Gimblett, William, 182, 192
girls' school proposed, 162, 217, 223
Glassie, Moe, 214
Glassie, Ngai, 214
Glassie, Samuel, 214, 221; and wife, 214
Goddard, Benjamin
  and Hawaii Temple dedication, 141
  and Maori Agricultural College, 122, 125, 177
  and mission home, 115
  as missionary, 67
  death of, 196
  hosts Maori Saints in Utah, 129, 159
  influence with First Presidency, 110
  nephew teacher at Maori Agricultural College, 146
  on daily karakia, 73–74;
  on interest of Europeans, 76
  on Maori emigration, 78, 154
  on Maori generosity, 74
  on Maori memorization ability, 68, 74
  on Maori oratory, 67
  president of New Zealand Missionary Society, 159
  supports permanent headquarters, 89
  teaches tithing, 56
  travels to hui tau, 72–73
  vice–president of Zion's Maori Association, 85
Goddard, Emma, 110
Goff, Jedediah, 85
Going, Cyril, 124
Going, Gertrude Cutforth, 139–40, 205, **206**, 207
Going, Lionel, 235
Going, Percy Stanley Connorton, 109, 139–40
  and Maromaku chapel, 205, **206**, 207
  ordained high priest, 202
  son killed in France in World War I, 139
Going, Stanley, 139
gold mines, Australia, 4–5, 11, 17–18
Goosman, William S., 234
Grace, T. S. (archdeacon), 76
Grant, Heber J.
  attends McKay's farewell dinner, 162
  death of, 220
  dedicates Hawaii Temple, 157
  on Maori Agricultural College, 182
  on Ratana, 180–81
  ordains Wiremu Duncan a high priest, 160
  promises to John Magleby, 193
Great Fleet, 22
Greening, Bessie, 132
Greenwood, Alma
  anoints self for chest pain, 112
  as missionary, 32, 34–37
  on fleas, 113
  on Maori hospitality and faith, 69–70
  on Otene Meihana, 37
Grey, George (governor), 36
Groesbeck, Joseph S., 64
Groesbeck, N. Harmon, 27–28
Gronlund, Neils J., 25
Groo, Isaac, 18, 22, 269
Grouard, Benjamin, 2
Groves, E. A., 12

H

Hafen, Bruce C., xv
Hagoth, and Maori belief, 47, 129–30
haka. *See* cultural conflict.
Hakopa, Mariana, 154
Hakopa, Ratima, 173
Hall, David, 136
Hall, Harata, 136–37
Halls, F. W., 103
Halversen, Andrew Reed
  as mission president, 174, 217, 219–25, 271
  checks temple ceremony translation, 257
Halversen, Luana, 219, 222
Hamer, John C., 8–9
Hamilton Branch, 244
  members from work on Auckland Chapel, 239
Hamon, Henare/Henry, 195, 211, 275
Hamon, Mildred, 221, 225
Hamon, Trevor, 221, 225
Hansen, Ben, 30
Hapeta, James, 236
Hapi, Charlie, 152
Hapi, Joe, 187
Hapi, Paora/Paul, **178**, 181, 191, 275
Hardy, Adelaide, 110, 116

312   *Tiki and Temple*

Hardy, Charles
  acquaintance with prime minister, 144
  and financial support, 26–27, 29, 85, 89, 109
  as president of Auckland Branch, 85, 115
  death of, 133
  on eruption of Mount Tarawera, 51
Hardy, Rufus K.
  and Maori Agricultural College, 122, 162, 177, 205
  as mission president, 110–11, 114–16, 194, 196–97, 270–71
  encourages missionaries to speak Maori, 197
  obituary of, 218
  visits New Zealand as General Authority, 201, 260
Hari, Ere, 95
Harold B. Lee Library, xv
Harris (missionary during flu), 154
Harris, Kelly, 210, 219, 220, 222
Harris, Rahiri, 159, **178**, 220, 229
Haslam, James V., 208
Hastings
  damaged by earthquake, 189–90, **190**
  hui tau, 216
  possible Church College of New Zealand site, 227
  visitors from tour Maori Agricultural College, 125–26
Hau Haus. *See* Pai Marire.
Hau–hau (religion), 75
Haughey, Thomas, 236
Hawaii, as Eastern Polynesian culture, 19 note 68
Hawaii Temple
  dedication, 139, 141, 157
  New Zealand Saints visit, 173, 184, 187, 198
Hawkes Bay District
  Relief Society in, 95
  Maori in, 44
  missionary work in, 36–37
Hay and Sons, 127
Hay, Joseph, 238, 252, 254
Hay, Muriel Going, 191, 238
healing, of chief's daughter, 32
Henderson, Thomas W., 105
Hendry, John M., 75, 84
Henry, Mii, 214

Heperi, Hohepa, 159, 181, 210, 229, 253, 275
Heperi, James, 174, **178**
Herd, Harriet, 54
Heremaia, Hirini, 181
Hetherington, J. R., 145
high priests, Maori ordained. *See* local members.
Hikurangi, Maori religion in, 22
Hinckley, Gordon B., 262
Hinckley, Ira Noble, 34–37
Hintze, A. Royal W., 134–35
Hintze, Jessie, 134–35
Hintze, Mildred, 134
Hippolite, Ben, 221
Hirihiti, Hirini Whaanga. *See* Christy, Sidney.
Hiroa, Te Rangi. *See* Buck, Peter.
Hislop, George T., 91
Hislop, John, 140, 142, 144, 163–64, 174
Hitler, Adolf, and genealogy, 203
Ho, Simon, 131 note 26
Hoagland, Louis Gerald
  and John Jury's genealogical volumes, 171–72
  and Maori Agricultural College, 108, 111, 185
  and mission paper, 108
  as mission president, 102, 270
  correspondence on schools, 107–8
  disapproved of haka, 260
  encourages missionaries to speak Maori, 188
  genealogy mission, 147, 153, 155
  in Hawaii, 157
  on Maori colony, 109
Hodge, Robert P., 184, 187–88, 191–92
Holbrook, Horace, 137
Holbrook, Leona, 137
Holder, Caroline Allington, 13, 15
Holder, Louisa. *See* Clark, Louisa Holder.
Holder, Martha Young, 7, 17
Holder, Thomas, 5–7, 13–15
Holland, Sidney (prime minister), 234, 237
Holyoake, Keith (prime minister), 234, 237, 248, 263
home missionaries, 60, 104. *See also* local missionaries.
Home Guard, World War II, 217
hongi
  McKay on, 163

with missionaries, 49
Hopper, T., 117
Howells, David P., 109–11
hui tau. *See also* individual locations.
  by years: 1887, 53; 1894, 75; 1896, 86; 1898, 87; 1904, 100; 1911, 118; 1912, 121; 1913, 123, 260; 1917, 141; 1918, 147; 1920, 158–59; 1921, 163–68, **167**; 1922, 169–70; 1926, 175; 1927, 177; 1928, 179; 1929, 183; 1932, 191; 1935, 198; 1936, 198, **199**; 1937, 199; 1938, 201; 1939, 202–3; 1940, 205; 1941, 210–11; 1943, 216; 1946, 220; 1947, 221–22; 1948, 224–25; 1949, 228–29; 1950, 236; 1951, 237; 1952, 242; 1955, 250; 1957, 253
  challenges of organizing, 53
  competition to host, 75
  food consumed at (1889), 65
  logistical problems, 198–99
  terminated, 266
Hui Atawhai. *See* Relief Society.
Hunt, Brian, xiii, 42
Hurst, Alfred, 5
Hurst, Aurelia, 18
Hurst, Charles Clement, 5, 17–21
Hurst, Frederick
  as missionary, 18–21, 29, 35
  baptized, 5
  gathers to Utah, 17
  preaches to Maori, 20, 29
Hurst, Mary Ann, 19–20
Hyde, Orson, 166 note 42
Hyde, William, 147
hymnals
  in Danish, 28
  in Maori (1910 and 1917), 69

I

Ihaia, Ema, 129–30, 141
Ihaia Hopu Te Whakamairu. *See* Te Whakamairu, Ihaia Hopu.
Ihaia, James, 153
Ihaia, Takarei, 37, 129–30, 132
Ihaka (chief), 72
infantile paralysis. *See* polio.
Institute for Polynesian Studies (Pacific Institute), xv

International Harvester Company, donates equipment to Maori Agricultural College, 122, 126
Invercargill Branch, 32, 90, 273
Iosepa, Utah, 78, 109
"itch," missionaries suffer from, 112

J

James, Ann, 24
Japanese Mission (Hawaii), New Zealand missionaries reassigned to, 210
Jenkins, Barbara, 174
Jenkins, Cora, 174
Jenkins, Donna, 174
Jenkins, J. Howard, **178**, 271
  and John Jury genealogical volumes, 173
  as mission president, 174, 178
  on Maori Agricultural College, 174–77
Jenkins, John, 174
Jenkins, Marion, 174
Jenny Ford (ship), 7
Jensen, Jens, 25–27
Jensen, Richard L., xv
Jenson, Andrew
  on Book of Mormon and Maori, 76
  on first Maori baptism, 30
  on Taramana Hei Watene, 52
  on Maori eagerness to participate, 69
Johnson, Edith, 122
Johnson, Elias, 49
Johnson, Eva, 122, 125, 128
Johnson, John
  and Maori Agricultural College, 122–126, 128
  as missionary, 85
  on College Board of Education, 123
  on haka, 260
  tours mission with Orson Romney, 123
Johnson, John, Jr., 122, 124
Johnson, Laura S., 118
Johnson, M. N., 119
Johnson, Matt, 135
Johnson, Vivian, 122, 124
Jones, John, 6, 269
Jones, R. A., attacked by mob, 92–93
Joseph Fielding Smith Institute for Latter-day Saint History, xv
Julia Ann (ship), 17
Jury, John Alfred (Te Whatahoro), 49–50, **59**, 72, 171 and note 62

and volumes of Maori genealogy and
    lore, 171–73
and Book of Mormon translation, 53, 58
invited to Salt Lake City, 172
on conversion, 70

K

Kaiapoi Branch, 15–16, 24
    Mormons in, 10, 18–19
    organized, 273
Kaikohe
    Church purchases forest land, 242, 246
    hui tau at, 141
    meetinghouse, 244–45
    multipurpose building proposed, 222–23
    sawmill at, 253
Kamau, Ani, 205
Kamau, David (Rawiri), 102
Kamau, Hamiora, 173
Kamehameha V (king), 130, 159
Kanab, Utah, 79, 81, 83
Karaitiana, Ka, 125
Karaka, Wiremu, 159
Karaki, Hone, 155
karakia (prayer meetings), 46, 49, 66, 103
Karori Branch, 7, 35 note 136
    Mormons at, 5–7, 10, 13–15
    numbers in, 45
    organized, 273
Katene, George, 217
kauri gum, 109
kauri tree, and Maromaku Chapel, 205–6, **206**
Kawakawa, missionaries attacked, 49
Kelly, Peter, 174
Kenneth, Esther, 146, 152, 238
Kenneth, Gertie, 146
Kimball, Spencer W., 261
Kimball, Stanley C., 179
King Country District, 70, 227
King, James, 96, 102
King movement, 23
Kiri Kiri
    debate at, 105
    hui tau at, 147
    meetinghouse, **148**
    missionary work at, 52
    Relief Society, 95
Kirkham, Francis W., 89
Knox College, 219

Kohunui Branch, 59
Kohunui, LDS school at, 118
Kopuawhara, Mormons in, 37
    possible college site, 108
Korean War, and missionary restrictions, 236, 238
Koroki (king), 203
Korongata
    and Maori Agricultural College, 121
    choir, 126, 201
    flu epidemic at, 152
    hui tau, 123, 221–22, 224–25, 228–29, 242, 260
    land ballot at, 197
    LDS school at, 118, 125
    Maori in, 44
    meetinghouse, 100–101, 110, 205
    Mormons in, 37
    proposed school site, 115–16
    Relief Society, 96
Kotahitanga. *See* Te Kotahitanga.
Krueger, Fritz Bunge, 214, 221
Krueger, Moririki, 214, 221

L

L. Tom Perry Special Collections and
    Manuscripts, xv
labour missionary program, 234, 242–44 and note 44
    and college construction, 255
    and temple construction, 250, 254–55
    missionaries released, 263
Laie Hawaii Temple. *See* Hawaii Temple.
Lambert, Claude, 137
Lambert, Edith Hunter, 137–38, **138**, 141, 149, 157
Lambert, James Needham **138**
    and Jury's genealogy volumes, 171–72
    and missionary visas, 155, 159
    as mission president, 137–40, **138**, 141–50, 270
    and Maori Agricultural College, 138, 160, 162
    and Spanish influenza, 151–54
    released, 157, 158–59
    RLDS slander, 148–49
Lambert, Phyllis, 137, 141
Lambert, Richard G., 30
land consolidation, LDS position on, 183–84

Index   315

land courts, religious services at, 46, 103
land, government "resumes" for veterans, 140
land titles, 100–1
Land Wars (1860–70s), 22–24
Larsen family, emigrates from Christchurch, 85
Larsen, Johanna, 24
Larsen, Norman V., 220
Latter-day Saints, The, in Maori, 88
Lauritzen (missionary during flu), 154
LDS Church Committee on Expenditures, 232
LDS Church, history of (1830–44), 1–2
LDS Church Welfare Program, 218
LDS Maori College. *See* Maori Agricultural College.
LDS missionaries. *See* missionaries.
LDS primary schools, 47, 107
   at Awarua, 118
   at Kohunui, 118
   at Kopuawhara, 118
   at Korongata, 101, 118, 125
   at Nuhaka, 47
   at Porirua, 118, 128
   at Taupo, 65–66, 118
   at Tauranganui, 118
   at Waiapu, 47–48
   at Wairau, 118
Le Bons Bay Branch, 32, 273
Leaves from My Journal, 68
Leavitt, Wayne, 220
Leonard, Glen M., 265
Liahona College/High School (Tonga), 235, 245
Lineham, Peter, 93
Lloyd, Ray H., 220
local members. *See also* members.
   as branch presidents, 66–67, 168
   as district and auxiliary presidents, 194–95, 227, 229, 245, 275
   as high priests, 160, 181 and note 105, 194, 202
   as missionaries, 37, 104, 174, 178, 196, 220, 229
   women as part-time missionaries, 196, 214
Locke, Thomas, 52
Logie, Charles, 17
London Missionary Society, 228
"Long Depression" in New Zealand, 79 note 142
Los Angeles Temple, 246
Love, Ngahuka, 212
Loving, A. L., 165–66
Lyman, Francis M., 26

M

Maaki, Arepa, 153–54
M.A.C. Old Boys Association, 183, 240
   concert, 205
   revived, 202–3
   Scholarship Fund, 217
"magic lantern" shows, 90
Magleby family and temple fund, 251
Magleby, Jennie, 179, 191, **195**
Magleby, John Ephraim, **195**
   and Maori Agricultural College activities, 188, 191
   and mission newspaper, 98
   and Ratana, 180–81, 183–84, 185–86
   and Relief Societies, 95–96
   appoints Maori district presidents, 181
   as mission president, 179–88, 193–195, 270–71
   as missionary, 51, 60, 63, 89–90, 102
   as schoolteacher, 47–48
   attacked, 49–51
   correspondence with Louis G. Hoagland, 188–89
   disapproves of haka, 260
   encourages retaining Maori language, 188
   emphasizes proselytizing Europeans, 91–92
   evaluation of presidency of, 193–94
   fluency in Maori, 50–51
   installs local district presidents, 275
   leads Hosanna Shout, 194
   suggests Mormon colony in New Zealand, 94
   sympathy with Maori culture, 107
Mahia Conference/District, 56, 83, 95
Mahia, Mormons in, 37, 82
Makarewa Branch, 273
Makura (ship), 147, 158
Manaia Branch, 36
Manawatu District, 104
Mangakahei, meetinghouse at, 100
Mangapai Branch, 273
Manihera (Sister), 61
Manihera, Edward, 64
Manwaring, Bernice, 179
Manwaring, Lawrence, 179

Maori
- as Lamanites/Israelites, 6, 35, 47, 129–30, 169
- choirs, 69, 118, 239
- converts threatened with death, 48
- culture. *See* cultural conflict.
- diet, 47, 61, 65, 74
- economic circumstances of, 44–45
- emigration. *See* gathering to Zion.
- ethnology, 27, 133
- faithfulness, 69, 71
- genealogy
  - ambilineal, 117 note 135
  - and Hawaiian genealogies, 159
  - books of appropriated by government, 171–73
- generosity/hospitality of, 47, 50, 53, 57, 64, 74–75
- giving children to childless, 65
- Maori Parliament. *See* Te Kotahitanga.
- memorization ability, 68, 74
- missionary work among authorized, 18–19, 27, 37
- move to cities, 90 note 31, 233
- numbers of, 95
- oratory among, 67
- origins, xiv, 129–131 and note 26
- prophets, x, 23–24, 37, 41–43, 169
- rangatira appointed district presidents, 181
- rangatira, influence on missionary work, 104
- resentment of treatment by Europeans, 45, 56, 60
- testimony meetings, 68, 159
- traditional marriages. *See* cultural conflict.

Maori Agricultural College, **127, 161**
- achievements during first year, 131
- aims of, 124
- and LDS Church School system, 174, 177
- baptisms at, 134, 162
- brass band and concerts, 133–36
- buildings at, 121–22, 173
- cadet corps at, 150, 160
- celebrates American holidays, **156**
- closure, 188, 190–92
- "commencement" at, 135
- construction of, 121
- crops and livestock, 137–38
- curriculum at, 125, 160
- dedicated, 126–27, **127**
- deficiencies of, 184–85
- earthquakes at, 134 (1914), 189 (1931)
- English language of instruction, 128
- faculty daughters admitted, 124
- first catalogue, 124
- funding/fees, 108, 124, 127, 136, 150–51, 160, 170, 175
- furniture at, 124
- graduates serve short-term missions, 179
- graveyard, 192
- inspection reports, 176–77 and note 89, 179, 182–83, 186–87
- land leased, 182
- member contributions to, 119–20
- memorial service in chapel ruins, 222
- missionaries as faculty, 145
- numbers enrolled, 133, 170, 186 and note 123
- origins of, 66, 99, 100–1
- Pakeha boys at, 124
- possible sites for, 110
- praised in newspapers, 126
- purchases more land, implements, 134
- school board appointed, 122–23
- scholarships, 187 and note 127
- student elections, 146
- Sunday School and Mutual Improvement Association, 151
- taxes on, 150
- "tidy dormitory" competition, 146
- uses American school year and texts, 128

Maori Antiquities Act (1908), 172
Maori Battalion, 215, 220
Maori Purposes Fund Control Board, 175, 182
Maori Secondary Schools Aid Fund, 175
Maori translations
- Articles of Faith, 53
- Book of Mormon, 53–60, 63–64, 147
- Doctrine and Covenants, 149
- "A Friendly Discussion," 177
- hymnal (1910), 69, 177
- Joseph F. Smith authorizes, 147
- *The Latter-day Saints*, 88
- Pearl of Great Price, 147
- temple ceremony, 257
- tracts, 29, 31–32, 53, 177
- written form of Maori, 67 note 98

Maori Wars. *See* Land Wars.
Mapuhi, Tamata, 179

Marama (ship), 162
Mariposa (ship), 201, 207, 210, 256
Maromaku Branch, 273
Maromaku meetinghouse, 205, **206,** 207
marriage celebrants, LDS, 98
Marriott, Georgiana Geertsen, 54–56, **55**
Marriott, Moroni Stewart, 54, **55**
Marriot, Winifred, 54
Marsden, Samuel, 47, 129
Marshall, Henry S., 211
Mason, Myra Going, 238
Mason, Norman, 238
Massey, William F. (prime minister), 143–44, 151, 156, 158
Masterton, Maori at, 42
Mata–aho (princess), 263
Matakowhai Branch, 232
Matthew Cowley Administration Building, 249, 252, 253
Maughan, Alvin T., 198, 271
Maughan, Eldora, 158
Maughan, Erma, 158
Maughan, Evelyn Going, 198
Maughan, Helen, 158
Maughan, J. Howard, 158
Maughan, Roy, 158
Maui Pomare (ship), 221
May, Fred J., 24, 270
McCune, Henry F., 30, 32–33, 71, 77
McDonnel, William John, 25, 32, 33
McKay, David O.
   and building program, 233
   and Church College of New Zealand, 253, 263
   and Maori Agricultural College, 168–69
   and New Zealand Temple, 168, 176, 248–49, 253, 261
   as Church Commissioner of Education, 161–62
   Auckland Stake organized, 263–64
   haka performed for, 260–61
   in New Zealand, 162–69, 167, 225, 246, 248
   meets evacuated missionaries, 210
   sermon on Church succession, 165
   suggests hui tau at Christmas, 168, 170
   tour of world missions announced, 161
McKay, Emma Ray Riggs, 248, 261
McKay, Hiria Katerina, 205
McKee, Leonard V., 220
McLachlan, William
   as missionary, 18–21, 29, 41
   on Maori society, 22
McMurray, Helena Harriet Weaver McKenzie, 220
McMurray, Joseph (father), 220
McMurray, Joseph Talmage (son), 220
measles, missionaries suffer from, 112
Meeks, Susan, 44
meetinghouses. *See also* individual locations.
   for Maori branches, 72
   stress on building, 232–36
   styles of, 108–9
   under construction, 252
Meha, Apiata, 170
Meha, Arapata, 70, 102, 123
Meha, Hohepa, 210, 211
Meha, Ivory (Ivy) Tepora Morris, 123 note 9, 196, 257
Meha, Meri Hineiturama Tapihana, 123 note 9
Meha, Rosina Jane Edith Morris, 123 note 9
Meha, Stuart (Tuati), **178**
   and Book of Mormon, 147
   and Doctrine and Covenants, 149
   and Maori Agricultural College, 123
   as home missionary, 132, 229
   biography, 123 and note 9
   Hawkes Bay District Presidency, 181, 229
   interprets McKay addresses, 164, 165 and note 37
   mission to Hawaii Temple, 195–96
   opposes gathering to Utah, 132–33
   president of Mission Genealogical Committee, 195, 211
   translates temple ceremony, 257 and note 106
   visits Utah, 129–31, 257
Meihana, Otene, 36–37, 46, 70, 104
Meldrum, Bert, 231–32, 236
Meldrum, Jeff, 131 note 26
members, *see also* local members.
   after mission division, 265–66
   in Mahia Conference/District, 82
   numbers of in New Zealand: 1885, 37; 1886, 48; 1888, 60; 1903, 99; 1907, 107; 1910, 118–19; 1911, 118; 1930, 189; 1931–32, 196–97; 1948, 225; 1955, 250; 1957, 257; 2011, xiii
   number of European branches/converts, 38, 45, 60, 85

Mendenhall, Paul, 247, 257
Mendenhall, Wealtha, 248
Mendenhall, Wendell B., **254**
   and building program, 247–48 and note 63
   and Church College of New Zealand, 248–51
   and New Zealand Temple, 248–51
   and organization of Auckland Stake, 263
   chairs Board of Education for the South Pacific, 255
   chairs Church Building Committee, 251, 254
Messenger, The, 110–11, 133
Mete, Watene. *See* Smith, Walter
Methodist Church, 15
Millennial Star, circulation in New Zealand, 13
Ministerial Association, anti-Mormonism of, 136
mission. *See* New Zealand Mission.
missionaries (American). *See also* local members.
   as district presidents, 102
   build meetinghouses, 100–1, 108
   compared to bishops, 103, 200
   debates with ministers, 104–5
   encouraged to learn Maori, 35, 43, 146–47, 188, 197, 200
   evacuated during World War II, 208–10
   female missionaries, 54–56, 104, 220–21
   financial support of, 56
   first in New Zealand, 5–7
   health of, 112
   illnesses of, 112, 225
   journals, letters, 44
   living among Maori, 44, 46–47
   mobbed, 92–93; mythologizing of, 93 and note 43
   numbers of, 43, 86, 99, 111, 145, 155, 178, 194–96, 198, 202, 250
   poverty of, 21, 34, 35
   proselytizing Europeans, 111–12
   quotas/visas, 142–45, 155, 160, 170, 174, 224
   replace local district presidents, 221–22, 227, 229
   travelling conditions, 45, 54–55, 60–61, 169
   visit branches, 102–3
   war work, 207
Moana (ship), 89

Moawhango
   hui tau at, 100, 105
   Mormons at, 101
moko. *See* tattooing.
Monowai (ship), 81
Monterey (ship), 196, 210, 220
Montgomery, W. B., 142
Moore, David, 217
Morgan, Samuel, 128
Mormon History Association, xv
Mormon Maid, The, 145–46
Mormon Tabernacle Choir, 240
"Mormonism in New Zealand: A Historical Appraisal," xiv
Mortensen, Hans Henrick, 27
Mortensen, Mette, 27
Mount Roskill, chapel site, 99, 253
Mount Tarawera, eruption of, 51–52; myth about, 52
Mountain Maid (ship), 7
Mulawa (ship), 124
Murdock, Della, 132
Murdock, John, 3, 6, 87, 269
Murdock, Reuben, 132
Muri Enua, Cook Islands, 222
Muriwai, 37, 53, 56, 97
Mutual Improvement Association, as missionary activity, 199

N

Napier
   damaged by earthquake, 189
   missionary work in, 25, 32
   visitors from tour Maori Agricultural College, 125
Napier Branch, 27, 273
Napier [Daily] Telegraph, 71
Nash, Walter (prime minister), 263
Nelson Branch, 221
networking, and missionary work, 15, 35, 38
Nevada (ship), 17
New Zealand
   as Eastern Polynesian culture, 19 note 68
   currency, xiv
   economy of, 79 note 142
   education system, 256
New Zealand Army, 221
New Zealand Company, 2
New Zealand Government Archives, xv
New Zealand Mission

challenges of, 85, 87
divided, 265
headquarters, 27, 89, 98–99, 115, **116**, 136–39, 226, 244, 253, 264
numbers. *See* members.
newspaper, 101, 109–10, 194. *See also Te Karere.*
photos of presidents requested, 125
reorganizations, 247, 269
New Zealand Mission Genealogical Committee, 195, 211
New Zealand Missionary Society. *See also* Zion's Maori Association.
  farewell dinner for David O. McKay and Hugh J. Cannon, 162
  fund–raising for temple, 251
  resists ordination of Maori district presidents, 191
  sponsors hymnal translation, 69
New Zealand, North Island, map, **8**
New Zealand, South Island, map, **9**
New Zealand Temple
  and David O. McKay, 168, 176, 248–49, 253, 261–62
  and Wendell Mendenhall, 248–51
  construction of, 250–55, 254
  dedication, xiii, 261–62
  openhouse, 261–62, **262**
  petition for, 176
  plans for, 250–51
  urged for New Zealand, 223
Newby, Edward, 77
Newton, missionary work in, 25
Nga Puhi, Mormons in, 60
Ngapuhi (tribe), 23, 36
Ngaruawahia
  hui tau, 177, 179, 202–3
  possible Church College site, 227
Ngata, Apirana, 110–11, 216, 220, 229
Ngataki (chief), 30 and note 116
Ngati Kahunguna (tribe)
  and new religion, 23, 36, 42
  welcome Mormonism, 37, 60, 81
Ngati Maniapoto (tribe), 23
Ngati Porou (tribe), 23, 48, 50, 58
Niagara (ship), 129, 137, 142, 157–58, 207
Nibley, Charles W., 139
Niue Island, 245, 247
Nopera, Eriata, **178**
  and wife, to Hawaii Temple, 159–60

death of, 222
on Paora's prophecy, 42
ordained high priest, 181 and note 105
president of Hawkes Bay District, 181, 211, 275
Nordstrand (family of Christchurch), 85
Norsewood Branch, 27, 273
Northwestern States Mission, 210
Nuhaka
  amusement hall, 173, 191
  as possible college site, 108
  carved house, 224, 226, 229
  conference at, 56
  hui tau at, 175, 198, 205, 210–11, 237
  LDS school in, 47
  Maori families return to, 154
  meetinghouse/amusement hall, 121
  members from work on Auckland Chapel, 239–40
  members in military service, 217
  Mormons in, 37, 83
  Primary organized, 132
Nye, Harriet, 55

O

Olpin, W. J., 137
Onedia Stake Academy, 122
Only Way to Be Saved, The, 19
Opotiki, missionary work at, 31–32, 41
Opuawhanga Branch, 273
Orakei, missionary work at, 29
Otene Meihana. *See* Meihana, Otene.
Otiria hui tau, 169
Ottley, Alice, 240
Ottley, Jerold, 135, 240
Ottley, Sidney J.
  as mission president, 240–50, 253, 271
  and Maori Agricultural College, 125, 128, 135
  sells property in Remuera, 264
Owaka Branch, 273
Owen, Robert, 14

P

Paea, Erana, 173
Paewai, Hineapa, 257
Paewai, Niki/Nireaha, 134, 173, 257
Paewai, Nitama, 218, 225, 257
Paewai, Wilson, 173, **178**, 181

Pai Marire (religion), 23, 81
Palmerston North, 28, 76
Palmerston North Branch, 273
Papanui Branch, 273
   LDS conference at, 24
   Mormons in, 21
Papawai Branch, 36, 68
Papawai, 35, 71
   hui tau at, 87, 118
Parihaka, 24, 30–31, 91
Parker, Rangi, xiv
Parr, James, 170
Parsons, Alfred, 98 and note 63
Parsons, Amelia McCormack, 98
patriarch, requested for New Zealand, 185, 194
Paxman, Kate, 54–58
Paxman, Sarah, 53–54
Paxman, William T.
   appointed to investigate conditions in Kanab, 83
   as mission president, 51, 53, 85, 270
   Book of Mormon translation, 53–54, 57–58, 60, 64, 76
   discourages emigration, 77–78
   on eruption of Mount Tarawera, 51
   on Maori temple work, 78
   president of Zion's Maori Association, 84
Paxman, William M., 101
Pearce, Elijah F., 24, 25, 270
Pearl Harbor, 212
Pearl of Great Price, Maori edition, 147
Peel, Leslie A., 144
Peeti, Luxford, 129–30, 132, 175, **178**
Pera, Hui Hui, 159
Pere, Baden, 156
Pere, Mafeking, 146, 155–56
Pere, Mahenga, 155
Perrott, William R., 211, 227, 237
Pesega, Samoa, elementary school at, 245
Peter (apostle), seen in vision, 33
Peters, John, 155
Petersen, Charles, 58, 85
petrol rationing, 207, 216–17
Phelps, William W., 1 and note 1, 4, 39
Piharau, K. N., 36
Plymouth Brethren, 104
Pohuhu, Nepia, 171
Poipoi, Ngawaea, 67
polio epidemic, 170 note 59, 175, 199, 225

polygamy
   among Maori chiefs, 63
   and RLDS missionaries, 148–49, 167
   hostility because of, 16, 20–21, 29, 91, 93
Polynesian origins, 27, 129–31, 159
   and Book of Mormon, 47. *See also* Hagoth.
   and DNA research, 131 note 26
Pomare, Apikara. *See* Whaanga, Apikara Pomare.
Pomare, Edna, 81
Pomare, Hara, 152
Pomare, Iraparete, 181
Pomare, Maui
   and Jury genealogical volumes, 172
   and missionary visas, 142
   and permission for Hawaii Temple visit, 140–41
   David O. McKay visits, 162
   speaks at LDS conferences, 96–97, 170–71
Porirua, resistance to British in, 23
Porirua Branch, 56, 67–68, 218
   hui tau, 170
   karakia in, 73–74
   LDS primary school at, 118
   meetinghouse, 244–45
   members from work on Auckland Chapel, 239
Port Nicholson. *See* Wellington, New Zealand.
Porteous, John, 182–83
Porter (family of Christchurch), 85
Potae, Henare, 58–59, 67
Potangaroa, Paora. *See* Te Potangaroa, Paora.
Poverty Bay, 37, 58
Powick, Joseph J., 205
Pratt, Addison, 2
Pratt, Orson, 14
Pratt, Parley P., 3, 222
praying with right arm raised, 42–43 and note 8
Prebbleton Branch, 24, 273
Prime, Ephraim, 215
prohibition, in New Zealand, 156
prophets. *See* Maori, prophets.
Protestant Political Association, 156
Puketapu, hui tau at, 163–68
Puriri family, 223, 226
Puriri, Ra/Rangikawea, 176, 212

R

Rainbow, Algernon, 216
Rakaututu
  Book of Mormon translated at, 57
Rama Rama Branch, 274
Randell, George, 202
rangatira. *See* Maori, rangatira.
Rangiora Branch, 274
Rangitane (tribe), 117
Rangitoto (Maori) Choir, 239
Rangitoto Branch (Auckland), 224, 233 and note 7, 237, 239
Rangitoto Branch (D'Urville Island), 70
Rarotonga, Cook Islands, 214, 221–22, 225, 228, 236
Ratana (prophet), 42, 43, 169–70, 180–81, 183–86
Ratana Pa, 183
Ratana, Tahupotiki Wiremu. *See* Ratana (prophet).
Reardon, Father (Catholic priest), 218
rebaptism, 10 note 26, 14 and notes 45 and 46, 15, 27
Reber, Meryl, 220–21
Red Cross activities, 207
Reform Party, 156
Reid, Thomas Ivan, 250
Relief Society
  activities of, 97–98, 151
  and Maori Agricultural College, 122, 124, 131
  building, in Tamaki, 97–98
  in Auckland, 29
  in Christchurch, 24, 25
  in European branches, 95
  in Hawkes Bay, 98
  in Huria, 136–37
  in Maori branches, 95–96
  mission conference, 148
  mission presidency and areas organized, 118
Remuera, mission home in, 226, 244, 264
Reorganized Church of Jesus Christ of Latter Day Saints, missionaries from, 148, 164–67
Rewiti, Erena, 104
Rewiti, Eru, 104
Rewiti, Mangu, 95
rheumatic fever, missionaries suffer from, 112

Rich, John T., 18, 20
Richards, Ezra Foss
  and Book of Mormon translation, 53, 57–58, 147
  as mission president, 86–87, 270
  as missionary, 48, 50
  ill health of, 112
  on eruption of Mount Tarawera, 51
  on Maori interest in emigration, 77
Richards, Franklin D., 12–13, 53, 77
Richards, LeGrand, 246
"ride and tie," 112 note 118
Ridgway family (of Carterton), 35
Rimmer, (first name not given), opposes Mormonism, 91
Ringatu (religion), 23
Roberts, William, 250, 256, 264
Rogers, Henry P., 153
Rogers, Noah, 2, 214
Romney, Emma, 118
Romney, Marion G., and wife, 261, 263–64
Romney, Melbourne, 118, 125
Romney, Orson D.
  and Maori Agricultural College, 121–25
  as mission president, 118, 132, 260, 270
  as missionary, 69
Romney, Orson Jr., 118
Romney, Vilate, 118
Romney, William, 118
Rosenvall, Erick Albert, 252, **254**, 258–59
Rosenvall, James, 252
Rosenvall, Lynn, 252
Rosenvall, Vernice, 252, 259
Ross, Hilda, 263
Rotorua
  Duke of York visits, 91
  members from work on Auckland Chapel, 239
Rotorua/Horo Horo Branch, 217
Ruahine (ship), 219
Ruatangata Branch, 274
Rudd, Glen L., xv, 208, **209**
Ruruku family, 189
Ruruku, Turi, 181, 211, 227, 275
Russell, Francis H., 263
Russell, G. W., 144–45

S

Salote Tupus (queen), 263
Samoa

David O. McKay visits, 168
LDS schools in, 107, 245, 255
Samoan
    members work on Auckland Chapel, 240
    Relief Society, contribution to temple, 251
    Saints in Auckland, 237
    students at Maori Agricultural College, 133, 146, 161, 168, 182
Samoan Mission, reorganization in, 247
Sanders, Sondra, Jr., 51, 53, 57–59, 123
Sarah and Mariah (ship), 14
Savage (RLDS missionary), 148, 165
Savage, Michael J., 203
Scandinavian immigrants
    converts, 28, 38
    in New Zealand, 25
schools. *See* LDS schools.
Schwendiman, Fred W., 159–60, 164, 271
Schwendiman, Lillian, 159
Schwenke, Albert ("Max"), 133
Scott, Patricia Lyn, xv, 114
Sears, Belle, 54, 56
Sears, Heber, 54
Sells, Albert E., 174, 177
Servicemen's Settlement and Land Sales Act, 231, 234
Sharp, Leo B., 170
shearing season, 245
sheep farming, New Zealand/USA compared, 132–33
Sheffield, Val, 214
Shortland, John, 146
Shortland, Willie, 179
Shreeve, Thomas A., 24–25, 270
Sierra (ship), 239
Simpson, Robert L.
    as mission president, 265
    as missionary, 200
    fluent in Maori, 197
    in U.S. Air Force in Egypt, 215
    on tohunga, 106–7
Singing Mothers launched, 205
Skull Valley, Utah, 78
Slater, James A., 51
Smith, David, 187
Smith, George Albert
    attitude toward haka, 260
    becomes Church president, 220
    speaks on Scouting, 201–2
    visits New Zealand, 201–2, 246

Smith, Hyrum, 2
Smith, Ida Mae Haley, 132, 134, 205
Smith, Joseph, 1, 2
Smith, Joseph F.
    authorizes Maori translations of scriptures, 147
    authorizes missionary work among Maori, 27
    and Maori Agricultural College, 108
    and Maori friends, 154
    death of, 156
    invitation to visit New Zealand Mission, 139
    missionary visas, 142
    on righteous war, 204
    pronounces Maori as Hagoth's descendants, 129
Smith, Joseph Fielding, and Jury's genealogy volumes, 172
Smith, Mary. *See* Whaanga, Mere Mete.
Smith, Mary Ruruku, 187
Smith, S. Percy, 171
Smith, Sidney W., 254
Smith, Walter.
    and Maori Agricultural College brass band, 133–35, 135
    member of Maori Agricultural College faculty, 132
    school song (MAC), 134, (CCNZ), 258
Smith, Wi, 181, 191, 275
Smoot, Reed, 142–43, 159
Snow, Lorenzo, 19, 94–95
softball, as missionary activity, 200
Solomon, Richard H., 97
Sorensen, John P., 25–28, 30–31
Sorenson, John L., 222
sores, missionaries suffer from, 112
South Africa, missionary visas for, 142
Southerton, Simon, 131 note 26
Southon family, 226
Southon, Jim, 189
Southwick, John A., 112
Spanish influenza, 151–54 and 152 note 105
Speech Day, 135
Spencer, Charles, 173–74, 181 note 105, 202
Spring-Rice, Cecil, 142–43
Spry, William, 129
St. Cuthbert's College, 213
Stapley, Delbert L., and wife, 261
Steed, Thomas, 18–21

Stephens, Julian R., 173–74, 178
Stephens, Trent D., 131 note 26
Stevenson, Ezra T., 56–57, 60, **66**, 122
   as mission president, 87–90, 270
Stewart, Alonzo, 61
Stewart, Andrew J., 269
Stewart, John Clarence, 53, 81
Stewart, William T.
   and Book of Mormon translation, 53
   as mission president, 46, 78–80, 270
   as missionary, 37, 46, 58
   concerns about Maori drinking, smoking, 71
   in Uawa, 75
   on Maori emigration, 78
   preaching among Europeans, 76
   to oversee Maori Saints in Kanab, 83
Stinson, Mick, 238
Stone, Howard B., 247
Stott, Franklin Earl, 146, 158, 160–61
Stott, Ida, 146
Stout, Robert, 110–11
street meetings in European cities, 194
Strickland, Harry T., 221
Strong, Thomas B., 182
Stuart, Edward Craig, 123 note 10
Sunday School, 67–68, 191
Suva Branch, 247
Swiss Temple, 250
Sydenham Branch, 24, 274

T

Tahiti
   as Eastern Polynesian culture, 19 note 68
   missionary work in, 2
   students from at Maori Agricultural College, 161, 168, 182
Tahoraiti, 158, 169
Tailby, William, 225
Takana, Pare. *See* Duncan, Polly.
Takana, Takare, 104
Takana, Wiremu. *See* Duncan, William, Sr.
Tamahau (chief), 118
Tamaki, hui tau at, 70, 86, 158–59, 198–99, **199**
Tamaki (Auckland) Branch, chapel, 252, 263
Tamaki (Hawkes Bay) Branch, 203
   chapel, 169
   Relief Society, 96–97

Tamihana, Waitokorau. *See* Te Awe Awe, Waitokorau
tangi (cry), at homecoming, 132
tangihanga (funeral rituals), 46, 51, 61–62, 163
   during flu epidemic, 154
Taonoke, 36–37, 46
Taranaki, 23, 24
Taranaki (ship), 20
Tararua (ship), 30
Tarawhiti, Heta, 103
Tarquinia (ship), 5, 17–18, 26, 27
Tasmania, proselytizing in, 14
tattooing, 105–6
Taumata o Tapuhi, resistance to Mormon missionary work in, 48
Taupo, Mormons in, 65
Tauranga, missionary work at, 117, 134
Tauranganui, LDS primary school at, 118
Taurau, Eruera, 181, 275
Taurau, Mane, 211
Tawa, Faafeu, 176
Tawhiao (king), 22, 29–31, 42
Taylor, Demar V., 204
Taylor, George S., **167**
   as missionary, 70
   as mission president, 160, 169–71, 271
   hosts David O. McKay and Hugh J. Cannon, 162–65, 167–169
   advice to Stuart Meha, 123 note 9
   on faith-healing by Ratana, 169–70
Taylor, Ida, 160
Taylor, John E., 91
Taylor, John W., 134 note 38
Taylor, Miriam, 160
Taylor, Priscilla, 160
Te Ahunga, Hakopa, 105
Te Ariki, deaths from volcanic eruption, 51
Te Aroha, Mormon school in, 47
Te Aute College, 95
   earthquake, 190
   Maori Agricultural College compared to, 111, 177, 183
   Stuart Meha educated at, 123
Te Awe Awe, Ada, 137
Te Awe Awe, Adelaide, 117–18
Te Awe Awe, Nora, 117, 137
Te Awe Awe, Tamihana, 117, **130**, 137, 153
Te Awe Awe, Waitokorau (Victoria) 117, **130**, 137, 141, 159–60
Te Hapara Branch, 245

Te Hatiwira/Hati (chief), 48–49, 52
Te Hauke
    conference at, 60, 63–64
    Relief Society, 96
Te Horo
    conference, 88
    meetinghouse at, 100, 109
    Mormons in, 104
    Relief Society at, 95
Te Hui Atawhai a Nga Wahine. *See* Relief Society.
Te Karere
    and Doctrine and Covenants, 149–50
    during World War II, 208, 210
    publication of, 110–11, 119, 133, 139, 192
    terminated, 266
    war news in, 212, 214
Te Katere, Hare (Harry Carter), 32, 34 and note 132
Te Kirihaehae Te Puea Herangi. *See* Te Puea.
Te Kooti, 23, 31, 75
Te Kotahitanga (Maori parliament), 59, 95
Te Kuiti, conference at, 223
Te Maare, Piripi, 58–59, 67, 70
Te Matorohanga, Moihi, 171
Te Ore Ore, 35, 36, 42
Te Potangaroa, Paora (prophet), 42–43
Te Puea (princess), 177, 179, 201, 203
Te Puru, 52
Te Rahui, hui tau at, 72–73
te reo (Maori language), missionaries learn, 146–47, 188–89, 197, 200
Te Rimu, 48
Te Ruruku, Hoera, 70
Te Ua Haumene, 23
Te Whakamairu, Ihaia Hopu, 35–36
Te Whatahoro, Hoani. *See* Jury, John A.
Te Whenuanui Rangitakaiwaho, Manihera, 35
Te Whiti-o Rongomai (prophet), 24, 29–31, 91
Teimana, Hare, 32
Teimana, Pare, 32
temple meetings as part of district conferences, 194
temple visits. *See* Hawaii Temple.
temple work, Maori, 77, 83, 88, 117
Temple View, village named, 244, 264
Tengaio, Pera, 215

termites, 233
Thames Branch, 169, 274
Thompson Brothers, 128
Thompson, Thomas, 115–16
Thompson, Una, 211
Thompson, William, 115–16
Thompson. *See* Te Awe Awe.
Thurston, Moses F., 10
Tiko Kino, 68
Timaru Branch, 24, 32, 274
Timoleon (ship), 2
Tirikatene, E. T., 218
tithing, 56–57, 74, 77–78, 85, 180
Tiwai, Ka Kariana, 205
Toaroa Pakahia (prophet), 42
Tohu Kakahi (prophet), 24, 30–31, 91
tohunga (priests),
    meaning of, 105–6
    mission presidents approach differently, 106–7
Tohunga Suppression Act (1907), 106
Tokomaru Bay, hui tau at, 98
Tonga
    LDS church schools in, 227, 235, 255
Tongan Mission, reorganization in, 247
Tongans
    attend Maori Agricultural College, 161, 169, 182
    in New Zealand, 237
    work on Auckland Chapel, 240
tongues, and interpretation of, 164–65 and note 35
tracting, 45, 86, 111
tracts. *See* Maori translations
transport regulations, 240–41
Treaty of Waitangi, 2, 23, 204–5
Trevarthen, W. E., 115
Tubuai, Addison Pratt in, 2
Tuhikaramea. *See* Church College of New Zealand.
Tunbridge, John Bennett, 92
Tungi (prince), 263
Tunuiarangi, Hoani Paraone (Major Brown), 172
Turei, Mohu (preacher), 48
Turnbull, Robert, 179
typhoid fever, missionaries suffer from, 112

U–V

Uawa

conference at, 46
hui tau, 89
LDS preaching at, 60, 71
Uawa-Tolaga Bay Branch, members in military service, 217
Union Steamship Company, 142, 184
University of Otago, 218
University of Sydney, xiv
Unto the Islands of the Sea: A History of the Latter-day Saints in the Pacific, xiii
Utah Agricultural College (Logan), 131
Utah, economic slump (1894), 79
Vili, Misitana, 174

W

W. M. Hay and Son, 121, 122, 124
Waa, Kewa, 95
Waddoups, William M., 158
Waiapu, Mormon school in, 47–48
Waikato
district conference, 223, 236–237
hui tau, 201
Maori at, 45
Mormon school in, 37
Waiomatatini, 50
Waipawa Branch, 102
Wairarapa Valley
Maori in, 42, 44, 59
missionary activity in, 35–36
Mormons in, 61
Wairau District, 216
Wairau, LDS school at, 118
Wairoa, 38, 54
Waiwhara, hui tau at, 75
Waitangi Centennial, 204
Walker, John M., 121
Walker, Luxford Peeti, 219
Wallace, Joseph, 30
Walton, W. D., 103
Wandell, Charles Wesley, 3–4, 269
Wanganui Branch organized, 28–29, 274
offer of land withdrawn, 108
Ratana at, 183
Waotu Branch, 34, 35
Warbeck, William Thompson, 29
Ward, Joseph (prime minister), 184
Warkworth, missionaries reach, 32
Warner (Protestant minister), 156
Watene family (of Kiri Kiri), 52
Watene, George, 210

Watene, Puti Tipene (Steve), 179
Watene, Taramana Hei, 52
Watene, Toke, 211
weddings, missionaries attend, 46
Wegener, Rose Marie, 221
Welch, Eulalia/Lalia, 152, 158
Welch, John S., 146–48, 150–54, 158
Welling, Job, 269
Wellington
British settlement of, 2
Mormons in, 13, 21, 45
Wellington Branch, 274
Wellington City Libraries, xv, 11
Wesleyan Methodist minister, 117
Whaanga, Apikara Pomare, 81, 123, 154
Whaanga, Hirini Te Rito, **82**
as branch president, 82
as missionary, 87–89
at Salt Lake Temple, 83–84, 117
death of, 102
disapproves of Sabbath-breaking, 83
gathers to Utah, 81
grandchild of, 132
monument over grave, **114**
Whaanga, Ihaiah/Ihaia, 81, 154
Whaanga, Ihaka Kanapa, 81
Whaanga, Mere Mete, **130**
as missionary, 110, 113–114
at Salt Lake Temple, 83, 117, 130
cares for missionaries, 82
death of, 154
gathers to Utah and returns, 81, 154
name added to monument, **114** note 126
Whaanga, Pirika, first Maori to Utah, 53, 81
whakapapa. *See* Maori genealogy.
Whakato cemetery, 53, 81
Whakato, Mormons welcomed at, 50
whare karakia. *See* meetinghouse.
whare wananga. *See* carved house.
Whata Whata, 246
Whatahoro volumes. *See* John Jury, genealogical volumes.
white slavery accusations, 155. *See also* anti-Mormonism.
White, Pamela Going, 206
White, Ra, **178**
Widerup, Johannes C., 27
Wihongi, Henare Pere, 181, 211, 227, 275
Wihongi, Pere, 155
Wihongi, Rupert, 174

Wiley, David Thomas, 58
Wiley family (of Carterton), 35
Wiley, Priscilla Fawcett, 35 note 136
Wiley, Robert, 58
William Denny (ship), 6
Williams, A. O. (supervisor of Maori ministers, Wanganui), 118
Williams, Henry (Anglican archdeadon), 111
Williams, Samuel (Anglican archdeacon), 111
Williams, William Leonard (Anglican archdeacon), 50
Williams, William, 155
Willie, Leon, 156
Wilson, Te Ao, 180
Wilson, W. J., 152
Wilson, Woodrow, 140, 142
Winslow, Alfred A., 141, 142–43, 158
Wishart, Alex, 251
Witehira, Hemi, 173, 181
women. See "firsts" *and* missionaries.
Woodruff, Wilford, 68, 78, 225
Woods, Charlene, 198
Woods, Elline, 198
Woods, Janet, 198
Woods, Moroni Charles
    as mission president, 198–201, 271
    and boys' school, 100–101
    plans for Korongata Branch chapel, 205
Woolley, M. Wallace, 117
Word of Wisdom
    adherence to, 105, 157
    and Relief Society officers, 96
    government support for, 97
    preached to Maori, 71
World War I
    American missionaries register for draft, 150
    American missionaries resented, 140–41
    end of, 151
    outbreak of, 134
    Maori Agricultural College cadet corps, 150
    mobilization in New Zealand, 139 and note 48
    Mormon supportive activities, 135–36
    New Zealand casualties, 167 note 46
    U.S. enters, 141
World War II
    effects of on mission and members, 204–17

evacuation of American missionaries, 207–10
return of "Zion" elders after, 220
Saints in armed forces, 217
Wreys Bush Branch, 274
Wright, Alexander, 96
Wright, Angus T.
    and Book of Mormon proofreading, 64
    and Jury genealogical volumes, 171–73
    as mission president, 64, 74, 174, 270–71
    letter to Millennial Star, 70
Wright, Emma, 96, 104
Wright, Francis H., 51
Wright, Martha, 171, 174

Y

yellow jaundice (hepatitis A), 225
YMCA and basketball league, 200
Young, Brigham, 2, 3–4, 27 note 102, 225
    McKay and Cannon testify of succession of, 165
    on Polynesian origins, 130
Young, Gordon Claridge
    American automobile of, 228
    ancestry of, 225
    and Church College of New Zealand, 226–27, 231–32, 234–36, 263
    and new meetinghouses, 232–36
    as mission president, 225–29, 271
    buys new mission home, 226 and note 118, 228, 264–65
    "housecleans" Maori traditions, 241
    interprets for McKay and Cannon, 164
    on local missionaries, 229
    prohibits haka, 260
    proselytizing among Europeans, 238
    temple ceremony translation, 257 and note 106
Young Maori Party, 95–96, 106
Young Men's and Young Ladies' Mutual Improvement Associations, 191, 200
Young, Thomas C., 47
Young, Virginia, 225, 240

Z

Zealandia (ship), 10, 25, 64
Zion in New Zealand: A History of the Church of Jesus Christ of Latter-day Saints in New Zealand, 1854–1977, xiii

"Zion" elders. *See* missionaries.
Zion's Maori Association, 122, 129. *See also* New Zealand Missionary Society.
  fundraising, 89
  monument to Hirini and Mere Whaanga 113–14, **114**
  organization of, 84
  relocates Whaanga family in Utah, 84
  sponsors missionary, 87
  sponsors translations into Maori
    of hymnal, 69
    of *The Latter-day Saints*, 88

About the Author

As a child in Sydney, Australia in the 1930s and 1940s, Marjorie Newton was raised on Church history stories by her fifth-generation LDS stepmother. This background grew into an interest in Mormon history in Australia and New Zealand. She pursued this interest when she finally realised a life-long dream of studying at the University of Sydney, including going on to post-graduate studies.

Her master's thesis was published in 1991 as *Southern Cross Saints: The Mormons in Australia,* and her doctoral dissertation, *Mormonism in New Zealand: An Historical Appraisal,* is forthcoming from Greg Kofford Books. Both won the prestigious Mormon History Association's Reese Award for the best thesis or dissertation, making her the only historian who has won the Reese Award twice.

Marjorie Newton has published award-winning articles in the *Journal of Mormon History, BYU Studies* and *Dialogue,* as well as several articles in *The Ensign.* She has been a member of the Mormon History Association since 1987 and has volunteered on the *Journal of Mormon History*'s editorial staff.

Also available from
GREG KOFFORD BOOKS

Knowing Brother Joseph Again: Perceptions and Perspectives

Davis Bitton

Paperback, ISBN: 978-1-58958-123-4

In 1996, Davis Bitton, one of Mormon history's preeminent and much-loved scholars, published a collection of essays on Joseph Smith under the title, *Images of the Prophet Joseph Smith*. A decade later, when the book went out of print, Davis began work on an updated version that would also include some of his other work on the Mormon prophet. The project was only partially finished when his health failed. He died on April 13, 2007, at age seventy-seven. With the aid of additional historians, *Knowing Brother Joseph Again: Perceptions and Perspectives* brings to completion Davis's final work—a testament to his own admiration of the Prophet Joseph Smith.

From Davis Bitton's introducton:

This is not a conventional biography of Joseph Smith, but its intended purpose should not be hard to grasp. That purpose is to trace how Joseph Smith has appeared from different points of view. It is the image of Joseph Smith rather than the man himself that I seek to delineate.

Even when we have cut through the rumor and misinformation that surround all public figures and agree on many details, differences of interpretation remain. We live in an age of relativism. What is beautiful for one is not for another, what is good and moral for one is not for another, and what is true for one is not for another. I shudder at the thought that my presentation here will lead to such soft relativism.

Yet the fact remains that different people saw Joseph Smith in different ways. Even his followers emphasized different facets at different times. From their own perspectives, different people saw him differently or focused on a different facet of his personality at different times. Inescapably, what they observed or found out about him was refracted through the lens of their own experience. Some of the different, flickering, not always compatible views are the subject of this book.

Saints of Valor: Mormon Medal of Honor Recipients

Sherman L. Fleek

Hardcover, ISBN: 978-1-58958-171-5

Since 1861 when the US Congress approved the concept of a Medal of Honor for combat valor, 3,457 individuals have received this highest military decoration that the nation can bestow. Nine of those have been Latter-day Saints. The military and personal stories of these LDS recipients are compelling, inspiring, and tragic. The men who appear in this book are tied by two common threads: the Medal of Honor and their Mormon heritage.

The purpose of this book is to highlight the valor of a special class of LDS servicemen who served and sacrificed "above and beyond the call of duty." Four of these nine Mormons gave their "last full measure" for their country, never seeing the high award they richly deserved. All four branches of the service are represented: five were Army (one was a pilot with the Army Air Forces during WWII), two Navy, and one each of the Marine Corps and Air Force. Four were military professionals who made the service their careers; five were not career-minded; three died at an early age and never married. This book captures these harrowing historical narratives from personal accounts.

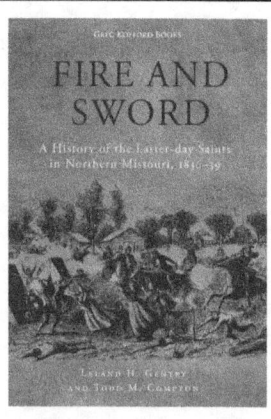

Fire and Sword: A History of the Latter-day Saints in Northern Missouri, 1836-39

Leland Homer Gentry and Todd M. Compton

Hardcover, ISBN: 978-1-58958-103-6

Many Mormon dreams flourished in Missouri. So did many Mormon nightmares.

The Missouri period—especially from the summer of 1838 when Joseph took over vigorous, personal direction of this new Zion until the spring of 1839 when he escaped after five months of imprisonment—represents a moment of intense crisis in Mormon history. Representing the greatest extremes of devotion and violence, commitment and intolerance, physical suffering and terror—mobbings, battles, massacres, and political "knockdowns"—it shadowed the Mormon psyche for a century.

Leland Gentry was the first to step beyond this disturbing period as a one-sided symbol of religious persecution and move toward understanding it with careful documentation and evenhanded analysis. In Fire and Sword, Todd Compton collaborates with Gentry to update this foundational work with four decades of new scholarship, more insightful critical theory, and the wealth of resources that have become electronically available in the last few years.

Compton gives full credit to Leland Gentry's extraordinary achievement, particularly in documenting the existence of Danites and in attempting to tell the Missourians' side of the story; but he also goes far beyond it, gracefully drawing into the dialogue signal interpretations written since Gentry and introducing the raw urgency of personal writings, eyewitness journalists, and bemused politicians seesawing between human compassion and partisan harshness. In the lush Missouri landscape of the Mormon imagination where Adam and Eve had walked out of the garden and where Adam would return to preside over his posterity, the towering religious creativity of Joseph Smith and clash of religious stereotypes created a swift and traumatic frontier drama that changed the Church.

"Swell Suffering": A Biography of Maurine Whipple

Veda Tebbs Hale

Paperback, ISBN: 978-1-58958-124-1
Hardcover, ISBN: 978-1-58958-122-7

Maurine Whipple, author of what some critics consider Mormonism's greatest novel, *The Giant Joshua,* is an enigma. Her prize-winning novel has never been out of print, and its portrayal of the founding of St. George draws on her own family history to produce its unforgettable and candid portrait of plural marriage's challenges. Yet Maurine's life is full of contradictions and unanswered questions. Veda Tebbs Hale, a personal friend of the paradoxical novelist, answers these questions with sympathy and tact, nailing each insight down with thorough research in Whipple's vast but under-utilized collected papers.

Praise for *"Swell Suffering"*:

"Hale achieves an admirable balance of compassion and objectivity toward an author who seemed fated to offend those who offered to love or befriend her. . . . Readers of this biography will be reminded that Whipple was a full peer of such Utah writers as Virginia Sorensen, Fawn Brodie, and Juanita Brooks, all of whom achieved national fame for their literary and historical works during the mid-twentieth century"
—Levi S. Peterson, author of *The Backslider* and *Juanita Brooks: Mormon Historian*

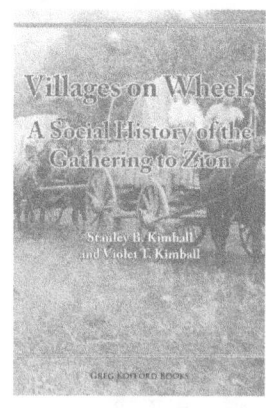

Villages on Wheels: A Social History of the Gathering to Zion

Stanley B. Kimball and Violet T. Kimball

ISBN: 978-1-58958-119-7

The enduring saga of Mormonism is its great trek across the plains, and understanding that trek was the life work of Stanley B. Kimball, master of Mormon trails. This final work, a collaboration he began and which was completed after his death in 2003 by his photographer-writer wife, Violet, explores that movement westward as a social history, with the Mormons moving as "villages on wheels."

Set in the broader context of transcontinental migration to Oregon and California, the Mormon trek spanned twenty-two years, moved approximately 54,700 individuals, many of them in family groups, and left about 7,000 graves at the trailside.

Like a true social history, this fascinating account in fourteen chapters explores both the routines of the trail—cooking, cleaning, laundry, dealing with bodily functions—and the dramatic moments: encountering Indians and stampeding buffalo, giving birth, losing loved ones to death, dealing with rage and injustice, but also offering succor, kindliness, and faith. Religious observances were simultaneously an important part of creating and maintaining group cohesiveness, but working them into the fabric of the grueling day-to-day routine resulted in adaptation, including a "sliding Sabbath." The role played by children and teens receives careful scrutiny; not only did children grow up quickly on the trail, but the gender boundaries guarding their "separate spheres" blurred under the erosion of concentrating on tasks that had to be done regardless of the age or sex of those available to do them. Unexpected attention is given to African Americans who were part of this westering experience, and Violet also gives due credit to the "four-legged heroes" who hauled the wagons westward.

Hearken, O Ye People:
The Historical Setting of Joseph Smith's Ohio Revelations

Mark Lyman Staker

Hardcover, ISBN: 978-1-58958-113-5

2010 Best Book Award - John Whitmer Historical Association
2011 Best Book Award - Mormon History Association

More of Mormonism's canonized revelations originated in or near Kirtland than any other place. Yet many of the events connected with those revelations and their 1830s historical context have faded over time. Mark Staker reconstructs the cultural experiences by which Kirtland's Latter-day Saints made sense of the revelations Joseph Smith pronounced. This volume rebuilds that exciting decade using clues from numerous archives, privately held records, museum collections, and even the soil where early members planted corn and homes. From this vast array of sources he shapes a detailed narrative of weather, religious backgrounds, dialect differences, race relations, theological discussions, food preparation, frontier violence, astronomical phenomena, and myriad daily customs of nineteenth-century life. The result is a "from the ground up" experience that today's Latter-day Saints can all but walk into and touch.

Praise for *Hearken O Ye People*:

"I am not aware of a more deeply researched and richly contextualized study of any period of Mormon church history than Mark Staker's study of Mormons in Ohio. We learn about everything from the details of Alexander Campbell's views on priesthood authority to the road conditions and weather on the four Lamanite missionaries' journey from New York to Ohio. All the Ohio revelations and even the First Vision are made to pulse with new meaning. This book sets a new standard of in-depth research in Latter-day Saint history."
    -Richard Bushman, author of *Joseph Smith: Rough Stone Rolling*

"To be well-informed, any student of Latter-day Saint history and doctrine must now be acquainted with the remarkable research of Mark Staker on the important history of the church in the Kirtland, Ohio, area."
    -Neal A. Maxwell Institute, Brigham Young University

www.ingramcontent.com/pod-product-compliance
Lightning Source LLC
Chambersburg PA
CBHW050200240426
43671CB00013B/2198